# THE SECRET HISTORY
# OF ROCK

# THE SECRET HISTORY OF ROCK

## THE MOST INFLUENTIAL BANDS YOU'VE NEVER HEARD

## RONI SARIG

Billboard Books

*An imprint of Watson-Guptill Publications/New York*

*To Tommy,*
*a most influential*
*brother*

Senior Editor: Bob Nirkind

Edited by: Sylvia Warren

Book and Cover Design: Robin Lee Malik, Buddy Boy Design

Production Manager: Hector Campbell

Photos by: Ebet Roberts

First Published 1998 by Billboard Books, an imprint of Watson-Guptill Publications, a division of
Billboard Productions, Inc., at 1515 Broadway, New York, NY 10036

**Library of Congress Cataloging-in-Publication Data**

Sarig, Roni.
   The secret history of rock  :  the most influential bands you've
never heard  /  Roni Sarig.
      p.   cm.
   Includes discographies and index.
   ISBN 0-8230-7669-5
   1. Rock music--History and criticism. 2. Rock groups.  I. Title.
ML3534.S27   1998
781.66--dc21

                                        98.6403
                                         CIP
                                            MN

Manufactured in the United States

1 2 3 4 5 6 7 8 9/06 05 04 03 02 02 01 00 99 98

# ACKNOWLEDGEMENTS

In bringing this book from a vague idea, to a huge pile of research materials, to a written and edited reality, many people have gladly given their help. I would like to thank those without whom I could not have made it through:

First, to my closest advisor, earliest editor, greatest supporter, and primary inspiration, my wife Danielle. And to all my family and friends for their support, particularly those with music business rolodexes: Tommy and Sabrina.

Thanks as well to my editors Bob Nirkind and Sylvia Warren, to my agent Sheree Bykofsky, and to my research assistants Jason Schepers, Chris Toenes, John Cline, and David Rosen. Also, to the nearby friends who provided advice and information, and helped track down albums, stories, and people: David Menconi, Tim Ross, Ben Goldberg, Joe and Elizabeth Kahn, Farnum Brown, and the music library at WXDU.

I am indebted to all the artists who, without anything to promote except the music they loved, enthusiastically agreed to be interviewed. Thanks especially to those who went out of their way to contact me and continued to make themselves accessible in whatever way they could: King Coffey, Jim O'Rourke, and Kate Shellenbach.

And of course, thanks to the many publicists, managers, label heads, and journalists who provided material and assistance. Particularly, those who went beyond the call of duty—Michael Shore, Carol Cooper, Bill Adler, Neil & Lucas Cooper—as well as those who did their jobs promptly and happily: Kathy Keely, Deborah Orr, Darcy Mayers, Sabrina Kaleta, Alison Tarnofsky, Mike Wolf, Beth Jacobson, Taylor Mayo, Bill Bentley, Steve Cohen, Bettina & Howard (at Thrill Jockey), Brian Bumbery, Renee Lehman, Karen Weissen, Andy Schwartz, Helen Urriola, Scott Giampino, Michelle Roche, Jennifer Schmidt, Tommy McKay, M.C. Kostek, Sarah Feldman, Marc Fenton, Cathy Williams, Glenn Dicker, Jason Consoli, Carl Munzel, Kurt (at Atavistic), Matt Hanks, Vicky Wheeler, Josh Mills, Julie Butterfield, Hallie (at K), Susan Darnell, Shawn Rogers, Tami Blevins, Colleen Mollony, John Troutman, Drew Miller, Jennifer Fisher, Heather (at Fire), Curtis (at Taang), Terri Hinte, Aaron (at SST), Josh Kirby, Heidi Robinson, Jen Boddy, Paula Sartorius, Carrie Svingen, Erica Freed, Susan Silver, Tony Margherita, Stacey Slater, Tracy Miller, Malik Bellamy, Claudia Gonson, Kevin O'Neil, Howard Weulfing, Jeff Hart, Jeff Tartikoff, Gene Booth, Jason (at Epitaph), Perry Serpa, Sandy Tanaka, Ali (at Cleopatra), Anne Pryor, Sandy Sawotka, and anyone else who helped out.

Final thanks go to the subjects of this book, who have not been thanked enough for daring to be original.

# TABLE OF CONTENTS

## INTRODUCTION

## 1
### 20TH-CENTURY COMPOSERS 7

Erik Satie 9
Raymond Scott 11
John Cage 14
Theater of Eternal Music (the Dream Syndicate):
LaMonte Young, Tony Conrad, John Cale 17
Philip Glass 21
Glenn Branca 25

## 2
### INTERNATIONAL POP UNDERGROUND 29

Van Dyke Parks 30
Scott Walker 33
Serge Gainsbourg 36
Big Star 39
Young Marble Giants 43
Beat Happening 45

## 3
### PSYCHOTIC REACTIONS AND GARAGE ROCK 50

MC5 51
The Stooges 53
Roky Erickson/13th Floor Elevators 57
Silver Apples 60
Syd Barrett 63

## 4
### ABSURDISTS AND ECCENTRICS 66

Captain Beefheart 66
The Residents 70
Pere Ubu 74
Red Krayola/Mayo Thompson 77

## 5
### NAÏVE ROCK 80

The Shaggs 81
Half Japanese 83
Daniel Johnston 86
Jonathan Richman and the Modern Lovers 90

# TABLE OF CONTENTS

## 6
### FRAYED ROOTS 94

Gram Parsons 94
Nick Drake 98
The Cramps 101
Gun Club 104

## 7
### KRAUTROCK 108

Can 109
Faust 112
Kraftwerk 115
Neu! 118

## 8
### SOUND SCULPTORS 121

King Tubby 122
Lee "Scratch" Perry 124
Brian Eno 128
Adrian Sherwood 133

## 9
### ORIGINAL RAPPERS 138

U-Roy 139
Last Poets 141
Watts Prophets 144
Gil Scott-Heron 147
Iceberg Slim 150

## 10
### NEW YORK ROCKERS 153

Suicide 154
Television/Richard Hell & the Voidoids 157
The Feelies 161
DNA 165
Swans 168

## 11
### MINIMALIST FUNK 172

Trouble Funk 173
ESG 175
Liquid Liquid 178

# TABLE OF CONTENTS

## 12
### THE POST-INDUSTRIAL WASTELAND 182

Throbbing Gristle 183
Einstürzende Neubauten 186
Chrome 189
The Birthday Party 191
Big Black 194

## 13
### BRITISH POST-PUNK 197

Public Image Limited 198
Wire 201
Buzzcocks 206
The Fall 210
Gang of Four 212
Swell Maps 216

## 14
### RIOT MOMS AND OTHER ANGRY WOMEN 219

Lydia Lunch 220
X-Ray Spex 223
The Slits 226
The Raincoats 228

## 15
### AMERICAN HARDCORE 232

The Germs 233
Black Flag 235
Dead Kennedys 236
The Minutemen 242
Hüsker Dü 246
Bad Brains 249
Minor Threat 252

## 16
### AVANT PUNK USA 256

Wipers 256
Mission of Burma 260
Flipper 263
Slint 265

# INTRODUCTION

When I read a flyer on the wall at a record store, or in the weekly classifieds, and it says something like "Looking for a bassist. Our influences are Megadeth, Nena, Bram Tchaikovsky, and Sting," I'm overcome with a strange combination of dread and embarrassment. No doubt this brand of "influence peddling" is practical—God forbid you should have a calypso guitarist show up for your death metal auditions—but it somehow seems shameful that any person or group would be willing to limit and define themselves that way. And yet I have composed an entire book in which I've asked dozens of contemporary recording artists to go forever on record with comments about their influences. Truthfully, it's not as perverse as it sounds. To explain the evolution of *The Secret History* as a concept, and then as a working process, I offer the following:

Nirvana may be heroes to some, but they came around at a time when I was just a little too old to connect with the band's angst and still too young to have grown nostalgic for my lost teen spirit. However, by laying in my path a more convincing rock sound than any I'd heard in the previous decade, Nirvana forced me to reevaluate the conclusion I had only recently reached, that rock music was dead. That's not to say that in the years before Nirvana's rise to national attention—say, 1987 through 1991—rock didn't have its moments, both in the underground (Sonic Youth) and mainstream (Guns N' Roses). But as I began thinking critically about popular music, it became a matter of great distress that, in a rock culture which derived power and liberation by confounding, even attacking, its elders (as in, "hope I die before I get old") the musical heroes of my peers were more likely to be our parents' age than our own. Absurd as it seems, the great rock figures of the late '80s—at least for the suburban white kids around me—were Led Zeppelin, Pink Floyd, the Who, and of course, the Grateful Dead. With nothing else in rock capturing my attention, but unwilling to accept the widely held notion that the enormously popular radio format known as "classic rock" was better than any current music, by 1991 I had simply given up on rock as a spent, exhausted form.

The culprits, in my mind, were the baby boomers who seemed to control the media with a form of cultural fascism, the radio programmers and entertainment marketers who were selling my generation the idea that the '60s had been the pinnacle of youth culture, that our own youth culture could never be as important or as exciting as it was back then. And for the most part it seemed we were happily buying it.

With the arrival of Nirvana (and on a smaller scale, bands like Sonic Youth) on the national scene, boomer hegemony began to break. Simply the enthusiasm with which the band was received seemed to revive rock. But more importantly, for the first time in ages a group that was neither a classic rock holdover nor a younger band steeped in that tradition was the focus of attention in rock. Nirvana's success paved the way for the mainstream breakthroughs of other punk-based groups like Green Day and heightened listeners' awareness of all underground music, as "alternative rock" became a hot marketing tool/pseudo-genre.

If it was not already clear from their sound that these bands were not defined by classic rock, Sonic Youth and Nirvana made a point of name-dropping the groups that had inspired them. Soon, little-known names like **Half Japanese, Glenn Branca, Wire,** and **Can** began popping up regularly in the pages of major magazines. With bands like Pavement and Stereolab, obscurity was at the very heart of the music, and identifying the references became something of a sport. Most young music fans in the '90s had not heard (or even heard *of*) the bands their favorite groups were citing, not just because many of these groups had disappeared before the fans had come of age as listeners, but because they had never made it onto classic rock radio. But as new bands have been inspired by Nirvana, R.E.M., and Sonic Youth (and Nine Inch Nails, Foo Fighters, Beastie Boys, and Butthole Surfers) to search out these forgotten groups, their influence has spread. They've been edited out of rock history, but their spirits are very much alive in current rock. To a large extent, it is modern/alternative/you-name-it rock's integration of these obscure elements that distinguishes the best of '90s popular music from previous decades and enables current bands to fashion their own generational identity.

In commerce as in war, history is written by the winners. So it shouldn't be a surprise to anyone that it's the big sellers—the Rolling Stones, the Beatles, Led Zeppelin, the Eagles, Bruce Springsteen, the Police, Talking Heads, U2, R.E.M.—who have found their way into the annals of popular culture. And in most cases, because popular groups reach the most ears, they truly deserve to be deemed historically significant. But it's also crucial to note that people inspired enough by music to make their own are usually the same people most motivated to dig beneath the surface in their own listening habits and absorb the influence of lesser-known groups. As **Brian Eno** once said of the Velvet Underground: They didn't sell many records, but everybody who bought one went out and formed a band.

What we have, then, are two histories of rock, one determined by what the mainstream public heard in the past and the other determined by what has had a recognizable impact on current music. Granted, the two are by no means mutually exclusive. No one would claim that the Beatles do not have a far greater impact on modern rock than an influential obscurity such as **Silver Apples**. Still, there is a significant segment of rock history made up of groups that were little known in their time (and perhaps even less known now), but nevertheless have helped define in some measure the music we listen to today. The tale of these bands essentially constitutes a secret history of rock.

My intention in writing *The Secret History of Rock* was to celebrate those groups, composers, and performers whose influence on modern music far outshines their commercial notoriety. To do this, I queried numerous current artists to elicit their opinions on the subject. My project was met with great enthusiasm by artists, many of whom were thrilled at the opportunity to pay tribute to their unsung heroes. As more and more artists expressed interest in participating, it became clear that their comments should be an integral part of the book. (To avoid confusion between my references to the current artists whom I interviewed and the past artists who are themselves influential, I will hereafter refer to the former as the "commentators" and the latter as the "subjects.")

The first step was to define the parameters of what constitutes a "most influential band you've never heard." I needed to provide the commentators with an idea of the kinds of subjects I planned to deal with in the book, in order to direct and limit the variety of responses I would get. But it was important that my own analysis not limit their responses, which would undermine my intentions in conducting a poll in the first place.

Establishing criteria proved difficult; what is perceived as obscure varies greatly depending on subculture, region, nationality, and a lifelong series of chance encounters. One seemingly obvious guideline—that none of the subjects could have any U.S. chart hits—proved to be of little help in narrowing the field. For one thing, thousands of bands meet this criterion. Even massively influential groups such as the Velvet Underground and the Sex Pistols—both of which I consider too well known to qualify for inclusion here—never had a hit. And in a few cases, such as with **Kraftwerk** and the **Last Poets,** having had one fluke hit more than 20 years ago did not seem to me a valid reason for disqualification.

In the end I formulated a list of approximately 250 bands, composers, and performers who seemed to represent the right combination of obscurity and influence, planning eventually to narrow it down to less than 100 (as it turns out, there are 80). Along with an explanation of my book project and a request for an interview, I sent this list to every current act I deemed in some way notable (more than 120 different artists in all).

The artists I contacted represent a cross section of musical styles (rock as well as hip-hop and dance music) and functions (e.g., drummers as well as songwriters). Although the commentaters are from bands at many levels of popularity, I did concentrate on the most critically significant—and to a large extent, the best known—bands of the '90s. The point, after all, was to argue the influence of obscure underground acts of the past on *popular* groups of the '90s. However, I found it worthwhile to include some lesser-known commentators. For instance, I contacted guitarist Jim O'Rourke, who noted that he was probably more obscure than most artists on my list. O'Rourke, though, is highly regarded in certain segments of underground music, and since he's still young and active, it seems likely that his influence will reach more and more young people as time goes on.

Between February and December of 1997, I interviewed approximately 80 commentators about their influences (some of the artists who declined to participate are nevertheless included through the use of previously published comments). In determining which subjects deserved to be included in *The Secret History* I looked first at the number of commentators who indicated the performer as an influence. Some artists often deemed influential (such as the Fuggs, Spacemen 3, and Television Personalities) were surprisingly cited by only one (or none) of the 80 commentators. On the other hand, the large number of responses for the **Stooges, Captain Beefheart,** or **Brian Eno** led me to reconsider just how obscure they really were (though in the end, no one was cut for getting too many votes). Artists not included on my initial list but later added at the suggestion of one or more of the commentators included This Heat, the Pop Group, United States of America, and Iannis Xenakis. A handful of these write-ins actually generated enough enthusiasm to make their way into the book, including **ESG, Scott Walker,** and **Tony Conrad**.

Other factors affecting the composition of the final list were these:

*The ratio of influence to obscurity:* An effort was made to provide a mix of bands such as **Television,** who are immensely influential but more likely to be a familiar name, with groups like **Neu!,** who are less influential but may present readers with a better chance for a new discovery.

*The popularity of the bands influenced:* An influence on a group like U2 weighed more heavily than an influence on a lesser known group. The reasoning was, first, more popular groups play a larger role in defining the sound of an era, and second, bands like U2 have themselves influenced bands, and thereby spread their own influences farther.

*The balance of genres and chapters:* In an attempt to touch on as many facets of modern music as possible, it was sometimes necessary to favor a subject who'd been cited less over one that fit into an already well-represented chapter. For instance, **Liquid Liquid** made it into the small "Minimalist Funk" chapter with only a few citations, while the often-cited groups Joy Division and Killing Joke were shut out of the crowded "British Post-Punk" chapter.

*The quality of the responses:* Merely citing an artist as an influence was not enough; the commentator had to give a compelling description of how the impact was felt. For instance, while many commentators cited Karlheinz Stockhausen as an inspiration, few could explain in even the simplest terms what they learned from him.

In choosing which quotes to use, I attempted to balance the responses that explicitly address "influence" with those expressing something less concrete—more a matter of inspiration. As I conducted the interviews, it became clear that influence is manifested in more ways than through direct stylistic appropriations, and it is exhibited through more than simply appearances on tribute albums. In fact, the very nature of influence and appropriation proved a fascinating undercurrent in the research of the book. Many of the commentators were able to elucidate their influences in very precise terms—even in some cases to an embarrassing degree, where it seemed they were deflating their own contributions. Others had a much more difficult time characterizing their influences, and a few seemed quite certain they were entirely original. Yet the terms in which the individual commentators described their growth as artists probably has little to do with the quality of their art; they simply represent different ways of processing information. Certainly every creative act is to some degree influenced by others, and is also in some measure original. How those two elements are integrated in an artist's mind would likely make a terrific subject of some other book.

Early on in this project, I was warned by a music professor, "Never claim someone was the first to do something—it'll get you into trouble every time." Sure enough, in this process of delineating the reference points and precursors to modern rock music, I'd repeatedly encounter artists credited with having discovered something completely original and revolutionary, only to dig a little deeper and find an earlier artist doing something similar. This doesn't mean there is no such thing as originality, but it underscores the constant flow of ideas between artists and art forms that makes the subject of influence such a dynamic issue. A quote from an interview with one of the book's subjects sums it up well:

*Helios Creed, Chrome:*

*Everybody inspires everybody else. Nobody has a corner on anything. So I'm not going to be all egoed out and say, "Yeah, we invented this kind of music." Actually, we're just one link in a chain. Maybe a rusty, unnoticed link, where the shinier links are on either side. I guess you're doing a book about the rusty, unnoticed links. You don't really have to write about the shinier links, because everybody already knows.*

# KEY TO FEATURES IN THE TEXT

The names of people and groups found in bold text are meant to signify cross-references. These artists have separate sections about them located elsewhere in the book.

The discographies are for the most part complete. Certainly all studio releases appear, as do all officially released live albums and retrospectives. Occasionally, EPs that have been tacked on to CD reissues are only noted in the reissue's commentary. Releases that are both long out of print and thoroughly unimportant are sometimes omitted as well. Names in parentheses before an album title signify either releases made under a name different from the main subject's name (either as part of a band or occasional solo projects) or releases done as collaboration (indicated by "w/" inside the parentheses)

In the parentheses following an album title are the label information and release date. The original label and year of release come first; the reissue (or most recent reissue) label and year, when applicable, come after the semicolon (a year without a label indicates that the original label also reissued the record).

# 1

# 20TH-CENTURY COMPOSERS

Theres long been a clear separation in Western culture between so-called "high art" (characterized by classical music) and low art (as in folk, or popular, music). It's made for a long-standing love-hate relationship between the two. Pop music fans see classical music as elitist; classical music audiences consider pop unrefined. At the same time, pop looks to classical music for what it can adapt and popularize, in hopes that some of the respect will rub off, and classical music looks to pop for freshness and informality, hoping to uncover and use pop's secrets to widespread success.

While ideas of high and low are very powerful social constructs, the actual division on a qualitative level is largely artificial and subjective. The differences between a symphony orchestra and a jug band are more about the training, professionalism, and cultural background of their members (and listeners) than about the music's inherent worth. To a large degree society's consciousness of "high" versus "low" indicates the insecurity of the middle class, who have traditionally overvalued the aristocratic culture they have striven to join and disparaged the folk culture from which they came. Passing freely between high and low—and often settling in an area somewhere between the two—are rock musicians with classical training, formal composers with their "ears to the street," and many unprejudiced listeners who simply enjoy a wide variety of musical styles.

This chapter focuses on some of the 20th-century musical personalities who are generally categorized as composers of high art and yet have exerted a sizable influence on recent rock music. Interestingly, all of these musicians were to some degree marginalized in the classical world (usually by choice), a fact that no doubt makes them all the more attractive as cult figures in the rock world.

Some notes on terminology: New explorations in music that would traditionally have been labeled as *classical* make the word somewhat inaccurate, and perhaps terms such as *concert* music, *art* music, and *serious* music are better (though far from ideal—many rock and jazz musicians also play concerts and consider themselves serious artists). Whatever the reality, all these terms continue to be used to denote a tradition that, for better or worse, is regarded as distinct from popular music.

Some modern music in the high art tradition is called *avant-garde*, or *experimental*. These terms are often used interchangeably, but are subtly different: "Avant-garde" is a general term for music on the cutting edge of culture; "experimental" refers specifically to music that is itself an experiment. For example, a piece of *aleatory* music is experimental because it is based on chance procedures, and therefore will turn out differently each time.

Other terms used here that are interchangeable in general usage, though distinct in more specific ways, include *atonal* music, *serialism*, and *12-tone* music. Each describes a major trend in 20th-century composition away from traditional tonality. For centuries, Western music has been written around a central note, or tone, and the seven other tones that appear in the note's scale. Atonal, serial, and twelve-tone music are not centered on a single tone but freely use all twelve notes available in an octave. A further development, *microtonal* music, rebels against the entire European system of equal temperament (from which both the 8-tone and 12-tone scales derive) and explores (as non-Western music has always done) the infinite number of tones found between the notes on the scale.

Not all developments in art music have directly impacted popular music; for instance, the vast majority of rock (aside from more extreme noise bands) still conforms to keys and traditional tonality. Indeed, it could be said that popular music (including folk, jazz, and rock) has had a much larger impact on art music than the other way around. Still, most major trends are in some way relevant to rock, whether they have trickled down from art music to pop, been soaked up from popular music by classical, or have impacted the entire spectrum of Western music. Key developments have included:

*The introduction of industrial sounds and noise:* Composers have always incorporated the sounds of their environment into music, and with the advent of the industrial age, a new sonic landscape presented itself. As early as 1915, Luigi Russolo's treatise "The Art of Noises" (a name later appropriated by a well-known '80s industrial pop band) defined a new esthetic where everyday street sounds—engines, sirens, clanging metal—would become music to our ears. Now, decades later, the proliferation of screeching electric guitars and booming drums (not to mention actual samples of these industrial sounds) in rock seems to be a logical end to a century dominated by noise.

*The influence of Eastern sounds and philosophies:* Traditionally, Western music, high and low, has been programmatic—that is, built along some defined course from beginning to end (as in a song or a symphony). Recent strains of music (including aleatory music and *minimalism*) have adopted Eastern ideas that focus on exploring indefinite paths to see where they lead rather than arriving at a predetermined destination; they emphasize concept rather than result. The influence of non-Western music has meant a greater use of rhythm (particularly percussion) and repetition (the basis of minimalism). These developments have fed back into popular music through what we call "world music," while newer drone rock and electronic dance music has adopted the East's more linear, exploratory approach to composition.

*The emergence of electronic music:* Recording technology, a 20th-century development, has changed the way we hear music in unimaginable ways. Recordings enable us to experience music from all over the world, and from every time period, repeatedly and inexpensively. This, perhaps more than any other factor, has shaped the way we make, hear, and think about music today. Beyond sound reproduction, electronic technology has also created new tools and techniques for composing music. The invention of tape recordings led to *musique concrète*, or tape music, where prerecorded sounds are manipulated and combined to make new music. The ideas of tape music pioneers such as Pierre Henry and Pierre Schaeffer are now used routinely in pop music through samplers, loops, and DJ turntables. More recently invented instruments such as synthesizers, capable of creating sounds electronically, are now commonplace in popular music as well.

*The distinction between high and low music is less relevant than ever:* Current composers not only draw from popular music (as composers have done for centuries), they actually work within it: Philip Glass plays in a band, Glenn Branca writes symphonies for electric guitar, John Zorn improvises freely, Cornelius Cardew composes for untrained musicians. On the other side, as popular music searches for new directions, rockers familiar with classical ideas (from the Beatles and Frank Zappa to Sonic Youth and Soul Coughing) allow what they've learned to inform their own music. And as new connections are made between long-separated musical traditions, outdated cultural barriers will surely fade away.

# E R I K   S A T I E

*Everyone will tell you that I am not a musician. That is correct. From the beginning of my career I classed myself as a phonometrographer.*

**Erik Satie, from "What I Am"**

Erik Satie was the product of a late 19th-century period that prized virtuosity, but he was an unremarkable pianist and cared little for the showy displays of Romanticism. He was not as well known as contemporaries Debussy and Ravel, yet he was an acknowledged influence on both. A true eccentric, Satie collected umbrellas, and wore one of seven identical gray velvet suits each day (thus earning his nickname "The Velvet Gentleman"). He was a popular figure in cafés of Paris, as idolized by a younger generation of composers as he was reviled by critics. In many ways, Erik Satie was the world's first alternative music star.

Unlike any composer before him, Satie is significant as much for his approach to music as for his music itself. In this way, he paves a path for the many conceptual composers that have defined 20th-century art music. Though his work was seldom performed during his lifetime—and is only slightly better known today—Satie's break from traditional ideas of composition influenced modern music styles from musique concrète to minimalism, from ambient techno to trip-hop.

---

**Eric Bachmann, Archers of Loaf/Barry Black**
*He was very minimalist and so spacious in a time when everything around was Romantic and elaborate. Something about doing less to make the music more focused and pretty, I would like to say I've learned that from him.*

---

Eric Satie (he changed the spelling of his first name later) was born in 1866 in the French port town of Honfleur, and moved to Paris at age 12 with his father, an amateur composer who owned a music shop. Soon after, the young Satie entered the prestigious Paris Conservatory, where he studied piano and composition. It was a disappointing experience for everyone involved. Feeling held back by the musical conventions of the day, he called the conservatory a "penitentiary bereft of beauty." Unimpressed by Satie's development as a pianist, teachers described him as "a very unimportant pupil."

By his late teens, Satie was frequenting the Bohemian cafés of Paris' Montmartre district and playing piano in nearby cabarets. The lively, melodic "pop" music he performed would prove influential when, around 1884, Satie began composing. Over the next decade he would pen what has turned out to be his best known material.

Satie's early piano compositions—including *Trois Gymnopédies* from 1888 and 1890's *Trois Gnossiennes*—are marked by their simple beauty and concise melodicism. Slow and hypnotic, but at times dissonant and full of unresolved chord progressions, these pieces sound strangely modern, even today. Their nonlinear, montage-like structure defied 19th-century rules of composition, and have more in common with modern collage styles. Tranquil and dreamy, the *Gymnopédies* have been adopted into the repertoire of New Age and Muzak, and seven decades before the minimalists adopted the modes and repetition of non-Western music, Satie's *Gnossiennes* reveal an influence of oriental music (which he likely first heard, as did Debussy, at the 1889 World Fair in Paris).

### Eric Matthews

*Satie's always been a part of my listening habit. It's tranquil, yet still harmonically challenging and exciting. He achieves a peaceful mood that I hope is in my music. The quietness, the solitude. It's effected some of us [pop songwriters] very deeply and become part of our own moods in our music.*

With 1893's *Vexations*, a short, neutral passage lasting one to two minutes, Satie created an important forerunner to avant-garde composition. *Vexations'* directions call for it to be repeated 840 times, which requires up to 28 hours to play. The piece may be the earliest example of a loop, those repeating musical phrases so common in electronic music.

### Alex Patterson, Orb

*At the end of the night, after going to the acid house clubs back in '88, coming home and putting Satie on was like touching heaven, really, on an ambient front. It gave me a lot of confidence to go in and put my hand on a piano and play sort of feminine chords.*

*Vexations* proved especially influential to **John Cage,** the leading figure in 20th-century experimental music. Taking literally Satie's instructions—"to prepare oneself beforehand, in the deepest silence, by serious immobilities"—Cage was inspired to compose *4'33"*, a piece where the performer sits silently at his instrument. And in 1963, Cage organized the first ever complete performance of *Vexations*, using an entire stable of pianists, including future Velvet Underground member **John Cale.** A more recent reprisal, in 1993, featured Soul Coughing's Mark De Gli Antoni and composer **LaMonte Young.**

Words were central to Satie's expression. He wrote absurdist prose, bits of which showed up in the titles of compositions (such *as Dried-Up Embryos* or *Three Pear-Shaped Pieces*) or were written on his scores as directions to the performer (for example, to play "like a nightingale with a toothache"). By the 1910s, these prose bits had become increasingly critical of 20th-century life. His *Bureaucratic Sonatina* (1917) contains ironic running commentary such as "he dreams of promotion."

In 1917 Satie composed the surrealist ballet *Parade,* a collaboration with Pablo Picasso (scenery) and Jean Cocteau (scenario). *Parade* utilized typewriters, rattles, steamships whistles, pistol shots, and sirens—sounds of the modern world. This musique mechanique would later be utilized by everyone from composer Edgard Varese to rappers Public Enemy.

---

*Mark De Gli Antoni, Soul Coughing:*
*Satie was a big, big influence philosophically. The way Satie stuck a typewriter in the middle of Parade. Take a Soul Coughing song like "Sugar Free Jazz": I was like, "Why can't a seagull become a lead guitar?" [The sample] still sounds like a seagull, but if I place it where traditionally some other lead instrument would speak, will you for a moment stop thinking it's seagulls and accept it as the lead melodic element, in a traditional song way?*

---

Three years after mixing outside sounds into *Parade*, Satie attempted the opposite: to write music that would itself blend into the environment. *Furniture Music*, as he called his series of compositions, was meant strictly as background music. It was functional music for a modern society, meant to soften an aural environment polluted with clanging silverware and car horns. It was, essentially, the root of ambient music.

Satie was still largely an outsider when he died of liver disease (he was a long-time alcoholic) in 1925, at age 59. By then, though, a small group of French composers known as Les Six (including Darius Milhaud and Arthur Honegger) had acknowledged Satie as their spiritual father. While Satie's work fell even further out of mainstream consciousness in the middle decades of this century, his music began to reemerge in the 1960s, thanks both to the influence of **John Cage** and to the popular recordings made by concert pianist Aldo Ciccolini of Satie's works.

In recent years, Satie has been discovered by a growing number of rock musicians. In one year (1995–1996) Satie's *Gnossienne No. 1* was sampled to great effect by both Folk Implosion (on the *Kids* soundtrack) and Drain, a side project of the Butthole Surfers' King Coffey. As modern music catches up with Satie's modernist visions, whole new generations are joining the Velvet Gentleman's musical cult.

## SELECTED WORKS

*Trois Gymnopédies* (1888).

*Trois Gnossiennes* (1890).

*Vexations* (1893).

*Pièces froides (Cold Pieces)* (1897).

*Trois Morceaux en forme de Poire*
  *(3 Pear-Shaped Pieces)* (1903).

*Le Piège de Méduse (Medusa's Trap)* (1913).

*Embryons desséchés (Dried-up Embryos)* (1913).

*Sports et divertissements (Sports and Diversions)* (1914).

*Parade* (1917).

*Sonatine bureaucratique (Bureaucratic Sonatina)* (1917).

*Socrate* (1918).

*Musique d'ameublement (Furniture Music)* (1920).

*Relâche* (1924).

*Cinéma Entr'acte symphonique* (1924).

# RAYMOND SCOTT

*Jazz historians have chosen to understate the importance of [Scott's band] in their histories of American music. The reasons for this rejection have much to do with [the band's] overt interest in classical music. This music lives in a zone somewhere between jazz and classical music. [Scott's group] accomplished this in a time when such a mix of influences was considered even more unusual than it is today.*

***Don Byron, jazz clarinetist [from his notes to Bug Music (Nonesuch, 1996)]***

Whether or not we realize it, we've all heard Raymond Scott's music; his manic, colorful vignettes appeared in over one hundred Looney Tunes cartoons (accompanying Bugs Bunny, Daffy Duck, and the rest). His primary influence lies in the way his music has reached young television watchers and shaped the way that generations have perceived the relationship between music and motion.

Scott's music is quintessentially modern. He was interested in mechanical sounds, even when made by humans. In his works, he took on the role of writer, arranger, player, conductor, engineer, and inventor, thus blurring the lines between composer, performer, and technician and creating a new paradigm for the roles a modern recording artist could assume.

By unapologetically injecting classical elements into pop and jazz, his music did much to relieve art music's burden of seriousness and break down the lines between high and low. His greatest contribution to 20th-century music was, ironically, also the reason for his relative obscurity. Deemed too classical (or else too goofy) for jazz and not sober enough for classical, Scott fell through the cracks of music history.

The son of Russian immigrants, Raymond Scott was born Harry Warnow in 1908 in Brooklyn. At school he studied to be an engineer, until his older brother Mark—conductor of the CBS Radio Orchestra—convinced him to pursue music. After attending Julliard, Harry became pianist in his brother's band and changed his name to Raymond Scott (which he picked from a phone book) to avoid charges of nepotism. Scott soon craved further artistic control and recruited five orchestra members to form his Raymond Scott Quintette. Though the group was actually a sextet—with saxophonist, clarinetist, trumpeter, bassist, drummer Johnny Williams (father of Star Wars composer/conductor John Williams), and Scott on piano—Scott preferred the sound of the word quintet. (In 1994, Stereolab—also a sextet—would name their record *Mars Audiac Quintet* in tribute to Scott).

Between 1937 and 1939, the Quintette's music appeared both on radio and in films. Songs like "Powerhouse" and "The Toy Trumpet" were fast and intricate, full of instantly gratifying melodies and caricaturesque instrumentation that makes them clear precursors to the hi-fi lounge sounds of Esquivel and Martin Denny. Evocative titles like "Dinner Music for a Pack of Hungry Cannibals" and "Boy Scout in Switzerland" complemented the whimsical, bizarre tunes. Though the music sounded closest to swing jazz, it borrowed classical melodies and was far too fast and disjointed for dancing. It became popular as novelty music, but was reviled by critics as fake jazz.

---

### Tom Maxwell, Squirrel Nut Zippers

*What Raymond Scott did was completely off the wall, very fucked up tonally. He brought in this weird, machine-like feel to music that's generally very loose and emotive. He was a nut out of left field who made sounds nobody else was making. "Powerhouse" kicks my ass; I love the changed times, the bizarre key, the weird drum breaks, the strange intervals, and it's really fun. I definitely took a page from his book [when] I wrote this orchestral song called "The Kracken." It's strange, angular jazz—but not bop—some other sort of 20th-century sounding thing.*

---

A perfectionist, Scott showed each musician exactly what to play and forbade any improvisation. In the studio, he pioneered the kind of creative techniques later used by Beatles' producer George Martin and the Beach Boys' Brian Wilson. An early adherent of overdubs and tape editing, Scott was also known to try things like dipping trumpets in water, or placing sea shells behind microphones, to get the sound he wanted.

In the early '40s, once the Quintette had expanded into the Raymond Scott Orchestra, Warner Bros. in-house composer Carl Stalling licensed a good deal of Scott's work. Over the next two decades, bits and pieces of Scott's tunes showed up in Stalling's Looney Tunes scores. The playful, exaggerated themes proved a perfect match for the cartoon world (decades later, they would appear on *The Ren and Stimpy Show* as well), and this music would prove Scott's most enduring legacy.

### Mark De Gli Antoni, Soul Coughing

*I loved cartoon music, but it wasn't until Soul Coughing put together "Bus to Beelzebub"—when we found this great cartoon that we had to [sample]—that I became aware Carl Stalling had taken stuff from Raymond Scott. [Soul Coughing's] "Disseminated" is consciously a Raymond Scott tribute: a short piece, a wacky little phrase from "The Penguin," completely built on his loop. And on "Zoom Zip," the trumpet part is taken from Raymond Scott's "The Toy Trumpet," but slowed down and edited.*

Scott, meanwhile, succeeded his brother as CBS bandleader and composed music for Broadway and commercials. All the while, his sense of humor continued to shine. In 1949, Scott's orchestra performed "Silent Music," a music-less, pantomimed swing tune, a full three years before **John Cage** offered his own silent work, *4'33"*. This wasn't the first—nor would it be the last—time Raymond Scott was ahead of those considered ahead of their time.

By the 1950s, as his music fell out of fashion, Scott focused more on electronics, an interest since his engineering days. He invented instruments such as the Electronium, which he described as "an instantaneous composition-performance machine," as well as an early synthesizer. Over the next two decades he would play a role in the development of both the sampler and sequencer, the basic tools of nearly all modern dance music. Scott's recording was sporadic, but typically ahead of its time. His 1963 synthesizer work, *Soothing Sounds for Baby*, featured keyboard patterns that predated similar work by minimalists such as **Philip Glass** and Terry Riley by decades (see also the 1996 album, *Music for Babies*, by U2 collaborator Howie B.).

### DJ Spooky

*Soothing Sounds for Babies is fucking brilliant. It's repetitive, with a beat pulse. I look to him as one of the originators of a techno aesthetic, in the way that techno comes out of the detritus of the industrial revolution.*

Scott continued composing and inventing until a stroke left him debilitated in 1987. By then, the influence of his avant-garde cartoon music could be heard in the quirky new wave of groups like

Oingo Boingo (whose Danny Elfman has composed very Scott-like material for *The Simpsons*) and They Might Be Giants. Recent tributes from both the jazz (Don Byron's *Bug Music*) and classical (Kronos Quartet's rendition of "Dinner Music") worlds indicates that today's musicians are finally walking across the bridges Scott built.

## DISCOGRAPHY

*Powerhouse: The Raymond Scott Project, Vol. 1* (Stash, 1991).

*Reckless Nights and Turkish Twilights: The Music of Raymond Scott* (Columbia, 1992).

# JOHN CAGE

*John Cage's influence has been so widespread for nearly anybody working in a certain type of music, it becomes part of what it means to make music in the 1990s or beyond. His influence comes from a few gestures: The idea that any sound is permitted. Something as simple as that, put to such terrific use in his works, just becomes a general fact of working with sounds.*

**David Grubbs, solo/Gastr del Sol**

To many familiar with concert music, John Cage is no secret at all. In fact, he's arguably the dominant personality in 20th-century experimental music. Studied in universities and performed by classical musicians all over the world, his work has shaped the course of modern music. Although Cage had no direct dealings in the world of rock music, his influence was so great that his presence—and that of his many disciples—is pervasive. So closely is Cage identified with the avant-garde as a whole, his name—as it shows up in R.E.M.'s "It's the End of the World as We Know It" or in Stereolab's "John Cage Bubblegum"—has come to signify an entire musical movement.

Like his hero, **Erik Satie,** Cage was colorful and good-humored, and often branded a charlatan by the classical orthodoxy. As perhaps he would have admitted, his work often seems more like a stunt than an actual composition; the ideas always stood out more than the music. Conceptually, though, Cage represents a complete break with the Western classical tradition, a total liberation of sound. His fundamental philosophy that "any sound is musical" would forever change the way we hear music.

Though nearly all Cage's work reinforces an "anything goes" ethic, his explorations took a number of distinct paths. As a young man in the early 1930s, he studied with two major composers, Arnold Schoenberg and Henry Cowell. Schoenberg, who sparked a revolution in classical composition with his use of 12-tone music (using all available notes rather than only those in a particular key), influenced Cage's earliest work. Cowell, however, would have a more lasting influence. Cowell was among the first to bring rhythm—which had long played a large role in Eastern music—to higher prominence in the West. Asian musical forms and Buddhist philosophies would play a central role in Cage's work. As much as any American artist, Cage presaged the flirtation of future generations—beatniks, hippies, and rock musicians—with Eastern culture.

**Thurston Moore, Sonic Youth**
*He was omnipresent as an influence on everybody in the arts, more as a theorist and teacher— his Eastern, Buddhist concepts—than for his actual pieces. Later I did go directly to his books*

*and works, though. His inspiration is really sublime in a way, you can't minimize his influence, even on people who don't know it.*

In 1937, Cage brought rhythm to the forefront by founding one of the country's first all-percussion ensembles. The physicality and tonal complexity of percussion attracted him; he believed that drumming was closer to natural human actions (hitting, tapping), and therefore a more direct musical expression, than other kinds of playing. He also recognized that percussion comes closer to the unintended sounds we hear in the world around us, otherwise known as noise. The eventual acceptance of noise elements into art music would have a significant impact on both modern jazz and rock.

Many of Cage's earliest works utilize percussion, most notably his *First Construction* (1939), which may be the first "industrial" song in its use of exclusively metal instruments (gongs, bells, metal sheets). From the beginning, Cage's rhythmic percussion works were closely tied to dance; in the '40s he began a lifelong collaboration with influential modern dance choreographer Merce Cunningham.

In search of a more economical way to present the varied sounds of a percussion ensemble, Cage began experimenting with the manipulation of piano strings. By attaching various small objects—bolts, nails, rubber bands—that distorted the notes and made them more percussive, Cage invented the "prepared piano," an instrument with a variety of exotic timbres. Cage's major prepared piano work, the trancelike *Sonatas and Interludes*, is perhaps his most beautiful and well-known piece. But the true significance of the prepared piano was, again, philosophical. The idea that not only was any sound permissible, but so was any instrument—or any use of an instrument—would inspire countless musicians, from Frank Zappa to Sonic Youth, to alter their instruments as well.

### Mark De Gli Antoni, Soul Coughing

*The psychological influence of "every sound around you is potentially a musical sound" was exactly the kind of thinking I needed for getting into the sampler. Take a song like [Soul Coughing's] "Is Chicago?": There was a building with great door squeaks, so I recorded them. And the question was: How do I take what I think are really musical sounds and fit them in a piece of music so they become not just random noise, but a real melodic, important element?*

By the 1950s, Cage had embarked on a new exploration that further employed Eastern and Buddhist ideas: aleatory, or chance, music. Instead of composing, Cage set up situations where chance determined the sounds created. The score of one well-known orchestral piece, *Atlas Eclipticalis,* is created by transposing astrological charts onto a musical staff.

One of Cage's greatest creations—and certainly his most notorious "composition"—combines elements of chance with nontraditional musical sounds. Cage's *4'33"* calls for a performer to sit at his instrument for 4 minutes and 33 seconds without playing. The silence enables the audience to focus on the "chance music" around them: the hum of the lights, the car horns on the street, the squeaking of chairs. The piece also illustrates as concisely as possible Cage's contention that, more than sound or structure, the only true determining element in music is time.

While Cage's chance operations have had little impact on popular music, the environment in which they were performed has. By the early '50s, Cage began to organize "intermedia events," where he held some of his more outrageous chance operations. *Theatre Piece,* for example, included a nude cellist smoking a cigar, balloons that were released and popped, and a man slung upside down with a watermelon. Events like these became the inspiration for the Fluxus art movement of the late '50s and early '60s, which included experimental composers **La Monte Young** and Yoko Ono, and artist Al Hansen (a student of Cage, who is also the grandfather of pop star Beck). Cage's intermedia events were also precursors to "happenings" such as the Velvet Underground's *Exploding Plastic Inevitable,* and later, '80s performance art.

---

### Joe Henry
*John Cage taught everybody a new way to look at art. And he was a big influence on John Lennon and David Bowie, people like that. He's still this tremendous figure. I wrote on my shaving mirror, in my wife's mascara, a quote from Cage: "Everything we come across is to the point." Cage talked constantly about getting your vanity out of the way. His idea of looking outward, I've tried so hard to work that way. For me, writing songs has less to do with self-expression than discovery. And I know a lot of my sensibility is informed by Cage.*

---

A last element of Cage's exploration with new sounds is his electronic and tape music. As early as 1939, his *Imaginary Landscape No.1* used two turntables (today's basic DJ tools). Later, with *Cartridge Music,* Cage amplified various materials (wire, pipe cleaners, feathers) by attaching them to a phonograph cartridge and running them across a variety of surfaces. The piece, recognized as the first electronic work designed for live performance, illustrated the potential for generating sound from even the most ordinary objects.

---

### DJ Spooky
*Pieces like Imaginary Landscape are supremely transitional moments in music. The piece uses radio signals, and if you think about it, radio acts as a network of frequencies just as instruments access a range of frequencies or tones. Playing with both of those he created this weird social piece. He was really advanced conceptually. For me, sampling acts as a theater of mem-*

*ory, and memory is its own network of frequencies—certain things trigger different memories. By putting them together in different bits and pieces you can build new memories, or imaginary memories. Which is like "Imaginary Landscape," where the psychology of human memory becomes its own landscape. That's what music is at its core.*

---

Though Cage was not the first to create musique concrète (or tape music, which like sampling, uses prerecorded sounds), pieces such as his *Imaginary Landscape No. 5* and *Fontana Mix* are innovative in their use of collage, which would play a large role in later pieces such as *Roaratorio* (1979) and his five *Europeras* (1988–1991). By the time he died, in 1992 at age 80, Cage's position as the preeminent representative of 20th-century musical experimentation was secure.

## WORKS

*Imaginary Landscape No.1*, for two turntables, frequency recordings, piano and cymbal (1939).

*Three Constructions*, for percussion (1939–41).

*Bacchanale*, for prepared piano (1940).

*Sonatas and Interludes for Prepared Piano* (1946–48).

*Imaginary Landscape No.4*, for 12 radios (1951).

*Music of Changes* (1951).

*4'33"*, for any instruments (1951).

*Williams Mix*, for tapes (1952).

*Fontana Mix*, for tapes (1958).

*Indeterminacy* (1958).

*Cartridge Music*, for amplified "small sounds" (1960).

*Music for Amplified Toy Pianos* (1960).

*Atlas Eclipticalis* (1961).

*HPSCHD*, for amplified harpsichord and 51 tapes (1967–68).

*Roaratorio, an Irish Circus on Finnegans Wake* (1979).

*Europeras 1–5* (1988–91).

TRIBUTE: Various Artists, *A Chance Operation: The John Cage Tribute* (Koch, 1993); an interesting collection—featuring Frank Zappa, Yoko Ono, Laurie Anderson, and other avant-garde figures—broken up into small fragments that, when played on a CD player's "random" mode, itself becomes a chance operation.

TRIBUTE: Various Artists, *Caged/Uncaged* (Institute of Contemporary Arts, 1993); produced by **John Cale,** the collection features Cage works interpreted by David Byrne, Lou Reed, Joey Ramone, Blondie, and Jello Biafra of the **Dead Kennedys.**

# THEATER OF ETERNAL MUSIC (THE DREAM SYNDICATE): LA MONTE YOUNG, TONY CONRAD, JOHN CALE

*The idea in my head was that the music had become so advanced that we didn't need composers at all. We were dismantling, destroying the Western tradition of composers by sitting in the middle of the music and just playing it.*

*Tony Conrad*

Between 1962 and 1966, a group of classically trained experimental musicians and composers came together under the direction of La Monte Young to create a hypnotic ensemble of endlessly droning sounds they called "dream music." They were informally called the Dream Syndicate (not to be confused with the '80s rock band of the same name), and later officially dubbed the Theater of Eternal Music. The partnership lasted only a short time and pursued a limited agenda, but the group would prove to be among the most significant outside contributors to the sound of modern rock.

The influence of La Monte Young's group on contemporary music is quite direct: It lies almost completely in one band, the Velvet Underground (and to a lesser extent, **Faust**), and one musical gesture, the drone. In the past 30 years, however, the Velvets' drone has inspired and informed countless bands, whether directly or through the many V.U.–influenced bands.

*Thurston Moore, Sonic Youth*

*The "existence" of La Monte Young was influential. I had no idea what his music sounded like until later, and at that point we were already playing music that was coming out of his lineage anyway. I found it really beautiful, but it didn't change my world. It had already changed my world through others.*

Young's earliest musical memory from his Idaho childhood in the '30s and '40s was the steady hum of an electrical transformer behind his grandfather's gas station. By his late teens, Young was in L.A. playing saxophone with free jazz experimentalists Don Cherry and Ornette Coleman, studying the serialist composition of Anton Webern, and discovering Indian music. By the late 1950s, Young had fallen under the influence of **John Cage** and was involved with what would become known as the Fluxus movement. With New York composers and visual artists such as Al Hansen and Yoko Ono, Fluxus set out to playfully blur the lines between different art forms (music, theater, visual art), as well as between art and life.

Young's work in this period was often more conceptual than musical. The score to his *Composition 1960 #10,* for instance, called for the performer to "draw a straight line and follow it." When it was musical, it retained an essential simplicity that came to define his work (his *Composition 1960 #7* consists of a single piano interval, "to be held a long time"), and Young is often recognized as the first major minimalist composer (a group that would include Steve Reich, Terry Riley, and **Philip Glass** as well).

Young's 1958 *Trio for Strings* served as a blueprint that he would use for his major life's work. Consisting of long, sustained viola notes, with other instruments joining for various durations to complete a chord, the droning strings created fascinating harmonic effects and psycho-acoustical phenomena. By 1962, Young had largely moved away from Fluxus and formed a group of like-minded musicians (including Terry Riley early on) to exclusively pursue these sounds, which he called "dream music."

One of his collaborators was Tony Conrad, a composer-violinist Young met in California who shared his fascination for Indian and experimental music and had been trained in harmonic theory. In addition to Conrad on violin and Young on saxophone (and later singing), the group dubbed the Dream Syndicate included poet (and original Velvet Underground drummer) Angus MacLise on percussion, future Warhol scenester Billy Name on guitar, and Young's wife Marian Zazeela singing and designing a light show. Rounding out the group on viola was John Cale, a young Welsh music student who had come to the United States on a Leonard Bernstein scholarship.

Expanding on the basic premise of slow, sustained tones and a limited number of pitches, the group produced *The Four Dreams of China,* an extended trancelike improvisation. The work's most developed section, called *The Second Dream of the High-Tension Line Stepdown Transformer,* explored the harmonic relationships between notes and used techniques such as amplification, throat singing, and a minimalist bowing style to emphasize certain harmonics.

By 1964, the group was renamed the Theater of Eternal Music to reflect the transcendental quality of the ever-lengthening performances. Conrad introduced new pitches based on notes in the harmonic series rather than the traditional Western system of equal temperament. *The Tortoise, His Dreams and Journeys,* which used the pitch of Young's turtle aquarium motor as the root frequency, was their first piece based on this harmonic tuning system, known as *just intonation.* That same year, Young's solo piano piece *The Well-Tuned Piano,* employed just intonation as well.

As the group's explorations grew, so did an inherent power struggle. On one side there was Young, who considered himself the Theater of Eternal Music's composer. On the other side was Conrad (along with his roommate Cale), who considered the group a collaboration and was openly disdainful of even the idea that this music could have a composer in the traditional Western sense. Though they would remain active for at least another year, Conrad and Cale were soon exploring other career options.

In the fall of 1964, Conrad and Cale became the bassist and lead guitarist for a rock band, the Primitives, where they backed up singer Lou Reed on an inane teenybopper dance song he'd written called "The Ostrich." The band was short-lived, but Cale and Reed soon began a musical partnership that would evolve into the Velvet Underground. Combining Cale's background in experimental music—particularly his droning viola work in the Dream Syndicate—with Reed's tough pop sensibility, between 1965 and 1967 the Velvets created some of the most original and most influential rock ever made.

---

### Sean O'Hagen, High Llamas

*I find John Cale fascinating insofar as he could actually write a happy song but convey an element of malice. That was very much an influence in Microdisney [O'Hagen's first band]. When he was investigating intervals and drones, that was something I love and we try to do a little with Turn On [O'Hagen's side project with Stereolab's Tim Gane].*

---

Conrad opted not to pursue rock with Cale and Reed (although he did name the Velvet Underground, after an S&M book he found in the street). Instead, Conrad got involved with avant-garde filmmaking, creating works such as *The Flicker,* a 1966 short that stands as a milestone of minimalist cinema. Currently a professor of video arts in Buffalo, Conrad never fully left music. In 1972, he traveled to Germany where he recorded *Outside the Dream Syndicate* with influential prog rock band **Faust** (it was from this record, not Young's Dream Syndicate, that the '80s group took its name). A decade later, Conrad embarked on a piece called *Early Minimalism* (released in 1997), which, like the Faust album, is an attempt to realize some of the harmonic ideas he first put forth with dream music. Conrad has also performed with rock experimentalists Gastr del Sol and recorded a further study of his anticompositional, anti-Western microtonal violin work, *Slapping Pythagoras.*

### Jim O'Rourke, solo/Gastr del Sol

*In Tony's music, the message is all laid out. There's no man behind the curtain, like there is in Stockhausen and Young.... If anybody gives me credit for helping Tony Conrad come back I've finally done something worthwhile on this planet.*

Cale, who left the Velvets due to creative and personal conflicts with Lou Reed, has pursued a solo career that bridges the worlds of classical and rock. His records run the gamut from orchestral (*Academy in Peril*) to hard rock (*Animal Justice, Sabotage*), and from tuneful and plaintive (*Paris 1919*) to cold and minimalist (*Church of Anthrax* with Terry Riley). Cale has composed song cycles around the life of Andy Warhol (*Songs for Drella*, with Lou Reed) and the poetry of Dylan Thomas (*Words for the Dying*), written with playwright Sam Shepard (*Music for a New Society*), and scored films (*I Shot Andy Warhol, Eat/Kiss, Basquiat*). As a producer, Cale is responsible for some of rock's landmark recordings, including the debut albums by **Jonathan Richman**'s **Modern Lovers,** Patti Smith, and the **Stooges**. Through collaborations, he has had a profound influence on the music of both **Brian Eno** (*Wrong Way Up*) and David Byrne.

### Brian Eno

*John Cale influenced me quite a lot. The way he works with musicians [in the studio] is very interesting. You get in there, you've just got yourself set up and the tape's suddenly rolling!... And this is something I've picked up, if you catch someone on their first time through they do some very odd things. You get this kind of liveliness to it which is a mixture of a sense of danger and excitement. I also picked up Cale's sense of arrangement. I started listening to the kind of instruments he uses; he uses a lot of orchestral instruments in a way that doesn't sound trite and sloppy.*

La Monte Young has continued to create drone works. In the late '70s, Young and Zazeela brought the concept of "eternal music" to a logical extension with their Dream House, an on-site installation of slowly evolving light and sound that runs continually, sometimes for several years at a time, in their New York studio. The Theater of Eternal Music has continued as well, in various forms including a brass ensemble and big band. In 1990, Young formed the Forever Blues Band to apply his drone and just intonation ideas to blues. "Dorian Blues in G," the group's extended jam originally composed in 1961, can go on for hours. The piece brings non-Western harmonic principles full circle by reuniting the just intonation developed in 20th-century classical music with the similarly microtonal folk music derived from African "blue" notes. In 1997, Pulp, Spiritualized, Nick Cave, and others participated in a benefit concert for Young and Zazeela, to help the couple pay for medical bills incurred during Zazeela's recent sickness.

Considering its impact, remarkably few have ever heard the original Theater of Eternal Music. Though Young often recorded the group's sessions, and likely still has many of the tapes, he has refused to release any of it officially. Some attribute this to Young's perfectionism—suggesting that he deems the recordings unacceptable for public circulation—while Conrad and Cale have contended for years that Young is only interested in protecting his reputation as "sole composer," which would be damaged if people heard what really went on. This feud, which has long strained Young's relations with Conrad and Cale, continues with no end in sight (Conrad was recently seen picketing a Young concert in Buffalo). Those willing to do some searching may be able to find a rare 1992 bootleg called the *White Album*, featuring an old radio broadcast of Young, Conrad, and Cale's Theater of Eternal Music. While the recording quality is only fair, it remains the only available artifact of this legendary group's dream music.

## DISCOGRAPHY

### YOUNG

*89 VI8 C.1:42-1:52 AM Paris Encore from "Poem for Chairs, Tables, Benches, Etc."/In "Fluxtellus"* (Tellus).

(w/Marian Zazeela) *The Black Record* (WG, Edition X, 1969).

(w/Marian Zazeela) *Dream House 78'17"* (Shandar, 1974).

*The Well-Tuned Piano* (Gramavision, 1987).

*90 XII 9C. 9:35–10:52 PM NCY, The Melodic Version of the Second Dream of the High-Tension Line Stepdown Transformer from the Four Dreams of China* (Gramavision, 1991).

*Forever Bad Blues Band: Just Stompin': Live at Kitchen* (Gramavision, 1993).

### CONRAD

(w/Faust) *Outside the Dream Syndicate* (Caroline, 1974; Table of the Elements, 1993).

*Slapping Pythagoras* (Table of the Elements, 1995).

*Four Violins* (Table of the Elements, 1996).

*Early Minimalism* (Table of the Elements, 1997).

### CALE

*Vintage Violence* (1970; Columbia, 1990).

(w/Terry Riley) *Church of Anthrax* (Columbia, 1971).

*The Academy in Peril* (Reprise, 1972; Warner Archives, 1994).

*Paris 1919* (Reprise, 1973; Warner Archives, 1994).

*Fear* (Island, 1974).

(w/Kevin Ayers/Brian Eno/Nico) *June 1, 1974* (Island, 1974).

*Slow Dazzle* (Island, 1975).

*Helen of Troy* (Island UK, 1975).

*Guts* (Island, 1977).

*Animal Justice EP* (Illegal UK, 1977).

*Sabotage Live* (Spy/IRS, 1979).

*Honi Soit* (A&M, 1981).

*Music for a New Society* (Ze/Passport, 1982; Rhino, 1993).

*Caribbean Sunset* (Ze/Island, 1984).

*John Cale Comes Alive* (Ze/Island, 1984).

*Artificial Intelligence* (Beggars Banquet/PVC, 1985).

*Words for the Dying* (Opal/Warner Bros., 1989).

(w/Brian Eno) *One Way Up* (Opal/Warner Bros., 1990).

(w/Lou Reed) *Songs for Drella* (Sire/Warner Bros., 1990).

*Even Cowgirls Get the Blues* (ROIR, 1991).

*Fragments of a Rainy Season* (Hannibal/Rykodisc, 1992).

*Seducing Down the Door: A Collection 1970-1990* (Rhino, 1994).

*The Island Years* (Island, 1994).

(w/Bob Neuwirth) *Last Day on Earth* (MCA, 1994).

*Walking on Locusts* (Rykodisc, 1996).

*Eat/Kiss* (Hannibal/Rykodisc, 1997).

# PHILIP GLASS

*[The Talking Heads] and a lot of other rock-oriented people really got into his trancelike repetition. We could relate to it. Like a lot of R&B—it's got a different kind of groove obviously—but it's still precise repetition with slight changes. Occasionally we would structure things with that repetition, maybe with an odd meter similar to something he would do....*

*David Byrne*

Beginning in the late '60s, as art rock aspired to a higher level of respect and academic acceptance, a new generation of classically trained composers became interested in accomplishing the inverse. Tired of Western musical traditions—even those, such as serialism, which had only been developed in this century—they looked to popular and folk music, particularly non-Western styles, for new inspiration. The most visible among these composers was Philip Glass.

While Western composers' attention to Eastern music was a trend that had been developing for almost a century, what made Glass and his peers different was that they were consciously a part of the rock era. Not content to sit around waiting for commissions from orchestras or become college professors, these young composers formed bands, played club gigs, and produced records. And having aligned themselves with the rock world, it was only a matter of time before rock musicians and fans took notice.

For at least three generations of musicians working in pop, Philip Glass was a key link to both classical and Eastern music. Over the last few decades, Glass has collaborated with artists from Paul Simon and David Bowie to Suzanne Vega and David Byrne to Aphex Twin. By meeting pop musicians half way, Glass has impacted not only rock, but ambient and techno music as well.

Born and raised in Baltimore, where Glass's father owned a radio and record store, Philip studied violin and flute at Peabody Conservatory as a kid, graduated from the University of Chicago at 19, then studied composition at New York's Julliard with Darius Milhaud in his early '20s. It wasn't until he went to France in 1964 to study with famed instructor Nadia Boulanger that Glass began to find his own musical voice.

In Paris, Glass was hired to transcribe the music of Indian composer Ravi Shankar (later a large influence on the Beatles) into Western notation. Glass was mesmerized by the music's timeless quality, and he was soon off to hitchhike through India and Africa in search of these new (to him, at least) approaches to music. By the time he'd returned to the U.S. in 1967, Glass was composing in a style that borrowed heavily from the structures, if not the sounds, of Indian music. He, along with a small group of composers taking a similar approach, became known as the minimalists.

The music of Glass and the other major minimalists—La Monte Young, Terry Riley, and Steve Reich—shared a number of traits. Profoundly influenced by Eastern music, minimalism was highly repetitive, with cycles of notes developing slowly and subtly, and continuing with no apparent end.

It could be cold and mechanical, and yet mystical and meditative. Though minimalism tended to be more traditionally tonal than the serial music that had dominated previous decades of concert music, the psycho-acoustic phenomena often resulting from the use of electronic instruments—such as Glass's preferred electric organ—could make it sound quite alien.

### Tim Gane, Stereolab

*Repetition and minimalism are the two major things we always come back to, from the first record to the last. Particularly in early Philip Glass and Steve Reich, I like the simple components. You can see how it starts, then hear as instruments are added. It lets you into the secret, but it doesn't take away from the beauty or wonder of the music. I always liked the idea of not covering up the music and allowing people to understand where the ideas come from. I think that's important.*

The minimalists also agreed that they themselves were the best performers of their own music. Each led small groups, or performed their works solo (Reich and Glass, former classmates, appeared in each other's groups early on). Soon after his return to New York, Glass formed the Philip Glass Ensemble, which included keyboards, wind instruments, and voices, all amplified and controlled through a mixing board. Too loud and "undignified" for most concert halls, the group played wherever it could, mostly the galleries and rock clubs of New York's downtown art scene.

Though Glass would later stray somewhat from his roots, the Glass Ensemble's earliest material—such as *Music with Changing Parts* and *Music in Fifths*—is quintessentially minimalist. By the early '70s, the group was playing to small crowds in the United States and Europe, and Glass began releasing work on his own record label, Chatham Square. The ensemble's format and volume made the music attractive to more adventurous rock fans, and early on musicians such as David Bowie and **Brian Eno** attended Glass concerts in London, while New York art bands like the Talking Heads became fans as well. Soon, an Eastern, minimalist quality could be heard in these bands' pop and rock music.

### Brian Eno

*It was a dense, strong sound, and that really impressed me, the physicality of that sound. There was no attempt to draw your attention by standard musical devices. It was just, here is the sound. Live in it.... A lot of people left that show, but it really bowled me over. I thought, Oh God, this is it! This is the future of rock music! [from Option, Nov./Dec. 1997]*

While Glass was developing a reputation in more progressive circles, it wasn't until 1976 that he broke through in the classical world. With the premiere that year of his first opera, a collaboration with scenarist Robert Wilson called *Einstein on the Beach,* Glass became a recognized composer uptown as well as downtown (though afterward, he was still forced to make a living driving a cab). *Einstein,* a four-hour theatrical piece without plot or well-defined characters, is still Glass's most celebrated work. It took Glass's music beyond strict minimalism, and laid the groundwork for a new, multimedia art form that would come to be known as performance art.

Over the next decade, Glass composed other theater works, including operas *Satyagraha* (based on the life of Gandhi) and *Akhnaten,* as well as film scores (*Powaqqatsi, Koyaanisqatsi*), dance pieces for choreographer Twyla Tharp, and even soundtracks for events (his music for the torchlighting ceremony at the 1984 Olympics in Los Angeles introduced his music to millions of television viewers).

---

### Toby Marks, Banco de Gaia

*I saw Powaqqatsi and I thought, "Wow, amazing." The way the music and the images marry together in that film is quite something. I was fascinated by the repetitiveness and small changes over time—and running different arpeggios against each other to get constantly shifting patterns—I definitely took something away from that, whether it was consciously or not.*

---

By the '80s, Glass's reputation had developed to a point where CBS Records offered him a recording contract (the first composer to receive one since Aaron Copeland). Subsequent records like *Glassworks* and *Songs for Liquid Days* moved Glass closer than ever to becoming an actual pop star. *Liquid Days,* which featured songwriting collaborations with Paul Simon, Laurie Anderson, Suzanne Vega, and David Byrne, is by design a rock record. In addition, he produced a record for new wave band Polyrock, and lent arrangements to both Simon and Vega on their own records.

---

### Jim O'Rourke, Gastr del Sol

*[Glass's music] was rock and roll to me. Complete headbanging music. People around me were listening to Rush and Metallica; to me that was the stuff that made me pump my fist in the air.*

---

Glass's full impact on rock has undoubtedly yet to be felt. Musical styles such as New Age, ambient, and techno have all embraced minimalist concepts in their repetition, slow development, linear structures, and layering of parts. In addition, Glass's 1995 collaboration with electronica star Aphex Twin connects him to yet another generation of pop explorers. And with his recent trilogy of symphonies based on David Bowie's late '70s work with **Brian Eno**—*Low Heroes,* and *Lodger*— Glass seems to be once again looking to rock music for inspiration.

## DISCOGRAPHY

*Music with Changing Parts* (Chatham Square 1972, Elektra Nonesuch 1994).

*Solo Music* (Shandar, 1972; Elektra Nonesuch, 1989).

*Music in Similar Motion/Music in Fifths* (Chatham Square, 1973; Elektra Nonesuch, 1994).

*Music in Twelve Parts 1 & 2* (Elektra Nonesuch 1974; 1996).

*Einstein on the Beach* (1976; CBS Masterworks, 1984; Elektra Nonesuch, 1993).

*Dance Nos. 1 & 3* (Tomato, 1976).

*North Star* (Virgin, 1977).

*Glassworks* (CBS, 1982).

*Koyaanisqatsi* (Antilles, 1982).

*The Photographer* (CBS, 1983).

*Mishima* (Elektra Nonesuch, 1985).

*Satyagraha* (CBS Masterworks, 1985).

*Songs from Liquid Days* (Columbia, 1986).

*The Olympian* (Columbia, 1986).

*Akhnaten* (CBS Masterworks, 1987).

*Dancepieces* (CBS Masterworks, 1987).

*Powaqqatsi* (Nonesuch, 1988).

*Mad Rush/Metamorphosis/Wichita Vortex Sutra*
  (CBS Masterworks, 1989).

(w/Allen Ginsberg) *Hydrogen Jukebox*

(Elektra Nonesuch, 1993).

*The Low Symphony* (Point, 1993).

*Heroes Symphony* (Point, 1994).

*La Belle et la Bete* (Nonesuch, 1995).

*Symphony* No. 2 (Nonesuch, 1998).

# GLENN BRANCA

*Branca was really interested in* **John Cage,** *but he was also completely into the Ramones. Which was heavy: equating this so-called D-U-M-B music with high-minded and intellectual ideas. I was really into that and the people I was playing with came out of that strain.... When I first saw him play, it was the most ferocious, incredibly transcendent, rampaging guitar thing I had ever seen. It was uplifting, completely unlike anything I'd ever heard. A lot of it sounded like what I always imagined would be great to play someday, but he was already doing it.*

**Thurston Moore, Sonic Youth**

Though the idea of a punk composer sounds strange, a quick glance at the history of classical music proves it inevitable. Composers like George Gershwin once used jazz to capture a contemporary mood in their pieces. And going back as far as composers existed, the "low" folk music of the common people was always primary source material for adaptation and appropriation.

Born in 1948, Glenn Branca was among the first generation raised on rock music. Like many rock musicians, Branca's main source of training and education came from listening to the radio, and later from working in a record store. By introducing the sonic barrage of electric guitars and noise rock into a formal art-music setting, Glenn Branca has created a place for himself as one of the most vital composers currently active.

As a teenager in Harrisburg, Pennsylvania, Branca rejected classical guitar lessons and opted to play in rock bands. Initially interested in mainstream rock, his experiences in the late '60s, while studying acting at Emerson College in Boston, broadened his perspectives. Exposure to experimental theater revealed new ways to incorporate music into stage pieces and led Branca to the avant-garde work of John Cage and the Fluxus composers, whose music was often theatrical by design. Soon after, he took a job in a record store, where he was exposed to a wide variety of sounds, from '70s glitter rock to the 19th-century Romantic composers. Inspired in equal parts by Roxy Music, Gustav Mahler, and new composers like Philip Glass, Branca made no distinction between high and low music. "As far as I was concerned, what the Who was doing was just as important as what Penderecki was doing," he says. "But at the same time, Penderecki was no less accessible to me than the Beatles. It was just music that worked for me."

In 1975, Branca formed his own experimental company, the Bastard Theater, which enabled him to pursue acting, directing, and playwrighting, as well as composing and performing his own theater music. When he heard about New York's downtown art scene, where punk poets like Patti Smith and minimalist composers mingled with the experimental theater world, Branca moved there in 1976. Soon he was hanging around rock clubs like CBGB and Max's Kansas City, and—on a whim—he decided to start his own band. Theoretical Girls featured Branca on guitar, co-songwriters Jeffrey Lohn and Margaret Deuys switching off on bass and keyboards, and drummer Wharton Tiers (who would later become Sonic Youth's producer). With their jagged guitar noise, Theoretical Girls fell in with the no wave scene of bands like **DNA** and **Lydia Lunch's** Teenage Jesus and the Jerks.

After releasing one single, "U.S. Millie," Branca formed a second band, the Static, to pursue his own musical ideas exclusively. The trio featured Barbara Ess, a visual artist and Branca's longtime girlfriend, and drummer Christine Hahn (who later played in CKM with Sonic Youth's Kim Gordon). In Static songs like "Inspirez Expirez," his first extended instrumental, and "The Spectacular Commodity," featuring a dense cluster of E notes, Branca began to explore more conceptual music.

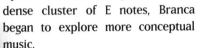

At Max's in 1979, Branca presented "Instrumental with Six Guitars," his first work as a composer. Featuring 12 minutes of minor intervals layered over each other to create a dense wall of noise, the repetitious music was clearly influenced by minimalism, though the guitar roar was all rock. Branca realized that working as a composer rather than in a rock band was a better way to express his highly dramatic themes. At the risk of sounding pretentious, Branca decided to call his extended sonic explorations "symphonies."

But while Branca made a conceptual leap into the world of art music, his material retained most of its rock roots. To maintain rhythm, Branca used a drummer and bassist, and to bolster the sound density he recruited a "guitar army" of up to a dozen musicians. Among the earliest members of his group was future Sonic Youth guitarist Lee Ranaldo (his bandmate Thurston Moore would soon follow). A bit later, Page Hamilton of Helmet joined the ensemble. Branca retained a theatrical element in his music by conducting in a very physical, dramatic style—writhing on the floor and flailing his arms madly—which he believed evoked better responses from the musicians.

---

### David Byrne

*I thought Branca's guitar orchestra performances were amazing. Very powerful and thrilling. It wasn't as loud as people said, it was more the immensity of the sound than the volume. At some point I tried to get elements of that kind of sound into what I was doing, though I wasn't very successful.*

---

Tuning individual guitars to a single note, Branca created intervals and chords by using a number of differently tuned guitars—11 in all for *Symphony No. 1*. It's easy to imagine the horror with which Branca, accompanied by performance artist Z'ev's industrial percussion, was greeted in classical music circles. Branca, however, offered more than just exercises in how to clear a room. While exploring the possibilities of guitar tunings and layering at extreme volumes, Branca began to hear phantom tones within the sheets of sound. He discovered that the guitars could produce natural effects that sounded like horns or choirs.

---

### Page Hamilton, Helmet
*Symphony Number 6 was a real sonic distorted guitar thing. Double strumming brought out different harmonics in the instruments. Live you hear all those guitars and all those harmonics popping out and it sounds sometimes like trumpet and also like voices. You definitely hear choirs. Being on stage with that is unreal.*

---

In the early '80s, Branca began to investigate acoustic phenomena and focused on the harmonic series, the string of notes (the root and overtones) that make up each musical tone. He began writing microtonal music, which uses tones that fall between the notes in the traditional 12-tone system. "People talk about the music of the 21st century. Well, this is it," Branca says. "It's going to be microtonal music, without a doubt." To accentuate the acoustic traits of microtones, Branca needed to create new instruments such as a mallet-struck guitar (for better resonance) and electric harpsichord (essentially guitars made into keyboards), as well as guitars refretted to play the harmonic series.

Branca became so obsessed with the mathematics of music that he began to lose interest in composing. Nonetheless, in 1983 his explorations bore fruit with *Symphony No. 3*. Subtitled, "Music for the first 127 intervals of the harmonic series," the piece attempted to amplify the sounds that occur naturally (though inaudibly) in nature. "At the time I saw the harmonic series as something that existed in nature, so I wanted to see, 'How did nature write music?'" he says. "Shouldn't it sound like chaos? And out of chaos comes order. The harmonic series is an infinite series, and it's also an infinite mind fuck."

After leaving influential downtown New York label 99 Records, which released his first recordings, Branca formed Neutral Records to release *Symphony No. 3*. During its brief life, Neutral released the debuts by both the **Swans** and Sonic Youth, as well as other post-no wave groups. Through these groups, younger bands were exposed to Branca's unconventional guitar tunings and dense guitar layering.

---

### Sean O'Hagen, High Llamas
*I'm very disinterested in guitar-based music, it constantly lets people down. Whenever music*

*starts to get interesting and experimental there's always a conservative rock-based movement to drag it back to year zero. But Branca held my confidence in guitars over the years. He was one of the people that redefined a tainted instrument, as far as I was concerned.*

Branca continues to use electric guitars in his compositions, though by 1985 he had begun writing for orchestral instruments as well (which required him, at 37, to learn to read music). Branca has also moved away from microtones toward a tonal style more focused on structure. His *Symphony No. 8* (1992), while composed for eight guitars, is clearly more melodic and dynamic than earlier guitar symphonies, as are his operatic and choral pieces. Now past 50, and able to boast commissions from Twyla Tharp's dance company and the 1992 World Expo in Seville, Branca is reintegrating his rock past with a more traditionally classical present. In the journey from punk clubs to symphony halls, Branca introduced rock esthetics into concert music and classical techniques into guitar noise. In doing so, he helped to further break down the artificial lines separating popular from art music.

## DISCOGRAPHY

*Lesson #1* (99, 1980); a debut EP showing Branca in transition toward composition.

*The Ascension* (99, 1981); another transitional piece, which unlike much of his later work, comes across well on record.

*Music for the Dance "Bad Smells"* (Giorno Poetry Systems, 1982); this Branca piece appears alongside work by John Giorno on the album *Who You Staring At?*

*Symphony No. 1 (Tonal Plexus)* (ROIR, 1983); composed in 1981, Branca's first guitar symphony explores his "emotional structure."

*Symphony No. 3 (Gloria)* (Neutral, 1983; Atavistic, 1993); Branca's creative breakthrough, his first to explore microtones in the harmonic series.

*Music for Peter Greenaway's Film "The Belly of an Architect"* (Factory [UK], 1987); Branca's first piece to appear on record that uses orchestral instruments.

*Symphony No. 6 (Devil Choirs at the Gates of Heaven)* (Blast First, 1989; Atavistic, 1993); a piece for 10 guitarists (including Helmet's Page Hamilton).

*The World Upside Down* (Les Disques du Crepuscule [Bel.], 1992; Atavistic, 1993); a full symphonic work in seven movements.

*Symphony No. 2 (The Peak of the Sacred)* (Atavistic, 1992); written a decade before its release, Branca's second symphonic work features percussionist Z'ev as well as his guitar army.

*Symphony Nos. 8 & 10 (The Mysteries)* (Atavistic, 1992); written in 1992 and '94 respectively, these guitar symphonies explore life and death.

*Symphony No. 9 (L'eve Future)* (Point Music, 1995); a work for orchestra and voices, Branca's first release on **Philip Glass**'s label.

*Songs '77-'79 (The Static & Theoretical Girls)* (Atavistic, 1996); a collection of recordings from Branca's early No Wave bands.

*Symphony No. 5 (Describing Planes of an Expanding Hypersphere)* (Atavistic, 1996); a guitar symphony from 1984.

*Indeterminate Activity of Resultant Masses* (Newtone, 1996); a lost recording from 1986 released for the first time.

# 2

# INTERNATIONAL POP UNDERGROUND

As a musical term, *pop* generally refers to *popular music,* all the stuff (rock, country, jazz, adult contemporary, etc.) that's not considered *classical.* Taken more literally, *pop* means *popular;* the stuff on the radio, on MTV, in the Top 40. But *pop* has another connotation, one more difficult to pinpoint. This is the sense in which we're going to use it in this chapter.

As a concept, Pop (with a capital P), can draw from many genres. Whether or not a particular piece of music is Pop doesn't depend on how many people hear it or how many copies it sells. Rather, it depends on sounds and attitudes and production styles. In this sense, an immensely popular band like Pearl Jam is not Pop, while an obscurity such as the Vaselines most definitely is Pop. And an undeniably creative musician like Jimi Hendrix is not Pop, while the Beatles surely are.

While Pop incorporates styles from all over, it retains an essential spirit. Pop is colorful, innocent, and melodic. It's not willfully noisy, gloomy, or rambling. Pop combines the song traditions of vaudeville, cabaret, Tin Pan Alley, English dance halls, Motown, bubblegum, and easy listening with the classic studio techniques of Phil Spector, Brian Wilson, George Martin, and Jeff Lynne. It ties Cole Porter to the Cardigans, the Monkees to Stereolab.

The two elements that each of the artists in this chapter share is that they are all (1) pop; and (2) not popular in the United States. Beyond that, they differ in styles, time period, nationality, language, and relative levels of success. Some were, in fact, immensely popular in other countries (**Serge Gainsbourg, Scott Walker**), but didn't translate well to American audiences. Others, like **Big Star,** had just about all the elements for popularity except luck and circumstance. Still others, such as **Van Dyke Parks,** were just too far out to connect in the mainstream, no matter how hard their label tried. A group like the **Young Marble Giants,** meanwhile, didn't stick around long enough to cross over. And some groups, like **Beat Happening** (who coined the term "International Pop Underground," which I've appropriated for my own purposes here), were too concerned with creating their own definition of what it meant to be a pop group to care much whether the mainstream took notice.

---

### Calvin Johnson, Beat Happening

*[The International Pop Underground] was the idea that there were people who were interested in pop music and making records all over the place, connected through the mail or through records. It was just a wide umbrella that wasn't necessarily a genre, not any one definition. It could be anything. Maybe it's people who are inspired by pop music, but basically it's just about taking over the media and calling the shots: "We're calling this pop music, and it is because we said it is."*

---

Whatever the reason these artists never became popular, their music lives on and thrives as part of a pop tradition that continues today, in both independent and some mainstream music. Unlike jazz or blues or even rock 'n' roll, this Pop is not exclusively American in origin, and it's certainly not culturally pure. Rather, it's an endearing musical mutt that's claimed by the entire modern world.

## VAN DYKE PARKS

*I was as influenced and as obsessed with Van Dyke Parks as I was with the Beach Boys. I loved that you could be avant-garde with traditional instruments and tunes. Some would say avant garde is for the elite, it's introverted, it happens in small rooms, it's subversive, but "Cabinessence" is a very strange piece of music that's melodically heartwarming and has a skip in its step. [Parks' influence] was definitely there in the back of mind [on the High Llamas' Hawaii], this bloody thing I wanted to get out of my system. It's derivative, I guess. I thought I was putting together a record that Van Dyke would've done."*

**Sean O'Hagen, High Llamas**

Van Dyke Parks draws on the entire American musical heritage, from 19th-century minstrelsy to psychedelic pop. While he has worked for decades just under the surface of our musical culture and his distinctive stamp can be heard in everything from film music to orchestral pop to experimental sounds, only a small cult of fans cherish him as a true American original. His influence can be heard both in bands like the High Llamas—who create lush, dizzyingly exaggerated pop—and more art-minded composers who work with pop idioms. Through his solo material—and through his ill-fated collaboration with Brian Wilson on the Beach Boys' aborted *Smile* album—Parks has elevated the modern pop tune into the world of the art song.

Parks was born in 1943 in Hattiesburg, Mississippi, the son of a distinguished doctor who had played in John Philip Sousa's band. Van Dyke played clarinet at age four, and sang in operas and choruses conducted by Arturo Toscanini before he'd reached his teens. He was also a child actor who appeared on Broadway and had bit parts on television and in films. After studying music composition in college, Parks played in a folk group called the Greenwood County Singers (with his brother Carson, who later wrote Frank Sinatra's hit "Something Stupid"), and worked as a session musician at Disney.

In his early twenties, Parks shifted his focus toward pop music. He became a songwriter (penning the often-recorded "High Coin"), session pianist (on records by the Byrds and Grateful Dead), and producer (for Judy Collins, Randy Newman, Arlo Guthrie, and others). In 1966, Parks met the Beach Boys' Brian Wilson, who had recently produced his most ambitious work, his band's *Pet Sounds* album. Wilson hoped his follow-up, *Smile*, would be far more sophisticated even than *Pet Sounds*, and invited Parks to collaborate with him.

In the face of growing national turmoil, Wilson wanted to explore innocence lost in America—a prevalent theme in Parks' own work—and create what he called "a teenage symphony to God." As promised, the first song Parks and Wilson wrote together, "Surf's Up" (which was not a surf song at all—note the title's double meaning), was miles beyond the band's signature beach music. Parks' lyrics—with surreal, deeply evocative lines like, "Columnated ruins domino/canvas the town and brush the backdrop"—were the perfect match for Wilson's music.

---

**Tony Goddess, Papas Fritas**
*They really took a literal picture of the sound. Like the song "Vegetables," where the downbeat would be accented by the sound of them biting through a carrot, or "Cabinessence," where they use rustic sounds like a banjo and a harmonica. Nothing we do is as developed as those guys, but like with "Live By the Water," I tried to make an island, calypso rhythm. I think Van Dyke Parks was directly responsible for pushing Brian Wilson toward that stuff. Some people really think he fucked up Brian Wilson, but I really like his lyrics. That's why we named our studio Columnated Ruins, from the lyrics to "Surf's Up."*

---

*Smile*, though, was plagued with difficulties. Brian's increasing mental instability and drug use were turning the recording process into a bottomless pit of expense that produced brilliant musical fragments but little completed work. The album was hyped as a masterpiece, but months passed without a release. It soon became clear Wilson was losing touch with reality. Meanwhile, the other Beach Boys wanted nothing to do with Parks' "incomprehensible" lyrics. When tensions mounted between Wilson and the band, Parks bowed out and *Smile* was abandoned altogether. Never officially released (though bits have shown up on later Beach Boys albums and on bootlegs), the legend of *Smile* has since assumed mythic proportions as pop's great lost album.

---

**Jeff Tweedy, Wilco:**
*His contribution to the Beach Boys is surreal, it's unbelievable. I'm a big fan of Smile. To me, it's not a record that could've become one of the best records ever made if it was finished. I think it is one of the best records ever made, unfinished. In a conceptual way, the idea of using strange instruments and intervals, horn and string parts, just an overall textural thing, was influential.*

---

After his break with the Beach Boys, Parks set out to explore his own pop artistry (as well as audition for *The Monkees*). Following a single he recorded under the alias George Washington Brown, Parks released his first album in 1968. Reputedly four years in the works, *Song Cycle* was a unified collection of richly orchestrated songs that drew from traditional music and themes. It was in many ways what *Smile* aspired to be—an American equivalent to *Sgt. Pepper's*. Though somewhat rambling and difficult, *Song Cycle* is full of great musical ideas. As with *Smile*, Parks' lyrics are rich in wordplay and explore Parks' own past as folklore. *Song Cycle*, however, was clearly not rock music, and so it isn't surprising the record sold dismally (despite its record company's considerable promotional backing). What Parks had created was an entirely unique chamber pop that drew freely from jazz, cabaret, show tunes, vaudeville, Tin Pan Alley, and the music of Stephen Foster, George Gershwin, and Charles Ives.

---

**Jim O'Rourke, solo/Gastr del Sol**
*Song Cycle is without doubt the greatest record ever made. At the time the guy was absolutely the greatest musical genius to walk the planet. It's my Holy Grail, everything I'd ever want is*

*there. It's music made by someone who's not dumb! There are great songs with the best damn lyrics he ever wrote, so incredibly articulate. Every bit of instrumentation makes sense, both musically and programmatically. It's the only thing I know of that's the logical extension of Charles Ives [early 20th-century American composer]. Van Dyke's records are the only link between the old way of Americana and the modern days.*

Parks' later albums explored similar territory, both thematically and in their highly intricate orchestrations. *Discover America*, in 1972, featured Van Dyke's arrangement of "Stars and Stripes Forever," but also added to the mix of styles, including steel drums and calypso songs. *Clang of the Yankee Reaper*, a 1975 collection of Parks' reworking other composer's music, also revealed a love for Caribbean music. Between solo recordings, Parks has worked as arranger for everyone from the Everly Brothers and Tim Buckley to Bruce Springsteen and U2, to Toad the Wet Sprocket and Fiona Apple. He also has scored films (including *Popeye, Bastard Out of Carolina, Private Parts*), played bit parts in movies, and even spent some time as a visiting lecturer at Harvard.

Parks' 1984 release, *Jump!*, based on the Brer Rabbit tales, simultaneously invoked his roots in Southern folklore and the bygone era of Hollywood musicals. *Tokyo Rose*, released in 1989, concerned itself with U.S.-Japanese trade relations, a somewhat bizarre, but nevertheless fascinating subject for a pop album.

### Eric Matthews

*Parks was another confirmation of what I wanted to do, or try to achieve. He introduced me to some instrument combinations that I hadn't even thought about before.*

In 1995, almost 30 years after *Smile*, Van Dyke reunited with Brian Wilson to create an album called *Orange Crate Art*. Featuring songs written by Parks and sung by Wilson, the album attempted to evoke the romantic image of California as a paradise that had drawn so many people there earlier in the century. Parks was still largely unsung, but still weaving his way through his American cultural heritage. And finally, he and Wilson had put a record out.

## DISCOGRAPHY

*Song Cycle* (Warner Bros., 1968); his best known record, a classic '60s album encompassing entire traditions of both pop and art music.

*Discover America* (Warner Bros., 1972); further cultural explorations, including the sounds of the Caribbean.

*Clang of the Yankee Reaper* (Warner Bros., 1975); featuring mostly covers reworked in Parks' unique orchestration style.

*Jump!* (Warner Bros., 1984); a show-tuney collection based on the Brer Rabbit folk tales.

*Tokyo Rose* (Warner Bros., 1989); a pop operetta on U.S.-Japan trade relations.

*Idiosyncratic Path: The Best of Van Dyke Parks* (Diablo, 1994); a compilation spanning Parks' work up until then.

*Orange Crate Art* (Warner Bros., 1995); a rumination on California's pastoral dream, featuring the vocals of Brian Wilson.

*Moonlighting: Live at the Ash Grove* (Warner Bros., 1998); a recently recorded live album.

## SCOTT WALKER

*Scott Walker is awesome. He's just got one of the biggest voices, and such a musical touch. I always think about Scott 3 as being the accelerated, futuristic version of what Sinatra and Nat King Cole were doing. It's the music of tomorrow in the old style. And if I put it on today, it's still the music of the future.*

**Eric Matthews**

If only for his seemingly backward career path—from '60s teen idol and cabaret crooner to his more recent underground experiments—Scott Walker would qualify as a unique and worthy cult hero. His reputation, though, can also proudly rest on his brilliant late '60s recordings, through which he carved his niche as a Sinatra-styled pop singer who could also handle—both as composer and performer—thoroughly contemporary, thoughtful, and engaging material. His unique style and abilities made him one of the few acts in post-Beatles rock to earn commercial and critical success in a "song interpreter" role that had essentially become outdated.

Walker's enigmatic reclusiveness and artistic eccentricities have only added to his myth. As his cult grows, his influence on modern music becomes more and more apparent: In the deep, showy vocals of David Bowie (who once tried to work with Walker), the eccentric pop of Julian Cope (who compiled a Walker retrospective), the dark swoon of Nick Cave (who included Walker in his recent soundtrack work), the pop fetishism of Marshall Crenshaw (who co-wrote liner notes for a Walker compilation), the mopey meanderings of Mark Eitzel (who had Walker Brothers songs played before shows), or the lush orchestral pop of acts such as Divine Comedy, Pulp, Eric Matthews, and Space.

---

**Chris Connelly, the Bells/Ministry/Revolting Cocks**

*He had a huge impact on David Bowie. When Bowie was first starting, the Walker Brothers were having hits and with all credit to Bowie, he recognized the darker and more experimental side of the band. What Bowie did with Scott Walker's music was drag out this sense of theater.... The way Scott Walker used the orchestra to play dissonance really appealed to me, because you don't find that in pop music, back then it was unlistenable. He was shamefully ignored at the time, but you can't really blame the public. He was Scott Walker, a pop figure, not someone you'd expect to experiment. It's like if somebody left the Spice Girls and went on to do a really radical, experimental record.*

---

Born in Ohio as Noel Scott Engel, the future Scott Walker moved around as a child before settling in Los Angeles in the early '50s. In his teens, he briefly fell under the tutelage of popular singer Eddie Fisher, who was interested in crafting young Scott into the latest teen sensation. When that failed to materialize, he began working as a bassist-for-hire for acts such as Ike and Tina Turner and lesser-knowns in the L.A. music scene. There, he met guitarist John Maus, who was performing under the name John Walker. They decided to team up, and with the addition of drummer Gary Leeds in 1964, the Walker Brothers were born. Originally styled after the Righteous Brothers (who weren't brothers either), with close harmonies and Phil Spector–like orchestration, the Walker Brothers recorded a few singles with Maus singing lead, but these failed to gain much attention. By the end of the year, the British Invasion was in full swing, and the band decided to head where the action was, so they moved to London.

Before long their single "Love Her," which featured Scott's operatic baritone as the lead voice, became a hit in the U.K. The Walker Brothers decided to stay, and signed with a British record label. With the help of producer Johnny Franz (who created a similarly orchestrated pop sound for Dusty Springfield), the Walker Brothers scored a string of big hits through 1965 and '66, including the #1 single "Make It Easy on Yourself," as well as "My Ship Coming In," as well as "The Sun Ain't Gonna Shine Anymore" (which was also a Top Twenty hit in the U.S.), and "Deadlier Than the Male." For a brief run, they were the biggest teen idols in Britain, complete with screaming mobs and fan-clubs, but the hysteria died off quickly, and in 1967 the Walker Brothers decided to disband. On their farewell tour of the U.K., they brought along Cat Stevens and Jimi Hendrix as supporting acts.

---

### Ron Sexsmith

*I love Scott Walker. Just the idea of Scott Walker—this guy who has a beautiful voice and puts out a record every ten years or something. There's your alternative artist for you, not that he sets out to be. His whole career is incredible, to be able to touch people that way, without tour-ing, without anything, and keep growing as an artist. He's an influence in that he doesn't fol-low any trends, he's always himself, and it's inspiring....*

---

Though each of the Walker Brothers pursued solo careers, only Scott had success (and only in the U.K.). Still working with producer Franz, between 1967 and 1969 Walker churned out a series of four landmark solo records— *Scott, Scott 2, Scott 3, Scott 4*—that remain his most enduring creations. Singing material that included works by the songwriting teams of Bacharach & David and Weill & Mann, as well as by renowned Belgian writer Jacques Brel, Scott established himself as a premier song stylist—a darker, more introspective Tom Jones; a Tony Bennett for the Age of Aquarius.

*Scott* restored Walker as a teen idol and made him a top draw in the cabarets of Europe. The record also featured, for the first time, Scott's own compositions. Even next to Brel's richly drawn pieces, songs such as "Montague Terrace (in Blue)" hold their own. But while Walker seemed to be growing as an artist, he remained firmly entrenched in an old-style career as a middle-of-the-road singer. For at least another year, Walker pursued a sort of musical double life; while he explored his more challenging material on increasingly artistic albums, he continued to please the masses (and his record company) with commercial singles such as "Johanna" and "Lights of Cincinnati."

With *Scott 2*, Walker had become the premier English interpreter of Brel's songs (which were translated by American songwriter Mort Shuman) and he enjoyed success with the somewhat unusual and risqué single "Jackie." By *Scott 3*, his own compositions filled the majority of the album. Songs like "Big Louise," "Rosemary," and in particular, "It's Raining Today"—with its disso-nant string orchestrations—showed that Walker was continuing to develop and stretch the bound-aries of what was acceptable in pop music.

When Walker released *Scott 4* in 1969 (under the name Noel Scott Engel), though, it seemed he had pushed a little too far. Consisting of all originals, the record contained challenging material such as the Ingmar Bergman–inspired "The Seventh Seal" and "The Old Man's Back Again (Dedicated to the Neo-Stalinist Regime)," a commentary on the recent Russian invasion of Czechoslovakia. The British public rejected the album, and Walker's stature quickly fell from marquee star to cult artist. And apart from his brief return to the pop charts, it was there it stayed.

In the '70s, Walker half-heartedly explored light country pop on forgotten records such as *The Moviegoer* and *We Had It All*. He briefly re-formed the Walker Brothers for three albums in the mid-'70s, and scored a U.K. hit with Tom Rush's "No Regrets." Tracks like "The Electrician," a 1978 song about the torture of prisoners in South Africa, proved Scott's songwriting as strong as ever and marked his advance into a more Bowie/Roxy Music mold.

For most of the past two decades, though, Walker has quietly concentrated on the solitary art of painting, away from public life. Twice, though, he has emerged with a new recording, and both have been as opaque and unorthodox as any music being currently produced. *Climate of Hunter*, in 1984, put Walker's moody, expressive vocals to use in a series of nebulous, ambient songs. And in 1995, *Tilt* came out of nowhere with an experimental pop opus—at times cinematic, at others industrial—that proves Scott Walker has not yet ceased to develop artistically.

---

### Will Oldham, Palace
*Tilt hardly even has a tangential relationship to anything you could describe in real life, which is pretty cool. It exists absolutely on a plane of its own, but it helps you recognize that there is a musical plane that doesn't have anything to do with any physical activity, or almost even with the medium itself.*

---

## DISCOGRAPHY

*Scott* (Philips [UK], 1967); the solo debut, full of terrific material and great singing.

*Scott 2* (Philips [UK], 1968); a record that further solidifies Walker as a first-rate song stylist and composer.

*Scott 3* (Philips [UK], 1969); an album coming at the peak of his success, but alluding to a more experimental direction.

*Scott 4* (Philips [UK], 1969); the start of Walker's slide toward obscurity, and his most challenging of the early solo albums.

*Til the Band Comes In* (Philips [UK], 1970); a slight return to former styles.

*The Moviegoer* (CBS, 1972); the first of a series of forgettable records, with country pop and bland standards.

*Any Day Now* (CBS, 1973); see above.

*We Had It All* (CBS, 1974); see above.

*Climate of Hunter* (Virgin, 1984); a surprisingly up-to-date and challenging return from self-imposed reclusion.

*Fire Escape in the Sky: The Godlike Genius of Scott Walker* (Zoo, 1981); compiled by Walker devotee, musician Julian Cope.

*No Regrets: The Best of Scott Walker and the Walker Brothers* (Fontana [UK], 1992); the only collection to include solo and Walker Brothers material together.

*It's Raining Today* (Razor & Tie, 1996); an excellent collection with key tracks culled from the first five albums, it's the only domestically available collection of Walker's early solo work.

*Tilt* (Fontana [UK], 1995; Drag City, 1997); critically adored recent return, available domestically on influential '90s indie label Drag City.

## SERGE GAINSBOURG

*I've always been interested in entertainers in other countries who aren't acknowledged here—for example, the Frank Sinatra of Chile. So I had that kind of appreciation for Serge.... [T]he content of his songs was pretty risqué—even for France. Which is what also endeared him to me. He expressed himself with such a mixture of disgust and passion. The combination is very tantalizing, and very '90s.... [Also], I'm rhythmically oriented, and a lot of his stuff was rhythmically based. He was very interested in African beats and Brazilian songs. He worked in many genres, and I do the same thing. He looked at music as a palette.*

**Beck [from *Interview* magazine, April 1997]**

Starting in the late '50s and continuing for decades, Serge Gainsbourg wrote and performed music—from cool jazz to slick disco, from mannered cha-cha to stylish mod beats—with lyrics that shocked, angered, and thrilled audiences in his native France. With his impeccably crafted songs, full of cynicism as well as humor—Gainsbourg chronicled the alienation of a modern rebel while mixing in enough sex, violence, and social commentary to keep the public captivated. "For me provocation is oxygen," Serge Gainsbourg once said. For over three decades, Gainsbourg so effectively played the role of bad boy provocateur that by the time he died in 1991 he was regarded as a national treasure.

Gainsbourg fancied himself an heir to young and restless French poets Baudelaire and Rimbaud—a Dylan of the Left Bank who played the part of both ugly duckling sex symbol and intellectual pop star. At the same time, he was also the archetypal sleazy lounge singer, the stereotypical French smoothie, the aging swinger who beds young models. The renewed interest in all sounds deemed kitschy (cocktail music, easy listening), has led to new notice of Gainsbourg in the English-speaking world. Indeed, his mix of retro sounds and thoroughly '90s polemics makes him a perfect antihero for the current revivals.

Beyond the trends, though, Gainsbourg was in essence a terrific songwriter whose ability to jump between various pop styles makes him an inspiration to modern-day eclectics. His growing influence in U.S. and British pop is implicit in the number of artists covering his material: Luscious Jackson [a version of Gainsbourg's "Soixante Neuf Année Erotique"—("69 Erotic Year")], Luna's Dean Wareham and Stereolab's Laetitia Sadier ("Bonnie and Clyde"), Free Kitten (featuring members of Pavement and Sonic Youth), and Mick Harvey of Nick Cave's Bad Seeds (two whole albums of Gainsbourg material translated into English).

His image as an angry outsider in France was not something Serge Gainsbourg needed to cultivate; it came naturally to him. He was born Lucien Ginzburg in 1928, the son of Jewish immigrants from Russia. As a teen during World War II, his family lived perilously under the Nazi puppet government in northern France and was forced to wear yellow stars, until they escaped to Limoges in the south. Though he returned to Paris after the war, Gainsbourg remained bitter about his experience, and disillusioned toward his fellow Frenchmen. He developed an arrogance and sense of fatalism about the world, and a keen desire to rebel against the repression he'd experienced under the Nazis. As a young man, he found kindred spirits in the bohemian scene of Montmartre, where he played piano in cabarets and studied painting.

By the late '50s, Gainsbourg had given up painting and began to earn attention for his songs, which he and others started performing in Paris clubs. He changed his name officially when he began his recording career in 1958 with the song "The Ticket Puncher," a jazz-based character study of the mundane workaday world. Other songs, such as "Intoxicated Man," "Ce Mortel Ennui" ("This Mortal

Boredom"), and "Indifferent," furthered Gainsbourg's image as a chronicler of bohemian angst and alienation and he became an antihero in an otherwise genteel French music world. Though his first album, *Du Chant à La Une!*, failed to gain much notice in mainstream French pop—which at the time was dominated by the "yé-yé" sound that borrowed heavily from American and British pop—Gainsbourg had become a favorite in the hip world of Paris' Left Bank.

### Dave Dederer, Presidents of the United States of America

*My wife spent a lot of time in Europe as a kid..., and she bought this set of stuff he did mostly in the '50s and early '60s, jazz trio with him singing. It's the most beautifully recorded music. Luscious, just so creamy, it makes you want to climb inside it. That's inspiring when it's time to record and you're trying to think of sounds and ways to invite the listener in.*

In the early '60s, Gainsbourg was reaching his mid-30s and was in search of a mainstream breakthrough. While remaining essentially a composer of jazz-pop, Gainsbourg began incorporating into his music the stylish sounds of the Caribbean and South America in songs like "Cha Cha Cha Du Loup," "Mambo Miam Miam," "Couleur Café." While his music became much more beat-oriented (1964's *Gainsbourg Percussions*), his world view remained dark ("End of the Rope") and he again failed to connect with pop audiences.

By the late '60s, the French public seemed ready for something a bit more risqué, and Gainsbourg was happy to comply. Though an innocent 18-year-old singer named France Gall had scored a hit with Gainsbourg's song "Les Sucettes" ("Lollipops"), it wasn't until Gainsbourg recorded his own version that the tune's dirty jokes became apparent. In no time, Gainsbourg went from cult favorite to bad boy of the French pop charts.

By then, Gainsbourg's music had shifted once again. Long enchanted by American popular culture, Gainsbourg now immersed himself in a mod-pop style, akin to Burt Bacharach and Lee Hazelwood/Nancy Sinatra songs, with colorful ditties such as the pop-art inspired "Comic Strip" (complete with sung sound effects—"Sh-bam! Pow! Whizz!") and the hipster society anthem, "Qui Est In Qui Est Out" ("Who's In Who's Out"). And having learned a valuable lesson from his success with "Les Sucettes," Gainsbourg set about creating his most provocative—and by no coincidence, his most successful—work.

Exploiting and exaggerating his outsiderness, Gainsbourg became Gainsbarre, a bad-ass rock star with an unkempt but fashionable junkie/lecher look, sneering derision at the world. He wrote songs about the fast life—"Ford Mustang," "Harley David Son of a Bitch," and gangster pop classic "Bonnie and Clyde"—and dueted with sexy younger women with whom he also had love affairs. Most notable was Brigit Bardot, who recorded two albums with Gainsbourg in 1967 and '68.

### Dean Wareham, Luna

*Laetitia [Sadier of Stereolab] picked that song, ["Bonnie and Clyde," to record as a duet] and it came out great. I always thought French music was just bad, but he had incredible production and the music was very sexy and really out there. The closest thing we have to that is Lee Hazelwood, another one of my heroes.*

A second young starlet, English actress Jane Birken, was Gainsbourg's partner on his best-known songs. In 1969, their hit "Soixante Neuf Année Erotique" played the current year for all its sexual potential and caused quite a stir in France. The follow-up, though, became an international incident. "Je T'Aime...Moi Non Plus" ("I Love You...Neither Do I"), with its suggestive lyrics ("I go and I come, inside you") and Birken's orgasmic moans, was banned throughout Europe at the urging of the Vatican. Nevertheless, the song was Gainsbourg's biggest hit; it turned Gainsbourg into a superstar at home, and even made the U.S. charts.

### Steve Shelley, Sonic Youth:

*There was this real innocence for Sonic Youth, or for myself, in discovering him. I compare it to first hearing about rock 'n' roll... At this point, we're so post-everything that I think we can really appreciate the way he put together all those cultures and sounds and words and feelings. It's much the same way that we appreciate Beck right now. I'm not into him for the kitsch value. What interests me is that he made such amazing sounds, and that takes me back to dealing with things simply on an aural level. [from Interview magazine, April 1997]*

With stardom opening up endless possibilities, Gainsbourg busied himself in the '70s with all sorts of creative pursuits: He composed soundtracks, acted in cheesy Italian films, directed his own movie, and even wrote a novel. Though he recorded less, his music was still controversial. He attempted a concept album with 1971's *Histoire de Mélodie Nelson,* a cult favorite, and took his jabs at government ("Rock Around the Bunker") and oil companies ("Torry Canyon"). He continued to exploit the latest sounds; in 1976 he traveled to Jamaica to record reggae with Sly Dunbar and Robbie Shakespeare, and three years later he released "Aux Armes Etcetera" with Bob Marley's Wailers as his backing group. The song, which amounted to the French national anthem "La Marseillaise" set to a reggae beat, was viewed as disrespectful and created an outrage in France.

Even into his late fifties, Gainsbourg continued to shock with songs—set to disco, funk, even hip-hop music—such as "Love on the Beat," about male hustlers, and 1985's "Lemon Incest," for which he made a video in bed with his daughter Charlotte Gainsbourg (now an actress). In the late '80s, Gainsbourg made news again when he told Whitney Houston, live on a French television talk show, "I want to fuck you." When Gainsbourg died of a heart attack on March 2, 1991, the entire nation of France mourned the loss of their most distinctive voice. Only posthumously would his influence truly blossom in the U.S., on the fringes of an exotica revival that he clearly transcends.

## DISCOGRAPHY

*Du Chant a la Une!* (Philips [Fr.], 1958).

*Jeunes Femmes et Vieux Messieurs* (Philips [Fr.], 1959).

*L'Etonnant Serge Gainsbourg* (Philips [Fr.], 1961).

*Confidentiel* (Philips [Fr.], 1964); a notable album from his jazz period.

*Gainsbourg Percussions* (Philips [Fr.], 1964); the album signaling his move toward Latin-flavored music.

*Bardot & S. Gainsbourg / Bonnie & Clyde* (Philips [Fr.], 1968); the first collaboration with Brigit Bardot, featuring their duet "Bonnie & Clyde."

*Initials B.B.* (Philips [Fr.], 1968); another album with Bardot.

*Jane Birkin & Serge Gainsbourg* (Philips [Fr.], 1969); a collaboration with Birkin, featuring "69 Erotic Year" and "Lollipops."

(w/Jane Birkin) *Je T'Aime* (Beautiful Love) (Fontana, 1969).

*Histoire de Mélodie Nelson* (Philips [Fr.], 1971); a concept album recorded with Birkin.

*Rock Around the Bunker* (Philips [Fr.], 1975); an album of politically provocative songs.

*L'Homme a Tete de Chou* (Philips [Fr.], 1976); a reggae album recorded in Jamaica.

*Love on the Beat* (Philips [Fr.], 1984); an electro-dance record.

*You're Under Arrest* (Philips [Fr.], 1987); Gainsbourg's final album, featuring the rapped title track.

*Jazz dans le Ravin* (Mercury, 1996); a collection of songs from Gainsbourg's jazz period in the late '50s and early '60s, released domestically in the U.S.

*Comic Strip* (Mercury, 1996); a collection of late '60s pop songs, including his best known songs "Je T'Aime...Moi Non Plus" and "Soixante Neuf Année Erotique,"

available in the U.S.

*Couleur Café* (Mercury, 1996); a collection of Gainsbourg's Latin-flavored songs from the late '50s and early '60s, released domestically in the U.S.

TRIBUTE: Mick Harvey, *Intoxicated Man* (Mute, 1995); first of two albums featuring Gainsbourg songs, translated into English and interpreted by Harvey, former **Birthday Party** member and currently in Nick Cave's Bad Seeds.

TRIBUTE: Mick Harvey, *Pink Elephants* (Mute, 1997); the second of Harvey's excellent Gainsbourg collections.

TRIBUTE: *Great Jewish Music: Serge Gainsbourg* (Tzadik, 1997); part of John Zorn's series highlighting Jewish musical figures, this features Faith No More's Mike Patton, Cibo Matto, Blonde Redhead, Kramer, and others in Zorn's "downtown" music circle.

# BIG STAR

*[Big Star] influenced me so much that when I was 21 I took a Greyhound bus from Los Angeles to Memphis just on the chance I might meet Alex Chilton. I spent a week buying him beer and cigarettes, trying to ask him about his music. But he was so bitter about music, it kind of bummed me out. I thought I would meet the voice behind those records, but the person was so different. Now I know how unfair that is, but I was young and idealistic. He was very cordial, and put me up a couple nights. But he was just so bitter about music, which is not what you hear in Big Star.*

**Steve Wynn, solo/Dream Syndicate**

In rock, Big Star was a freak of nature. While most British bands of the '60s tried to sound like they were from Memphis, here was a group of white kids from Memphis (in the '70s) who couldn't get enough of Beatles harmonies and Kinks riffs. Their records mixed Brit-pop with middle-of-the-road production, bits of garage and glam rock, and an inescapable Memphis country-soul sound that came across as unfashionable at the time and helped to keep them obscure.

By the end of the '70s, though, Big Star's take on rock would serve as a blueprint for the "power pop" that connects '80s bands like the dBs to current acts, from Matthew Sweet to Fountains of Wayne. And with the emergence of postmodern rock, Big Star's technique of constructing new songs out of various classic pop building blocks made them natural reference points for young musical historians. Their quirky blend of styles, along with undeniably catchy tunes, would make them heroes to scores of later groups interested in pursuing pop in all its shades: R.E.M. and the Dream Syndicate have sighted them as a big influence; the Replacements, the Jayhawks, and Letters to Cleo have all named songs after the band or its members; the Bangles, Afghan Wings, and tons of other groups have covered Big Star songs; while Teenage Fanclub and the Posies have outright copied their sound.

Back in 1971, Memphis singer/guitarist Chris Bell, bassist Andy Hummel, and drummer Jody Stephens were playing Badfinger and Led Zeppelin covers in a band called Ice Water. Though all three were heavily into British pop music, they couldn't escape the influence of local Memphis soul groups like the Bar-Kays. Alex Chilton, Bell's childhood friend who had recently moved back to Memphis after spending

some time in the New York folk scene, attended an early Ice Water gig. Chilton, who as the sixteen-year-old lead singer for the Box Tops had scored a number one hit with 1967's "The Letter," was something of a local celebrity, and already a music biz veteran at twenty-one. In search of a new project, Chilton accepted Bell's invitation to join his band. Renaming themselves after a supermarket chain, Big Star was born.

Around the same time, local producer John Fry had decided to start a record label based around his recording studio, Ardent, and was looking for acts. Ardent had already become a hangout for the small community of mostly white, mostly suburban Anglophiles on the fringes of the Memphis music scene, and Big Star quickly emerged as the most promising of the pack. Without bothering to do gigs or coalesce as a band, Big Star began recording.

What they created in 1972, a debut record they optimistically called *#1 Record,* was the product of a collaboration between two very talented songwriters, Chilton and Bell. The tracks combined elements of all the music that had touched them: the light blues rock of "Feel," Byrds' jangle of "In the Street," the folk picking of "Thirteen," country boogie of "My Life Is Right," the soft rock of "Try Again," tied together with M.O.R. arrangements and well-crafted Beatlesque harmonies. *#1 Record* was hardly revolutionary, but the skill with which it navigated styles made it an early model for future underground pop packrats like the Pooh Sticks and Papas Fritas. And the songs, taken at face value, could be quite effective emotionally.

Immediately after the debut's release, cracks began to appear in the band. While Bell wanted to keep the band a studio project, Chilton wanted to tour. In addition, Bell was battling depression, which only worsened when he began to sense that Chilton was emerging as the dominant figure in the band. "With the first album we got a lot of great press, most of which was focused on Alex, and I think Chris thought he was going to have to live in the shadow of this famous band member," drummer Stephens says. "That first record was primarily the result of Chris's vision of what the band should sound like, and somebody else was getting the spotlight for it." As Big Star began to make their follow-up to *#1 Record,* Chris Bell quit the band.

### Eric Matthews

*Big Star directed me to a new sound and style. There was something incredibly haunting and strange to it. It's strange to discover music that you're just not aware of that has existed for so long. It's really the new wave of the time.*

While Bell returned for a brief period to work with Chilton on new songs, they soon divided the material they'd written and split up for good (some of the final Bell/Chilton material, including, "Back of a Car," eventually showed up on Big Star's second record). As a three-piece, Hummel and Stephens' creative impact increased, but Chilton was clearly the main force in the band. *Radio City,* their 1964 follow-up to *#1 Record,* is predictably more raw than the debut, and also more consistently Beatlesque, with songs like "Way Out West" and "She's A Mover" harking back to '60s Brit pop. In 1974, though, this sound was almost a decade out of fashion, and it would be a number of years before "power pop" (which would adopt *Radio City*'s "September Gurls" as its Rosetta stone) brought these sounds back.

### Tony Goddess, Papas Fritas

*Radio City is one of my all-time favorite records. Alex Chilton shaped my ideas a lot. I read a quote from [producer] John Fry about how they got a couple guitars together to use in an orchestral way. And it got me thinking. On Radio City there's so many guitars, but it's never like a wall of guitars. There's one percolating, one strumming. Also, I was a huge Replacements fan and when I finally got Big Star records I was like, "Oh, there it is. That's the whole thing right there."*

Big Star's problems, though, were deeper than just being out of step. While they received terrific reviews and even got some radio play, they had terrible luck with record companies that always seemed to be in a state of transition, or bankruptcy, when it came time to promote and distribute their records. *Radio City,* like *#1 Record* before it, got lost in the shuffle. Fed up that artistic acclaim was not leading to commercial success, Andy Hummel quit the band and went back to school, leaving only Chilton and Stephens from the original Big Star.

Nevertheless, the remnants of the group went ahead with a third album in 1975. Though Stephens played drums, wrote one of the songs, and was responsible for introducing string arrangements to the band's sound, for the most part the record turned out to be an Alex Chilton solo project (with help from new producer Jim Dickinson). Attempts were made to produce a richer, more orchestrated sound, with the addition of back-up singers and strings. But Chilton, disappointed by his lack of success, had reached a low point personally, which is reflected in the dark, subdued feel of songs like "Holocaust" and "Big Black Car."

### Matthew Sweet

*Big Star just sounded so great to me it was my total inspiration. With all my teenage emotions I could really get into "Big Black Car," feeling really morbid. I don't know if I ever tried to do stuff like Big Star in the way bands that are obsessed with them do—like the way Teenage Fanclub would do something that was SO Big Star—but I was really influenced by Alex Chilton's writing, the way anything goes, even though it's really melodic and poppy.*

Ardent Records folded before the album called *Third* and/or *Sister Lovers* (because Stephens and Chilton had been dating twins) was completed, and the record was not released until three years later (and then only in the U.K.). Once the record was complete, Stephens quit and Big Star ended. As such, *Third* serves both as an appropriate end to a troubled band and as a telling prelude to a moody, uneven Alex Chilton solo career.

### Dean Wareham, Luna

*It's amazing that Big Star didn't become famous. I discovered them around the time Galaxie 500 [Wareham's first band] was forming. Those records are beautifully produced. I know they're an influence on a lot of people, but I don't think anyone has really come close to the haunting qualities of their Third record. People have emulated their production, but not gotten the "scraping the bottom of the barrel" feeling of that record.*

After leaving Big Star, Chris Bell struggled through depression to launch a solo career. Though he made a solo record in 1976, it went unreleased for decades (*I Am the Cosmos* was eventually issued in 1992). Tragically, Bell died in a 1978 car crash, never having achieved the stardom and recognition he deserved.

Alex Chilton moved back to New York and in 1977 made an EP, then a couple of inspired but uneven solo albums (*Like Flies on Sherbet, Bach's Bottom*) into the early '80s. By then, Big Star's legend had grown, and Chilton became a popular draw in New York rock clubs. Though he'd resurface over the years as the producer of early **Cramps** records, or to release a sloppy EP (often full of cover songs), for the most part Chilton has continued in a no-man's land between cult hero and has-been. He made an art out of lazy, underachiever music, and became a hero to bands like the Replacements (who recorded a song called "Alex Chilton" in Ardent Studios) and other "slacker" bands. Though he returned, along with the Ardent label, in the early '90s to make new records with occasional moments of brilliance, he remained bitter and enigmatic, an oft-cited example of wasted talent in rock. Recently, Chilton was back on the road with his first (and most successful) band, the Box Tops.

While Andy Hummel became an engineer for General Dynamics, Stephens continued drumming with Chris Bell and other local musicians before going back to school for a degree in marketing. In 1987 he was hired by Ardent Studios and, as projects manager, oversaw Alex Chilton's recent solo records. Stephens also plays with Golden Smog, a side band for members of the Jayhawks, Soul Asylum, and Wilco.

---

**Gary Louris, Jayhawks:**

*When I grew up I wanted to be in Big Star, not Buffalo Springfield. My roots are in bands like Big Star, and I think we have something in common with them in that they were a little bit out of step with the times. On his solo record, Chris Bell—someone very influential who was never recognized in his time—sounds like somebody who's frustrated, who can't understand why he isn't understood musically.*

---

In 1993, Chilton and Stephens re-formed Big Star, with the help of Jon Auer and Ken Stringfellow of the Posies. A reunion concert (released as a live album) and short tour followed, though there are no plans to continue the band.

## DISCOGRAPHY

*#1 Record/Radio City* (Ardent, 1972/1974; Stax/Fantasy, 1992); the reissue of Big Star's first two albums is the classic document of the band at the peak of its powers, especially on *#1 Record,* which features Bell.

*Third/Sister Lovers* (Ardent, 1978; Rykodisc, 1992); dark and pain-ridden, the band's final record (reissued with bonus tracks) was essentially an Alex Chilton solo project, and certainly his finest at that.

*Big Star Live* (Rykodisc, 1992); taken from a 1974 radio broadcast, the live set includes Chilton solo and acoustic, as well as full band performances and an interview.

*Columbia: Live at Missouri University* (Zoo, 1993); featuring members of the Pixies along with Chilton and Stephens, this Big Star reunion show was historic but adds little to the band's legend.

TRIBUTE: *Big Star Small World* (Ardent, 1998); a collection of Big Star covers, done by Juliana Hatfield, Whiskeytown, Afghan Whigs, Teenage Fanclub, Gin Blossoms, and Matthew Sweet, plus a new track by a reformed Big Star.

# YOUNG MARBLE GIANTS

*One of the things that really shaped the way I structure my own music was Young Marble Giants. I heard them around 1979 or '80, when I first discovered punk rock. I guess you'd call the record low-fi, but the Young Marble Giants in particular was so sparse. They used that cheesy percussion of old organs, and this cool, edgy, clipped guitar sound, with beautiful female vocals soaring over-top. But the songs were really short and compact. From the first time I heard them it just absolutely made sense to me. It sounded like this perfect music in a small scale.*

**Lou Barlow, Sebadoh/Folk Implosion**

They were a small band with a small sound. And having existed for only three years—with only a single album to show for it—the Young Marble Giants barely registered a blip on the screen of pop music history. Somehow, though, they cast reverberations that are still heard today—in the simplicity of indie pop bands like **Beat Happening,** the evocative synths of Magnetic Fields, the beat minimalism of Luscious Jackson, and the spare folk of Frente! and Billy Bragg.

The Young Marble Giants formed in 1978, just as Britain's indie punk movement had spread across the U.K. and reached their remote hometown of Cardiff, Wales. Empowered by the "do-it-yourself" ideas of post-punkers like Swell Maps and Desperate Bicycles, the trio of two brothers and their female friend helped put together a local music compilation, *Is the War Over Yet?*, which featured two of their songs. One listen to the curvy melody of the Young Marble Giants' "Searching for Mr. Right," though, and it was clear: They may have been D-I-Y, but they were closer to pop than punk. While they were miles away from the Bee Gees or anything else on the pop charts in 1979, they somehow possessed all the essential elements of pop: a steady and simple rhythm, a pure and beautiful melody. And like all the best pop, the Young Marble Giants' music was easy to understand, right away. The elements were clearly defined and stripped to their bare essentials: Stuart Moxham's muted guitar stabs or warbly organ, Philip Moxham's tuneful bass, Alison Statton's lilting voice, and, at times, a pulsating electronic beat.

### Tracy Thorn, *Everything But the Girl*
*[The Marine Girls, Thorn's first band] didn't know anyone who could play drums...so we decided to take our cue from the Young Marble Giants and play minimalist quiet music. Colossal Youth was our favorite record.* [from EBTG website]

*Colossal Youth,* the group's 1980 debut, sounded like nothing else before it. A hushed, ghostly shell of a record on the surface, it proved surprisingly deep on closer inspection. While remaining coolly restrained and consistent, the album covered a wide enough range that no songs sounded the same: from playful and fluid ("Colossal Youth") to intense and abrupt ("Include Me Out"), and from melancholic ("Salad Days") to menacing ("Credit in the Straight World," which was later covered by Hole). All 15 songs (written mostly by Stuart) are memorable, though none conformed in any way to accepted formulas.

### Dean Wareham, *Luna*
*We used to do "Final Day" in Galaxie 500 [Wareham's first band]. Colossal Youth is a unique and special record, and there's never been anything like it. The sounds, the instrumentation. It was really spare and quiet, but really powerful. Being in a trio, it showed you could get away with sparseness.*

*Colossal Youth* was not to have a follow-up. The Giants made the U.K.'s indie charts in 1981 with an instrumental EP called *Testcard,* but amicably disbanded that year, before another record was ever produced. Following the Giants' break-up, Stuart and Philip Moxham formed the Gist, which released one album in 1983. Sporadically, Stuart also produced bands such as **Beat Happening** and the Marine Girls (which featured Tracey Thorn of Everything But the Girl). For most of the '80s, though, Stuart worked as an animator, contributing to films including *Who Killed Roger Rabbit?* In the '90s, Stuart, Philip, and a third Moxham brother formed the Original Artists and released three albums (the first containing Stuart's duet with Alison of the Giants). A 1995 Stuart Moxham solo album featured acoustic guitar versions of older material, including some from *Colossal Youth*.

Alison Statton continued singing, first with loungy jazz poppers and exotica revivalists Weekend, then as half of Devine & Statton. In the '90s, she reunited with Weekend guitarist Spike as Alison Statton & Spike, and released three albums in Japan. The duo's final live recording featured Stuart and Philip in what essentially was a Young Marble Giants reunion.

## DISCOGRAPHY

*Colossal Youth* (Rough Trade, 1980; Crepuscule, 1994); the astounding first album, reissued with the instrumental EP and two other nonalbum songs.

*Testcard* EP (Rough Trade, 1981); originally an instrumental 7-inch, this record has been tacked onto the reissue of *Colossal Youth*.

*The Peel Sessions* EP (Strange Fruit, 1988).

## BEAT HAPPENING

*I like Calvin's outlook about music and life, he's sort of a righteous person. He's made up his mind about things he feels strongly about, even though it's sometimes difficult. To me, it's an affirming thing, like, "This is cool what we're doing. It's special, important." And to be around people who actually realize that and make it that way is important.*

**Doug Martsch, Built to Spill/Halo Benders**

Before Seattle was known for grunge, and before female bands from the Northwest were labeled riot grrrl, Calvin Johnson was doing his own thing up in Washington state. In fact, the example and support of Calvin's label K Records helped encourage the formation of a self-sufficient punk feminist movement. And though Beat Happening's skeletal ditties had little in common with Nirvana's metallic roar, Kurt Cobain felt sufficiently inspired by Johnson's do-it-yourself ethic to have the K Records logo tattooed on his body. From a home base in Olympia, the college town/state capitol 50 miles south of Seattle, Johnson did as much as anyone to ignite a regional music scene that would become the most recognized of the '90s.

The influence of Calvin, Beat Happening, and K, however, is not limited to the Northwest. Combining the childlike innocence of **Jonathan Richman** with the unschooled roughness of **Half Japanese,** Beat Happening is the progenitor of a style—known variously as cuddle-core, tin-can pop, or love-rock—that's been adopted to varying degrees by everyone from L.A.'s That Dog to Louisville's King Kong, and from D.C.'s Tsunami to Chicago's Veruca Salt. In defining an indie-pop aesthetic that incorporates humor and melody with punk's willful obscurity—and by forming alliances with like-minded acts such as Australia's Cannanes, Japan's Shonen Knife, and Scotland's Vaselines—Beat Happening has landed at the heart of a worldwide network of subterranean music, dubbed (by Calvin) the International Pop Underground.

In the early '8os, Johnson got involved with Olympia's community radio station KAOS and a related music zine called *Op*, which introduced him to the then-radical concept of independent music as an alternative to the entertainment/culture fed by major corporations. Soon he began collaborating with fellow DJ Bruce Pavitt on a new zine dedicated to the Northwest's underground music scene called *Subterranean Pop*, which Pavitt later abbreviated to *Sub Pop* (their slogan—"We're here to de-centralize pop culture") and turned into the famed Seattle record label. *Sub Pop* began covering the local scene by releasing not only conventional fanzines but also "cassette" zines, compilation tapes that allowed readers to hear the music they'd been reading about.

---

### Carrie Brownstein, Sleater-Kinney

*The first time I heard Beat Happening, I was just blown away. I was still in high school and I went to their show. It was the first time I saw a woman playing guitar up close. I would go to punk shows all the time, but I never really saw women. And they brought this kind of sexiness back to rock music. In terms of performance, it wasn't about this kind of tense maleness. It was really fluid, feeling the music in a way that wasn't about all this angst. In Olympia, and in general, they were really an important band.*

---

"There was the general idea of taking control of the media," Johnson remembers of the indie/punk scene at the time. "Put on your own shows, make up your own songs, do your own radio show, make your own magazines, start your own label, start your own club, those are all basically the same idea." Greatly aiding their crusade were the two unsung heroes of indie culture: the cassette tape and the photocopier, which by the early '80s had become sufficiently high-quality, inexpensive, and easy to find that they presented a feasible way of producing and distributing music. "Cassette culture in the early '80s was oriented toward experimental and industrial music, not to rock music or underground pop," Johnson recalls. "But cassettes provided an accessibility that just didn't exist before. It was obvious to us."

Branching out from *Sub Pop* in 1982, Calvin formed his K label and began releasing cassettes of mostly a cappella and folk music that stood in sharp contrast to the strictly defined hardcore that began to dominate the indie world. At the same time Calvin began playing in bands, first with the Cool Rays and 003 Legion, then with two friends as Laura, Heather and Calvin. When Laura dropped out of this last group, Calvin and Heather Lewis, whom he'd met at Olympia's Evergreen State College, recruited Bret Lunsford and Beat Happening was born. In an Olympia tradition that continues today with groups such as Sleater-Kinney, Beat Happening had no bassist. Instead, the trio featured a singer, drummer, and guitarist; because none of them was particularly proficient at any one role, they alternated instruments and vocals between them from song to song.

With the **Wipers'** Greg Sage producing, Beat Happening recorded and released two five-song cassettes in '83 and '84 (later collected on the *Beat Happening* and *1983-85* compilations). The music was spare and sloppy, and the singing—Calvin's froggy baritone and Heather's artless lilt—was often flat. There was plenty of low-fi production and punk attitude, but Beat Happening still had an innocence and melodicism in songs like "What's Important" and "I Spy" that identified the group as pop. Beat Happening's affinity for **Cramps**-style rootsy rock was clear, as was the group's love for **Jonathan Richman**'s kiddy songs. Their colorful album covers, featuring stick figure drawings and hand-written liner notes, reinforced the warmth and charm of the music.

---

### Jenny Toomey, Tsunami/Licorice

*People talk about them as the mothers and fathers of this sort of "shamble pop" style, which is like two chords, same melody over and over, lots of easy rhymes. And there's a million bands that started making music like that because they were inspired by Beat Happening. I think we were inspired by Beat Happening in the beginning—like "Ski Trip" or "Candyman"—random songs that used lots of objects, written really fast, and we also tried to have a dark side.*

---

K continued to release compilations such as *Let's Together, Let's Kiss,* and *Let's Sea,* which featured regional bands such as the Fastbacks, Mecca Normal, and the Melvins, as well as similarly-minded groups from around the world that Beat Happening befriended through the mail and while touring. The group also continued to record somewhat sporadically throughout the late '80s. A debut album in 1985 collected more recordings with Sage, and a 1988 EP grouped Beat Happening with their friends Screaming Trees for a four-song collaboration in the spirit of the **Black Flag/Minutemen** record, *Minute Flag.*

---

### Van Conner, Screaming Trees

*They were kind of like the hub of the whole Northwest-do-it-yourself rock scene. There really wasn't anything going on in Seattle at the time. Soundgarden and Green River [which evolved into Pearl Jam] were just starting. But Calvin was putting out all these tapes. They influenced a lot of people, just in how you go about it. They didn't have a bass player, and they didn't care. Their attitude was that you don't have to wait around for some label to sign you, and you don't have to be great musicians. Calvin actually booked Screaming Trees' first paid show ever, in Olympia. The day before we went, my brother Lee [Conner, Trees guitarist] said, "I wonder if that's the same Calvin Johnson I was in seventh grade with?" It was, and Lee remembered he was really weird. For his seventh grade science project, Calvin drew a picture of a flying saucer with an alien guy hanging out the top shooting laser beams at little stick people. We got the first Beat Happening record and Lee was like, "This looks like that type of drawing!"*

---

In 1987, K began releasing a series of singles by their favorite indie bands, which they called the International Pop Underground. Like Beat Happening, I.P.U. bands were not necessarily pop, but rather groups inspired by pop music. Like punk rock, it was just another way for bands to define their own terms and express their independence. Through K, which held an I.P.U. convention in 1992, bands asserted their ability to be friendly and accessible without having to conform to mainstream ideas of what pop was.

**Tim Gane, Stereolab**

*When we did Duophonic [Stereolab's record label], we definitely had something like K Records in mind. Someone who would do their own thing, their own singles, they controlled themselves.*

Between 1989 and 1992, Beat Happening released four full albums of new material. The first, *Jamboree*, was produced by members of the Screaming Trees and Steve Fisk (of Pigeonhead and Pearl Jam spin-off Brad). The record shows the band greatly improved as songwriters, though still unapologetically amateurish. Songs like the two-chord "Indian Summer" (covered at various points by Luna, Spectrum, Yo La Tengo, and Eugenius) and the irrepressibly cute "The This Many Boyfriends Club" are among the group's most memorable works.

**King Coffey, Butthole Surfers**

*Calvin, Beat Happening, and K Records are incredibly influential on the U.S. scene as a whole. The entire K ethic was really a shot in the arm for the do-it-yourself thing, they really had their act together as far as putting out tapes, supporting the local scene, doing things on their own terms and own level. There was a vision and style very unique to K, best personified by Beat Happening. All their albums are just brilliant, very primitive and minimalist. Gibby [of the Butthole Sufers] and I have talked about doing a Beat Happening cover band.*

*Black Candy*, also released in 1989, was just as tuneful and perhaps a touch more polished than *Jamboree*, while 1991's *Dreamy* is similar, but less successful. By 1992's *You Turn Me On* (produced by Fisk and the **Young Marble Giants**' Stuart Moxham), Beat Happening had been at it for nearly a decade and it showed in the band's confidence and improved musical chops. Despite its relative polish, songs like "Teenage Caveman" and "Tiger Trap" have all the classic Beat Happening charm of their earliest recordings.

Since the release of *You Turn Me On*, the trio has not released any new music, though Calvin says the group has not broken up. Bret has played in the group D+ and owns a bookstore/café in Anacortes, Washington. Heather does set design and visual art in Seattle. Calvin, meanwhile, continues to operate K Records with his partner Candice Pederson. In 1993, K released Beck's *One Foot In the Grave*, which Calvin produced and to which he lent his distinctive vocals. The following year, Johnson built an eight-track studio in his basement, called Dub Narcotic, and embarked on two new bands. The first, a loose garage rock group called the Halo Benders, features Doug Martsch of Built to Spill. The second is Dub Narcotic Sound System, a group centered around Calvin's studio and featuring a revolving cast of collaborators. DNSS was among the first indie rock groups of the '90s to embrace and incorporate dub techniques into their music. While he seems confident Beat Happening will one day resurface, in the meantime Calvin keeps busy orchestrating new revolutions in independent music.

## DISCOGRAPHY

*Beat Happening* EP (K, 1984); a five-song cassette-only debut, collected on both later compilations.

*Three Tea Breakfast* (K, 1984); a second five-song cassette-only release, also included on the compilations.

*Beat Happening* (K, 1985; 1996); the first full-length; later reissued with lots of bonus tracks as a compilation that's virtually identical to the *1983–85* collection.

*Beat Happening/Screaming Trees* EP (K/Homestead, 1988); the band's contribution consists of four tracks of electrified acid pop.

*Jamboree* (K, 1989); their first proper album, and perhaps their best; featuring the often-covered "Indian Summer" and other classic Beat Happening material.

*Black Candy* (K, 1989); a slightly darker, and nearly as terrific, follow-up to *Jamboree*.

*1983–85* (K/Feel Good All Over, 1990); collects the first two EPs, the debut album, and assorted rarities onto one CD; made somewhat irrelevant by the expanded CD reissue of the 1985 debut.

*Dreamy* (K/Sub Pop, 1991); a relative low point, though still full of catchy and worthwhile songs.

*You Turn Me On* (K/Sub Pop, 1992); leaving off a good note, this record is full of strong and confident material.

TRIBUTE: *Fortune Cookie Prize: A Tribute to Beat Happening* (Simple Machines, 1992); Beat Happening covers done by Velocity Girl, Superchunk, Unrest, members of Sonic Youth, Tsunami, and others.

# 3

## PSYCHOTIC REACTIONS AND GARAGE ROCK

Once the British Invasion of the mid-'6os brought hard-rocking white-blues bands like the Rolling Stones, the Yardbirds, and the Who to the U.S., kids across the country convened in suburban garages and set out to imitate or else outdo their heroes through an irrepressible assault of power chords and wake-up-the-neighbors drum pounding. Though most were too awful to ever get heard, many of them did manage to cut a record or two before disappearing from sight. Most of these one-hit (or none-hit) wonders would today be forgotten were it not for great psychedelic garage compilations like *Nuggets* or *Pebbles*.

The underground garage movement had a huge impact on later generations of rock—from punk to noise-rock to grunge—and although few of the individual bands had enough impact to qualify for inclusion in these pages, as a whole, bands like the Count Five, the Seeds, and dozens of others deserve credit for their part in shaping rock as we know it.

*King Coffey, Butthole Surfers:*
*The Pebbles compilation, and before that the Nuggets compilation, opened the doors to the whole idea of punk rock.*

For a variety of reasons, some American garage rock bands stood the test of time and have been rediscovered by later rock generations. The **13th Floor Elevators,** who stuck around long enough to release more than one record (and even scored a minor hit), are remembered as a quintessential psychedelic rock group. The **MC5,** by closely tying themselves to the larger student/anti-war movement of the '6os, also became a musical signpost of the time. Other groups, like the **Stooges,** are remembered in part because a band member went on to more mainstream success. But mostly, these garage bands stood out as the most extreme, colorful, and outrageous of their time.

A second, peripherally related, movement is the psychedelic underground, which has flowed across oceans and over decades. Though Pink Floyd has emerged as the most recognizable psychedelic rock band of its time, their original lead singer **Syd Barrett** left the group before worldwide success came knocking. In his solo work he assumed legendary status to his cultlike fans but otherwise languished in semi-obscurity. Barrett's tripped-out heritage continued through the punk years of the '7os with bands like the Soft Boys, who in turn linked an entire community of American post-punk bands—from R.E.M. in Georgia to the Paisley Underground bands in Los Angeles—to the psychedelic rock tradition.

**Steve Wynn, solo/Dream Syndicate**
*The whole thing we came out of in L.A., called Paisley Underground, that was really a bunch of bands that liked '60s music and weren't hearing it anywhere. Other bands like the Bangles and the Three O'Clock picked up on it even more than we did.*

# MC5

*We knew the times were serious. We knew civil rights was a real important issue, that ending this war was real important. So there was no way to separate a political consciousness from rock and roll. It became exactly the same thing.*

*Wayne Kramer, MC5*

At their peak, in 1968 and '69, the MC5 were louder, harder, and faster than any rock band before. Though groups like the Who and Jimi Hendrix Experience could rival them sonically, none could match the MC5's revolutionary bad-ass spirit. They were a product of late '60s counterculture, but the MC5 were not flower-power hippies. Their aim—"total assault of the culture"— spoke of a darker side of the youth movement. Therefore MC5 has often been ignored in music histories focused on the "peace and love" aspects of the era.

The spirit of the MC5 can be heard in the muddy blues rock of the Jon Spencer Blues Explosion, the free jazz-inspired noise of Sonic Youth, and the screaming agitprop of Rage Against the Machine. Most significantly, the MC5's mix of heavy electric blues and aggressive rock made them forerunners to both heavy metal and hardcore punk. Thus, they were an important reference point for bands like Dinosaur Jr and Screaming Trees when metal and punk met in the early '90s as grunge rock.

**Lou Barlow, Sebadoh**
*I got into the MC5 when I was first in Dinosaur [Jr]. We really slowed down a lot from when we were into hardcore. We hit this mid-tempo groove and stuff like MC5 really hit me.*

Formed in the Lincoln Park area of Detroit in 1965, the Motor City Five (soon shortened to MC5) evolved from the Bounty Hunters—which featured vocalist Rob Tyner and guitarists Wayne Kramer and Fred "Sonic" Smith—when drummer Dennis Thompson and bassist Michael Davis joined. Right away it was clear they were the product of their hometown. "It was a really unique scene in that there were no dividing lines between color," Kramer remembers. "The influences were all blending together and there was an esthetic developing, a Detroit sound, that combined the best of Motown R&B and white rock guitar of the Who and the Yardbirds, and then ultimately the free jazz movement."

**Thurston Moore, Sonic Youth**
*The name Sonic Youth is a cross between Big Youth, a reggae toaster guy, and Sonic Smith, the MC5 guitar player. We wanted to bridge these two strains of influence, high energy Detroit rock and dub.*

In 1967 the MC5 met their mentor/manager John Sinclair and began on their path as a revolutionary rock band. Sinclair, an underground journalist, jazz critic, and leader in the radical White Panther Party, recognized the group's untamed energy and set out to mold the MC5 into something of a trumpet call for youth revolution. "John was able to bring clarity," Kramer says. "Things we knew on a gut level—this society's fucked-up, this war is fucked-up—he was able to put into a political context. And musically as well, he opened the doors to our understanding of free-jazz."

By the summer of 1968, when the MC5 fearlessly rocked for the riotous demonstrators at the Democratic Convention in Chicago (a concert the Grateful Dead, Jefferson Airplane, and Country Joe canceled out on), the group's reputation had spread and record companies started taking notice. Because they were known for particularly powerful live shows that mixed John Coltrane and Who covers with their own extended jams like "Black to Comm," Elektra Records made the unusual decision to release a live record as their debut. Recorded at a Detroit theater in October 1968 and released the following year, *Kick Out the Jams* was an audacious introduction. Though much of the group's best material was left off, songs like "Motor City Is Burning" and a cover of Sun Ra's "Starship" are representative of the MC5's mix of political agitation and musical experimentation.

**Van Conner, Screaming Trees**
*MC5 to me are kind of the superheroes of rock. Every record totally kicks ass. They were so cool, like how the guitarists would get down on their knees at the same time in concert. When Warrant does it, it's cheesy, but when they do it's cool. I think that gave the Trees license to be a little bit stupid and tongue-in-cheek in our live shows, like, "Well MC5 did it, and they're fucking cool.*

Though the album was well received and even made a showing on the charts, the opening track's revolutionary call to arms—ending with the infamous charge to "Kick out the jams, motherfuckers!"—soon had the band embroiled in a disastrous controversy. Once word spread of the record's profanity, many stores refused to stock it and radio stations avoided the group entirely. When the band released "Kick Out the Jams" as a single, "motherfuckers!" was replaced with "brothers and sisters!" Still, the damage had been done. Elektra dropped the band soon after.

**Chris Cornell, Soundgarden**
*I could draw a comparison between us and the MC5, in terms of the things they sang about and the attitude they had. If I would think of Soundgarden strictly as an over-the-top rock band, the MC5 would've always been the band that I would've held up as the pinnacle. If you're going to be a rock band, this is it.*

Further compounding their troubles, by late 1969 John Sinclair was on his way to jail on marijuana charges (sentenced to nine years for possessing two joints). Though without Sinclair the MC5 were losing their initial focus, the band was nevertheless picked up by Atlantic Records to make a second album. With producer John Landau (a rock critic who soon after became Bruce Springsteen's manager), the MC5 created *Back in the U.S.A.*, a more refined and song-oriented take on the Chuck Berry-styled guitar rock they loved. Although the album was a commercial flop, it was to be just as influential as the debut. "Where some didn't care for *Kick Out the Jams* because it was so over-the-top and raucous, many fans—especially in England, guys like the Clash, the Damned, and Elvis Costello—have all told me that *Back in the U.S.A.* was the yardstick for the kind of music they wanted to make. It was all concise, two-and-a-half minute pop songs."

A third record, 1971's *High Time,* attempted to synthesize the wildness of the first album with the studio refinement of the second. It also flopped, and soon Atlantic dropped the MC5 as well. In 1972, after a failed attempt to resuscitate the rapidly disintegrating group by seeking stardom in England, the MC5 went through a bitter breakup.

Though the MC5's reputation in the underground grew steadily with the advent of punk, no one in the band was able to translate their notoriety into a viable career. It wasn't until Rob Tyner's death in 1991 that the remaining MC5 reconciled and played a benefit concert together. The years in between is mostly the stuff of rock footnotes: Michael Davis played with the **Stooges'** Ron Asheton in Detroit's Destroy All Monsters, and Dennis Thompson played in a band called the New Order (not to be confused with the better-known British group), while Fred Smith formed Sonic's Rendezvous Band and married punk poet Patti Smith. He died in 1994.

The one exception, it seems, has been Wayne Kramer. After a drug conviction sent him to jail in the late '70s, Kramer cleaned himself up and returned to music. In 1995, three decades after he formed the MC5, Kramer began releasing solo albums on Epitaph, an indie label connected to MC5-inspired punk band Bad Religion. Sharp and vital, Kramer has proved himself a viable '90s rocker.

## DISCOGRAPHY

*Kick Out the Jams* (Elektra, 1969); the controversial and thoroughly raucous live debut.

*Back in the USA* (Atlantic, 1970; Rhino, 1992); the stripped-down studio follow-up.

*High Time* (Atlantic, 1971; Rhino, 1992); the final album, which attempted to find a cohesive middle ground between the first two records.

*Babes in Arms* (ROIR, 1983); a collection of outtakes and rarities.

*Power Trip* (Alive, 1994); a mix of live and rare studio recordings, including the 18-minute freak-out "I'm Mad Like Eldridge Cleaver."

*Teen Age Lust* (Total Energy/Alive, 1996); a live recording from a 1970 concert.

*Ice Pick Slim* (Alive, 1997); more live recordings, these from 1968.

# THE STOOGES

*They were more relative to my world. "No Fun," a song about a girl hanging out smoking a cigarette, spoke volumes about what was going on in my world, as opposed to "Lord I was born a ramblin' man" by the Allman Brothers, which was what everybody in my school was listening to.... When Iggy came to New York in '76, he met people like the Ramones and the Dead Boys and they were like,*

*"Your albums are so important to us, we've started bands because of those albums." They sold thirteen copies of their records, but those thirteen people went on to form bands that were themselves influential, who influenced **Black Flag**, who influenced Nirvana, who influenced Green Day.*

**Thurston Moore, Sonic Youth**

W ithout the burdens of artsiness (like the Velvet Underground) or political conviction (like the **MC5**), the Stooges and their leader Iggy Pop barreled into the late '60s hippie rock scene, taking white trash garage rock to the ultimate point of frenzy, where it sounded so brutal and depraved it had to be ignored by all respectable society. Yetl it managed to catch on all over the place in the '70s, influencing early New York pre-punk bands like **Suicide** and the New York Dolls, British punks like the Sex Pistols and the Damned, and L.A. punk and hardcore groups like the **Germs** and **Black Flag**. In the '80s, the Stooges' raw power was tapped by metal bands like Guns 'n' Roses, and then, in the '90s, by the grunge bands

### King Coffey, Butthole Surfers

*There's no denying they're the grand influence. I'm pretty sure the bands that today get credited with being grunge will very quickly credit the Stooges as being an influence. Basically the Stooges played grunge music, I guess, with a kind of abandon. They were definitely coming out of the drug culture of Michigan in the late '60s, so there's a psychedelic underpinning to what they're doing. But Iggy Pop is a true punk rocker as we all know.*

Before he became Iggy Pop, James Osterberg grew up in a trailer park in Ypsilanti, Michigan. Through high school Osterberg was a fairly straight, intelligent, socially adjusted kid, at least compared to his juvenile delinquent classmates Ron and Scott Asheton. He played drums with a few garage bands in the nearby college town of Ann Arbor—including the Iguanas, which gave Osterberg the nickname Iggy—and even attended the University of Michigan for a short time. He dropped out in 1966, though, and went to Chicago to pursue his dreams of being a blues musician. Realizing that he needed to find his own means of expression, he returned to Ann Arbor and formed the Psychedelic Stooges—Iggy, bassist Dave Alexander, and the guitar and drum playing Asheton brothers.

### Van Conner, Screaming Trees

*I remember being a complete idiot about the Stooges when I was about 18. We played Ann Arbor and Ron Asheton actually came to the show. We talked to him and over the years got to be friends. We have this dream of flying him out to play on a couple Trees songs. That night he was there we played "Real Cool Time" by the Stooges. We'd always do a Stooges cover as our last song, like "Raw Power" or "Search and Destroy." We listened to those records so many times somebody would just start playing the line and Mark [Lanegan] would start singing.*

After a period of rehearsal and indoctrination during which Iggy played for the others all the obscure free-jazz albums that inspired him, the band (soon to be simply the Stooges) debuted on Halloween, 1967. By then, Iggy had become a devotee of the Doors—particularly Jim Morrison's intensely physical stage persona. The Stooges, though, far outdid the Doors when it came to on-stage anarchy. While the others banged out loud and sloppy blues-rock riffs, a shirtless (and sometimes pantless) Iggy cavorted madly while spewing uptight teen anthems—his own take on the blues. Creating a spectacle the likes of which no audience had seen, Iggy Stooge (as he was known) would smear peanut butter and hamburger meat on his body before performing rock's earliest stage dives.

Though the Stooges had absolutely no interest in any political movement, early on they aligned themselves with the more established Ann Arbor rock revolutionaries, the **MC5**. When Elektra Records came to town to sign the MC5 in early 1968, members of that band recommended the label check out their "little brother band," the Stooges. Impressed, Elektra signed both bands at the same time, though they offered the Stooges—who'd only been a band for six months—one quarter the money that the MC5 got.

The Stooges' self-titled debut album, released in 1969, was produced by the Velvet Underground's **John Cale** (Velvets' singer Nico was present at the recordings as well, and soon began an affair with Iggy). Though they hardly had enough material for a whole album, the few songs they'd worked out later became punk rock classics. Among the highlights were "No Fun" (covered by the Sex Pistols) and "I Wanna Be Your Dog" (covered by just about everyone else), two roughnecked paeans to teen looserdom. Though on record the group sounded significantly more polished than they did live, the album's primal riffs and pissed-off singing mark it as one of punk rock's primary sources. It proved much too raw for mainstream tastes.

---

### Lou Barlow, Sebadoh

*There wasn't anyone like them at the time. The Stooges cut everything down to such a basic level no one could really handle them. I was always drawn to the Stooges because they were playing in Ann Arbor, near where I grew up. My dad actually worked with Iggy's mom. And I remember when I was, like, nine I used to think all hippies were violent and wanted to kill everybody. I thought the rock bands coming out of Detroit were the state of rock. Later on I realized they were the exception.*

---

For the following year's *Fun House,* Iggy Stooge renamed himself Iggy Pop. Ironically, the record is much less pop-oriented than the debut. Though the tunes were perhaps less memorable, songs like "Down On the Street" and "T.V. Eye" certainly rocked harder. While their friends in the **MC5** were stripping down their sound, *Fun House* songs like "L.A. Blues" and the title track seemed to pick up where the MC5's earlier wah-wah guitar and free-jazz freakout had left off. A truer expression of the band's muscle, the addition of saxophone showed the band willing to grow musically. For Elektra, though, *Fun House* merely convinced them that the Stooges would never be a salable group. After hearing material for the band's third album, the label decided to drop them.

Intent on continuing to refine its sound, in late 1970 the band fired Alexander (who died in 1975) and hired guitarist James Williamson (Ron Asheton switched to bass). But by then most of the group was heavily into heroin and Iggy himself was in no condition to front a group. (He even turned down the Doors' offer to become singer when Jim Morrison died.) The Stooges broke up, and in 1971 Iggy headed down to Florida to clean himself up.

A year later, Pop met David Bowie, a rising pop star who had been a fan of the Stooges. As Bowie had recently done with Lou Reed, he offered to help Pop resurrect his career. Signing with Bowie's management company, Pop went to England, with Williamson, and started work on a new album. Unable to capture the sound he wanted, he eventually brought the Ashetons over as well and re-formed the Stooges. With Pop clearly the focal point, however, the band became known as Iggy & the Stooges.

### Nick Cave

*The way Iggy presented himself as the ultimate individual, someone who would not be bound down by anything—the audience, the apparatus of the music industry—and he was just god-like to me in that way.*

In 1973, the band produced *Raw Power*, a record so true to its name the group's new label, CBS, called Bowie in to remix the record. Bowie's mix satisfied the label, but didn't really do justice to the music (Pop remixed it again for its 1997 reissue). Still, the best tracks, like "Search & Destroy," combined the mad intensity of *Fun House* with the hook-filled songwriting of the debut. Acoustic guitar and keyboard touches expanded the sound somewhat, but mostly it was pure hard electric guitar rock—the kind that would be tapped in the creation of both punk and heavy metal in coming years.

Bowie's support exposed the group to a larger audience than ever, but upon relocating to L.A. old drug habits resurfaced and Stooges' short-lived return ended. Pop, who was essentially a solo artist by then anyway, hooked up with Bowie in Berlin (after checking into a mental hospital to detoxify himself) and produced two strong pop-oriented albums in 1977, *The Idiot* and *Lust for Life*. By then, he was widely acknowledged as an elder statesmen of punk rock, a distinction he'd continue to enjoy through the '80s and '90s. In addition to an ongoing recording career, Pop has acted in a number of films, including John Waters' *Cry Baby*.

### Fred Schneider, B-52s

*A lot of the new wave bands were really influenced by a lot of the garage bands. Iggy probably had a big influence, that real rough, raw, in-your-face thing. Really loud and snotty. It influenced a lot of the new wave bands everywhere. I loved listening to Iggy. Just all that energy.*

The other Stooges have been less visible. Williamson recorded one album, *Kill City*, in collaboration with Pop. Ron Asheton played in a variety of little-known bands, including New Order (U.S., not U.K.) with MC5 drummer Dennis Thompson, and Destory All Monsters. Recently, Asheton remade a number of Stooges songs with Thurston Moore and Steve Shelley of Sonic Youth, Mudhoney's Mark Arm, and former **Minutemen** Mike Watt for the film *Velvet Goldmine*.

*Mike Watt, Minutemen/Firehose/solo*

*The Stooges were irrepressible. They had a big effect on L.A. punk. Iggy was there right at the beginning of our scene. Iggy was a big fertilizer, a lot of people were growing their crops in his soil, man.*

## DISCOGRAPHY

*The Stooges* (Elektra, 1969); a great first burst of dumb, primal rock.

*Fun House* (Elektra, 1970); a follow-up with an even heavier guitar attack and the addition of some skronky saxophone.

*Raw Power* (Columbia, 1973; 1997); originally produced by David Bowie and recently remixed by Iggy Pop, this strong final studio recording was issued under the name Iggy & the Stooges.

*Metallic K.O.* (Import, 1976); a live album that includes the group's final gig in 1974, augmented by the double album *Metallic 2 X K.O.*

*Rough Power* (Bomp!, 1994); for Stooges completists, this is *Raw Power* in its original, rougher version before the Bowie mix.

*Open Up and Bleed!* (Bomp!, 1995); collects post–*Raw Power* material, live and in rehearsals, previously available on import.

*California Bleeding* (Bomp!, 1997); collects live material, most never before released, from '73 and '74.

*Year of the Iguana* (Bomp!, 1997); a collection drawn from Bomp!'s "The Iguana Chronicles" releases.

TRIBUTE: Various Artists, *We Will Fall: The Iggy Pop Tribute* (Royalty, 1997); a tribute to the band's leader that includes many Stooges songs as well as Pop solo favorites, recorded by Red Hot Chili Peppers, Sugar Ray, Joey Ramone, Joan Jett, 7 Year Bitch, and 15 others.

# ROKY ERICKSON/13TH FLOOR ELEVATORS

*There are a lot of parallels between the psychedelic underground of the '60s and punk as far as being creative and anti-establishment. What the Butthole Surfers were doing in the '80s—being experimental, pushing the envelope—I thought was parallel to what the 13th Floor Elevators did. Maybe it's giving ourselves a lot of credit, but I got a sense I could relate to the Elevators. It's interesting how punk rockers, especially in Texas, took to Roky Erickson. I really can't think of anyone in American music who's as mythical to me. And the guy never got his fair due. He even had to go on welfare. He really touches me in a lot of different ways. Working with him was a great thrill, really rewarding.*

### King Coffey, Butthole Surfers

As one of the earliest (and perhaps the very first) psychedelic rock bands, the 13th Floor Elevators certainly influenced the course of music history through their steady output of red hot rock and input of LSD. It wasn't until later generations came to appreciate the tortured genius of the Elevators' frontman Roky Erickson, though, that the band's true impact was felt, in everything from southern dream poppers R.E.M. to garage punks Mudhoney to Texan wackos the Butthole Surfers—was felt. Like **Syd Barrett** and **Daniel Johnston,** Erickson's eccentricities have added to his status as cult icon, but the realities of his mental illness have, tragically, limited his ability to prosper creatively and financially.

---

### Curt Kirkwood, Meat Puppets

*I love Roky. He's one of the most fantastic poets, and the greatest singer. In the same way that Roy Orbison is an influence, he is. In terms of, like, space-aged doo-wop, R&B. I've always been really influenced by weird stuff from Texas. I was born there and moved away when I was pretty young, but was always really into the stuff from there.*

---

In 1965, University of Texas student Tommy Hall decided to form a rock band as a mouthpiece for his radical philosophies on the uses of mind-altering chemicals. Because he was not a musician himself, Hall recruited capable instrumentalists to surround him while he relegated his own duties to lyric-writing and playing the "electric jug." Having heard the local hit "You're Gonna Miss Me," by Austin group the Spades, Hall invited that band's singer/songwriter—a 17-year-old prodigy named Roger Kynard (Roky) Erickson—to join as well. When he accepted, the band—called the 13th Floor Elevators in some oblique reference to marijuana—was complete.

Signing to the Texas-based International Artists label, the Elevators re-recorded "You're Gonna Miss Me," which became a minor hit in 1966 and a garage rock classic. Early on, though, Hall wired the group into his own agenda, which included daily doses of LSD for everyone in the band and writing songs that encouraged psychoactive drug use as a way of life. On trips to San Francisco, where the Elevators played regularly, their friend Janis Joplin (who nearly joined the band while still living in Texas) introduced them to the similarly acid-friendly music of the Grateful Dead and Jefferson Airplane.

The band's 1967 debut, *The Psychedelic Sounds of the 13th Floor Elevators*—reputed to be the first musical use of the term "psychedelic"—came complete with liner notes that outlined Hall's program: "Recently, it has become possible for man to chemically alter his mental state. He can then restructure his thinking and change his language so that his thoughts bear more relation to his life and his problems, therefore approaching them more sanely. It this quest for pure sanity that forms the basis of the songs on this album." An early acid rock classic, the record mixed Erickson's bluesy constructions and strong singing with Hall's drug advocations. It sold well despite it's still-controversial subject matter, though soon Texas law enforcement had their eyes on the Elevators as the state's leading hippie troublemakers.

On the follow-up, *Easter Everywhere*, the Elevators got even more adventurous, with mesmerizing songs like "She Lives (In a Time of Her Own)" and "Levitation." Unfortunately, in early 1969 the Texas authorities caught up with the band, arresting Roky for possession of one marijuana joint. Erickson pleaded innocent by reason of insanity and was sentenced to a hospital for the criminally insane. Thus the Elevator's third studio album, *Bull of the Woods*, written mostly by guitarist Stacy Sutherland, proved to be their last.

---

### Van Conner, Screaming Trees

*Easter Everywhere and Bull in the Woods are really hypnotic. I've listened to them a billion times and still put them on. There's a heart and vibe to them that can freak you out. We have quite a few songs we didn't put out because we thought they sounded too much like 13th Floor Elevators. The last song on [the Trees'] Uncle Anesthesia has their spacey feel. And Mudhoney had a song called "Thirteenth Floor" that was a total rip-off.*

---

Over the next four years in the psychiatric hospital, Erickson was given electroshock treatment and various drug regimens, the benefits of which were dubious at best. By the time he emerged in 1973 Roky had written a book of messianic poetry and declared himself a Martian. With the slight notoriety engendered by the Elevators' appearance on 1972's *Nuggets* compilation, Erickson briefly attempted to re-form the group, but soon began fronting a series of bands over the next decade with names such as Bleib Alien, the Nervebreakers, Evil Hook Wildlife E.T, and the Resurrectionists.

Away from Hall, Roky began writing new songs—with titles like "I Walked with a Zombie," "Bloody Hammer," and "Don't Shake Me Lucifer"—that came straight out of the fantasy and horror comic books he devoured. Though his thematic fascination with the occult and Satanism would be echoed in escapist heavy metal music, the demons chasing Roky were quite palpable to him. Yet while Erickson's obsessions had clearly become twisted, his effortless singing and songwriting abilities—capable of producing a classic rocker like "Don't Slander Me" or a sweet Buddy Holly-esque tune like "Starry Eyes"—were amazingly intact.

---

### Jean Smith, Mecca Normal

*I saw an article on him and he seemed to be pretty scattered in his thinking. I was interested what this person's music sounded like. There's some very disturbing stuff, like "Bloody Hammer." This maniacal accusation against the psychiatric world he's had to deal with. It's super-personal—not polite stuff to talk about—and he obviously means it. His sincerity comes through to the degree that it's uncomfortable. I like that his songs reveal something and get a reaction. I don't know that music's mandate is to make you feel good or tap your toe.*

---

Erikson continued to perform and sporadically record into the mid-80s, but has never achieved more than a small cult following. By 1987, a discouraged Roky retired from music entirely. Without any income from the many bootleg releases of his music, he was forced to live on social security outside Austin. The '90s have been a bit kinder to Roky. With the help of family, friends, and advocates, Erickson improved his financial situation, and a tribute album further raised his profile. Following a 1993 return to the stage at the Austin Music Awards, Roky entered a recording studio for the first time in a decade. Working with local musicians such as Charlie Sexton, Lou Ann Barton, and the Butthole Surfers' Paul Leary, Erickson recorded six new songs released in 1995 on King Coffey's Trance Syndicate label (with an accompanying book of lyrics on Henry Rollins' 2.13.61 publishing company). As Roky entered his forties, *All That May Do My Rhyme* proved he was still one of Texas's finest singers and songwriters.

## DISCOGRAPHY

### 13TH FLOOR ELEVATORS

*The Psychedelic Sounds of...* (International Artists, 1967; Charly, 1991); a founding document of the psychedelic era.

*Easter Everywhere* (International Artists, 1968; Charly, 1991); an adventurous follow up that pointed in new directions.

*Elevator Live* (International Artists, 1968; Charly, 1991); a good early live recording.

*Bull of the Woods* (International Artists, 1969; Charly, 1991); recorded as the band was splitting up, it contains few Erickson songs.

### ROKY ERICKSON

*The Evil One* (415, 1981; Restless, 1987); studio album

originally released with unpronounceable rune title (later released as *I Think of Demons*).

*Don't Slander Me* (Pink Dust, 1986); songs recorded 1983–84.

*Gremlins Have Pictures* (Pink Dust, 1986); a mix of live and studio recordings from the late '70s and early '80s.

*You're Gonna Miss Me—Best of Roky Erickson* (Restless, 1991); a widely available collection of Erickson's '80s studio work and live recordings.

*All That May Do My Rhyme* (Trance Syndicate, 1995); a surprisingly solid return to the studio, with a mix of songs from a 1985 EP and brand new recordings.

*Roky Erickson & Evil Hook Wildlife E.T.* (Sympathy for the Record Industry, 1996); includes live recordings from the '80s, studio work, and interviews.

TRIBUTE: *Where the Pyramid Meets the Eye* (Sire, 1990); a collection featuring Erickson's songs recorded by ZZ Top, R.E.M., Jesus & Mary Chain, Butthole Surfers, and many more.

## S I L V E R   A P P L E S

*It's like what happened to Rip Van Winkle. Twenty years were sliced out. There's some sort of social/musical thing that links the '60s to the '90s in how it perceives itself through art. So you can skip the '70s, skip the '80s, and jump to the '90s and there's this beautiful interchange. The guys I'm working with now weren't even born when I recorded those albums.*

**Simeon, Silver Apples**

While many obscure groups are granted the consolation that they were "ahead of their time," few groups were quite as palpably precocious as Silver Apples. When they recorded in the late '60s, their metronomic beats and oscillating synth textures sounded like absolutely nothing that had come before. And though they've subtley infiltrated underground music through krautrockers like **Kraftwerk** and keyboard punks like **Suicide,** only now—three decades later—is the rest of the world truly catching up. The Silver Apples' organic and psychedelic electronica is heard today in the space rock of Spectrum and Jessamine, the post-rock of Laika, the digital hardcore of Atari Teenage Riot, and the futurist pop of Stereolab and Yo La Tengo, all of whom have paid tribute to the group in recent years.

Simeon, the central figure behind Silver Apples, was a hippie artist from New Orleans who came to New York in the '60s to work as a painter. To supplement his income, he sang in Greenwich Village clubs and coffee houses. Though the music he performed was generally standard blues and rock, on the side Simeon was interested in avant garde music, particularly the early electronic music of Karlheinz Stockhausen. One day in 1967 a composer friend showed Simeon an old World War II laboratory test oscillator, which had been used to send sound waves through equipment in order to check the effectiveness of circuitry. When Simeon heard the warbly tones the oscillator produced, he asked if he could borrow it. "I started thinking this had serious possibilities," Simeon remembers. "If you had a halfway decent ear, you should be able to play this thing the same way you'd play a trombone or any instrument with a slide thing, where you could play notes between notes and do the whole spectrum." That night Simeon's group, the Overland Stage Electric Band, was performing at the popular Village hangout Café Wha? (where Bob Dylan had started years before). During one of the group's extended instrumental jams, Simeon pulled out the oscillator and began playing it. Though Simeon liked what he heard, most of his bandmates didn't and quit in disgust. Soon all that remained of the quintet was Simeon and the group's drummer Dan Taylor, a gifted beat-keeper who'd played with Jimi Hendrix. Simeon and Taylor decided to continue on as a duo, writing original music for drums and oscillator.

---

### Tim Gane, Stereolab

*We did a single that was kind of an homage to Silver Apples called "Harmonium"/"Farfisa." They were just inspiring and awe-inducing. It shows how so many things are there if you just look for them. Any kind of strange music which you'd never imagine, to some degree someone's already done it. The music is like a happy accident. Two people happened to meet and they couldn't form a band so they did this. That's what makes it interesting.*

---

Simeon and Taylor called themselves Silver Apples, taking the name from a line in a poem by W. B. Yeats ("The silver apples of the moon/The golden apples of the sun"). Though they were without guitars, basses, and keyboards, Silver Apples were anything but minimalist. Expanding on the principles of the first oscillator, Simeon constructed an instrument, The Simeon, made of a dozen or so audio oscillators, with all sorts of amplifiers, sound filters, and radio parts, operated by 86 telegraph keys and a "whammy bar" type handle. While singing, Simeon played the bleeping midrange rhythm patterns with one hand, the whirly-sounding lead part with the other hand, and the pulsating bass lines with his feet. Because Simeon was untrained as a musician, he devised a system of color coding the controls; rather than playing in a particular key, each song was played in a color.

---

### Lou Barlow, Sebadoh/Folk Implosion

*I think they're inspirational. Their use of synthesizers is great. We sampled a few of their beats for the Kids Soundtrack and slowed them down.*

---

Taylor's setup was similarly complex. He used a 20-piece drum set, with 10 different tom-toms tuned to match Simeon's oscillator tones. Though there was nothing electronic about his equipment, Taylor took a mechanical approach to playing and his intricacy only added to the group's techno-futurist sound. "He talked constantly about the mathematical structure of his drumming," Simeon says. "I used to say, 'Why don't you fucking just drum! Put some power into it and let's rock and roll!' But he wanted to do it computerized. In his head he was a computer. He loved the idea of the interaction between man and machine."

---

### Alec Empire, Atari Teenage Riot

*I was always looking for music like that, psychedelic with synthesizers, and I think there's a certain punkiness to the drums that I really like. The way they approach psychedelic is exactly what I like, it's just so extreme, and there's also the humor that I understood about them. That's why I've started on a record with Simeon.*

---

Doing gigs in downtown New York, Silver Apples became part of an art and music scene centered around the Max's Kansas City club that included the Velvet Underground and Andy Warhol (who did a portrait of Simeon). Their big break came almost immediately, though, when they got themselves booked opening for the Steve Miller Band, Chambers Brothers, Sha-Na-Na, and Mothers of Invention in front of 30,000 people in Central Park. Silver Apples received enough critical attention from the show that record companies began offering contracts. In early 1968 Silver Apples signed a deal with Kapp Records (whose roster included acts such as Burt Bacharach and Louis Armstrong) and released a self-titled debut album in June of '68.

*Silver Apples* was a strange and mysterious debut. The original cover offered no title or band name, and the music, recorded roughly on a four-track machine, was completely alien. Never before on record had music so entirely based around electronics been put in a rock setting. The lyrics, written by poet Stanley Warren, were of the hippie-dippy variety (sample: "seagreen serenades awaken me to dream") and Silver Apples was rooted in current psychedelia. However, songs like "Program," which used sampled bits from the radio, and the group's signature tune, "Oscillations," with lyrics about "electronic evocations," offered something that approached avant-garde. Kapp, unsure how to promote so unusual a band, booked Silver Apples in high school auditoriums more suited to bubblegum pop. Not surprisingly, they were often booed off stage.

---

**Bob Pollard, Guided by Voices:**
*I liked their sound. It was just two guys. They talk about us as being the pioneers of low-fi but I think of bands like Silver Apples, they were way before us.*

---

Still, Kapp was a large label, with good distribution and strong radio connections, and was able to turn both *Silver Apples* and "Oscillations" into minor hits. But by the band's 1969 follow-up, *Contact,* Kapp was on the verge of folding. Though in some respects the record—made in a 24-track studio, with the addition of banjo and Simeon's own, darker lyrics—was even more ambitious than the debut, without Kapp fully behind the album it quickly disappeared. A lawsuit filed by Pam Am Airlines (*Contact'*s cover depicted Simeon and Dan in a Pan Am cockpit surrounded by drug paraphernalia) put the final nail in both Kapp's and Silver Apples' coffins. By early 1970, Simeon and Dan had gone their separate ways.

Legend has it that in the group's final months, they recorded a third album, with Jimmy Hendrix contributing his guitar work to some of the songs. But, unable to secure a new recording contract, Silver Apples were unable to pay their recording costs. The studio kept the tapes, and they were eventually lost.

After a brief attempt to revive Silver Apples in 1971, Simeon returned to painting and moved to Mobile, Alabama. He stored his "Simeon" under a friend's house in Mobile, and when his friend moved years later the new tenants disposed of the large gadget. Simeon believes the oscillator was auctioned off for charity by the local Veterans of Foreign Wars, though its current whereabouts have never been determined. Dan Taylor, whom Simeon last saw in the '70s, is also missing in action.

After decades of obscurity, in 1994 a German company reissued a bootleg of the Silver Apples records, and the following year another label put together a tribute album (MCA finally made the original albums available on domestic CD in 1997). Inspired by the new interest, Simeon resurfaced and formed a new Silver Apples with two younger musicians. Recreating the Simeon machine (now using a keyboard instead of telegraph keys to operate), the new Silver Apples picked up where the old one left off and worked with artists such as **Big Black's** Steve Albini (Nirvana's producer), Space Needle, and Meat Beat Manifesto. Thirty-years later, the group's electronica finally seems to fit in with current sounds.

## DISCOGRAPHY

*Silver Apples* (Kapp, 1968; MCA, 1997); this amazingly advanced record was reissued with *Contact* on an essential CD that now features all available recordings of the band.

*Contact* (Kapp, 1969); the extremely rare and long out-of-print second album is now included with the first on the reissue.

*Beacon* (Whirlbird, 1998); the group's first new album in almost thirty years features Simeon with two younger band members.

TRIBUTE: *Electronic Evocations: A Tribute to the Silver Apples* (Enraptured, 1995); a mini-album featuring Windy and Carl, Third Eye Foundation, and others.

# S Y D   B A R R E T T

*Probably the first adult album I heard was The Piper at the Gates of Dawn, so I grew up thinking that was normal music. And I was really into both Syd Barrett albums. I used to go to my local folk club and do "Effervescing Elephant" on acoustic guitar, which was quite appalling I'd imagine. There's the whole mythos of the man: Was he mad? Is he a genius? Did he burn himself out? Is he really living with his mum in Cambridge? Does he watch television all day? It's interesting. Now I look back and it's quite sad the way someone who had great talent became just a myth. It's a bit of a warning.*

**Toby Marks, Banco de Gaia**

Nothing builds a legend like a tragically shortened career, and Syd Barrett's career was nothing if not tragically short. What he left behind, though—the internationally famous rock band he founded and two unique solo albums—puts him among the most influential figures in rock. Though he hasn't recorded in almost 30 years, Syd Barrett can be heard in the music of each generation to follow: In the glam-rock of David Bowie and T. Rex; in the punk-inflected pop of the Soft Boys (whose Robyn Hitchcock wrote "The Man Who Invented Himself" in tribute to Barrett); in the '80s alternative music of Love and Rockets, Jesus and Mary Chain, and R.E.M. (who covered his song "Dark Globe"); and in recent groups such as the Gigolo Aunts (named after a Barrett song) and scores of young psychedelic rock bands.

Roger Keith "Syd" Barrett grew up in Cambridge, and at 18 moved south to London to attend art school. He quickly fell in with a crowd of other Cambridge expatriates, including architecture student Roger Waters, with whom he formed Pink Floyd in 1965. Named after two old bluesmen in Barrett's record collection, the original band was very much Barrett's creative vehicle: he sang and played guitar, and wrote most of the early material, including the initial singles "Arnold Layne" and "See Emily Play." The most popular of London's original psychedelic bands, Barrett's Pink Floyd put on shows that featured elaborate light shows and sounds inspired by the group's LSD experimentation.

With the release of their debut album *The Piper at the Gates of Dawn* in 1967, Pink Floyd broke into the British charts and were rising fast. Though Barrett had played the dominant role on the record, both writing and mixing most of the songs, his abundant and often brilliant creativity began to suffer from his excessive acid intake. Combined with what may have been a predisposition to mental illness, Barrett's nearly constant tripping was causing a mental meltdown. He became distant, unreliable, easily freaked, and sometimes violent.

### Tim Gane, Stereolab

*I was a massive fan, I still am. I used to get all the bootlegs and magazines. His music is very touching, especially his solo records. They're an amazing summing up of someone's state of mind at the time. Creativity tinged with mental disturbance can create something that's very human. Every single song he wrote has something unusual about it. I also like the way he composed his songs. Simplistic but not simplistic. He had a very good ear for chords and melodies, very focused. And the first Pink Floyd record is just an amazing record, with amazing insights into how you could do things that hadn't been done before. And that was all due to him really.*

When it became clear the band could not count on Barrett to be a consistent frontman, the other members of Pink Floyd recruited a new guitarist, Syd's childhood acquaintance David Gilmour. Though the initial plan was to keep Barrett as singer and songwriter, within weeks the five-person line-up proved impossible and the band kicked Barrett out of the group. Though left without a creative leader, in time a more angst-ridden Pink Floyd led by Roger Waters would become one of the biggest bands in the world. Though Syd Barrett would continue to play an important role in Pink Floyd's music, it was not as creator but as subject. The band's 1975 record *Wish You Were Here* (particularly the song "Shine on You Crazy Diamond") is often cited as a tribute to Barrett.

Upset by his dismissal, but not yet so far gone he couldn't make music, Syd Barrett soon entered a recording studio to begin work on his first solo album. By 1969 he signed a record contract, and in January of 1970 his debut, *The Madcap Laughs,* was released. Produced by Syd's former bandmates Gilmour and Waters, the record is a loose and shambly affair (what we might call low-fi today, with its audible guitar pick clickings) but contained a terrific set of playful and eccentric folk ditties. As schizophrenic as its maker, *The Madcap Laughs* could be trippy and rambling but remained consistently tuneful. The music, which combined Pink Floyd psychedelia with a more innocent skiffle pop style, mixed solo acoustic performances with the light accompaniment from members of the British prog band Soft Machine. Barrett's lyrics were at times unintelligible and other times focused and clever; they could be mystical and literate, or quite base.

### Marcellus Hall, Railroad Jerk

*It affected me a lot, especially in the songs where he makes mistakes. Like he turns the page in the middle of singing, and there's a song where he starts way off key then goes, "No, wait, wait," and then starts again. The way he does it was so much an influence to me because it showed a lot of humanness. It was a revelation to know you could do that on record and let it be.*

A second album, produced by Gilmour with Pink Floyd keyboardist Richard Wright, *Barrett* was released in November of 1970. Though more consistent than the debut, with tighter and more structured arrangements, the record sounds stilted and somewhat joyless in places. Barrett's eccentricities still abound, though, particularly in the record's many animal-themed songs: the devious "Rats," the lethargic "Maisie" (about a cow), the plodding "Effervescing Elephant," and others. With Syd losing grasp on reality and often failing to show up at the studio, *Barrett* was too difficult an album to make for anyone involved to contemplate further recordings. It was to be Syd's last album of new material.

---

### Chris Cornell, Soundgarden

*He had an amazing way of taking dour experimental music, singing strange carnivalesque happy lyrics over top, and making it work in a non-pretentious way. So you're being pulled in two different directions at once. On his solo records there's plenty of situations where I've learned from him as far as the sparseness, and the somber quietness with a frantic edge. There's been a number of times where I've tried to achieve that in a song, making it my own but wanting to feel for my song the way he would feel for his songs.*

---

Barrett left London in 1971 and returned to his mother's house in Cambridge. A 1974 return to the studio led absolutely nowhere and he has been virtually silent for the last two decades. Now in his fifties and using his given name, Roger Barrett continues to live quietly in Cambridge. Under the care of relatives, he lives off pension and record royalties, and tends his garden with little contact from the outside world. Meanwhile, the Syd Barrett personality cult contines to thrive.

## DISCOGRAPHY

*The Madcap Laughs* (Harvest, 1970; Capitol/EMI, 1990); produced by his former bandmates, this is a rough-cut and eccentric folk pop gem.

*Barrett* (Harvest, 1970; Capitol/EMI, 1990); a second recording, released only months later, with weaker material and less charm, but not without its finer moments.

*Opel* (Capitol, 1989); a collection of outtakes and alternate versions, including the standout title cut.

*Crazy Diamond: The Complete Recordings* (Harvest/EMI, 1993); just like it says, this box set contains everything Barrett released, plus a bunch of unreleased material.

TRIBUTE: Various Artists, *Beyond the Wildwood* (1987); featuring the Shamen, Death of Samantha, Plasticland.

# 4

# ABSURDISTS AND ECCENTRICS

Somewhere along the line of rock history a small, rebellious contingent stopped making music that conformed to a steady beat, grooved on a fluid melody, and made any sort of lyrical sense. Not surprisingly, the most radical of these convention-twisters were largely overlooked. But while the most committed bizzaros never had a hope of impacting mainstream tastes, the sounds they introduced have slowly been adapted and assimilated into rock through the music of bands they influenced.

In terms of breaking new ground with the structures and arrangements in rock, **Captain Beefheart** is the man who launched a thousand skronky and jagged rock bands. Two of his most accomplished pupils, **Pere Ubu** and the **Residents,** would further spread the word with their own uniquely perverse music. And somewhere on the side there's **Red Krayola,** a colorful footnote to psychedelic art rock whose flirtations with the absurdist avant-garde go back even further than Beefheart's. Red Krayola, in the end, may prove to be the missing link in the progression from early Dadaist shenanigans to austere '90s post-rock.

## CAPTAIN BEEFHEART

*My music isn't that much different from the music that's in [people's] minds. Because I conceive it so naturally, it's bound to be in their minds. Sooner or later, they'll catch on; they'll learn to enjoy it without understanding why.*

**Don Van Vliet (Captain Beefheart) [LA Times, 1971]**

Captain Beefheart's take on American music endowed the blues with an entirely new palette of colors and offered art rock some emotional roots. With his irregular rhythms, peculiar melodies, and all-around perversity, Beefheart is the father of surrealist rock. As such, he's an important reference point for many of the bands scattered throughout this book—the **Residents, Public Image Limited, DNA, Half Japanese,** the **Minutemen**—and his influence includes just about anyone who's broken away from steady rock beats, traditional tonality, and literalist lyrics. Songwriters quote his absurd lyrics (PJ Harvey, Aztec Camera), singers imitate his gruff Howlin' Wolf voice (Tom Waits), and bands adapt his herky-jerky arrangements (Talking Heads, Sonic Youth). Still, no one sounds quite like the man born Don Van Vliet outside Los Angeles in 1941.

### David Yow, Jesus Lizard

*I really dig his shit, man. There are times I've tried to write a song and have not been able to come up with something I like. And I kind of go, "Well, gee, what would the Captain do?"*

Van Vliet's creative genius was evident early on. He was a recognized sculptor by the age of 4; by 13 he'd been offered scholarships to study art in Europe. Declining the invitations, Don's parents moved him to Lancaster, California, in the Mojave Desert, where among his schoolmates he found a kindred eccentric in a young Frank Zappa. By the time they graduated from high school, Zappa and Van Vliet—who by then was playing saxophone and harmonica—intended to form a band and make a movie. Neither the band (the Soots) nor the movie (*Captain Beefheart Meets the Grunt People*) ever materialized, and Zappa soon left for Los Angeles to form the Mothers of Invention. In 1964 Van Vliet, renamed Captain Beefheart, formed his own group, the Magic Band.

The original Captain Beefheart and the Magic Band was a fairly straightforward blues and R&B group, though their outrageous outfits and antics earned them local attention and A&M Records released their cover of Bo Diddley's "Diddy Wah Diddy" in 1965. An album was to follow the next year, but as Beefheart's eccentricities started to show, A&M rejected the band's new recordings as "too negative." Collected as the album *Safe As Milk*, these songs were finally released on a smaller label in 1967. The record features a young guitarist named Ry Cooder, who would go on to play with Eric Clapton and the Rolling Stones as well as record albums and movie soundtracks on his own. Other Beefheart sidemen would go on to play with acts such as Red Hot Chili Peppers, PJ Harvey, Frank Black, and Joan Osborne.

Beefheart encountered more record company problems with his second album, 1968's *Strictly Personal*, and might have given up on music altogether had not his old friend Frank Zappa re-emerged to offer him a contract—and complete artistic control—with Zappa's own label, Straight Records. Beefheart wrote 28 new songs in 8½ hours, then assembled a new Magic Band with exotically named "musicians" such as Zoot Horn Rollo, the Mascara Snake (Beefheart's cousin), and Antennae Jimmy Semens. What came out after eight months of rehearsing and recording, *Trout Mask Replica*, was radically different from anything that had been attempted in rock. It was immediately acknowledged as the work of a musical visionary.

### Chris Cornell, Soundgarden

*He's definitely influenced me lyrically, just thinking about the color and depiction of an idea without being straightforward. In fact, when I'm sitting around writing lyrics and having trouble getting into the flow, I'll always grab the CD booklet to Trout Mask Replica and read some of it. It's not trying to get someone else's rhythm and copying it. Just listening to any record that you're influenced by opens up the possibilities that your brain can close to you. You forget what you can get away with.*

Though clearly influenced by Ornette Coleman's free jazz, *Trout Mask* was a rock album and had absolutely no improvisation. Beefheart, who composed each instrument part either on piano or in his head, dictated exactly how each musician should sound. Whatever training the Magic Band had, it needed to be unlearned to grasp the music in Beefheart's brain. With songs full of clashing rhythms, relentless dissonance, and asymmetric riffs—and complemented with some of his most inspiringly grotesque lyrics—*Trout Mask* is often difficult to sit through. At at its most successful (for instance in songs like "Pachuco Cadaver"), the instrumentation seems to move in all different speeds and in all different directions, yet makes some sort of twisted sense.

### David Byrne:

*Trout Mask Replica was a huge influence. It's just an amazing piece of work. At first, it sounds like two different bands playing in the same room or something. Then when you listen to it closer you realize everything is organized and worked out. There's no accidents here. The whole thing is orchestrated. It has all the rock and blues textures, but totally reinvented and made fresh again.*

With the next year's *Lick My Decals Off, Baby*, Beefheart and his Magic Band created another absurdist masterwork, with perhaps even more confidence and control than in *Trout Mask*. *Decals*, though, marked the end of Beefheart's most extreme period of musical dementia, and with two records in 1972—the blues/rock-oriented *Spotlight Kid* and *Clear Spot*—Beefheart offered a somewhat more commercial sound.

Despite Beefheart's change of emphasis, his albums were still too eccentric to achieve more than moderate sales. Increasingly frustrated, Beefheart next made two records that aimed directly at a pop audience. *Unconditionally Guaranteed* and *Bluejeans and Moonbeams* were widely regarded—even by Beefheart himself—as his worst records. Unable to make a decent living with the Magic Band, in 1975 the Captain toured as a vocalist with Zappa's group (he appears on Zappa's *Bongo Fury* live album).

### Curt Kirkwood, Meat Puppets

*Beefheart was a major influence, more than an influence. Conceptually, where would I be without that? It's not so much the style, but where it gets you. But in Beefheart's case, the medium is so intense it's no surprise when you get where you're going with it.*

Surprisingly, as younger Beefheart-inspired bands like Talking Heads and B-52s were emerging, the Captain was on the verge of a second career peak. In 1978, he formed a new Magic Band and released *Shiny Beast (Bat Chain Puller)*, a stunning wake-up from Beefheart's mid-'70s slumber. Full of burning blues licks, stuttered rhythms, and vital singing, the album integrated the best elements of past records to create a sound that was both accessible and engaging. In the early '80s, Beefheart produced two more bright and energetic records. Even more off-center than *Shiny Beast*, these albums completed a most unusual career arc—from aggressive weirdness to somewhat uninspired product and back to a challenging angularity that fit right in with the most dynamic postpunk groups.

### Joe Henry

*When I was making the last record we talked about Beefheart a lot. Not that I was trying to make a record that sounds like him, but I really like his treatment of sounds and where he puts them. I always think of mixing not as an incidental thing you do to wrap up a project, but as one more color on your palette.*

In 1982, Captain Beefheart retired from music and, with his wife, moved back to the Mojave desert. Having developed a reputation over the years for his paintings (which appeared on many of his record covers), Beefheart became Don Van Vliet once again and dedicated his time to visual art. While his records still haven't reached a large audience, his paintings now bring thousands of dollars apiece. Rumor has it that Van Vliet is terminally ill. But even if we never hear music from Captain Beefheart again, his overwhelming influence on modern rock means that it will be almost impossible to miss the sounds of his musical children and grandchildren.

### Lou Barlow, Sebadoh/Folk Implosion

*I know with Folk Implosion, John [Davis]'s guitar playing is pretty influenced by Beefheart, those kind of stuttering rhythms. That guitar style is actually the precursor to stuff like Gang of Four, so I was probably more influenced by things that were influenced by Captain Beefheart. I don't even think I've fully realized his influence, but it's going to continue to inspire me in the future.*

## DISCOGRAPHY

*Safe as Milk* (Kama Sutra, 1967; Unidisc, 1992).

*Strictly Personal* (Blue Thumb, 1968; Liberty/EMI UK, 1994).

*Trout Mask Replica* (Straight, 1969; Reprise, 1970); Beefheart's breakthrough as a musical visionary, a double-album from another planet.

*Lick My Decals Off, Baby* (Straight, 1970; Rhino, 1991); a slight refinement of *Trout Mask*'s approach, with equally (if not more) successful results.

*Mirror Man* (Buddah, 1970; Unidisc, 1992); features four bluesy, jam-filled songs recorded in 1968.

*The Spotlight Kid* (Reprise, 1972; 1991); a record of fairly straightforward blues rock, now available on one CD with *Clear Spot*.

*Clear Spot* (Reprise, 1972; 1991); a more pop- and rock-oriented record.

*Unconditionally Guaranteed* (Mercury, 1974; Blue Plate/ Caroline, 1990); an even deeper dive into the mainstream, with mixed results.

*Bluejeans and Moonbeams* (Mercury, 1974; Blue Plate/Caroline, 1990); a record widely regarded as Beefheart's lowpoint.

*Shiny Beast* (*Bat Chain Puller*) (Warner Brothers, 1978); a second career peak, incorporating the best elements of his most challenging and most accessible work.

*Doc at the Radar Station* (Virgin, 1980; Blue Plate/Caroline, 1990).

*Ice Cream for Crow* (Virgin-Epic, 1982; Blue Plate/Caroline, 1990); the final album, that ended Beefheart's career on a decidedly high note.

*The Legendary A&M Sessions* EP (A&M, 1984); featuring five songs from 1965, these are Beefheart's earliest available recordings.

*I May Be Hungry But I Sure Ain't Weird: Alternate CB* (Sequel, 1992); the restored version of *Strictly Personal*, which was altered by producers against Beefheart's wishes.

TRIBUTE: *Fast'n'Bulbous: A Tribute to Captain Beefheart* (Imaginary,1988); a tribute album in days before it was so common, these covers by Sonic Youth, XTC, and others celebrate a musical mind truly deserving of it.

# T H E   R E S I D E N T S

*We owe a lot to them.... I'd never heard anything as fucked up as the Residents that wasn't just experimental or avant-garde for the sake of being that way. Those guys were just wicked, and so mysterious. Originally we tried to cop a lot of that from them. There were no pictures of us or credits on our records. The whole "Gene Ween" and "Dean Ween" idea came from the Residents. We were influenced as much by the Residents as any other band in the world.*

**Micky "Gene Ween" Melchiondo, Ween**

The Residents are outsiders among outsiders, strict adherents to a "Theory of Obscurity" that contends the best and purest art is made without any consideration for, or feedback from, an audience. They've produced dozens of albums over the past three decades and managed to maintain anonymity by disguising themselves in all public appearances. Their trademark disguise, large eyeballs they wear on their heads, along with a standard top hat and tuxedo, is a brilliant deconstruction of pop music's cult of personality; the costume makes it impossible to identify and define band members (apparently four of them) in terms of age, race, gender, beauty, charisma, or sexuality and forces listeners to deal exclusively with the music itself.

While constantly operating on the periphery of pop, the Residents offered themselves as a powerful symbol of artistic independence and substance over celebrity. They pioneered a low-fi Dadaist style with no constraints except a commitment to the unusual. With bits of quirky-jerky noodling, electronic and industrial sound collages, a twisted Zappa/Beefheart humor, an avant-garde compositional sense, and childlike playfulness, the Residents prefigured the essential elements of punk, post-punk, new wave, and post-rock—and informed the styles of current groups from Primus to They Might Be Giants—without ever becoming part of a definable musical movement. And as bands and genres have come and gone, the Residents remain a step ahead of popular currents.

*Dave Dederer, Presidents of the United States of America*
*Discovering records like the Residents in high school was like finding another world. It was*
*truly alternative at the time. If you had the records, you were one of a handful of people who*
*did. It had an appeal on that level.*

All we know of the the Residents' early history is what they've told us: The members attended high school together in Shreveport, Louisiana, and moved to San Francisco in the early '70s. They made four albums' worth of material before their first release—before they even had a name. They sent one of their early tapes, unsolicited and unidentified, to the Warner Bros. executive that signed **Captain Beefheart**. When it was returned to "Resident" at their address, they had found their name.

It was clear that to maintain the desired level of anonymity, the Residents would have to handle all business operations themselves. They set up their own label, Ralph Records, to release Residents material, and their own design company, Pore No Graphics, to create album art. And soon after, four "friends from Shreveport" arrived to form Cryptic Corporation, a marketing and management company that served as an umbrella organization for all

Residents-related projects. Cryptic members such as Jay Clem and Homer Flynn have served as band spokespeople as well. By keeping close control over both the creative and business affairs of the group, the Residents served as an important model for future generations of do-it-yourselfers.

*Tim Gane, Stereolab*
*It's music that came from another solar system. The way the Residents recorded wasn't like*
*anybody else, it was just so special. They sum up all sorts of reactions and emotions and I*
*can't see really why. It's very poignant music. We had this design [on our early self-released*
*singles], which I liked because I thought it looked like the guy from Ralph Records.*

Throughout their more than 25-year career, the Residents' primary order of business has been the mangling of pop convention. They immediately took aim at the top: their 1973 debut, *Meet the Residents,* parodied the Beatles' first album. The follow-up, *The Residents Present the Third Reich and Roll,* featured classic '60s songs redone as if from a Nazified parallel universe and offered an outrageous but potent satire of pop music as fascism for youth. Perhaps the group's most cutting stab at the heart of music culture came with 1980's *Commercial Album.* Featuring 40 one-minute songs (to fit in ad slots which they bought on local radio stations), the record explored music as a sales tool and mocked the Top 40 format that made music's emotional value meaningless by ranking songs according to commercial success.

### Sean O'Hagen, High Llamas

*I like the anonymity they've maintained without being totally faceless. I don't like the idea of pictures or people knowing what we look like or who's actually in the band. We've never had any pictures of us on our records. I like the idea of having a floating membership, with a name, a musical community, and the sound. The Residents managed to do that.*

Later works continued to offer the Residents' bizarre perspective on otherwise familiar material: The *Eskimo* album practiced phony ethnomusicology; their American Composers Series (offering Residents-style covers of Gershwin, Sousa, Hank Williams, and James Brown) and Cube E series (attacking early American music and Elvis songs) were good for kicks as well. A deranged cover of the Rolling Stones' "Satisfaction" in 1976 came right in time for the Residents to emerge as a visible outside influence on punk irreverence, and later, with the semipopular *Duck Stab/Buster & Glen* album, on new wave eccentricity.

### David Byrne

*Their influence was in just the fact that they existed. Not directly musically, but the fact that they are doing such original work is encouragement. You can take it as, "It's okay to go that far out, to push things that far. Somebody else is doing it in their way, so I can do it in my way."*

Video has been at the forefront of the Residents' work from the start. Acknowledged as one of the first groups to develop narrative music video, the Residents weaved together visual and musical ideas years before MTV existed. And unlike today's videos, work such as *One Minute Movies* (a companion to their *Commercial Album*) had more in common with avant-garde film than cola advertisements. By the early '80s, when the group went on tour with their Mole Show—a fantasy "opera" about the struggles between the immigrant laborer Moles and the industrial xenophobe Chubs—the Residents were pioneering a concept that blurred the lines between concert, theater, visual art, video, animation, and dance.

In the '90s, the Residents have increasingly incorporated computer technology in their work. Recordings have become less of a focus, and the group has made a reputation for itself in the world of CD-ROM. Beginning with 1993's *Freak Show,* the Residents have produced award-winning discs that mix music with software design, computer animation, video, and narrative. In 1994, they were one of the first groups to offer an enhanced CD that could be played in both a disc player and drive. As removed from mainstream music as ever, the Residents have also managed to maintain their place at the forefront of art.

## DISCOGRAPHY

*Meet the Residents* (Ralph, 1974; ESD, 1988); the defiantly eccentric debut album, reissued with the initial four-song release, *Santa Dog.*

*The Third Reich and Roll* (Ralph, 1976; ESD, 1987); a parody of fascism in the commercial culture of pop music.

*Duck Stab/Buster & Glen* (Ralph, 1978; ESD, 1987); the closest they came to a pop record, this was reissued with the *Goosebump* EP.

*Not Available* (Ralph, 1978; ESD, 1988); a 1974 recording that was made with no intention of release.

*Eskimo* (Ralph, 1979; ESD, 1987); a bit of fake ethnomusicology that is nevertheless one of their most musically successful recordings.

*Diskomo/Goosebump* (Ralph, 1980); a disco remix of *Eskimo,* with an added EP of nursery rhyme—based songs.

*The Commercial Album* (Ralph, 1980; ESD, 1988); the best-known album, a collection of 40 one-minute songs (increased to 50 on the reissue).

*Mark of the Mole* (Ralph, 1981; ESD, 1988); the first installment of the Mole Trilogy, including the *Intermission* release.

*The Tunes of Two Cities* (Ralph, 1982; ESD, 1990); the second part of the Mole Trilogy.

*Residue of the Residents* (Ralph, 1983); a compilation.

*George & James* (Ralph, 1984); the first of the American Composers Series, featuring the music of George Gershwin and James Brown.

*Whatever Happened to Vileness Fats* (Ralph, 84; ESD, 1993); soundtrack to a documentary about the band's aborted *Vileness Fats* project, reissued with their *Census Taker* soundtrack.

*The Big Bubble* (Black Shroud-Ralph, 1985; ESD, 1990); skipping the third part, this is the "fourth" and final part of the Mole Trilogy.

*Heaven?* (Rykodisc, 1986); a random and decontextualized compilation.

*Hell!* (Rykodisc, 1986); same as *Heaven?*, but with worse songs.

*Stars & Hank Forever* (Ralph, 1986); the second of the American Composers Series, spotlighting the music of John Philips Sousa and Hank Williams.

*The Eyeball Show (13th Anniversary) Live in Japan* (Ralph, 1986)

*God in Three Persons* (Rykodisc, 1988); a record investigating sexual obsession, also released in excerpted instrumental form as *God in Three Persons Soundtrack.*

*Buckaroo Blues & Black Barry* (Ralph cass., 1989); the combined first and second parts of Cube E, a Residents-style deconstruction of early American music.

*The King & Eye* (Enigma/Restless, 1989); the third part of the Cube E project, a collection of Elvis songs done in the Residents' inimitable style.

*Stranger Than Supper* (UWEB Special Products, 1991); a collection of live recordings and rarities.

*Freak Show* (Cryptic Official Product, 1990; ESD, 1995); the band's first CD-ROM project.

*Our Finest Flowers* (Ralph/ESD, 1993); a "greatest hits" collection to celebrate the group's 20th anniversary, it features reconstructed and recombined bits of past songs.

*Gingerbread Man* (ESD, 1994); an Enhanced CD, also released as music-only, featuring a series of character sketches.

*Bad Day on the Midway* (Inscape, 1995); a CD-ROM game, released in music-only form as *Have a Bad Day* (ESD, 1996)

*Hunters: The World of Predators and Prey* (Milan/BMG, 1995); the soundtrack to a Discovery Channel series on wild animals.

*Our Tired, Our Poor, Our Huddled Masses* (Rykodisc, 1997); a terrific two-CD 25-year retrospective.

TRIBUTE: *Eyesore: A Stab at the Residents* (Vaccination, 1996); a collection of quirky post-Residents artists such as Primus, Stan Ridgeway, Cracker, and Thinking Fellers Union Local 282 doing Residents songs.

# PERE UBU

*The vision is to create modern music. If indeed we are not going to reach the future, somebody better bring the future now.*

**David Thomas, Pere Ubu (from Search & Destroy #6, 1978)**

In their mix of classic '60s rock with wheezy synthesizers, harsh found sounds, fractured and angular song structures, and absurd humor, Pere Ubu was a pre-punk band with a post-punk sound. More organic and tuneful than most experimental music, but too stark and disjointed for consideration by the mainstream, they were purveyors of strange folk music for a post-industrial age. Commonly branded "avant garage" for their duel loyalties to down-home rock and out-there noise, Pere Ubu's imprint can be detected on husky-voiced guitarists such as Frank Black and Bob Mould (as well as their respective original bands, the Pixies and **Hüsker Dü**), and on newer obscurantists like Pavement and Guided By Voices.

### Bob Pollard, Guided By Voices

*They swam in a sea of their own, they did their own thing. Along with that whole Cleveland thing, Pere Ubu were way ahead of their time.*

At its core, Pere Ubu is a Cleveland band. Its roots were in the suburban Midwestern tradition of garage rock, but they played like a band of intellectuals lost in a post-apocalyptic no-man's land (which in the pre–urban renewal '70s, was just what Cleveland looked like). Pere Ubu arose in 1975 out of the ashes of Rocket from the Tombs, one of a small group of local bands (including the Electric Eels and the Mirrors) that played original music. Two Rocket alums, David Thomas (whose stage name was Crocus Behemoth) and Peter Laughner, put together a group of local musicians (which Thomas named Pere Ubu after a character from a play by the French absurdist Alfred Jarry) as a one-time only studio band to record two Rocket favorites, "30 Seconds over Tokyo" and "Heart of Darkness."

### Bob Mould, Sugar/Hüsker Dü

*Their music sort of scared me the first time I heard it, it's really ominous and different. Pere Ubu seemed to really capture what it would be like to live in an industrial city. Their music was like industrial soundscapes. They really presented the whole thing well, you couldn't tell if they were factory workers or artists. The lyrics were really oblique, the melodies were different. It wasn't punk rock but it was really energetic.*

When Thomas released the songs as a single, it became necessary to play a live show to promote the record, and Pere Ubu got together again. One show led to another, then another, and by the time they recorded a second single in 1976, the band had settled into semipermanent status. Still, Pere Ubu was far from stable. The first notable departure was original bassist Tim Wright, who moved to New York and joined the no-wavers in **DNA**, a band that took Pere Ubu's disjointed and dissonant sound to a new extreme. Laughner, who had been one of the group's songwriters and creative leaders also left, to form his own band, Friction. In June of 1977, at the age of 24, Laughner died, succumbing to the excesses of substance abuse. He is best remembered for early Pere Ubu compositions as well as the Dead Boys' "Ain't It Fun" (which Gun N' Roses covered), and two albums of Laughner's solo recordings have been released posthumously.

While in Pere Ubu, Laughner had been a force toward more traditional rock styles. With him gone, Thomas's more avant leanings gradually took hold—though Thomas preferred to define himself as pop. "I personally consider Pere Ubu to be a pop band, totally the same as Wings or the Archies," Thomas told the punk zine *Search & Destroy*. "It's just that we're doing more modern and therefore better pop music. We're not concerned with the pop music of the past."

### Scott Kannberg, Pavement
*They were a huge musical reference. Their songs are warped. To me they're like classic rock, just as classic as Boston or whatever. I see a lot of similarities in our early stuff, with the tape loop electronic stuff running with a classic song.*

With two standout albums released nine months apart, 1978 was the year Pere Ubu finally took off. Like their earlier singles, *The Modern Dance* and *Dub Housing* were well received in England and proved a major influence on post-punk. Though still capable of rocking, Pere Ubu's quirkier side emerged: Thomas's yelping and squealing of fractured melodies; abrasive, industrial sound effects (such as the seeping steam in "The Modern Dance"); Allen Ravenstine's inventive synth playing; and a bizarre stage presence that seemed to come (like the band's name) straight out of absurdist theater. Anchoring it all was Tony Maimone's dubby bass and Scott Krauss's always on-the-mark drumming.

### Marcellus Hall, Railroad Jerk
*They were doing artistic things with instruments that had never been done before. Angular rock and high, dramatic singing. He had this way of singing I thought was cool because he was trying to sound helpless at times. That kind of desperation in the voice appealed to me then, and it still does.*

Following 1979's *New Picnic Time*, Pere Ubu underwent another significant change. When Tom Herman, whose angular guitar work helped define the group, quit the band, he was replaced by **Mayo Thompson**, who had been and continued to be leader of **Red Krayola**. Thompson's presence, added to Thomas's already well-defined eccentricities, made the albums *The Art of Walking* and *Song of the Bailing Man* Pere Ubu's most challenging work.

By 1982's *Bailing Man*, Krauss had been replaced by Cleveland-via-New York drummer Anton Fier, who'd just finished stints with the **Feelies** and Lounge Lizards. The band was plagued by infighting and, worse, a lack of inspiration. Thomas, who released his first solo album in 1981, decided to concentrate on his solo career, and Pere Ubu entered an extended period of inactivity. Though they would reconvene in the late '80s, their influence on subsequent generations of avant-rockers was already secure.

David Thomas's 1987 solo album *Blame the Messenger* featured a band (called the Wooden Birds) that included former Ubus Allen Ravenstine and Tony Maimone (who later played with They Might Be Giants and Bob Mould), as well as Cleveland guitarist Jim Jones. Somewhat by default, this band—with the return of Krauss and addition of second drummer Chris Cutler (of Henry Cow)—became the re-formed Pere Ubu that resumed recording in 1988. Though initially they sounded quite close to their last incarnation, by 1989 the band had taken a more pop approach. In the early '90s, however, former **Captain Beefheart** guitarist Eric Drew Feldman (who later played with Frank Black, PJ Harvey, and Belgian band Deus) joined the group, reaffirming their idiosyncratic roots. In 1998, after a period where Thomas led a band with none of the original members, Tom Herman and Jim Jones returned for the album *Pennsylvania.*.

## DISCOGRAPHY

*The Modern Dance* (Blank, 1978); an adventurous and fully realized debut.

*Datapanik in the Year Zero* EP (Radar, 1978); a collection of the pre–*Modern Dance* singles, not to be confused with the identically named box set.

*Dub Housing* (Chrysalis, 1978); the creative peak of the early Ubu records.

*New Picnic Time* (Chrysalis [UK], 1979).

*The Art of Walking* (Rough Trade, 1980); with the addition of **Mayo Thompson,** the band digs deeper into eccentricity.

*390 Degrees of Simulated Stereo* (Rough Trade, 1981); a live album capturing the early Pere Ubu lineup in all its ragged glory.

*Song of the Bailing Man* (Rough Trade, 1982); the final studio album before the extended hiatus.

*Terminal Tower: an Archival Collection* (Twin/Tone, 1985); an interim collection of early singles.

*The Tenement Year* (Enigma, 1988); the strong return after a six-year absence.

*Cloudland* (Fontana, 1989); a reflection of Thomas's more conventional approach to songwriting.

*One Man Drives While the Other Man Screams* (Rough Trade, 1989); a second set of live recordings, this one from the '78–'81 incarnation.

*Worlds in Collision* (Fontana, 1991); a less successful pop-oriented album.

*Story of My Life* (Imago, 1993); their major label peak that ironically coincided with a return to eccentricity.

*Ray Gun Suitcase* (Tim/Kerr, 1995); called their final album, it returned to a more challenging era of Ubu music.

*Datapanik in the Year Zero* (Geffen, 1996); a five-CD box set that includes the first five studio albums, rare live recordings, and a disc featuring recordings of Ubu members' side projects and other bands.

*Pennsylvania* (Tim/Kerr, 1998); features the return of Tom Herman and Jim Jones.

# RED KRAYOLA/MAYO THOMPSON

*We came from an avant-garde tradition that tries to push limits. We saw ourselves connected to an intellectual tradition more than a musical one. We didn't want to be the same as everybody, just popular and part of the youth movement. We wanted to be the greatest and most radical of all. We saw our competition as **John Cage** and Miles Davis. We'd look at some of these '60s bands and say, "Oh, you think you're wild? Have you heard Albert Ayler? Get serious."*

**Mayo Thompson, Red Krayola**

The Red Krayola (or Red Crayola as they were known in Europe, outside the reach of crayon trademark lawyers) has been around for over 30 years. Through each of its four distinct incarnations two things have remained constant: first, the inspired leadership of Mayo Thompson; second, obscurity. Despite the latter the Red Krayola have left their mark on a few key bands who've distilled certain elements and passed them on to a wider audience. It can be heard in the warbly eccentricities of **Pere Ubu**, in the psychedelia of Spacemen 3, in the Texas freakiness of the Butthole Surfers, in the Marxist pop of Stereolab, and in the post-rock music of Tortoise and Gastr del Sol.

Thompson formed the Red Crayola as a quintet in Houston in 1966, though the group was soon pared down to a trio featuring Thompson on guitars and vocals, Steve Cunningham on bass, and Frederick (Rick) Barthelme (now a well-known author of minimalist fiction) on drums. Gigging through 1966 and early '67, the group developed a dedicated core of fans, friends, and associated artists that called themselves the Familiar Ugly. A sort of Texan version of Ken Kesey's Merry Pranksters, the group participated on stage in the Red Crayola's "free form freakouts," massive spontaneous cacophonies that also appear six times on the group's debut, *The Parable of Arable Land*. The record also featured their International Artists labelmate **Roky Erickson** (of the **13th Floor Elevators**), who played harmonica and organ on more structured garage psychedelia such as "Transparent Radiation" and "Hurricane Fighter Plane."

Though *Parable* captured the group in its early stage as a conventionally structured—though certainly unusual—rock band, the Red Crayola wanted much more. As art students without much musical experience, from the start the group intended to work more in an avant-garde art context than as a rock band. Their reference points were experimental music and free jazz, as well as their "general revulsion for the lack of nerve of most people in the world."

After collaborating with guitar improviser John Fahey in California, the group returned to Houston at the end of '67 and made a second record, a radical departure they called *Coconut Hotel*. A vigorous deconstruction of traditional pop elements, the record featured tracks like "Vocal," "Piano," and "Guitar"—formless demonstrations of the various sounds each instrument could make—as well as 36 different "One-Second Pieces" that explored the various permutations a band could represent in a single instant. It was closer to the experiments of **Cage** than a rock album, and the group's label wasn't sure what to do with it. When Barthelme left the group and Thompson returned to California, the record was shelved, not to be properly released until 1995.

---

**David Grubbs, solo/Gastr del Sol**

*I was very fortunate to hear the Red Krayola first when I was in high school. Their songs prompted question after question. Why fragments? Where are the handrails? What is that sound on "The Shirt?" (This was an important adolescent acousmatic experience.) The song "Music" obviated punk's fourth wall. I was scandalized by it in the best possible way.*

---

In 1968, International Artists convinced Mayo to return and make one more album. *God Bless the Red Krayola and All Who Sail with It,* which featured Thompson and Cunningham (and a new spelling of Krayola to avoid trademark infringement), was slightly less extreme than *Coconut Hotel* but sufficiently bizarre to ensure its commercial failure. Though it was the most successful integration of the group's experimentation and art song style, by the time it was released the group had ceased to exist. *God Bless* did, though, point to the more acoustic, song-oriented approach Thompson took when he made a solo album in 1970. The tuneful *Corky's Debt to the His Father* featured the cream of Houston musicians, but, like *Coconut Hotel,* was not formally released at the time. A lost classic for many decades, it was finally made domestically available in 1994.

---

### Jim O'Rourke, solo/Gastr del Sol

*Corky's Debt to His Father helped increase my interest in songwriters. It always struck me how wonderful that record's arrangements were. It helped move me away from wanting to do tape music, and into producing records and making arrangements. Mayo has so many divergent interests—sociological, linguistic, musical—and the music is so much a result of him trying to put it together.*

---

Thompson relocated to New York in the early '70s and, through an association with artist Robert Rauschenberg, met a radical collective based in New York and London called Art & Language. "They were the nastiest piece of work around as far as conceptual art was concerned," Thompson recalls. "The hatchet boys, the hit men, with the fastest tongues and sharpest language." Soon Mayo was writing songs to the group's poetry, which was full of obscure philosophy and Marxist theory. "I gave them a copy of *Corky's Debt* and asked them what they thought. 'The lyrics are highly personal and don't mean anything to anybody but you.' And I said, 'That's probably true. Do you have a better idea for lyrics?' And they gave me the material for *Corrected Slogans.*"

Credited to Art & Language and the Red Crayola, 1976's *Corrected Slogans* featured a cast of a dozen writers, singers, and musicians doing songs like "The Mistakes of Trotsky," "Thesmorphoriazusae," and "Don't Talk to Sociologists." Both philosophically and musically, the record had little to do with any rock tradition before it (though decades later, Stereolab's lyrics come close).

Because Thompson was more closely aligned with the European branch of A&L, he moved to London in 1977 and made two more records with the group, 1981's *Kangaroo?* and '83's *Black Snakes.* Thompson also got a job with influential indie label Rough Trade, for whom he produced records by the **Raincoats,** the **Fall,** and **Pere Ubu** (a band he would also join in the early '80s). And he continued making Red Crayola records with guest musicians such as Lora Logic (of **X-Ray Spex**), Gina Birch (of the Raincoats), Epic Soundtracks (of **Swell Maps**), and Allen Ravenstine (of Pere Ubu). Following 1984's *Three Songs on a Trip to the United States* (which featured regular Crayolas Jesse

Chamberlain and Ravenstine), Thompson put the group aside once more while he worked as an executive for Rough Trade (he marketed the Smiths' *Queen Is Dead*). By the late '80s, Thompson found himself in Dusseldorf, Germany, where he worked as a jingle writer and made another Red Crayola album with German collaborators.

---

### Mike Watt, Minutemen/Firehose
*Like Beefheart, they were about having your own voice. They were a big influence on us. We used to listen to those records all the time. Mayo played with that wiry, trebly style too. It left more room for the bass, that's why D. Boon dug it.*

---

In the early '90s, Thompson met Gastr del Sol guitarist David Grubbs, who had been in Louisville's Squirrel Bait (with members of **Slint**) and was heavily influenced by Mayo's work. "Hearing Gastr del Sol's music I thought, 'Yeah, this has something to do with what I know, some tradition I understand,'" Thompson says. Soon, he was back in the U.S., teaching art at a college in California and collaborating with Grubbs on new music. In 1994, a re-formed Red Krayola—featuring Grubbs and his Gastr bandmate Jim O'Rourke, as well as Tortoise's John McEntire, members of Slovenly, and **Minutemen** drummer George Hurley—began releasing new material. Though it undeniably retains Mayo's distinct voice, the '90s Red Krayola, still out of bounds 30 years after, completes a circle that runs from Thompson's early avant rock to today's leading experimenters.

## DISCOGRAPHY

*The Parable of Arable Land* (International Artists, 1967; Collectibles, 1993); the debut, featuring "free form freak-outs" and psychedelic rock songs.

*Coconut Hotel* (unreleased, 1966/67; Drag City, 1995); an unreleased album of mostly instrumental experimentation.

*God Bless the Red Krayola and All Who Sail on Her* (International Artists, 1968; Collectibles, 1993); the final recording of the original Houston-based band.

(Mayo Thompson) *Corky's Debt to His Father* (unreleased, 1970; Drag City, 1994); Thompson's only solo record, a great collection of songs by a mostly acoustic band.

(w/Art & Language) *Corrected Slogans* (Music Language, 1976; Recommended, 1982); this eccentric batch of political songs is Thompson's first collaboration with the artist collective.

*Microchips & Fish* (Rough Trade, 1979).

*Soldier-Talk* (Radar, 1979).

(w/Art & Language) *Kangaroo?* (Rough Trade, 1981; Drag City, 1995); a more accessible collaboration, with an all-star underground line up.

(w/Art & Language) *Black Snakes* (Rec-Rec/Pure Freude, 1983).

*Three Songs on a Trip to the United States* (Recommended, 1984); a mini-album, partially live.

*The Malefactor* (Glass, 1989); a record made by Thompson and musical collaborators in Germany.

*The Red Krayola* (Drag City, 1994); the first record of Krayola's '90s incarnation, featuring members of Gastr del Sol, Tortoise, and other bands.

*Amor & Language* (Drag City, 1995); a mini-album with model Rachel Williams on the cover.

*Hazel* (Drag City, 1996).

# 5

# NAÏVE ROCK

In the world of classic art, qualifications such as discipline, training, and mastery of form have been used to identify the masters. Classical music, for instance, generally requires a certain level of virtuosity to perform successfully, and the best musicians are usually among the most technically accomplished. With folk art, though, such determinations are less important, since most folk artists are self-trained. While technique is still prized in folk traditions, creative vision and expressiveness are valued more.

In recent decades, as American folk traditions have dwindled—many being relegated to museums and preservationists—a specific type of folk art has emerged. Variously called outsider art, visionary art, or naïve art, it describes current work made by people with no connection whatsoever to the mainstream or academic art world. These artists—often poor and uneducated, from rural areas— make art simply to fulfill their natural need to express themselves. The most impressive works of naïve art, predictably, are those that come out of a natural gift and a truly eccentric vision.

In music, there is an analogous genre that could be called naïve rock. As with outsider art, makers of naïve rock are eccentrics and visionaries whose talents of expression more than overcome their limited training. With naïve rock, not only are technical considerations not important, they can be a disadvantage. Primitive and innocent, the music is free of self-conscious creative restrictions and post-modern cynicism.

---

### Amy Rigby

*If you're just looking at someone like Madonna or the big stars, you can't really see yourself in that same place, doing it the same way. But the more outside people make it seem more possible, to someone like me, anyway.*

---

Hearing the naïve rock music of groups like the **Shaggs** or **Half Japanese**, it's natural for experienced ears to perceive it is as noisy, inept, or just plain worthless. And those who champion such music above more easily digestible fare can easily be seen as praising "the emperor's new clothes." But at its best, this music challenges listeners to allow themselves to hear completely foreign sounds with unprejudiced ears. To even try to compare these groups to more accomplished rock bands is to miss the point; these are truly alternative artists that demand a complete reappraisal of what makes music valuable.

It should be noted that **Jonathan Richman** is included in this chapter, despite his mastery as a songwriter and performer, on the basis of his success in capturing an undistilled innocence in his music. Though he's hardly an outsider from mainstream pop music in intellectual terms, Richman's music overcomes the "disadvantages" of his technical capabilities with an eccentric charm that makes it fundamentally naïve.

## THE SHAGGS

*I find the Shaggs inspirational, just listening to them express themselves, without fear of being wrong or being bad, just doing something with the confidence that if you're true to yourself then something good will come out. A lot of young bands have a fearlessness to just do things and not really care, but our band has gone through a bizarre evolution. We get more fearless as we get older, which is kind of backwards. The Shaggs are inspirational in our approach to playing guitar and organ and drums: You don't have to know what you're doing. And the things you know are not by definition better than the things you don't know. Just be brave.*

*Ira Kaplan, Yo La Tengo*

It's hard to prove that the Shaggs have musically influenced anyone, since it's impossible to consciously recreate what they innocently captured on record. However, with their example of absolute purity of expression and integrity, the Shaggs have taught a valuable lesson to many bands that, in rock, heart is always more important than technical ability. What's more, the Shaggs' example has encouraged more capable rock bands to see that approaching their music unselfconsciously is a way to keep the sounds fresh and the feelings honest.

---

### Amy Rigby
*They definitely moved me, the way they sang in real voices instead of thinking, "I'm a singer, so I have to sing like a singer." It was like they were talking amongst themselves, and the naïveté was charming. The name of the Shams [Rigby's former band] was taken from mixing the Shaggs and the Tams ['60s R&B group]. The Tams were so smooth and soulful and really had it together. And the Shaggs were kind of the opposite. We took a lot of inspiration from the Shaggs.*

---

Before the Shaggs were a band, they were three sisters in the Wiggin family of Fremont, New Hampshire, who had been raised to be music lovers by their dad, Austin Wiggin Jr. By the late '60s the teenage Wiggin girls had developed a love for pop groups like Dino, Desi & Billy, and Herman's Hermits, and when they expressed an interest in playing music, Austin was happy to help. He bought electric guitars for his eldest daughters, Dorothy (Dot) and Betty, and a drum set for the younger Helen, then enrolled the girls in voice and instrumental lessons.

To speed along their transition from musical novices to pop stars, the three girls stopped going to school. They took home courses through the mail in order to dedicate as much time and energy as possible to music lessons. Within a year, Dot had written a dozen songs and the sisters were hard at work learning to play them as a band. Though the girls hardly considered themselves ready,

Austin—determined to "get them while they're hot—booked time in a recording studio.

On March 9, 1969, the Wiggins girls and their dad drove over to the studio in Revere, Massachusetts, and in a matter of hours the Shaggs, as the sisters were calling themselves, had put all 12 songs on tape. Austin Wiggins had made a deal with a local entrepreneur to press an album from the tapes, and as simple as that, The Shaggs were a recording group. Before their debut, *Philosophy of the World*, was released, however, the businessman skipped town with the Wiggins' money. Still, the family managed to come away with a single box of albums, and Austin set about distributing the record wherever he could.

Listening to *Philosophy of the World*, it's clear that although the Shaggs may have been a lot of things in 1969, "hot" was certainly not one of them. However, Austin's misjudgment was responsible for capturing a truly remarkable moment on record. *Philosophy* is a masterpiece of American primitivism, a one-of-a-kind artifact of outsider music. Song after song, the girls flatly murmur deadpan odes to the radio, sports cars, boys, lost pets, parents, Halloween, and God, while they delineate their philosophy of the world. They'd yet to learn chord progressions or how to tune their guitars—and Helen's drums pound away oblivious to tempo or rhythm—but the sheer ineptitude of the playing only works to enhance the record's disarming intimacy and complete innocence. The three girls, completely removed from the rules and conventions of music, had created their own take on pop music, one that was unlike anything else.

---

### Lou Barlow, Sebadoh/Folk Implosion

*I heard Philosophy of the World and was like, "Oh my God!" That record is totally damaged, it's so perfect. The lyrics are so complete, the playing is so determined, but so off. I loved to play it for people to see the look that crossed their faces. I played it for my mother and she loved them, she said, "It's so cute!" And my mom has very little patience for stuff that's willfully obscure. It was cool to see someone like my mother hearing the Shaggs and just realizing the human part of it. That's really what the Shaggs are about. It's really emotional, not novelty.*

---

Of course, few ever heard the record when it came out. And most who did simply laughed. The Wiggin sisters, though, continued to practice and eventually they were good enough to earn a steady gig Saturday nights at Fremont Town Hall. They even returned to the studio in 1975 and recorded a new batch of songs they called *Shaggs' Own Thing*. By then, the young women had improved considerably, and a younger sister, Rachel, had joined on bass. The album, not released until 1982, includes covers of the Carpenters' "Yesterday Once More," as well as a remake of "My Pal Foot Foot," a favorite track from *Philosophy*. The highlight of *Shagg's Own Thing*, though, is undoubtedly the title track, on which the four Wiggins sisters accompany their dad and brother Robert, who playfully trade off vocals. And it's clear where the girls have inherited their (lack of) musical abilities.

---

### King Coffey, Butthole Surfers

*I first thought "what in the hell is this trash?" But when I looked upon it in the sense that these were simply people encouraged by a loving father to make music for the love of playing, it's really touching. It's really a beautiful record. Really experimental in a way. I don't think they were trying to be, but they were pursuing a path of music that had no formal basis, it just made sense to them.*

---

Austin Wiggins died not long after the second album was made, and the Shaggs faded from view At some point in the late '70s, the Shaggs' first record caught the attention of the band NRBQ, who turned fellow musicians from Bonnie Rait to Frank Zappa on to their discovery. In 1980, NRBQ reissued *Philosophy of the World* on their Red Rooster label. That year, to the astonishment of the Wiggins sisters and the entire town of Fremont, *Rolling Stone* magazine voted the Shaggs "Comeback of the Year."

## DISCOGRAPHY

*Philosophy of the World* (Third World, 1969; Rounder, 1980); the ultra-rare debut album that was heralded as "comeback of the year" when it was reissued.

*Shaggs' Own Thing* (Rounder, 1982); a second album of songs recorded in 1975, when the Wiggin sisters had become more polished.

*The Shaggs* (Rounder, 1988); a CD compilation of all known recordings of the Shaggs, including the two albums and some home tapes.

# H A L F   J A P A N E S E

*I used to listen to [Half Japanese] on my walkman while strolling round the supermarket, right there at the heart of American culture. I though if other people got into listening to this music, they'd start to melt, to go crazy, to jump right out of their skins. So then I'd turn it up full, and imagine the music was coming from the store's loudspeakers.*

**Kurt Cobain, Nirvana [from French zine *Inrockuptibles*]**

Sometimes it's the folks that don't know anything who can teach us the most. That's certainly the case with Half Japanese. Armed with only their hyperactive creativity and natural enthusiasm, brothers David and Jad Fair—two nerdy punk savants—created some of the most liberating rock music ever put to tape. Though few musicians could hope to capture the unschooled innocence of Half Japanese, hearing them has given other bands a glimpse of a world that operates on completely different rules than most rock, if indeed it has any rules at all. Experiencing Half Japanese's inspiring freedom, even vicariously, has allowed groups such as Sonic Youth and Nirvana to expand the limits of their own music as well.

David Fair and his younger brother Jad grew up in southern Michigan in the '60s and early '70s. Though they listened to the Beatles and Motown groups on the radio, they also loved little-known garage bands that were making noise over in Detroit, such as the **Stooges** and **MC5**. During college, the brothers moved together into a house, where they found a guitar and amp someone apparently left behind. Though they'd never played music before, they decided to get a drum set as well, and before they could bother taking lessons David and Jad had formed a band.

Half Japanese, as the brothers called their band, immediately set on their quest to become the greatest rock 'n' roll band in the world. Though they didn't know how to play chords, keep a prop-

er beat, or sing on key, they managed to rock quite well on irrepressible energy alone. Though they made noise like free jazz skronkers, Half Japanese were not pursuing any particular musical concepts. "I thought it sounded great," Jad remembers. "I didn't think of it as noise, it was what came most natural to me, like folk music in a way. Only after the record came out, listening to it in a record store between two other records kind of brought to light for me that it was very different."

### Thurston Moore, Sonic Youth

*In retrospect they were highly crucial. It was just these two Half Japanese brothers, banging on pots and pans and screaming out their love for Patti Smith. It was something I could relate to, like "Wow, this is like me if I didn't control myself!" When I first saw Half Japanese in the '80s I was converted by the complete originality, and a certain bizarro quality that was really authentic. It wasn't a put-on or a show, this guy was just a kind of strange cat who really wore his heart on his sleeve. Jad Fair and Half Japanese were a major influence on the whole K Records scene and I remember Kurt [Cobain] was really into them.*

Their first release in 1977, a nine-song 7-inch EP titled "Calling All Girls," was a burst of rock primitivism and physicality that took familiar rock themes—hating school, feeling misunderstood, failing with girls—to a nearly psychotic, but disarmingly raw, level. By then, David and Jad had finished school and moved with their parents to Maryland. Their familiarity with underground music had led them to the **Residents** and the Los Angeles Free Music Society, groups who were producing independent music sold through the mail. Following suit, Half Japanese began making tapes of themselves.

By 1980, they'd amassed a large cassette collection of their tuneless and structureless songs and decided to compile them onto a three-record box set, to be released as their debut album, *Half Gentlemen/Not Beasts*. Though the collection was a bit much for anyone to listen to all the way through, their mix of untuned guitars with bits of electronics, and bizarre originals with barely recognizable covers, was a stunning document of homemade, completely free music, brimming with the childlike joy of making noisy music and musical noise.

---

### Ira Kaplan, Yo La Tengo

*Half Gentlemen/Not Beasts is astonishing: the lyrics, the noise. It was, on one hand, so impenetrable, but also so inviting at the same time. That's just a trip. Great, great record. I've been a big fan ever since. In the [Half Japanese documentary] there's an amazing scene where David Fair explains how easy it is to play guitar as long as you understand the science of it, but they didn't know any traditional ways of playing. They were just playing with all the exuberance and fearlessness that they had.*

---

As Half Japanese progressed into the '80s, their music became more cogent—thanks to the addition of other musicians and to David and Jad's growing experience—while retaining all of its unassuming charm. *Loud*, in 1981, added saxophones, which brought the band even closer to a free jazz no-wave sound, while *Horrible* delivered adolescent thrills with horror songs like "Rosemary's Baby" and "Thing with a Hook." Two albums in 1984, the mostly David-penned *Our Solar System* and the mostly Jad-penned *Sing No Evil*, proved Half Japanese was a seemingly endless well of inspiration, with no loss for material.

*Charmed Life*, with smooth and catchy songs like "Red Dress" and "One Million Kisses," was to be Half Japanese's breakthrough, but label problems kept the record unreleased for years (it finally came out in 1988). Surrounding themselves with capable sidemen such as Don Fleming (later of Gumball), by the mid-'80s the Fairs had evolved Half Japanese from radical naturalists into a reasonably competent garage group. In 1987, David fulfilled a long-standing intention to quit the group when he turned 35, and retired from Half Japanese (he now works as a librarian on a bookmobile in rural Maryland). With Jad the sole voice in the band, and Bongwater's Kramer producing, Half Japanese made the outrageous *Music to Strip By*, with clever, often hilarious songs such as "My Sordid Past," "Sex At Your Parents House," and "U.S. Teens Are Spoiled Bums."

---

### Steve Malkmus, Pavement

*They're just these cacophonous things. Hearing this guy that couldn't really sing or play his instrument exactly, and just didn't give a fuck, was inspirational to me. It was just noisy and bratty, and made us think that we could make a record too.*

---

To keep up with his prodigious songwriting, Jad also released solo records. Beginning with *The Zombies of Mora-Tau* EP in 1980, his solo material ranged from confessional (1982's *Everybody*

*Knew But Me*) to experimental (1988's *Best Wishes*, featuring 42 short instrumentals, titled either "O.K." or "A.O.K."). For 1992's *I Like It When You Smile*, Jad's guests included members of Sonic Youth, Dinosaur Jr., and Yo La Tengo. Over the years, Jad has also collaborated on record with fellow eccentric **Daniel Johnston,** avant-garde composer John Zorn, former Velvet Underground drummer Moe Tucker, the band Mosquito (featuring Sonic Youth drummer Steve Shelley), and countless others. And between gigs and recording sessions, Jad has worked as a teacher in a daycare center and in a factory, making things he was never able to identify.

In the '90s, Jad has continued Half Japanese with an ever-changing cast of backup musicians and a steady stream of releases, while David returned to music with an album by his '50s-style band, Coo Coo Rocking Time. In addition, Half Japanese was the subject of a 1994 documentary, titled *The Band That Would Be King,* and Jad has been the focus of two musical tributes, in songs by Pee Shy and the Spinanes.

In 1996, David and Jad reunited for the touching *Best Friends* record, and followed in early '98 with the playful *Monster Songs,* which features one horror rocker for each letter of the alphabet ("Abominable Snowman" to "Zombie"). Twenty years after he began playing, Jad still doesn't know a single guitar chord. Perhaps their still-intact musical innocence is what has allowed the Fair brothers, now in their forties, to retain their youthful exuberance as well.

## DISCOGRAPHY

*Calling All Girls* EP (50 Skidillion Watts, 1977); a nine-song single without any regard for convention.

*Half Gentlemen/Not Beasts* (Armageddon, 1980; TEC Tones, 1993); the triple-album debut, a classic document of unschooled noise rock.

*Loud* (Armageddon, 1981); still rough, but slightly more cohesive with four other band members joining the Fair brothers.

*Horrible* EP (Press, 1982); a collection of gruesome and twisted horror songs.

*Our Solar System* (Iridescence, 1984); an album heavy on David's material.

*Sing No Evil* (Iridescence, 1984); an album heavy on Jad's material.

(w/Velvet Monkeys) *Big Big Sun* (K [cassette], 1986).

*Music to Strip By* (50 Skidillion Watts, 1987); the first HJ record without David, Jad holds the fort with smart and funny tabloid-obsessed lyrics.

*Charmed Life* (50 Skidillion Watts, 1988); their best-known and most accessible record, released a few years after it was made.

*The Band That Would Be King* (50 Skidillion Watts, 1989); a record featuring saxophonist/composer **John Zorn** and guitarist Fred Frith.

*We Are They Who Ache with Amorous Love* (TEC Tones, 1990).

*Fire in the Sky* (Safe House, 1993); a good recent collection, featuring the Velvet Underground's Moe Tucker.

*Boo! Live in Europe* (TEC Tones, 1993).

*Greatest Hits* (Safe House, 1995); a terrific collection of material spanning the group's entire career.

*Hot* (Safe House, 1995).

*Bone Head* (Alternative Tentacles, 1997).

*Heaven Sent* (Trance Syndicate, 1997).

# DANIEL JOHNSTON

*I knew that I was an artist. I just didn't know it would be music. If I didn't do it, I'd be in pretty sorry shape, 'cause my imagination gets carried away.*

**Daniel Johnston [in the *Austin American-Statesman,* 9/24/92]**

Having been blessed with the gift of crafting great songs, Daniel Johnston could have been a huge success as a songwriter or musician. But his curse—a severe bipolar disorder that has kept Johnston in and out of institutions for decades—has to a large degree marginalized his music. Ironically, the condition that has kept him suffering and made him obscure is the very thing that motivates him to continue writing songs. As someone whose sanity literally depends on the music he makes, Daniel Johnston's work—most of it only available on low-fi homemade cassettes—is an inspiring example of passion and honesty for musicians to emulate.

And they do: His songs have been covered by Pearl Jam, the Dead Milkmen, Built to Spill, Wilco, and P (which features Gibby Haynes of the Butthole Surfers and actor Johnny Depp). Sonic Youth and Yo La Tengo have recorded with Daniel, while Nirvana's Kurt Cobain mentions him in the liner notes to the album *Incesticide*. Though Johnston's eccentricities have no doubt contributed to the cult around him, much of his music stands on its own. To focus solely on his mental instability is to do disservice to Daniel's underappreciated talents.

Johnston grew up in West Virginia in a strict fundamentalist Christian family that viewed rock and roll as the devil's music. Regardless, Daniel idolized the pop stars he heard as a kid in the late '60s and '70s—Bob Dylan, Neil Young, and in particular, the Beatles. Though music had been an important refuge for him since his first bouts with severe depression in junior high, it wasn't until college in 1980—in an attempt to impress a female classmate—that he began writing songs. When she responded favorably, Daniel made songwriting (and the girl) an obsession.

From the start, Johnston documented his music. Recording himself on a simple hand-held tape recorder, he sang in a high quavery voice while he accompanied himself, on piano, chord organ, toy guitar, or any other instrument at his disposal. In the mid-'80s, he moved to eastern Texas to live with siblings, and after some time spent working as a carny, Daniel wound up in Austin. Inside his tiny apartment Johnston spent time expressing himself and exorcising the demons of mental illness that continued to haunt him. Over the years, he'd write and record hundreds of songs and create at least as many drawings. On the streets of Austin, or through his job at a local McDonald's, Daniel would pass out tapes and pictures to anyone who'd take them.

### King Coffey, Butthole Surfers

*He was definitely an eccentric, but a good eccentric, a great Texas pioneer. Daniel Johnston's songs stick with you, they're so unique and incredibly moving. There's a sense of drama and sadness, wonder and humor, in his songs. Everyone in Austin had these homemade Daniel Johnston tapes. He was controversial in Austin. You either thought he was a genius or a joke. I'm with the camp that thinks he's an amazing songwriter.*

Johnston's early tapes, with titles like *Songs of Pain, Don't Be Scared,* and *More Songs of Pain,* were disarmingly intimate. With sound quality ranging from decent to awful, his tapes bundled together songs—often great, but not always—with snippets of phone calls, family fights, toilet flushes, TV shows, and anything else that seemed appropriate. The songs ranged from confessions of anguish ("Going Down") to hopeful advice ("Don't Let the Sun Go Down on Your Grievances") and from hilarious character studies ("Pothead," "Harley Man") to sincere tributes ("The Beatles"). Though amateurish and childlike, they undeniably contained the seeds of really good pop tunes. Where Johnston could be unselfconsciously enthusiastic, he was also a showman with a great knack for songcraft.

Among those in Austin who recognized Johnson's unrefined talent was film director Richard Linklater, who included Daniel's music in films such as the Austin-based *Slacker*. At gigs, local bands like Glass Eye (featuring Kathy McCarty, who'd later record a tribute album to Daniel) invited him to perform his songs between their sets. Whether the audience was laughing at him or cheering him on, Johnston reveled in the attention. His ultimate dream, to be a famous rock star, seemed to be coming true. But by 1986, Daniel had taken to using LSD, and it was destroying his already fragile psyche. He eventually became delusional and suffered a mental breakdown that sent him home to West Virginia for recovery.

### Chris Cornell, Soundgarden

*There's so much humor and pain all in the same line, it's pretty devastating and pretty amazing. This is somebody making music just because he wants to or because he has to. That itself is such a big influence to somebody in my situation, where everything has to balance in the books at the end of the year, that kind of crap. To stop and think that this guy made a record on his boom box that's one of my all-time favorites. To remember that what matters is the process, and not if anyone buys it or hears it.*

Meanwhile, Johnston's reputation continued to grow and in 1988 indie label Homestead began professionally releasing the best of Daniel's tapes, 1983's *Hi, How Are You* and *Yip/Jump Music*. Safely on medication, and with a newfound religious zeal in his music, Johnston recorded his first studio albums with producer Kramer (released on his Shimmy Disc label). The album, *1990*, featured an appearance by Steve Shelley and Lee Ranaldo of Sonic Youth. But, again, Johnston fell apart just at the point he was nearing a breakthrough. Having stopped taking medication to curb his manic depression, Johnston started to believe he was on a mission of world salvation; he became combative with his label and incoherent in concert. Soon, he was back in West Virginia.

---

### Lou Barlow, Sebadoh

*[Barlow's first band] Dinosaur did a tour with Sonic Youth, and I heard Kim [Gordon of Sonic Youth] playing a Daniel Johnston tape. I immediately recognized the way he recorded it because I'd been doing the same thing. But I was totally floored because his songs were really developed in a way that I hadn't developed my own. He was obviously completely enamored with the Beatles, and songwriting. He was making his own Billboard Top 300 at home, making his own legacy to keep himself entertained or keep himself sane. He made the definitive hand-held tape recordings, so hearing Daniel made me want to concentrate on really crafting my four-track recordings.*

---

After more time spent in a psychiatric hospital, Daniel amazingly bounced back and signed a contract with a major label, Atlantic Records. Returning to Austin, he recorded 1994's *Fun;* Paul Leary of the Butthole Surfers produced and other local musicians, including King Coffey and members of Lyle Lovett's band, appeared as well. But Daniel was too fragile to be a pop star. Unable to promote the record through the normal routes of promotional tours and interviews, Atlantic could not convert Johnston's cult status into anything like mainstream success.

Though there has been some talk of a second Atlantic album, prospects seem dim. However, his reputation as a visual artist, in the world of folk and outsider art, has grown, and his drawings have been known to sell for hundreds of dollars.

## DISCOGRAPHY

*Songs of Pain* [cassette] (Stress, 1980–81); the best of the early recordings that are still available only on cassette.

*Don't Be Scared* [cassette] (Stress, July 1982).

*The What of Whom* [cassette] (Stress, August 1982).

*More Songs of Pain* [cassette] (Stress, 1982–83).

*Yip/Jump Music* (Stress, Summer 1983; Homestead, 1989); the best-known early release, featuring Daniel on chord organ and favorites like "Casper the Friendly Ghost."

*Hi, How Are You* (Stress, September 1983; Homestead, 1988); the first nationally available release, featuring "Walking the Cow," a signature song.

*The Lost Recordings* [cassette] (Stress, 1983).

*The Lost Recordings II* [cassette] (Stress, 1983).

*Retired Boxer* [cassette] (Stress, December 1984).

*Respect* [cassette] (Stress, January 1985).

*Continued Story* (Stress, December 1985; Homestead, 1992).

(w/Jad Fair) *Jad Fair and Daniel Johnston* (50 Skadillion Watts, 1989); a spotty collaboration with the **Half Japanese** leader.

*Live at SXSW* [cassette] (Stress, March 14, 1990).

*1990* (Shimmy-Disc, 1990); the first studio recordings, featuring members of Sonic Youth giving minimal accompaniment.

*Artistic Vices* (Shimmy-Disc, 1992); recorded in West Virginia with a full band.

*Fun* (Atlantic, 1994); Daniel's only major label effort is an uncharacteristically clean recording, but doesn't contain his best material.

TRIBUTE: K. McCarty, *Dead Dog's Eyeball* (Bar/None, 1994); an excellent collection of Johnston's songs, fleshed out by a sympathetic performer.

**Note:** The Stress releases are all homemade cassettes, unavailable in stores; they can be ordered directly from Stress, 4716 Depew, Austin, TX 78751.

# JONATHAN RICHMAN AND
# THE MODERN LOVERS

*The honesty and sincerity of what he's doing is undeniable. He's really a genius. The main thing you get from Jonathan Richman is to be loose, be yourself. It's really enjoyable to watch someone who doesn't have any problem with being on stage. He's totally comfortable and having a great time, as opposed to someone who's staring at the floor and obviously has some major hang-ups about people looking at them.*

**Jeff Tweedy, Wilco**

Though he hasn't come close to any mainstream commercial success in his nearly 30 years as a songwriter and performer, Jonathan Richman can claim to have profoundly influenced rock music—not once but twice. With early '70s songs like "I'm Straight," "Pablo Picasso," and "Roadrunner," Richman created a prototype for the cynical, hippie-hating, phony-exposing young punk rocker that would emerge half a decade later.

---

**Dean Wareham, Luna**
*That History of Rock and Roll series on PBS, the punk episode started with Jonathan Richman, which I thought was very appropriate. Because before any of it happened, here was this guy with short hair singing about being straight. Then the Sex Pistols covered "Roadrunner." That first Modern Lovers record is one of the ten best records ever made.*

---

Soon, though, Richman outgrew his teen angst and embraced innocence—not because he couldn't do anything else, like the **Shaggs,** but by conscious choice. Writing silly songs that bring out the kid in us, and love songs that connect in very simple and direct ways, Richman created a unique style that shows up in the music of everyone from the Violent Femmes and Talking Heads to They Might Be Giants and Beck. Well-crafted and without a trace of irony, his songs celebrate the things ('50s pop, suburban life, romance) that so many musicians have parodied or mocked.

By the time Jonathan Richman released his first album in 1976, he'd already left behind a career's worth of great music that would secure his place as a key link between late-'60s American garage rock and the late-'70s British punk explosion. In 1970, the 19-year-old Velvet Underground fanatic moved back home to Boston from a year in New York and formed his first band, the Modern Lovers. Within a year, the band—which featured future members of the Talking Heads (Jerry Harrison) and Cars (David Robinson)—were being courted by major record companies. In 1972 they recorded two sets of demos, one with former Velvet **John Cale** producing. By then, though, the group was on the verge of splitting up.

---

**David Byrne**
*Obviously they were an influence, we hired one of them. They were doing really spare, bare-bones stuff, that spoke in a rock vocabulary but was very honest.*

---

As it turned out, the original Modern Lovers never completed a record and the '72 recordings demos remain the band's only studio documents. When the recordings were finally released four years later, it was as if they'd fallen into a time warp: the youthful energy and dark humor of Velvets-influenced songs like "Hospital" and "Old World" turned up in England to inspire a new generation.

Ironically, at the same time the Sex Pistols adopted the Modern Lovers' classic "Roadrunner" as a rocking proto-punk anthem of teenage freedom, Jonathan Richman had taken to writing quieter, less aggressive songs. "By the age of 22, having played a few hospital shows for kids and an elementary school or two with just acoustic guitar," Jonathan later wrote in a record company bio, "[I] was convinced that high volume was not a necessity but a hindrance to communication and intimacy."

In 1976, a few months before the early demos were belatedly released as *The Modern Lovers* album, Richman had put out his first "proper" record, called *Jonathan Richman & the Modern Lovers,* which featured Jonathan fronting an entirely new backing band and singing—with his nasal sincerity—songs like "Hey There Little Insect" and "Abominable Snowman in the Market." Just when he could have embraced the arrival of punk as a movement, Jonathan had opted for something entirely different.

---

### Tony Goddess, Papas Fritas

*He offered examples from his world that anyone can relate to, when he sings about the suburbs and the Museum of Fine Arts in Boston. You think it's just these kiddy songs, but then you realize it's much bigger, this whole aesthetic. I like his innocence. And I get along with my parents. I want to be able to play them music that won't offend them, that won't make my mom jittery while she's driving.*

---

Moving to California in the late '70s to record for the Beserkley label, Richman made albums such as *Rock 'n' Roll with the Modern Lovers* and *Back in Your Life.* In sharp contrast to his rocking early years, the new Modern Lovers—featuring the stand-up bass of Curly Keranen (later Asa Brebner), D. Sharpe's muted three-piece drum kit, and Leroy Radcliffe's softer acoustic guitar sound—perfectly captured the wide-eyed wonder of Richman's songs.

### Tjinder Singh, Cornershop

*We did a cover of "Angels Watching Over Me" [from Rock 'n' Roll With the Modern Lovers]. It's a religious, sort of traditional song, and I certainly like a lot of religious stuff, because it inspires people immediately. And it's very good to see how they're put together.*

With record sales always minimal, Richman concentrated on touring, and by the early '80s he was performing around the world to a growing cult of fans. It was in concert that Richman's charms shone brightest. A great storyteller and unselfconscious dancer, with a quick wit that made for terrific audience interactions, Jonathan could hold a crowd's attention with just his guitar and stage presence—sometimes without the guitar at all.

### Marcellus Hall, Railroad Jerk

*He would just say things off the top of his head, free form ad-libbing, and he relied and trusted in it and it yielded results. That helped me create, because I could trust that kind of stuff when it came out instead of being fearful. He was singing about simple things, the same way Woody Guthrie might. He was trying to grab a hold of the suburban American myth, the greatness and the boredom of it. That was a big influence.*

The next time he recorded, for major label Sire in 1983, it was with an extended band that included keyboards and backup singers. Though the record, *Jonathan Sings!* contained playful tunes like "The Tag Game," the large band wasn't able to reflect Richman's spontaneity. For his next two records, *Rockin' and Romance* and *It's Time For...*, Jonathan stripped down his sound again, with songs like "The Baltimores" relying more on classic vocal group harmonies than instrumentation.

By releasing his late '80s records on roots label Rounder, Richman completed his devolution from fast rocking garage kid to folk singer/songwriter, although his subject matter—which ranged from childhood remembrances ("Harpo Played His Harp") to everyday love ("Closer") to hilarious buffoonery ("I Eat With Gusto, Damn! You Bet") made him a folkie like none other. He'd also settled into a touring schedule that took him, either alone or with a drummer, around the country once a year or more. His stripped-down live show made touring logistically simple and inexpensive, and also perfectly suited his improvisational, spontaneous performance style.

### Dave Dederer, Presidents of the United States of America

*I love the way he tours: He just rents a Ford Taurus or something, picks up his guitar, gets in the car, and he's on tour. I really envy that, it's total genius in business terms. It's just so cool and admirable that he's created this career for himself, because the music business is a total nightmare, and he's found a way to do it without having to deal with any of the bullshit. And that's a real life accomplishment.*

Richman has continued touring regularly in the '90s; his concerts are frequently sold out, regardless of whether he's promoting a new album. His recording career has slowed and become increasingly driven by old material and novelties (he's made Spanish-language and country records). Yet recent songs such as "You Must Ask the Heart" and "To Hide a Little Thought" are proof that Richman has not lost his gift for communicating emotional subtleties in disarmingly simple ways. In 1996, Jonathan signed with Neil Young's record label, Vapor, on which he released *Submit to Jonathan*.

## DISCOGRAPHY

*The Modern Lovers* (Beserkeley, 1976; Beserkley/Rhino, 1986); the belatedly released, hugely influential early '70s recordings, featuring Richman's original band.

*Jonathan Richman and the Modern Lovers* (Beserkley 1976; Rhino, 1986); Richman's first properly released album.

*Rock'n'Roll with the Modern Lovers* (Beserkley, 1977; Rhino, 1986); a highlight of the late '70s period, heavy on the children's songs.

*Modern Lovers Live!* (Beserkley, 1978).

*Back in Your Life* (Beserkley, 1979; Rhino, 1986).

*The Jonathan Richman Songbook* (Beserkley, 1980); a compilation of the Beserkley albums.

*The Original Modern Lovers* (Bomp, 1981); a bootleg featuring further material from the Modern Lovers of the early '70s.

*Jonathan Sings!* (Sire, 1983); a major label effort featuring a fuller band and back-up singers.

*Rockin' and Romance* (Twin/Tone 85); a collection of new material, recorded in an intimate live setting.

*It's Time for Jonathan Richman and the Modern Lovers* (Upside 86); a largely acoustic record, heavy on nostalgia songs like "Double Chocolate Malted."

*The Beserkley Years: The Best of Jonathan Richman & the Modern Lovers* (Beserkley/Rhino, 1986); another compilation of songs taken from the Beserkeley albums.

*Modern Lovers 88* (Rounder, 1987); a terrific collection of songs played with a small group.

*Jonathan Richman* (Rounder, 1989); a largely solo guitar collection of quite varied material.

*Jonathan Goes Country* (Rounder, 1990); a novelty, featuring new and reworked songs in a vaguely western style.

*Havin' a Party with Jonathan Richman* (Rounder, 1991); a fine re-creation of Jonathan's free-flowing live performances.

*I, Jonathan* (Rounder, 1992); a '90s highlight, featuring Richman's tribute, "Velvet Underground."

*¡Jonathan, Te Vas a Emocionar!* (Rounder, 1994); Richman's songs done in Spanish.

*Precise Modern Lovers Order: Live in Berkeley and Boston* (Rounder, 1994); a collection of two live performances from the early '70s' Modern Lovers.

*You Must Ask the Heart* (Rounder 95); a mix of older songs with some great new ones.

*Submit to Jonathan* (Vapor 96); Richman's first for Neil Young's record label.

# 6

## FRAYED ROOTS

The development of modern rock music has not been a matter of linear progression so much as it has been a path determined by the convergence of disparate styles and the cyclical reintegration of older forms. That is to say that while rock and roll could be called a synthesis of blues and country music, both blues rock and country rock are after-the-fact outgrowths of rock music. While the artists in this chapter range widely in terms of sounds and associations, each is significant in part for integrating traditional, or roots, music into current rock styles. In doing so, each in effect transformed an older form of music into an expression of their own creativity and their own times.

Gram Parsons and Nick Drake made music during roughly the same years. Though both were born into privilege, made widely influential music based in traditional styles, went largely unsung in their day, and died—within a year of each other—at age 26, their music and lifestyles were very different. Parsons virtually invented country rock by merging the '60s rock sensibility of friends and associates like the Rolling Stones and Byrds with the country music he loved growing up in the American South. Drake came out of the late '60s British folk revival spearheaded by groups like Pentangle and Fairport Convention, but adapted folk song elements to create intensely personal and remarkably beautiful music.

The Cramps and the Gun Club both stem roughly from the punk era, but their music reached back to older rock and pre-rock styles. Both bands were based in Los Angeles in the early '80s—and even shared a guitarist at the time—but were better appreciated in England. The Cramps came first and updated rock's earliest and rootsiest manifestation—the wild hillbilly style known as "rockabilly"—by infusing it with punk attitude and a postmodern sense of art and humor. The Gun Club, formed a bit later, went even further back for its references; the band's leader, Jeffrey Lee Pierce, applied the Delta blues to a post-punk sound in creating music that exposed the dark underbelly of American life.

Heirs to the music made by Gram Parsons and the Gun Club are often lumped together as representatives of a style most loosely defined as Americana but sometimes called "alt country" or "insurgent country." Nick Drake's most direct influence has been on British pop songwriters, though his inspiration has reached much farther. And the Cramps can claim scores of "psychobilly" imitators. Interestingly, Parsons, Drake, and the Gun Club's Pierce all died prematurely. The ghoulish Cramps, meanwhile, have long been considered among the living dead.

## GRAM PARSONS

*Nothing has impacted on me as hard as that guy. The day I heard him I was like, 'Oh shit!' It was really heavy. He had such a sweet voice that betrayed his Southern accent, and the fact that he had Emmylou Harris as a singing partner blew my mind. They just sing like angels togeth-er. He was the thing that finally pushed me in that direction, toward country. If I had never heard of that guy, there's a lot I would never know about music. He understood so much about rock and roll too. For me it was never like I was going country because I considered it cool, it was more that when I listened to him I realized there was so much more to learn.*

**Ryan Adams, Whiskeytown**

Although Gram Parsons hated the label "country rock," and preferred to call his blend of honky-tonk, hippie rock, and southern soul "cosmic American Music," he was the single biggest force in forming the genre in the late '60s and early '70s. And though neither the name nor his music ever caught on with a mainstream audience, few musicians have had as direct and substantial an impact on the course of rock music.

Through his involvement with the Byrds and Rolling Stones, he steered both bands toward a country sound, and then inspired bands like the Eagles and Poco (both of whom have written songs about Parsons) to adopt a countrified West Coast rock that would take them to middle-of-the-road fame and fortune. In the late '70s and '80s, Parsons' legacy inspired performers like Tom Petty and Elvis Costello, as well as hipper country artists such as Dwight Yoakam and Jimmie Dale Gilmore. In the '90s, with the development of Americana as a radio format and the resurgence of country rock, bands like the Jayhawks, Son Volt, and Whiskeytown claim Parsons as their patron saint.

**Gary Louris, Jayhawks**
*I grew up listening to rock and pop music, and it was something different for me at the time. It was obviously heartfelt music, he wrote great songs and had a lot of character to his voice. He didn't have big pipes, but I'm attracted to that kind of voice, maybe because I don't have them either.*

Gram Parsons was born Ingram Cecil Connor III in Winter Haven, Florida; his mother was a wealthy citrus heiress, and his father was just back from World War II. Growing up in Georgia, Gram first heard many of his musical heroes: Hank Williams, the Louvin Brothers, Buddy Holly, and especially Elvis Presley. After his father's suicide in 1958, Gram returned to Florida with his moth-er, where she married a man named Robert Parsons who would legally adopt Gram. By his early teens, Gram was playing in rock bands, and at 18 he'd already recorded with a folk-oriented group called the Shilohs. He had just graduated from high school and was headed north to attend Harvard University when his mother died of alcohol poisoning. A trust fund set up to ensure Gram's finan-cial security allowed him to pursue music without worrying about money.

At Harvard, Parsons immediately formed a quartet called the International Submarine Band, through which he hoped to integrate his earlier love of country music with his interest in rock and R&B. When the group began performing, Parsons lost interest in school and dropped out after one semester. The quartet relocated to New York, where they recorded one single, then moved on to Los Angeles in 1967. After making a cameo in a Peter Fonda film, *The Trip,* the Submarine Band recorded their debut album for Lee Hazelwood's LHI Records. By the time the record was released, however, Parsons had befriended Byrds' guitarist Chris Hillman, who shared Parsons' desire to inject country elements into his music. Soon, Hillman invited Parsons to join the Byrds.

Thrilled at the prospect of being part of an already established folk rock group, Parsons left the Submarine Band and they soon folded. When their record, *Safe At Home,* came out in 1968, the label had no interest in promoting a defunct band and the album went virtually unnoticed. Only in retrospect is *Safe At Home* significant as arguably the first ever country rock album, and Parsons' earliest full-length attempt to apply rock's driving beats and soul singing to country songs.

With Hillman on his side, Parsons quickly exerted a huge influence on the Byrds. Within months of joining, the band entered a Nashville studio to record *Sweetheart of the Rodeo,* a classic album which marked the group's shift from psychedelic folk rock to rootsy country rock. Two Parsons songs, "Hickory Wind" and "One Hundred Years From Now," appear on the record, though some of his vocals were removed due to lingering contractual problems from the Submarine Band. But while Parsons' impact on the Byrds was substantial, it would not last long. After only three months in the band, Parsons decided to quit rather than join the group on its tour to South Africa (at the time run by a racist apartheid government).

### Jeff Tweedy, Wilco

*Parsons' contribution to Sweetheart of the Rodeo, in particular, is undeniably a big part of Uncle Tupelo [Tweedy's former band with Jay Farrar of Son Volt].*

When Hillman quit the Byrds soon after, the two decided to form their own group, the Flying Burrito Brothers. It was here that their vision of a country band with a rock setup and counterculture attitude was most consciously manifested. Along with bassist Chris Ethridge (from the Submarine Band) and steel guitarist "Sneeky Pete" Kleinow, the Burrito Brothers released a remarkable debut in 1969 called *The Gilded Palace of Sin.* The album cover perfectly conveyed the image they were after: The long-haired band was dressed in the gaudy Nudie suits that were fashionable among country stars, while Parsons' suit was decorated with marijuana leaves. Inside, the record collected countrified soul covers ("Do Right Woman"), straight country originals ("Juanita"), and tunes about draft-dodging and war protests ("My Uncle," "Hippie Boy"). Like many of today's alternative country acts, the Burrito Brothers fans (though there weren't many) came almost exclusively from the rock audience.

### Jay Farrar, Son Volt

*The Gilded Palace of Sin album was pivotal for a lot of my ideas. At the time I had been play-ing rock music, but I grew up around country music. I never put the two together to do both, though.*

By the time the Burrito Brothers released their second album, the similar but less successful *Burrito Deluxe,* Parsons had lost interest in the group. Hillman would soon follow, as would new guitarist Bernie Leadon (to join the Eagles), though the band would continue in name for decades.

Parsons, who by then had fallen in with the fast-moving drinking and drugging rock star crowd, took the next few years off. He spent his time hanging out with friends such as Keith Richards of the Rolling Stones, either at Richards' French villa or in Parsons' favorite getaway, Joshua Tree National Park. Inspired by Parsons' music, Richards and Mick Jagger wrote the song "Wild Horses" (which Parsons recorded for *Burrito Deluxe*) and took a country-influenced approach on their album *Let It Bleed* (which Parsons helped arrange).

In 1972, after forming a singing partnership with up-and-coming country star Emmylou Harris, Parsons returned to writing and playing his own music. With Harris and a backing band made up of Elvis' touring musicians, Parsons recorded two solo albums within a year of each other, *GP* and *Grievous Angel*. While the records included Parsons' most soulful work yet, they toned down the rock elements in favor of a more traditional country sound. *Grievous Angel* featured covers of Tom T. Hall and the Louvin Brothers, as well as Parsons' most sophisticated originals, "Return of the Grievous Angel" and "$1000 Wedding." Standing out above all else, though, were Parsons and Harris's heavenly harmonies; their vocal inflections and arrangements are still imitated by bands like the Jayhawks and Whiskeytown.

---

### Matthew Sweet

*Gram Parsons is probably one of my biggest idols. I just love his songs, both solo and with the Burrito Brothers and International Submarine Band. I've listened to every little thing. I didn't care about country music at all until I got into him. I think vocally he had some influence on me, sometimes I'll bend notes in a way I picked up from Gram. It's taken out of context, so it might not be easy to spot. But there's other ways, like hearing Sneaky Pete's pedal steel guitar made me want to use pedal steel on my records. I would be a good example of Gram's influence even way outside the realm of country rock.*

---

Before *Grievous Angel* could be released, Parsons overdosed on a mix of morphine and tequila; he was 26. When friends highjacked his coffin en route to New Orleans for burial and burned his body, as he had requested, in the Joshua Tree desert, the Gram Parsons legend had begun.

## DISCOGRAPHY

(w/International Submarine Band) *Safe at Home* (LHI, 1967; Shiloh, 1987); though hardly acknowledged, this was essentially the first country rock album.

(w/the Byrds) *Sweetheart of the Rodeo* (Columbia, 1968); recorded during Parsons' brief stay in the band, it strongly bears Parsons' imprint in its country flavor.

(w/Flying Burrito Brothers) *The Gilded Palace of Sin* (A&M, 1969); the fullest realization of Parsons' "hippie country" vision.

(w/Flying Burrito Brothers) *Burrito Deluxe* (A&M, 1970); a less-inspired follow-up to *Gilded Palace*, it features Parsons on his way out of the group.

(w/Flying Burrito Brothers) *Close Up the Honky Tonks* (A&M, 1972); a compilation.

*G.P.* (Reprise, 1973; 1990); Parsons' first solo album, with a slightly more traditional approach to country songwriting.

*Grievous Angel* (Reprise, 1974; 1990); posthumously released, and reissued on one CD with G.P., this last Parsons' recording was his most sophisticated effort yet.

*Sleepless Nights* (A&M, 1976; 1990); a mix of Flying Burrito Brothers songs recorded just before Parsons' departure and outtakes from *Grievous Angel*.

*Gram Parsons: The Early Years 1963–65* (Sierra, 1979); a collection of tracks from early Parsons bands such as the Shilohs.

*Gram Parsons and the Fallen Angles Live, 1973* (Sierra, 1982)

(w/Flying Burrito Brothers) *Dim Lights, Thick Smoke and Loud Loud Music* (Edsel, 1987); this collects all the band's Parsons-era recordings not included on the two studio albums.

*Warm Evenings, Pale Mornings, Bottle Blues 1963–1973* (Raven, 1991); a compilation covering Parsons' entire career, both solo and as part of bands.

(w/Flying Burrito Brothers) *Farther Along: The Best of the Flying Burrito Brothers* (A&M, 1988); contains nearly the entirety of *Gilded Palace*, plus an assortment of other songs from the Parsons-era band.

TRIBUTE: Various Artists, *Conmemorativo: A Tribute to Gram Parsons* (Rhino, 1993); features Uncle Tupelo, Bob Mould, Victoria Williams, Steve Wynn, members of R.E.M. and the dBs, as well as Parsons' daughter, Polly.

# NICK DRAKE

*Fame is but a fruit tree, so very unsound/It can never flourish, 'til its stalk is in the ground.*

**Nick Drake, "Fruit Tree"**

The archetypal lonely songwriter who pours his heart into music, Nick Drake has been an inspiration for countless musicians. A dark and romantic troubadour whose thin frame and soft features convey vulnerability, Nick Drake is today the focus of a sizable cult attracted to his intimate music and enigmatic personality. While it could be argued that Drake's example has created far too many self-indulgent guitar-wielding weepers, those who've grasped the purity and beauty in his songs are generally better songwriters for it.

An early admirer, Elton John recorded Drake's music in the late '60s, and artists as diverse as Lucinda Williams, Run On, and the **Swans** covered his songs later. Drake has been the subject of tributes by three generations of performers, from Richard Thompson to Robyn Hitchcock to indie rock band Ida. In the '80s, English pop groups such as the Lilac Time (named after a Drake lyric) and the Dream Academy (who dedicated their hit "Life in a Northern Town" to Drake) were clearly influenced by Drake, as were other gloomy Brits such as Morrissey and the Cure's Robert Smith. More recently, singer-songwriters like Jeff Buckley and folk-oriented bands such as Red House Painters and Bell and Sebastian have mined similar stylistic territory. Decades after his death, Nick Drake remains one of the most vitally inspiring musicians in popular music.

### Gary Louris, Jayhawks

*Nick Drake's stuff was an influence on us in the late '80s. He was a little off-kilter, in-between styles. And it was pretty emotional stuff, beautifully arranged. "Take Me With You" is definitely patterned after a Nick Drake song, even though it sounds quite a bit different.*

The son of a British lumber industry executive stationed in the Far East, Nick Drake was born in Rangoon, Burma, though his family returned to Tamworth-in-Arden, a village in the English

Midlands, while Nick was quite young. Along with his parents and older sister, Gabrielle (who would go on to become a well-known actress in the U.K.), Nick grew up in a house large enough to have a name—Far Leys—where he was exposed early on to classical music through his mother, a singer and composer. Though he'd played piano since childhood, and later tried saxophone and clarinet, it wasn't until Drake was 16 and away at boarding school that he first started playing guitar. An exceptionally gifted musician, the shy and lonely teenager took to the instrument immediately and was soon comfortable with advanced fingering techniques and innovative open tunings.

### Chris Cornell, Soundgarden

*Everyone talks about the introspective, shy, quiet, tragic Nick Drake, but if you listen to his records and the way he plays guitar, he was incredibly forceful and aggressive on it. He'd just pull on the strings. There was some underlying thing going on that was almost angry. I don't know if a lot of people get that, but I got it and it was kind of a surprise. For me as a guitar player, he's someone I would think of as a guitar god.*

While attending college in Cambridge, Drake became interested in the work of poets such as William Blake and the French Symbolists, and their influence began to show up in the songs he started writing. Soon he was performing in local coffeehouses, which had become a center for the blooming British folk revival of acts like Fairport Convention, Pentangle, and John Martyn. Drake proved to be a capable, if uneasy, performer of folk and blues standards, Dylan covers, and his own originals. He attracted the attention of Fairport Convention's manager, Joe Boyd, who signed Drake to his Witchseason label (which was soon bought by Island Records). As he began to work on his first album, Drake dropped out of college to focus on his music.

Released in 1969, *Five Leaves Left* was an impressive debut for the 21-year-old musician. While the songs featured lush string arrangements or the light jazz-folk accompaniment of musicians from Pentangle and Fairport Convention (including guitarist Richard Thompson), the album remained predominantly acoustic and focused on Drake's rich singing and guitar work. Songs like "River Man" and the eerily prescient "Fruit Tree" combined a romantic melancholy with wide-eyed enchantment, sung with perfect clarity and intimacy. Though *Five Leaves Left* was received warmly by critics, it failed to catch on with the public. Drake's discomfort with performing made it difficult to promote the record through a concert tour, and by 1970 Drake gave up on playing live altogether.

### Eric Matthews:

*I had an immediate affection for his voice. Five Leaves Left is all solace and peace and quietude. The string arranging and the guitar, I think it had an influence on my direction. People think maybe I'm consciously trying to sing like him, though what I get from him mostly is the whole package, the string arranging. But if people think I'm influenced by Nick Drake, well they're right.*

Soon, Drake began work on a second album, *Bryter Layter,* which he released in 1970. It featured many of the musicians that had joined him on *Five Leaves Left,* with the addition of the Velvet Underground's **John Cale** on keyboards and viola. The record fleshed out Drake's songs with brighter, fuller arrangements that included horns and more prominent drums. Some of the songs, including "Hazey Jane II" and the title track, actually came closer to '70s light pop—a sound adopted by more recent bands such as Belle and Sebastian and the Cardigans—than Drake's earlier folk compositions. Again, however, Drake's music failed to connect with a large audience. Drake had long suffered from depression, and this perceived rejection of his work made the condition much more acute, to a point where it became debilitating. Following *Bryter Later*'s release, Drake left the flat he'd taken in London and, after a retreat to Spain, returned to his parents at Far Leys.

### Moby
*I almost feel foolish counting him as an influence because so many people—at least among people making records—cite him as one. He had such a beautiful voice and was such a phenomenal songwriter. On Bryter Later especially, the arrangement and orchestration is wonderful. Very vulnerable and very emotional.*

Back in his childhood home, Drake became more withdrawn than ever. Rarely seeing friends—and at times alienating them—Drake spent most of his days sitting in his favorite orange armchair and listening to records of classical music; at night he stayed up trying to write. Then one day Drake entered producer John Wood's studio and, barely uttering a word, proceeded to record 11 new songs with only his own guitar and piano accompaniment. Declining to add anything to the spare tracks, Drake took the master tapes and dropped them off unannounced at his record company's reception desk.

Though Island was delighted to have Drake's third album, which they released as *Pink Moon,* the label had no illusions that this collection of gorgeous but desolate music would succeed commercially. When their fears were realized, Drake's mental state worsened to a point where he briefly entered a psychiatric facility. He decided to quit music altogether, and even looked into a job as a computer programmer, but was soon unable to work at all.

### Jim O'Rourke, solo/Gastr del Sol
*One of the greatest songwriters ever. Very pure and specific, with a very simple use of language. The ability to use a few words to say so much is a gift only given to certain people, and he was definitely one of them. He was a beautiful singer, and he meant it. Whenever I hear someone who's genuine, it helps me keep going.*

By 1973, Drake had begun taking antidepression medication and his condition eased enough for him to begin writing songs again. Encouraged by French chanteuse Françoise Hardy's interest in recording his music, and wanting to make another album of his own, Drake recorded four new songs and went to live in France. There, Drake tried to see Hardy, but she was not at home and he was turned away. In November of 1974, while returning for a visit to Far Leys, Drake overdosed on his medication and died in the night. His death was ruled a suicide, though his family says it was an accident. Either way, the fragile 26-year-old never lived to witness the slow bloom of his "fruit tree."

## DISCOGRAPHY

*Five Leaves Left* (Island; 1969; Hannibal, 1986); this debut album features Drake at his most mystical, with light accompaniment.

*Bryter Later* (Island, 1970; Hannibal, 1986); this record dresses Drake's songs up with drums, strings, and horn arrangements, and is his brightest, most pop-oriented record.

*Pink Moon* (Island, 1972; Hannibal, 1986); recorded in two days and featuring only Drake accompanying himself, this is his most spare and depressed work.

*Time of No Reply* (Hannibal, 1986); a collection of early recordings and demos for a never completed fourth album.

*Fruit Tree: The Complete Works of Nick Drake* (Hannibal, 1986); a box set containing all of Drake's available music.

*Way to Blue: An Introduction to Nick Drake* (Hannibal, 1994); a compilation drawing from all of Drake's albums.

TRIBUTE: Various Artists, *Brittle Days: A Tribute to Nick Drake* (Imaginary Records, 1992); this English release features Drake's songs done by the High Llamas, Nikki Sudden (of **Swell Maps**), Loop, and others.

# THE CRAMPS

*My initial exposure to the deranged universe of the Cramps severely affected my psychological circuitry, displacing all previously known parameters of the Rock 'n' Roll medium. For the next year and a half of my pimple-fighting adolescence, I played my Bad Music for Bad People cassette until it sounded like Duane Eddy being blasted through an underwater PA system on the 20,000 Leagues Under the Sea ride at Disneyland. When I finally witnessed the Cramps live, my alien genetic code was quickly re-sequenced during the chaotic sonic centrifuge of the show-terminating "Surfin' Bird." Without question, my perception was forever thereafter permanently askew: The essence of potent music lies not in technology or endless hours of practiced virtuosity, but in energy, lust and obsession.... My final stage of Crampdom was manifested in actually being a chem-activated exothermic stage-warmer-upper for those aforementioned "Lords Who Indeed Taught Us Songs." Obviously, this was a thrill unable to be described in any non-direct-nerval communication.*

**Birdstuff, Man or Astroman?**

Though they looked like a bunch of goons who'd just emerged from a cemetery crypt, the Cramps are covertly some of the most astute connoisseurs and musicologists in rock. They reintroduced to a post-punk world the characteristically American weirdness and insanity just under the surface of early rock 'n' roll. They were among the earliest indulgers in a "junk aesthetic" of white trash, fast food, Vegas lounge acts, late-night horror films, and low-budget teen rebellion that extends through current art and entertainment, from Tarantino films to Elvis sightings. The Cramps' cultural significance lies in its disposable idiocy.

The band's black leather, rock-animal approach to punk can be seen today in bands like D-Generation, Dash Rip Rock, and Jon Spencer Blues Explosion, and their skill in unleashing rock's forgotten primordial ooze inspired the recent proliferation of twangy guitar bands with tongue-in-cheek concepts, from the space-age surfers of Man Or Astroman? to the trailer park tramps of Southern Culture on the Skids. Still going strong after more than two decades, Cramps' disciples now constitute a genre—coined from early Cramps gig posters—known as "psychobilly."

### Kate Schellenbach, Luscious Jackson

*They haven't really gotten the credit that's due, as far as influence on today's alternative bands. Jon Spencer Blues Explosion owes a lot to the Cramps, especially with the guitar-only line-up. They were very entertaining, horror-rock monsters. They played New York so often in the early '80s that their shows were like this really fun social scene.*

Erick Purkhiser and Christine Wallace—who'd met during college in California—conceived the Cramps while living in Purkhiser's hometown of Akron, Ohio. Hearing about the outrageous costumes of the New York Dolls and the thriving punk scene around CBGB, the couple moved to New York in 1975, then recruited guitarist Bryan Gregory and his sister, drummer Pam "Balam" Gregory. When Erick remade himself as the "Elvis crossed with Vincent Price" singer known as Lux Interior and Christine became the guitar-wielding icy vixen called Poison Ivy Rorschach, the Cramps became reality.

### David Yow, Jesus Lizard

*I liked the Cramps quite a bit. Watching Lux Interior was a real blast. I can imagine that working its way into my thing. I liked how Elvis Presley had obviously had a big impact on his voice. I think I liked his Elvis more than Elvis's Elvis.*

By the time the Cramps started gigging at CBGB, the Dolls were long gone and the band's haunted-house theatrics were quite out of place around the sober poetics of acts like Patti Smith and **Television**. But the Cramps' hyperactive rockabilly—inspired by '50s guitar madmen such as Link Wray and Hasil Adkins—provided just the energy release (and comic relief) the scene needed. After some personnel changes, Nick Knox became the group's steady drummer, and the band emerged as one of the city's premier live draws. Having developed a name for themselves, the Cramps journeyed to the heart of twisted old-time rock and roll—Memphis, Tennessee—where they recorded a series of singles (collected as *Gravest Hits*) with former **Big Star** leader Alex Chilton.

*Gravest Hits*, which consisted mostly of covers, provided only a taste of what was to come. Returning to Chilton's studio in 1980, the Cramps recorded their debut album, *Songs the Lord Taught Us*, which fully mined the aesthetic that would define them for years to come. With originals that celebrated trash television ("TV Set"), trash movies ("I Was A Teenage Werewolf"), and just plain trash ("Garbageman")—and covers of twisted garage rock obscurities (the Sonics' "Stychnine") and mangled pop classics ("Fever")—the Cramps' kitsch obsessions and rock 'n' roll exaggerations were sufficiently original and infectious to spark a genre of punk rockabilly—or psychobilly—that continues to thrive.

### King Coffey, Butthole Surfers

*We played with them once and I was star struck. They ARRIVED for sound check dressed in full regalia, and a few hours later their fuzz guitars and echo boxes filled the room. Rarely have I been happier. Songs the Lord Taught Us is a great, scary album—they were able to fuse such distinctly American stuff to make their own weird thing. Later people copied what they were doing and it became known as psychobilly, but really the Cramps were in their own league. Sometimes the Butthole Surfers can go into a rockabilly thing, and I think we're tapping into "songs the Cramps taught us."*

As the Cramps ventured out on national and international tours, word quickly spread of their highly entertaining rock/freak show. Audiences were thrilled by Lux's seemingly endless energy on stage—where he'd often end up mostly naked in a frenzy of microphone-swallowing howls—while Ivy projected cool sexuality and stayed in character by never cracking a smile. They caught on particularly well in England, where, oddly, they were coupled on tour with the Police and Morrissey was an early member of their fan club, Legion of the Cramped.

### Nick Cave

*I remember seeing a Cramps show in the very early days, the first time they came to England. That was an extraordinary event, just the anarchy of the performance. It was mind-blowing, really hilarious and irreverent. The **Birthday Party** [Cave's first band] were similar in some respects. And what England was going through was just so boring and safe.*

In 1980, the band moved to Los Angeles. After Bryan Gregory left the band (for a variety of pursuits, including witchcraft and acting), Kid Congo Powers of the **Gun Club** joined for the second album, *Psychedelic Jungle*. While tracks like "Goo Goo Muck" and "Voodoo Idol" were certainly along the lines of what fans had come to expect from the band, the record suffered from being somewhat slower and more polished in places. Frustrated by their label's inability to parlay the band's growing following into larger record sales, following *Psychedelic Jungle* the Cramps sued IRS Records to be released from its contract. The issue was settled out of court, and in 1981 the Cramps, for better or worse, parted ways with IRS.

Through most of the '80s, the Cramps focused on nearly constant touring, while much of the group's album releases were either compilations of previously

released material or live records. What studio recordings they made—such as 1986's *A Date with Elvis*—were at first released only in the U.K. While the Cramps maintained their psychobilly sound and image, the late '80s saw the group's themes shift slightly away from horror movies and more toward the glittery sleaze of Las Vegas and the sexploitation of Russ Meyer films. Songs like "Can Your Pussy Do the Dog?" and "Bikini Girls with Machine Guns" (from 1989's *Stay Sick*) parody misogyny so convincingly they're apt to offend, though behind it all was Ivy, as producer and star of the group's increasingly ridiculous album covers.

### Ian MacKaye, Fugazi/Minor Threat

*I saw the Cramps in my junior year of high school and it was life-altering. Period. It was the most incredible show I'd ever seen. It sort of came to me in a rush that this was what I was looking for in music. All the times I'd seen Ted Nugent and Queen, where it was always such a spectator sport, I was actually participating in this Cramps concert. And I also found this underground world where people were willing to really question and confront life on many different levels. Challenging the conventions of sexuality, or politics, or religion.*

In the '90s, the Cramps have continued doing what they do best. While band members—including **Lydia Lunch**/Nick Cave drummer Jim Sclavunos, and current rhythm section of Slim Chance and Harry Drumdini—have changed, Lux and Ivy remain constants, and so have the group's hypersexual, high-octane roots rock and demonic bad-ass schtick. For over 20 years they've told the same joke, but with such brilliant energy and style that one was all they needed.

## DISCOGRAPHY

*Gravest Hits* EP (IRS, 1979; 1989); a five-song EP collecting the groups earliest singles.

*Songs the Lord Taught Us* (IRS, 1980; 1989); produced in Memphis by **Big Star**'s Alex Chilton, this record laid out the course the band has followed since.

*Psychedelic Jungle* (IRS, 1981; 1989); a slightly toned down collection, reissued together on one CD with *Gravest Hits*.

*Smell of Female* (Vengeance, 1983; Restless, 1990); a live mini album recorded at the Peppermint Lounge in New York, later expanded to a full album with bonus tracks.

*Bad Music for Bad People* (IRS, 1984; 1987); a compilation of the group's IRS material.

*A Date with Elvis* (Big Beat, 1986; Restless/Vengeance, 1994).

*Rockinnreelininaucklandnewzealandxxx* (Vengeance, 1987; Restless, 1991); a live album recorded in 1986 that well represents the band's stage show.

*Stay Sick!* (Enigma, 1990); from this point on, the Cramps offered pretty good imitations of their earlier records.

*Look Mom No Head!* (Restless, 1991).

*Flamejob* (Medicine, 1994; Epitaph, 1994).

*Big Beat From Badsville* (Epitaph, 1997).

TRIBUTE: *Songs the Cramps Taught Us* (Born Bad); more of a reverse tribute, this record collects the obscure original versions of twisted songs the Cramps later appropriated.

# GUN CLUB

*Just in the past few months, I've remembered the one thing that made me fucking want to start a band was hearing the first Gun Club record. I remember thinking, "Shit, I could play drums like that." So I did. It was the middle of winter, I was living in a storage shed with my drums, a couch and that was it. My friends would come over, plug in their guitars, and we'd play all the slow songs off the first Gun Club record. And now Jeffrey [Lee Pierce, Gun Club leader] is gone... at 36.*

**Mark Lanegan, Screaming Trees [Melody Maker, 7/13/96]**

Though it came out of the L.A. punk scene, the Gun Club was in love with the dark romance of Louisiana swamps and Mississippi blues. By marrying his group's reality with his fantasy, Gun Club mainstay Jeffrey Lee Pierce created a southwestern gothic that has influenced other—mostly foreign—songwriters to play on notions of "bad America" that come more from folklore than personal experience: Nick Cave, early Waterboys, Simon Bonney. Back home, the Gun Club have also inspired would-be punks from the Screaming Trees to the Geraldine Fibbers and from Morphine to Sixteen Horsepower to get in touch with their blues roots.

### Moby

*I loved the Gun Club. They were obviously very influenced by American roots music, but it was their own personal interpretation of it.... They reminded me there was a lot of really wonderful stuff coming from that world. I loved the Americanness of it: showing how perverse and corrupt—and at the same time wonderful and emotional—mainstream American culture could be.*

Jeffrey Lee Pierce was born in Texas but moved as a kid to Los Angeles, where he fell in with the early punk scene centered in Hollywood. After working a variety of odd jobs, including some time at famed punk store/label Bomp Records, Pierce formed a band with his friend, guitarist Brian Tristan. Called at first Creeping Ritual, then renamed the Gun Club, the band followed L.A. groups X and the Blasters with a sound that mixed punk with more roots-oriented and early rock sounds. And unlike the plainclothes assault of suburban hardcore groups, the Gun Club—Pierce in particular, with his peroxide blonde mane and western/gothic outfits—adopted the more glam-influenced look of Hollywood rock bands. Pierce's appearance made his passion for playing blues music seem all the more incongruous, though his impudence in freely appropriating a tradition so clearly not his own was a bold punk statement in its own right.

By the time the Gun Club released their debut album in 1981, Tristan had left to join the **Cramps** (and renamed himself Kid Congo Powers) and Ward Dotson had replaced him. Still, *Fire of Love* presented the Gun

Club at their purest and most inspired. With punked-up covers of blues songs like Robert Johnson's "Preaching the Blues" and scorching originals such as "She's Like Heroin to Me," the group reimagined punk as bottle-necked voodoo music, conjuring phantoms on the highway and hellhounds on their trail.

### Mark Sandman, Morphine

*That first Gun Club album was a big influence in the way it went back to the blues and came up with a really fresh way of playing the songs and the getting the feel, but skipping twenty-five years of blues clichés that really dragged it down.*

For the next year's *Miami*, the Gun Club enlisted as producer Chris Stein of Blondie, Pierce's favorite band (Blondie's Debbie Harry adds backing vocals as well). Stein steered the band to a slightly more accessible style by cutting down on the punk aggression, while accentuating Pierce's lyrics and howl to fine effect. *Miami* retained the guitarists' distinctive slide thrash style to some extent, but Pierce's sin-and-salvation lyrics evoked the blues more in spirit than in sound. With 1984's *Las Vegas Story*, the band (once again featuring Kid Congo Powers) moved even further away from its early sound, and in its place developed a western-style rock that could be as dry and blistering as the desert sun and as expansive as the Big Sky landscape.

### Ryan Adams, Whiskeytown

*I've been listening to the Gun Club since I was 15. I think Jeffrey Lee Pierce is a huge influence on a lot of people. Any rockabilly I hear these days sounds to me like the Gun Club. They had a lot to do with me wanting to play faster, with bigger chords, and holding out verses longer. I was also really affected by his imagery. It's really dark and swampy, like he might have crawled out of a New Orleans graveyard. He seemed like an American spiritualist, like Jack Kerouac on heroin.*

By 1985, Pierce's own dark side—a drinking problem—had gotten the best of him and he broke up the Gun Club. While Dotson formed the Pontiac Brothers (and later, the Liquor Giants) and Powers joined Nick Cave's Bad Seeds, Pierce moved to England and put together a solo album called *Wildweed.* Then after two years away, Pierce re-formed the Gun Club, with Powers (who also remained in the Bad Seeds, and later formed his own group Congo Norvell) and Japanese bassist Romi Mori (whom Pierce later married). In 1987, they entered a Berlin studio with Robin Guthrie of the Cocteau Twins producing, and made *Mother Juno.* The record was the band's most polished, but marked a resurgence of vitality that had waned steadily in past Gun Club records. The album was warmly greeted by the group's fans (who by then were also centered in the U.K.), and the Gun Club seemed destined for a larger success than it had ever had. But instead the band's label went out of business—pulling the record off the shelves—and Pierce's drinking problems worsened.

The story of the band in the '90s continued to be one of ups and downs. When Pierce was sober and in good health—as with 1990's *Pastoral Hide & Seek* and 1993's *Lucky Jim*—the Gun Club produced strong music. Pierce's continuing battles with alcohol, though, took their toll, making it difficult to work regularly. By 1996, things had once again begun to look up; Pierce re-formed the band and had begun collaborating with Mark Lanegan of the Screaming Trees. While visiting his father in Utah, however, Pierce suffered a cerebral hemorrhage. He died at 36.

## DISCOGRAPHY

*Fire of Love* (Ruby, 1981; Slash, 1993); a searing blend of blues and punk.

*Miami* (Animal 1982; Animal/IRS, 1990); an expansion of the debut's sound palette, without sacrificing the energy.

*Death Party* EP (Animal, 1983); recorded by Pierce and an assortment of musicians while he was in New York.

*The Las Vegas Story* (Animal, 1984; Animal/IRS, 1990); a strong continuation of *Miami,* with an even greater thematic focus on America's dark side.

*The Birth the Death the Ghost* (ABC, 1984; Revolver, 1990); a live collection of more recent material.

*Danse Kalinda Boom: Live in Pandora's Box* (Dojo, 1985; Triple X, 1994).

*Mother Juno* (Red Rhino/Fundamental, 1987; 2.13.61/Thirstly Ear, 1996); a strong return after a few years away, this record finds the new band more mature and polished, but retaining Pierce's initial spark.

*Pastoral Hide & Seek* (Fire, 1990); recorded in Brussels, this record moves Pierce away from his home country, literally as well as thematically.

*Divinity* (New Rose [France], 1991); a more sonically adventurous studio effort.

*In Exile* (Triple X, 1992); this compiles Pierce's later work with the reformed group.

*The Gun Club Live* (Triple X, 1992).

*Lucky Jim* (Triple X, 1993); Pierce's final studio recording, which hinted at a possible creative resurgence that he would not live to realize.

# 7

# KRAUTROCK

For some, the thought of German popular music brings to mind either the cheese metal of groups like the Scorpions or the Eurotrash pop of Milli Vanilli. Fortunately, that's not the whole story. In fact, for a period in the late '60s and early '70s, Germany produced rock music rooted in the best underground and avant-garde traditions, variously hypnotic and thrilling, melodic and funky. Kosmische ("cosmic") music, as it was known to the Germans, was even more progressive, adventurous, and extreme than the underground music being made in the U.S. and Great Britain, a fact that certainly didn't help it win fans around the world. As the music has slowly filtered into the English-speaking world, journalists have generally dubbed it "krautrock." Today, krautrock's relative obscurity, utter foreignness, and amazing prescience—not to mention it's overall quality—make it an attractive reference point for current rock and techno bands.

Kosmische music began as a natural outgrowth of the cultural climate in post-War Germany. Two forces worked simultaneously: First, the Nazis had wiped out large segments of the liberal artistic tradition in the country, and second, the large presence of American and British soldiers in Germany meant an influx of Anglo culture during the '50s and early '60s. Young German bands, disconnected from their own culture, generally imitated the rock music they heard coming out of the English-speaking world. Sometimes—as in the case of the Beatles' early stint in Hamburg—they heard it even before we did.

As rock music bloomed in the mid-'60s as a vehicle for social change, German students were quick to notice. Though the American struggle between the youth movement and the establishment was strong at the time, German kids were faced with an even more personal struggle in the knowledge that their parents' generation had been accomplices, victims, or apathetic bystanders to the Nazi atrocities. They wanted nothing to do with Germany's recent past and desperately yearned to reestablish German culture as they envisioned it.

With this backdrop, a new generation of German band emerged in the late '60s that borrowed from the art rock of Frank Zappa and the Velvet Underground (and even sang in English most of the time), but infused the music with its own, distinctly German character. A lot of the earliest Kosmische bands were quite psychedelic and formed as extensions of communes, such as Amon Düül. Others had a more formal music school background, such as **Can,** the first group to have widespread exposure. By adopting the cultural elements on hand—such as the stark minimalism of the Bauhaus design school or the early electronic music of avant-garde composer Karlheinz Stockhausen—these groups created some of the most complex, experimental, and visionary rock music of their time.

The golden age of Kosmische/krautrock music spanned the years 1968–1974, when—in addition to the bands discussed in this chapter—groups like Popol Vuh, Tangerine Dream, Ash Ra Temple, Guru Guru, Brainticket, and Cluster flourished. Many released records on adventurous German labels like Ohr and Brain, with inventive cover art and designs that have been appropriated by later indie rock and electronic groups (such as the adaptation of Guru Guru's *Kanguru* for Pavement's *Wowee Zowee* cover). By 1975, many of the bands—with the exception of **Kraftwerk,** who had its most successful years in the late '70s—had either split up or passed their prime.

Of course, little Kosmische music ever reached the U.S. at the time (though it did play a larger role in the British glam, punk, and post-punk music scene). But over the years, word of this freaky foreign music spread in underground circles and even showed up in the music of mainstream artists such as David Bowie and U2. Now, two decades after its German peak, krautrock has established itself as an important element in '90s music.

## CAN

*I grew up being pretty rational and intellectual, so I always analyzed music in terms of scales and chord sequences and rhythmic structures. But "Yoo Doo Right," I just couldn't figure out how they'd make twenty minutes out of this two-note riff and bad singing. It just felt right. They're one of the bands that gave me the idea you don't have to explain it. You don't have to think about it for music to be evocative and effective. It's all about feel rather than intellect.*

**Toby Marks, Banco de Gaia**

The undisputed kings of krautrock, Can's music is so influential it can be said to have transcended its ghettoization as krautrock and joined the ranks of rock's most important work. Like the Velvet Underground, Can was a primary meeting ground between music traditionally defined as high and music deemed low, and in its ability to make experimental sound groovy—and dance music intricate—Can helped wipe away the distinctions between the two. Blending a modern classical background with '60s psychedelic rock and free jazz, Can serves as a precursor and inspiration to the funky world music of **Brian Eno** and David Byrne, the post-punk exploration of **Public Image Limited** and the **Fall,** the '80s progressive pop of the Eurhythmics and U2, the trippy dance rock of the Happy Mondays, the space-age sounds of Stereolab and Moonshake, the electronic trance music of the '90s, and scores of other groups you'd never expect to have been touched by them.

**Gary Louris, Jayhawks**

*A song on our album [Sound of Lies], "Dying on the Vine," has this great throbbing bass intro that was influenced by Can. Sometimes you listen to something and say, "I like the idea." I don't want to write a song that sounds like Can because we're not like that, but little snippets can lock into some little piece of the puzzle.*

In the late '60s, Holger Czukay and Irmin Schmidt worked in the world of modern classical music; between them they'd studied and performed with **John Cage** and **LaMonte Young** and were classmates together under Karlheinz Stockhausen. Though already in their thirties, by 1968 they'd become interested in the artistic possibilities of popular music. When Michael Karoli, one of Czukay's students, played him the Beatles' "I Am the Walrus," Czukay was inspired to form a band. Inner Space, as they were called, included Karoli on guitar and Schmidt on keyboards, along with a jazz drummer named Jaki Leibezeit. Schmidt's wife, who became the group's manager, brought in an African-American painter living in Germany named Malcolm Mooney to sing. Because it was the only rock instrument not taken, Czukay took up playing bass, though his primary role in the group was as recording engineer, conceptualist, and tape editor.

By year's end, the group changed their name to Can and moved into a castle near Cologne, where they immediately began recording their improvisations. This early material—later released on both the *Delay 1968* album and on parts of *Unlimited Edition*—included Velvet Underground-style minimalist rock and "samples" of recent student protests. Also captured were the first installments of the group's "Ethnological Forgery Series," which appropriated bits of world music, as Western artists like Peter Gabriel and David Byrne would do decades later.

---

### Karl Wallinger, World Party
*They've definitely influenced me in the sense that, though they wanted to make it, there was a lot more of "We really want to make this music." They had weird, great rhythms.*

---

The band's first true release was 1969's *Monster Movie*, which they recorded live in their castle/studio. By then the band's vision and delivery had been substantially refined. Songs like the insistent opener "Father Cannot Yell" sustain linear tension, with bass throbbing steadily, and sharp—almost mathematical—drumming. Most impressive, though, is the 20-minute finale, "Yoo Doo Right," a classic example of what the band called "instant composition," a process where they sculpted and edited an extended improvisation into a cohesive (though expansive and free-flowing) song. A tight, minimal funk groove beats out hypnotically and steers "Yoo Doo Right" on its course, while Mooney's vocals explore rhythmic and melodic possibilities.

---

### Scott Kannberg, Pavement
*I think I read some interview with **Public Image** where they said Can was their favorite band and so I went and checked them out. First I thought it was just hippie dribble, but as I listened to it more and more I thought it was amazing. On Wowee Zowee, "Half a Canyon," that kind of has a Can-like groove on the second part of the song.*

---

After the interim release of *Soundtracks*, a collection of the group's contributions to low-budget and soft-core porn movies, the band returned in 1971 with *Tago Mago*. By then, Mooney had returned to the United States to work out emotional problems and pursue his original path as a painter. After months without a lead singer, Czukay approached Damo Suzuki, an adequately eccentric Japanese street musician he saw in Munich, and invited him to join the band for that night's sold-out concert. Having no plans for the evening, Suzuki accepted. And though he managed to clear out the audience with his spastic samurai-scatting, Damo remained Can's new lead singer. Unlike Mooney's more disciplined vocals, Suzuki's style—later copped by singers such as the **Fall**'s Mark E. Smith (who wrote a song called "I Am Damo Suzuki")—blended into the instrumental mix and allowed the others more opportunity to explore.

*Tago Mago*, Can's first album with Suzuki, was not surprisingly the group's most extreme in sound and structure. At over 70 minutes (it was originally a double album), the record charts a descent into madness. After a relatively conventional and melodic first side, the 18-minute "Halleluhwah" and 17-minute "Aumgn" (named after an Aleister Crowley magic spell) fill sides two and three with a trancelike rhythm that degenerates into dissonance. "Aumgn" and "Peking O," which feature Czukay's tape and radio experiments (a trick he'd learned from Stockhausen and **Cage**), bring the group as close as it ever got to avant-garde noise music.

Surprisingly, 1972's *Ege Bamyasi* headed in the opposite direction. Can's first album recorded at their new Inner Space studio (and first released in the U.S.), it plunged the band into much more accessible territory. When "Spoon" was used on a popular German television show, it even yielded the group's first European hit. With its cover art—a can of okra—and songs like "Vitamin C," "Soup," and "I'm So Green," *Ege Bamyasi* is Can's most literally unified and consciously organic work. Having discovered their sound, the members of Can settled back into a comfortable blend of surreal sound sketches and disciplined funk rhythms.

---

### Thurston Moore, Sonic Youth

*I found Ege Bamyasi in the 49-cent bin at Woolworth's. I didn't see anything written about Can, I didn't know anything about them except this okra can on the cover, which seemed completely bizarro. I finally picked that record up, and I completely wore it out. It was so alluring. Something about it made Can seem to be playing outside of rock 'n' roll. It was unlike anything else I was hearing at the time.*

---

With 1973's *Future Days*, Can delved into atmospherics as never before, with the gentle synth pulsations, gull chirps, and watery rushes of songs like "Spray" and "Moonshake" (a name later adopted by a British post-rock group). The 20-minute "Bel Air" radiates the kind of space-age ether/undersea solemnity that still sounds ultra-modern in the hands of a band like Stereolab today. After *Future Days*, Suzuki left the group, and was not replaced. Karoli and Schmidt split what little vocal work appears on the mostly instrumental, and even more ambient, *Soon Over Babaluma*.

Though Can would produce six more albums during the '70s, by 1975 their strongest work was behind them. After *Landed* (which featured "Hunters and Collectors," another song that later became a band name), the group branched out into reggae, country, and other styles with 1976's *Flow Motion* and had a British hit with the disco funk of "I Want More." For *Saw Delight*, Can added two former members of the band Traffic—percussionist Reebop Kwaku Baah and bassist Rosko Gee—who were no doubt meant to steer the group toward more mainstream success. But as Gee freed Czukay from his bass responsibilities, he began to focus more on tape and radio experiments that were not compatible with the group's increasingly commercial approach. It was a contradiction that was never resolved, and after a self-titled album in 1979, the members of Can went their separate ways.

Can reunited in the late '80s with original singer Malcolm Mooney to record the surprisingly good *Rite Time,* but the reunion was short-lived. Though each member has remained active on his own, Czukay's post-Can career is most distinctive. In his collaborations with the Eurythmics, PiL's Jah Wobble, U2's Edge, and Japan's David Sylvian during the '80s, Czukay transmitted Can's legacy onto a new generation of progressive rockers who would in turn define the styles we hear today. This, along with extensive reissues of Can albums and a record of electronic remixes, has considerably raised the band's profile in the '90s and moved them closer to receiving their due credit as one of rock's most distinctive and visionary bands.

## DISCOGRAPHY

*Monster Movie* (United Artists, 1969; Spoon/Mute, 1995); the debut, featuring original singer Malcolm Mooney and their classic "Yoo Doo Right."

*Soundtracks* (United Artists, 1970; Spoon/Mute, 1995); a collection of tracks recorded for various movies.

*Tago Mago* (United Artists, 1971; Spoon/Mute, 1995); a double album, Can's most experimental record.

*Ege Bamyasi* (United Artists, 1972; Spoon/Mute, 1995); their most accessible album which, not surprisingly, was something of a commercial breakthrough.

*Future Days* (United Artists, 1973; Spoon/Mute, 1995).

*Soon over Babaluma* (United Artists, 1974; Spoon/Mute, 1995); a more ambient effort, their first without a lead singer.

*Landed* (Virgin, 1975; Spoon/Mute, 1989).

*Unlimited Edition* (Caroline, 1976; Spoon/Mute, 1991); an expanded version of *Limited Edition,* collecting previously unreleased material spanning their entire career up to that point.

*Flow Motion* (Virgin, 1976; Spoon/Mute, 1989); the band ventures into styles such as disco and reggae, to varying results.

*Saw Delight* (Harvest, 1977; Spoon/Mute, 1989); the addition of two ex-Traffic members makes the sound slicker and fuller.

*Out of Reach* (Peters Intl., 1978); a hard-to-find album generally regarded poorly.

*Cannibalism 1* (United Artists, 1978; Spoon/Mute, 1995); a compilation of songs culled from the first six albums.

*Can* (Laser, 1979; Spoon/Mute, 1991); the final studio album.

*Can Delay 1968* (Spoon, 1981; Spoon/Mute, 1995); featuring original singer Mooney, this contains never before released recordings that predate the first record.

*Rite Time* (Spoon, 1989; Spoon/Mute, 1994); a short-lived reunion in the late '80s yielded this album.

*Cannibalism 2* (Spoon/Mute, 1992); a second compilation covering the later albums.

*Anthology: 25 Years* (Spoon/Mute, 1994).

*Cannibalism 3: Solo Edition* (Spoon/Mute, 1995); a compilation of Can members' solo work between 1979 and 1991.

TRIBUTE: *Sacrilege: The Can Remix Album* (Mute, 1997); Sonic Youth, the Orb, **Brian Eno,** members of **Wire** and the **Buzzcocks,** and others reconceive Can originals— sometimes changing them beyond recognition.

## FAUST

*What is this avant-garde? We're not avant-garde. We're not trying to be ahead, to be beyond our time. We're just trying to be here now.*

**Jean-Hervé Peron, Faust [N.M.E, March 1973]**

hough Faust was the most radically experimental of the krautrockers, their modern compositional approach left enough room to incorporate acid rock, funk grooves, and Beach Boys pop
with the required dose of Stockhausen. By applying the techniques of musique concrète as a
central element of their work, Faust laid the groundwork for later rock collage artists in the industrial and post-punk worlds. And through their influence on bands like **Throbbing Gristle,** word of
the dark and mysterious band Faust has spread, where it now informs the music of groups from
Pavement to Stereolab to Gastr del Sol.

### Tim Gane, Stereolab:

*The first German band I got into was Faust, because I was really into Cabaret Voltaire and*
***Throbbing Gristle*** *and I saw a review of some Faust reissues that said, "if you like those bands,*
*these are their forefathers, and this is far wilder." I was really into music where I couldn't*
*understand where the person's brain was at when they were doing it. And Faust were the epit-*
*ome of mysterious creative nutcases. They were so brilliant and so advanced. When I heard*
*their record it was everything I'd imagined I wanted to do in music, already done.*

Strange as it seems, those krautrock experimentalists were as prefabricated as the Monkees. But
where the Monkees were designed to look good on TV, the members of Faust were picked to be
musical revolutionaries, rewriting the rules of rock. The producer behind the group was journalist
Uwe Nettlebeck, who in 1970 formed Faust with backing from a German record label. Nettlebeck

recruited musicians he knew from Hamburg
bands, and named the group after the legendary German doctor and literary character (the word also means "fist" in German).
Using the record company's money, he converted an old schoolhouse in the nearby
town of Wümme into a studio, and the eight
or so members of Faust set on their way
toward creating music like none before.

Though Nettlebeck remained the group's
producer, manager, and spokesman
throughout, Faust were quick to establish
themselves as a viable band. Some members
even designed their own instruments.
Within a year, Faust had produced their
first album, which came in a striking package: clear vinyl inside a transparent lyric
sheet, inside a clear record jacket that had an x-ray image of a fist on it. The music was no less
unusual. Though it contained just three songs that averaged over 10 minutes each, the tracks compiled many, often unrelated, fragments and cut them together on the editing table. "Why Don't You
Eat Carrots," for instance, jumped from radio static and snippets of the Beatles, to strange low-fi

acid rock clearly influenced by Frank Zappa, to classical piano lines, to marching-band horns, to singing passages of melodic absurdities, to sound bites of random conversations. Though it had more in common with Stockhausen than anything going on in pop music, the album had a modest success in the U.K.

The second album, 1972's *So Far*, was designed as the debut's polar opposite. Packaged in black, except for illustrations that corresponded to the songs, this album offered something more recognizable as rock. The opening track, "It's a Rainy Day (Sunshine Girl)," had a strong Velvet Underground feel to it, while "On the Way to Abamäe" was a sprightly acoustic guitar piece. In other places, the band slipped into a dance beat or jazz progression. Though the lyrics were just as nonsensical as those on the debut (example: "Daddy, take the banana, tomorrow is Sunday!"), *So Far* was neither as fractured nor as difficult as that album.

Following the release of *So Far*, Nettlebeck arranged for the group's core members—Werner Diermaier, Jean-Hervé Peron, and Rudolf Sosna—to record with **Tony Conrad**, a minimalist composer/filmmaker who had played an important role in the formation of the Velvet Underground. Their collaboration, *Outside the Dream Syndicate*, was something of an attempt to place the "dream music" Conrad had created with **LaMonte Young** in the early '60s in a more rock environment. Featuring Conrad's sustained violin tones with Faust's bass and percussion, the music pursued a trancelike drone for more than 70 minutes. In the end, it expressed more of Conrad's artistic vision than their own. (And it was this record, rather than the Conrad/Young group, from which the '80s rock band Dream Syndicate took its name.)

Shortly after, the group produced *The Faust Tapes*, an apparent effort to amalgamate the editing efforts of the first record with the eclectic art rock of the second. Offering over 20 song fragments but no title listing, the album was one long mix tape of material taken from the group's large library of unreleased recordings. Combining noise effects with guitar jams and conventional songs, *The Faust Tapes* attempted to use creative editing to mold disparate elements into a fluid whole.

---

### David Grubbs, solo/Gastr del Sol

*The Faust Tapes were important to me in how it was assembled. With fragments, the music is composed after the fact. Grouping performances as material, to be completed later, that's a basic fact of the way I work. And it was done with extreme sensitivity and grace on The Faust Tapes.*

---

Though *The Faust Tapes* was at times group's most difficult music, it became their best-selling release in Britain due to its more-than-affordable price of a half-pound (roughly one dollar!). It even led to a U.K. tour, featuring a colorful stage show in which the band played pinball machines that triggered sampler-like instruments to help reproduce their music live.

---

### Sean O'Hagen, High Llamas:

*The Faust Tapes was really weird, but for 50 pence, it was an album you could afford and everybody at school bought it. Hearing this bizarre music when I was nine or ten, I didn't have a clue what was going on. But I just thought all rock music was great because it wasn't Bing Crosby. These tapes of people rummaging around and these strange, badly recorded riffs, to us it was like, "Well these guys are out there doing it, this must be what [rock music] is about."*

*Faust IV*, the group's fifth release in three years (counting the Conrad collaboration), swung back again to more accessible sounds, including the reggaeish "The Sad Skinhead" and the psychedelic "Jennifer." Though it was the first album recorded in England, where the group's fan base was now centered, it failed to take hold. When the next album was rejected by the group's label, Nettlebeck lost interest in the band. By 1975, Faust had broken up.

Little was heard from the band members over the next decade, though Faust's influence on experimental and sample-based music continued to be felt. In 1990, Diermaier and Peron resurfaced as a reunited Faust. After touring for years with an industrial/hippie-style stage show, the group hired post-punk guitar improviser (and **Tony Conrad** cohort) Jim O'Rourke to compile a collage work to their tapes. The result, *Rien*, was released in 1995.

## DISCOGRAPHY

*Faust* (Polydor, 1971; 1991); the striking debut, featuring long songs full of editing, low-fi effects, and absurdity.

*So Far* (Polydor, 1972; 1991); a more accessible effort that revealed the band's eclecticism.

(w/**Tony Conrad**), *Outside the Dream Syndicate* (Caroline, 1972; Table of the Elements, 1995); a collaboration with composer Tony Conrad that built on the earlier work he'd done with **LaMonte Young**'s Dream Syndicate.

*The Faust Tapes* (Virgin, 1973; Recommended, 1991); their classic collage of song fragments into one complete album-length work.

*Faust IV* (Virgin, 1973; 1992).

*Munic and Elsewhere/The Return of a Legend* (Recommended, 1986); recorded between 1973 and 1975, after the band stopped releasing new music.

*The Last LP (Faust Party Three)* (Recommended, 1989); a collection of previously unreleased material.

*71 Minutes of...* (Recommended, 1996); combines the *Munic and Elsewhere* album with *Faust Party Three*.

*The Faust Concerts Vol. 1* (Table of the Elements, 1994); a live recording from 1990.

*The Faust Concerts Vol. 2* (Table of the Elements, 1994); a live recording from 1992.

*Rien* (Table of the Elements, 1995); the first new Faust recording in decades, made by editing together recordings from recent concerts.

*You Know Faust* (Klangbad, 1996).

# KRAFTWERK

*I've always loved them. I don't think anyone doing electronic music can say Kraftwerk wasn't an influence.*

**Richard James, Aphex Twin**

While it's hard to consider any group that had a Top Five album and Top Forty single to be part of a "Secret History," Kraftwerk makes the cut because of how overwhelmingly influential they've been to people who weren't even born at the height of their commercial success—and because of how inaccurately they've been perceived in the United States. When their futuristic pre-techno single "Autobahn," and album of the same name, became hits in 1975, they shared the charts with acts like B. J. Thomas, John Denver, and the Captain & Tennille. It was no wonder they were perceived as a freakish novelty act from some distant time and place, and soon suffered the fate of most novelty acts (they never returned to the pop charts).

---

### Sean O'Hagen, High Llamas

*I was attracted by the fact that Kraftwerk were using classic pop writing, which is one thing you didn't do when you were into progressive rock. But Kraftwerk were just like, "Hang on, we do what we do, and we start off with pop writing." Even today there's lessons to be learned.*

---

But while "Autobahn" may have been the beginning and end of the Kraftwerk story in the eyes of the mass market, for followers of krautrock and electronic music it was neither. They had been making progressive pop music since the beginning of the '70s, and were soon to become one of the primary roots nourishing nearly all the new computer-based music to arrive in the coming decades: disco (where they continued to thrive), techno (through their acknowledged influence on Detroit dance pioneers Juan Atkins and Derrick May), electro-funk and early hip-hop (through Afrika Bambaataa's appropriations), new wave (in Gary Numan's robot-man pose), and synth pop (with the stylistic borrowings of Depeche Mode and other groups). So important was Kraftwerk to even the more mainstream pop world, David Bowie dedicated a song to the group's co-founder ("V-2 Schneider") and even Michael Jackson expressed interest in working with them (they declined).

---

### Alex Paterson, the Orb

*Even back in '74 I was really influenced by them. The 22-minute version of "Autobahn" I imagine brought me in line with making big Orb records early on. You can cram a lot of stuff into a three-minute pop song, but you can make much better music if you give yourself ten or fifteen minutes. When they split up a few years ago two of them ended up around here checking out me and [Orb member] Thrash to see if they could work with us. That was quite weird, I assure you. Them sitting on the floor cross-legged, listening to me deejay in my own flat. They were all dressed in black! And they didn't undo their top buttons either! That was strange—two people you idolize when you're little, sitting there watching you deejay, asking silly questions.*

---

Kraftwerk's principle members, Ralf Hütter and Florian Schneider, studied together at the Düsseldorf Conservatory in the late '60s, where they were exposed to the early electronic compositions of Karlheinz Stockhausen. Their first foray into popular music came in 1970, when their quintet the Organisation released an album called *Tone-Float*. Within the year, Hütter and Schneider decided to pare down the group to become a duo and renamed themselves Kraftwerk (which means "power station"). By the time they'd recorded the first Kraftwerk record, though, the group had expanded to include percussionists Klaus Dinger and Thomas Hohman. While the album, recorded at their own KlingKlang studio, had hints of the ambient techno-pop sound Kraftwerk would arrive at years later, it mostly sounded like exotic art rock that had been heavily influenced by their avant-garde backgrounds.

### Tim Gane, Stereolab

*The whole thing of the "stereo-lab," with references to scientific experiments and mixing chemicals, that's been my approach to music in a tongue-in-cheek way. I always wanted the image of the band to be that, rather than a pop group. It all comes from Kraftwerk. Our early records had the same sleeve design, with slight variations, just as Kraftwerk had done. I like the idea of records being reports, not so much individual records as an ongoing discovery. I just thought Kraftwerk was the highest point you could do in music, the whole thing influenced me. The throbbing, hypnotic music just struck a chord in me.*

Following the release of Kraftwerk's debut album, Hohman was replaced by a friend of Dinger's, guitarist Michael Rother. The team of Dinger and Rother began to move the group's sound into more rhythmic guitar-groove territory, a direction Hütter found so distasteful he quit the group for a while in 1971. The trio of Schneider, Dinger, and Rother lasted only about six months; then Hütter returned while Dinger and Rother left to form **Neu!**. Temporarily a duo once more, Kraftwerk turned to drum machine accompaniment on their *Kraftwerk 2* and *Ralf & Florian* albums. Ironically, even after Dinger and Rother left Kraftwerk their influence remained, as Hütter and Schneider began to produce a more synthesized version of **Neu!**'s propulsive and metronomic "motorik" beat.

With 1974's *Autobahn*, Kraftwerk entered a new phase. Recognizing a need to more effectively communicate an image for their esoteric music, the group—once again a quartet, with electronic percussionist Wolfgang Flür and guitarist/violinist Klaus Roeder—conspired with visual director Emil Schult to recast themselves as robotic man-machines that celebrated technology through synthesized music. Another thread running through the music was a nostalgia for lost European pre-War cultural institutions, such as the minimalist school of design called Bauhaus, that had been suppressed under the Nazis. With their 22-minute "Autobahn" (which, in shortened form, became an international hit), Kraftwerk fused a love for technology with German scenery, and turned it into what was essentially a futuristic "Born to Run" (released the same year!).

With their new image (or maybe anti-image, since it masked their real personalities behind the cold veneer of hardware) Kraftwerk became the only German band of the era to cross into the American mainstream. Though their follow-up *Radio-Activity* failed to take hold the way *Autobahn* had, 1977's *Trans-Europe Express* was a return to form that made a splash on the disco charts. The title track and "Europe Endless" offered more continental musings, while "Metal on Metal" made a strong impact on early industrial music. Similarly, the following year's *The Man-Machine* produced standouts such as "The Robots," with its vocoder voice synthesizer, and the Euro-chic hit "The Model," which reached number one in England and anticipated the arrival of new wave artists like Human League and Gary Numan.

*Doug Firley, Gravity Kills*

*Kraftwerk was really the avenue that I initially wanted to explore and it took me many, many years trying to reproduce music like that. And I guess I found I was really bad at it, or that there was no way to reinvent the wheel. So I got a sampler and thought instead of trying to recreate the parts, I'd just go ahead and sample them.*

As more groups adopted Kraftwerk's sound and the computer age dawned, the music became less alien and the group's robot gimmickry began to wear thin. By the early '80s the band was recording only sporadically and veered toward anachronism and self-parody. Though they continued to show up in dance clubs doing songs like "Tour de France," they produced little material of note during a decade when their legacy would sprout a variety of new directions in music. With their 1991 remix album, *The Mix,* Kraftwerk—reduced again to the duo of Ralf and Florian—were taking their cues from artists for whom they'd paved the way.

## DISCOGRAPHY

*Kraftwerk 1* (Philips, 1971, Germanophon, 1994).

*Kraftwerk 2* (Philips, 1972; Germanophon, 1994).

*Ralf and Florian* (Vertigo, 1973; Germanophon, 1994).

*Autobahn* (Vertigo, 1974; Elektra, 1988); the international breakthrough.

*Radio Activity* (Capitol, 1975; Cleopatra, 1996); a challenging but largely unsuccessful follow-up, coming at the height of their success.

*Trans-Europe Express* (Capitol, 1977; Elektra, 1988); a strong return to the stuff that made *Autobahn* a success.

*The Man-Machine* (Capitol, 1978; Elektra, 1988); further explorations into techno-futurism.

*Computer World* (Warner Bros., 1981; Elektra, 1988); no longer so ahead of its time, the group now sounds strangely dated.

*Electric Cafe* (Warner Bros., 1986; Elektra, 1988); a mid-'80s release, barely noticed and never followed up.

*The Mix* (Elektra, 1991); an album that remixes past material into '90s dance tracks.

*The Model* (Cleopatra, 1992); a compilation of the group's best known material.

*Three Originals: The Capitol Years* (Cleopatra, 1994); collects the group's post-*Autobahn* records.

TRIBUTE: *A Tribute to Kraftwerk: All in a Day's Work* (Mute, 1991).

TRIBUTE: *Trancewerk Express Vol. I: A Tribute to Kraftwerk* (Cleopatra, 1995); features European electronic acts such as Audio Science, Purity J., and Kirk.

# N E U !

*I think Neu! has been the main proto-influence on Stereolab because it was completely primitive and simplistic on the surface. I loved the way the drumming would stay the same 4/4 for 20 minutes. That was really powerful, and I thought we could do something with it. The more simple and unchanging you make the music the more possibilities there are for melody and things on top.*

**Tim Gane, Stereolab**

As early as 1971, Neu! (pronounced "noy" and translated into English as "New!") provided the prototype for the avant-garde minimalist pop sounds of '90s post-rock bands. With their distinctive motorik beat and gently coerced guitar effects, Neu! offered a comforting glimpse into a future ambient bubblegum sound that was so inspiring to David Bowie he came to Germany in the late '70s and made three Neu!-influenced albums that stand among his finest recordings. Neu! also impacted, perhaps indirectly, the first generation of British punk, and continued to impact Bowie clones and post-punk bands up through Ultravox, Sonic Youth (who titled a song "Two Cool Rock Chicks Listening to Neu!"), and Buffalo Daughter.

### David Bowie

*I thought the first Neu! album, in particular, was just gigantically wonderful. Looking at that against punk, I had absolutely no doubt where the future of music was going, and for me it was out of Germany at that time. [from Mojo magazine]*

Neu! began in 1971 as part of the band **Kraftwerk**. Guitarist Michael Rother and drummer Klaus Dinger had briefly joined that group, and even made an appearance on German television as two-thirds of the band, until Kraftwerk's leaders—Ralf Hütter and Florian Schneider—decided to go it alone as a duo. Rother and Dinger also decided to carry on as a twosome, and Neu! was born. Making the most of the tools they had on hand, Neu! created entire soundscapes using little more than a drum set and an effects-heavy guitar.

Within a year, they recorded a debut album—the critically acclaimed *Neu!*—with well-known krautrock producer Conrad Plank. The sparsely designed cover art—"NEU!" brush-stroked in bold red against a solid white background—perfectly captured the minimalism of the music. Opening with the 10-minute voyage of "Hallogallo," the duo virtually perfected the steady driving, metronomic motorik beat that would later be associated with Kraftwerk's most successful music. "Hallogallo, and other, less rhythmically propulsive tracks like "Lieber Honig" and "Weissensee," cast an irresistible spell, while slipping in enough traces of melody to move the mostly instrumental music along. "Negativland," with its wall of industrial noise deflecting a funk-dub guitar line, prefigured post-punk—and provided the name for San Francisco's culture-jamming group.

After some time spent touring with members of Guru Guru, Neu! started work on its second record, *Neu! 2*, which would feature virtually the same album cover as the debut, but with a large "2" now spray-painted on top. The 11-minute "Für Immer" opened the record by recapturing "Hallogallo"'s incessantly hypnotic forward motion, and added churning guitars to make it even more dramatic. The misleadingly titled "Lila Engel (Lilac Angel)" closed the first half of the record with a savage tribal punk assault, complete with Dinger's grunted vocals. At this point in the making of the album, Dinger and Rother's recording budget ran out and the two were forced to use prerecorded material to fill side two. Making the best of a bad situation, they offered sped-up, slowed-down, and switched-around versions of their earlier non-album single "Neuschnee"/ "Super." Fortunately for the group's reputation, the two terrifically aggressive and modern rock cuts were among their best work.

### Mark Hosler, Negativland:

*In the late '70s, I was 17 and totally thrilled to discover this world of unusual, independent music from Germany, it was so exotic and wild. Among them was Neu!. You put on Neu!2 and you hear the sound of someone putting on a record. It just blew my mind, it was so weird beyond weird. It wasn't even breaking any rules, it was as if the rules didn't even exist. Back then, it was like hearing some music that was from another planet.*

Embittered by their experience recording *Neu! 2*, the duo split up after the album's release. Rother started a band called Harmonia with yet another German musical duo, Cluster's Dieter Moebius and Hans Joachim Roedelius. Dinger formed his own band, La Dusseldorf, a more aggressive proto-punk trio that included his brother Thomas and Hans Lampe. Before they could release an album, though, Rother approached Dinger with a desire to make one last Neu! record to end the group on a more positive note. Along with Thomas Dinger and Lampe, Rother and Dinger produced *Neu! '75*, which overwhelmingly achieved its goal. The first side, dominated by Rother and clearly informed by his work with Harmonia, featured a more ethereal take on Neu!'s signature sound. The Dinger-controlled second side was a blueprint for La Dusseldorf's soon-to-be revealed style. Klaus's ferociously whining vocals on "Hero" and "After Eight" would have an influence on Johnny Rotten's singing style in the Sex Pistols.

### Julian Cope

*You know, I can say this over and over till I'm a boring old git but Side 2 [of Neu! 75] is punk as fuck and two years ahead. Not the **Stooges**, not the Dolls, not American at ALL. You hear "Hero" and "After Eight" and British punk suddenly makes sense. For a few beautiful months before old-prick Johnny Thunders brought heroin-injecting into the punk scene, it was really the Neu!-driven sound of the Sex Pistols that turned on the young punks. And it was Klaus Dinger & Michael Rotter who deserved the credit and never got it. [from Cope's book Krautrocksampler]*

Having brought Neu! to respectable closure, Dinger continued with La Dusseldorf (who in 1979 David Bowie called "the soundtrack of the '80s") and had success expanding on *Neu! '75*'s breakthroughs. Rother made another Harmonia record, and produced a record for his Harmonia-mates in Cluster (another, previously unreleased, collaboration between Harmonia and **Brian Eno** was recently released as well). Aside from a brief reunion in the '80s, Rother and Dinger have pursued solo careers ever since.

## DISCOGRAPHY

*Neu!* (Brain/United Artists, 1972; Germanophon [CD reissue]); the mesmerizing debut.

*Neu! 2* (Brain/United Artists, 1973; Germanophon [CD reissue]); one-half of a terrific follow-up, though marred by a hastily thrown together second side.

*Neu! '75* (Brain/United Artists, 1975; Germanophon [CD reissue]); a final album that highlighted the distinct personalities of the duo.

*Neu! 4* (Captain Trip [Japan], 1995); material recorded by Dinger and Rother, along with other musicians, in 1985 and '86.

*Neu! '72 Live* (Captain Trip [Japan], 1996); not a concert, but rather a recording of an early rehearsal/jam session by the group.

# 8

# SOUND SCULPTORS

From the time recording studios first appeared earlier this century, the conventional approach to recording music has been to create the truest possible reproduction of the sounds made by the musicians. While this kind of sound engineering can require a great deal of skill and technical knowledge, for the most part it exists not as an art in itself but rather as a means of conveying the art of the performer.

As the technological capabilities of the recording studio advanced, the room for creativity in recording increased. Sound engineers, record producers, and the artists themselves began to conceive of ways to express themselves in the areas of sound treatments, tape editing, and the mixing of multitrack recordings. The studio moved from being a mere device for documentation to becoming a tool for creation.

The very idea that a producer can be an artist—and a recording studio can be an instrument—represents a significant conceptual leap in music. Precedents go back to the development of musique concrète in the '40s, when experimental composers such as Pierre Henry and Pierre Schaeffer began manipulating prerecorded sounds to create new compositions. It wasn't until the '60s that these ideas were applied to popular music, and they did not trickle down from the high art concept of musique concrète. Instead, this most revolutionary aesthetic development in late 20th-century popular music came from Jamaica, a relatively poor country whose recording facilities were quite primitive at the time.

In search of new ways to thrill their listeners with limited material, Jamaican producers such as **King Tubby** and **Lee "Scratch" Perry** began to rework previously recorded music in ways that made the songs sound fresh—or even like entirely new pieces of music. Dub, as this studio-based derivation of popular rock steady and reggae styles was called, caught on in Jamaican dance halls. For the first time in popular music, producers who did not necessarily sing, play an instrument, or write songs—who simply reshaped the sounds of songs—could be recognized as the primary artist in a piece of music.

Now, all varieties of music can be manipulated by "remixers" who reimagine the work of others—often to make it more danceable—and who are given as much credit as the original artist. In hip-hop and techno, nonmusician DJs have become recognized artists for merely *playing* records in new and unusual ways, such as scratching and elongating breakbeats. Digital sampling technology has made it easier than ever to create new music from previously recorded sounds, to a point where a significant number of today's recording artists—particularly in electronic music, but in rock as well—are not musicians at all, but essentially producers.

While more mainstream rock has maintained the primacy of the performer and songwriter in the creative process, it too has been deeply affected by the emergence of the producer as artist. In the '60s, producers such as Phil Spector (with his many "girl groups") and George Martin (with the Beatles) established a tradition of the producer as a vital force in the creation of sophisticated pop music. In the '70s, **Brian Eno** emerged (as had Martin) from an art music tradition familiar with the ideas of music concrète. Though Eno was not primarily a producer at the start of his career, his ability to integrate all types of recording and compositional techniques—as well as his stylistic innovations and high-profile production work—have made him a model for the new type of recording artist who uses all available tools, from acoustic instruments to digital effects, in music.

Like Eno, **Adrian Sherwood** is a white British producer, though Sherwood emerged a generation later, in the punk era of the late '70s. Early on, English punk bands were attracted to reggae's political content and expressed solidarity with the Jamaican immigrant underclass. As post-punk artists stretched out and began to incorporate nonrock styles, they discovered a natural affinity with the more adventurous reggae sounds found in dub music. Sherwood, who'd been a reggae fan for years, found himself at a crossroads between post-punk and dub, and merged the two in his work as producer and ringleader for an entire collective of like-minded musicians. The precedents he set for applying dub studio techniques to post-punk styles have become part of the vocabulary in genres such as techno, industrial, and post-rock.

# KING TUBBY

*Tubby had a much broader impact than all of [the dub producers]. He was able to really do version, taking one song and creating a different or ideal version while keeping the song structure in back. It's really monumental stuff—like generative or process music—but going on in an implicit social situation in Jamaica. Where you can have Warhol making multiple prints of the Mona Lisa, you can have King Tubby making multiple prints of a song.*

*DJ Spooky (Paul Miller)*

Though King Tubby didn't play an instrument or write songs, the Jamaican producer has nevertheless exerted a tremendous influence on popular music. While his use of certain effects and his mixing style are often adopted in bass-heavy dance music such as trip-hop and drum 'n' bass, Tubby's larger contribution has been conceptual. In developing the system of in-studio musical manipulation that came to be known as "dub," Tubby moved the creative focus from musician (who creates the musical components of songs) to producer (who augments and arranges or rearranges musical components in distinct and artful ways). As such, dub paved the way for the common practice of remixing in dance music, and for the collage constructions in hip-hop and electronica. More recently, these ideas have become increasingly important to rock-oriented, or post-rock, bands.

*Johnny Temple, Girls Against Boys*

*The mixes on all of King Tubby's albums are serene and bizarre—the product of a brilliant, twisted mind. Tubby was able to make delays, flanges, and other cheesy effects sound organ-*

*ic. I didn't so much learn to play bass by listening to King Tubby as I learned to conceive of bass, and truly appreciate its role as a powerful undercurrent, bubbling beneath the rest of the music. And in terms of mixing, Tubby's work illustrates how an instrument can sometimes best be appreciated by yanking it out of the mix for several measures, something that the average rock and roll ego is hard pressed to comprehend.*

The man who became known as King Tubby was born Osborne Ruddock in Jamaica, in 1941. As a young man, he worked as an electronics engineer in Kingston, where he became involved with the world of sound systems. The Jamaican sound systems that arose in the late '50s featured mobile deejay setups that brought music and entertainment to neighborhoods and towns at a time when few homes had radios or record players. Ruddock built equipment for sound systems, and by the late '60s he was operating his own, the Home Town Hi-Fi sound system.

As competition grew between Kingston systems, Ruddock—who by then had adopted the nickname King Tubby—developed his own echo and reverb effects to make Home Town's sound distinctive and exotic. Other systems, though, were acquiring exclusive tracks from local studios, which gave them an advantage. Tubby wanted to offer something even more special.

In addition to running Home Town, Tubby worked at Kingston's Treasure Isle Studios as the engineer in charge of cutting the master copies of recordings onto acetate discs. It had become common practice in Jamaica for new singles to feature on the B side a "version," which was a test recording of the same song but mixed without vocals in order to set the instrument levels. While cutting a version one day, instead of dropping the vocals entirely Tubby began alternating between the vocals and instruments (on the primitive two-track recordings), sliding vocals in and out of the mix at opportune times. The effect was thrilling; the absence of voice, or the sudden disappearance of the music, added a dynamic tension to the song that didn't exist before. Tubby took these acetates to play on his sound system, and dub music was born.

Soon Tubby began experimenting more with the possibilities of the version. In the studio he added homemade effects like echo, delay, reverb, and flange, while accentuating the bass and drums in the song to make it more appealing to dancers. Meanwhile, Home Town's star deejay **U-Roy** began filling up the space that the dropped vocals left behind with his own rhythmic chanting, and developed the style known as "talkover" or "toasting." Accompanied by Tubby's reworked acetates (known as dub plates), U-Roy became what's recognized as the first rapper.

### Wyclef Jean, the Fugees

*Our whole production style, myself and my cousin Jerry, since we've been little has been drum and bass dub-style, and the vibe King Tubby gives me is the dub-style, scientifically. King Tubby was to dub what Thelonious Monk was to jazz.*

As **U-Roy** began recording his toasts onto Tubby's dubs, both talkover and dub records appeared for sale commercially and the new styles emerged as popular genres. By the early '70s, entire albums of dub such as Carl Patterson's Tubby-produced *Psalm of Dub* emerged. In a stroke of self-promoting genius, in 1970 Tubby used his knowledge of electronics and radio transmissions to jam the national Jamaican Broadcasting Company and replace their programming with hours of his own dub music.

By the time Tubby moved into his own four-track Dynamic Studio in 1974, he had created an entire industry around his production techniques. Reworking the music of artists such as Augustus Pablo and Yabby U, as well as recordings made by his house band the Aggrovators (which featured the legendary reggae rhythm section of drummer Sly Dunbar and bassist Robbie Shakespeare), Tubby churned out hundreds of dub tracks over the years. As other producers got into dub, Tubby stayed ahead of the competition with new innovations. Reggae producer **Lee "Scratch" Perry** became Tubby's rival, but they were also collaborators and friends.

Through the late '70s and into the '80s, as Tubby focused on the overall administration of his studio, other dub producers whom Tubby personally trained became his successors. By 1985, when Tubby opened a new, modern studio, his assistant Prince Jammy (Lloyd James) had become dub reggae's leading producer. Four years later, King Tubby was gunned down by a robber outside his Kingston home, ending a brilliant career of studio advances that had stretched around the world and changed the shape of popular music.

## DISCOGRAPHY
## (WIDELY AVAILABLE RECORDINGS)

*Roots & Society* (Lagoon Reggae, 1993).

*If Deejay Was Your Trade: The Dreads at King Tubby's 1974–1977* (Blood and Fire, 1994); features I. Roy, Tappa Zuckie, and other toasters.

(Augustus Pablo) *King Tubby's Meets Rockers Uptown* (1976; Shanachie, 1994).

*Dub Gone Crazy: King Tubby and Friends* (Blood and Fire, 1994); features Tubby and his protégés, Scientist and Prince Jammy.

*King Tubby Special 1973–1976* (Trojan, 1994); features Niney, Dennis Brown, and others.

*Shining Dub* (Lagoon Reggae, 1994).

(Yabby U) *King Tubby's Prophesy of Dub* (1976; Blood and Fire, 1995).

*Roots Dub* (Lagoon Reggae, 1995).

*Dancehall Style Dub* (Abraham, 1995).

(w/the Aggrovators) *Creation Dub* (Lagoon Reggae, 1995).

(w/Soul Syndicate) *Freedom Sounds In Dub* (Blood & Fire, 1996).

(w/Prince Jammy) *Dub Gone 2 Crazy* (Blood & Fire, 1996).

*Dangerous Dub* (Greensleeves, 1996).

*King Tubby's Meets Scientist at Dub Station* (Burning Sounds, 1996).

*King Tubby's Meets Scientist In a World of Dub* (Burning Sounds, 1996).

(w/Glen Brown) *Termination Dub (1973–1979)* (Blood and Fire, 1996); features Bunny Lee's rhythms played by the Aggrovators.

*Morwell Unlimited Meet King Tubby's: Dub Me* (Blood and Fire, 1997).

*Dub Gone Crazy: The Evolution of Dub at King Tubby's 1975–1979* (Blood and Fire, 1997).

(w/Lee Perry) *Megawatt Dub* (Shanachie, 1997).

*Rod of Correction* (Musicrama, 1998).

*Upset the Upsetters* (Musicrama, 1998).

TRIBUTE: Sly & Robbie, *A Tribute to King Tubby* (Rohit, 1990).

# LEE "SCRATCH" PERRY

*Lee Perry is one of the geniuses of contemporary sound. His fearlessness in the face of technology is remarkable when you think he came from an agrarian society. This guy was taking tape machines, space echoes, and reverbs, fashioning them into what he wanted them to be, and using them to create a whole new sound. Using the studio as an instrument was revolutionary. A lot of times I'm trying to create an ambience and space for the lyrics to fit in. He'd create a mood or a tension, not by adding to the track but by taking things away.*

**Michael Franti, Spearhead**

Lee "Scratch" Perry's career, which has spanned five decades of Jamaican music, has touched on R&B, ska, rock steady, reggae, dub, dancehall, and beyond. He's done it all: sound system operator, talent scout, songwriter, singer, producer, record executive, and studio owner. Though he'd probably be a music legend based only on his eccentricities and his long list of nicknames—Scratch, Upsetter, Super Ape, Pipecock Jackson, to name a few—Perry's most important contributions to modern music came through his production work. He set Bob Marley & the Wailers on their reggae path, added some low-end to blue-eyed funkster Robert Palmer, and helped the Clash create rude-boy punk. More significantly, Perry's own dub creations in the '70s forever expanded the language of sound and defined the art of the mixing board. As a mad scientist of the studio, Perry inspires knob-twiddlers in all genres to create a mix that adds up to more than the sum of its parts.

**Tjinder Singh, Cornershop**
*...The madness and weirdness of his production techniques. We try to keep things pretty raw and simple like he did.*

Rainford Hugh Perry was born in 1936, the son of laborers in the Jamaican countryside town of Kendal. Perry quit school at 15 and drifted through a variety of occupations—including dominoes champ and dancer—before hearing a voice in his head that called him to the capital city, Kingston. Arriving in the late '50s, Perry sought out the R&B music he loved as a dancer, and was hired as errand runner for Clement "Coxsone" Dodd, owner of the popular Downbeat Sound System. Soon he was in charge of running the system.

By the early '60s, as Dodd's Studio One label began producing ska records by indigenous artists, "Little" Lee served as talent scout (discovering, among others, Toots & the Maytals), songwriter (for early stars like Delroy Wilson), and producer. In 1965 he scored a ska hit of his own with "Chicken Scratch," the song which gave Perry his most enduring nickname. With other, sexually suggestive songs like "Doctor Dick" and "Puss in Bag," Perry set a precedent for "slack" reggae lyricists such as Shabba Ranks decades later.

Feeling unappreciated by Dodd, Perry left Studio

One in 1967 to join producer Joe Gibbs' Amalgamated label, where he had another hit (and earned another nickname) with a song attacking Dodd, "The Upsetter." He quickly became dissatisfied with Gibbs as well and in 1968 started his own label, Upsetter Records. With his new backing band, the Upsetters, Perry scored a hit with "People Funny Boy," a song aimed at Gibbs. Slower in rhythm than most ska and rock steady of the time, the song is recognized as one of the earliest tracks in the evolution of reggae.

As the Upsetters got rolling, they achieved great success with novelty songs like "Return of Django" that mixed reggae rhythms with western soundtrack music. In 1969 Perry began working with the Wailers, a vocal trio led by Bob Marley. Under Perry's production and direction, the Wailers developed into a full reggae band. Though they left Perry in 1971, after their second album—and Perry threatened to kill Marley for stealing the Upsetters' rhythm section—the two patched things up and even collaborated in the late '70s on the reggae-punk solidarity anthem "Punky Reggae Party."

Through the early '70s, Perry continued recording with the Upsetters, collaborating with dub pioneer **King Tubby,** and producing artists such as early toasters **U-Roy** and I-Roy. Stretching the possibilities of the studio, Perry spliced sections of other songs into new ones (an early, manual form of sampling) and took Tubby's dub advances to new levels of sophistication. In 1973, Perry built his own studio in the Kingston suburbs. Black Ark, as he called it, soon earned a reputation as Perry's mystical sanctuary, where anything was possible. As the self-mythologizing Perry would say, "It was only four tracks written on the machine, but I was picking up 20 from the extraterrestrial squad. I am the dub shepherd."

---

### David Byrne

*Lee Perry blew my mind. He took dub to a whole new level, where it really became textural and musical, and it wasn't just throwing reverb on a rhythm track. He saw how he could create a whole new piece of music out of somebody else's track, and sometimes what he did was better than the original. You don't hear it [in my music] in a way that sounds like what he does—but when you think in terms of what he's doing structurally, emotionally, texturally, you learn from that.*

---

During the mid- and late '70s, Black Ark produced hundreds of tracks, including politically conscious reggae hits such as Max Romeo's "War Ina Babylon" and Junior Murvin's "Police and Thieves" (later covered by the Clash). Even more notable, though, was the dub made by Perry and the Upsetters on records like *Super Ape*. Employing early drum machines, phase shifters, and all manner of psychedelic wizardry, Perry took the Upsetters' music and infinitely reimagined it as some of the most mind-warping dub sounds ever created.

By 1979, Perry's life was unraveling. With his marriage falling apart and record sales steadily declining as his music became more esoteric, Perry was drinking heavily and smoking huge amounts of marijuana. When local gangsters started extorting protection money from him, Perry cracked. Visitors recall seeing him walk backwards, eat money, and pray to bananas. Then, after covering the walls of Black Ark in small graffiti, Perry burned the studio to the ground.

After that legendary episode, Perry adopted an eccentric, lunatic lifestyle (perhaps an act, perhaps the result of a real mental breakdown), spouting half-mystical, half-nonsensical statements and dressing in junkyard costumes. He left Jamaica, and spent the '80s working in the U.S., then England, where he produced acts such as Simply Red and Terence Trent D'Arby, and updated his own sound through collaborations with more electronically oriented dub producers such as Mad Professor and **Adrian Sherwood**.

---

### Mase, De La Soul:

*We did a show with Lee "Scratch" Perry in Belgium. He ripped it. I've been inspired by the way he mixes his music. The warmness of the songs. I'm always inspired by good production, but reggae definitely has something in common with hip-hop in that it's always been really low-end and bassy, really deep and thick. That was something that we applied to our style of music as well.*

---

Now in his '60s and living in the Swiss Alps, Perry has come back in the public eye. In 1995, the Beastie Boys made him the cover story of their magazine, *Grand Royal,* and Perry reissues have increased since. In 1997, Perry did his first U.S. tour in over 16 years and appeared at the Tibetan Freedom Concert. Alongside musicians who weren't born when Perry had his first hit, the Upsetter not only held his own but seemed to occupy a space as timeless as his music.

## DISCOGRAPHY
## (AVAILABLE RECORDINGS)

(the Upsetters) *The Upsetter* (Trojan, 1969; 1996); Perry and group's earliest tracks.

(the Upsetters) *The Return of Django* (Trojan, 1970; 1996); features the group's early western-inspired instrumentals.

(the Upsetters) *Eastwood Rides Again* (Pama, 1969; Trojan, 1996); more spaghetti western reggae.

(the Upsetters) *Africa's Blood* (Trojan, 1971; 1996); a soulful early reggae album.

(the Upsetters) *Blackboard Jungle Dub* (Upsetter, 1973; RAS, 1988).

(the Upsetters) *Double Seven* (Trojan, 1974; 1996); features **U-Roy,** I-Roy, and other toasters.

(the Upsetters) *Kung Fu Meets the Dragon* (DIP, 1975; Lagoon, 1995); dub inspired by Bruce Lee movies.

(the Upsetters) *Super Ape* (Mango, 1976; 1993); a classic dub album at Black Ark's highpoint.

(the Upsetters) *Return of the Super Ape* (Mango, 1977; VP, 1990); Perry's classic dub at its most extreme.

*Roast Fish, Collie Weed and Corn Bread* (1978; VP, 1994); features late Black Ark material.

(the Upsetters) *The Upsetter Collection* (Trojan, 1981;

1994); a good compilation spanning 1969–1973.

(w/the Majestics) *Mystic Miracle Star* (Heartbeat, 1982; 1990); recorded in the U.S. with a white reggae backing band.

*History, Mystery, & Prophecy* (Mango, 1984; 1993); recorded during Perry's early '80s slump.

*Reggae Greats* (Mango, 1984; 1993); a compilation featuring Perry and his productions for others.

*The Upsetter Compact Set* (Trojan, 1988); combines three early albums: *Africa's Blood, Rhythm Shower,* and *Double Seven.*

*Battle of Armageddon* (Trojan, 1986, 1994); an '80s comeback, and his last to feature the Upsetters.

(w/Dub Syndicate) *Time Boom X De Devil Dead* (On-U Sound, 1987; 1994); a strong collaboration with **Adrian Sherwood**'s dub group.

*Give Me Power* (Trojan, 1988; 1994); a compilation of Perry productions.

*Some of the Best* (Heartbeat, 1988); a compilation of Perry's early reggae works, including an early Bob Marley track.

*Scratch Attack!* (RAS, 1988); combines two early albums.

*Chicken Scratch* (Heartbeat, 1989); a collection of early Perry ska songs from 1964–66, backed by the Skatalites.

*Open the Gate* (Trojan, 1989); a two-CD compilation of Black Ark material.

(w/Mad Professor) *Mystic Warrior* (Ariwa, 1990); a collaboration with UK dub star, also released in a *Mystic Warrior Dub* version.

*From the Secret Laboratory* (Mango, 1990); another collaboration with **Adrian Sherwood**.

*Lee Scratch Perry Meets Bullwackie in Satan's Dub* (ROIR, 1990).

*Public Jestering* (Attack, 1990); a compilation from 1972–76.

*Lord God Muzick* (Heartbeat, 1991); a new album recorded in Jamaica.

*Out of Many—The Upsetter* (Trojan, 1991); a compilation of early '70s material.

(the Upsetters) *Version Like Rain* (Trojan, 1992); a compilation from 1972–76.

*The Upsetter and the Beat* (Heartbeat, 1992); a late '80s reunion with producer Coxsone Dodd.

*Soundz from the Hot Line* (Heartbeat, 1992); a compilation from the Black Ark days.

(w/**King Tubby**) *Dub Confrontation Vol. 1* and *Vol. 2* (Lagoon, 1994; 1995); a mixing battle between the two dub greats.

(w/Mad Professor) *Super Ape Inna Jungle* (RAS, 1995); a wacky dub-techno creation.

(w/Mad Professor) *Black Ark Experryments* (Ariwa, 1995).

(w/Mad Professor) *Experryments at the Grass Roots of Dub* (Ariwa, 1995).

(the Upsetters) *Upsetters A Go Go* (Heartbeat, 1995); features lost tracks from Perry's original band, remixed.

*Who Put the Voodoo Pon Reggae* (Ariwa, 1996).

*Technomajikal* (ROIR, 1997); a collaboration with Yello's Dieter Meier.

*Upsetter in Dub* (Heartbeat, 1997); a collection of Black Ark dubs.

*Arkology* (Island, 1997); a three-CD box set documenting the work at Perry's Black Ark studio between 1975 and 1979.

# BRIAN ENO

*Some bands went to art school; we went to Brian Eno.*

**Bono, U2**

As an independent musical adventurer, Brian Eno has been alternately the most artfully sophisticated mind in pop and the catchiest composer in experimental music. A musical creator with truly equal-opportunity ears, his huge body of work serves as a meeting ground for minimalism and glam rock, techno and pop, European intellectualism and non-Western folk styles, obscure composers and stadium rock. Eno has stood at ground zero in the development of art rock, ambient, new wave, no wave, New Age, trance-dance, and mannered pop. As a producer, he has played a critical role in the careers of some of rock's most significant acts. As an inspiration, he has been cited by artists in all forms of contemporary music.

---

### Mark De Gli Antoni, Soul Coughing

*When I was in, like, sixth grade, I went ape over Roxy Music's second record. The credits said Brian Eno did "treatments," and I thought, "Wow, what does that mean?" Then I got [Genesis'] The Lamb Lies Down on Broadway, and the credits called the way the piano was treated "Enosification," and I was like, "So what did Eno do there?" It was such a big deal to me, all those things. It started the spark. Through learning more about what Eno was doing with tapes, I started playing with that stuff.... Soon after I heard Music for Airports, I gave away all my records and decided to start from scratch. I only listened to Music for Airports for two or three years.... And I really liked working with unfamiliar sounds and musique concrète, but I also really liked pop music. Eno was very important to solving the problem of living in both worlds at the same time.*

Brian Peter George St. John le Baptiste de la Salle Eno grew up in a middle-class neighborhood in Suffolk where his father was a postman. At a young age Eno began tuning in American radio broadcasts from the nearby U.S. Air Force Base, where he first heard sounds that seemed to come from another world: early rock 'n' roll, doo-wop, easy listening pop. Eno also became fascinated with tape recorders as a kid, and when he finally got one he constantly investigated its possibilities. The tape recorder, essentially, became Eno's first instrument.

As Eno entered art school in the mid-'60s, he began hearing the work of modern composers such as **John Cage** and **LaMonte Young**. Soon he fell under the influence of British composer Cornelius Cardew, with his collective of anarchic musical experimenters the Scratch Orchestra, and joined a similar group, the Portsmouth Sinfonia. Simultaneously, Eno pursued rock music with Maxwell's Demon, a band for which he sang and operated electronics.

In 1971 Eno settled on a single musical pursuit when he formed Roxy Music, an eccentric art rock band that took its cues from the Velvet Underground and early German krautrock bands. Eno was nominally the keyboardist, but his true function was something closer to sound engineer, handling "treatments." Eno's musical direction and freakish glam look—with makeup, glitter suits, and feather boas—dominated Roxy Music's first two albums and tension developed between Eno and singer Bryan Ferry. In 1973, Eno decided to move on.

### Scott Kannberg, Pavement

*We had all these electronic keyboards on our first single, and I think that came from him. I was in a record store and I heard this amazing electronic solo on a Roxy Music bootleg. Eno was just going off on this warped accompaniment. A week later I was like, "Oh, we gotta have something like that on our song."*

Eno's first stop was *(No Pussyfooting)*, an experimental guitar album with King Crimson's Robert Fripp, on which the two developed a system of delayed tape looping (called "Frippertronics") that enabled Fripp to layer guitar parts and essentially accompany himself. Eno also embarked on a solo career with 1973's *Here Come the Warm Jets* and the following year's *Taking Tiger Mountain (By Strategy)*, two excellent records—both playfully melodic and sonically adventurous—that at different points seemed to prefigure both punk rock and synth pop.

### Eric Bachmann, Archers of Loaf

*If you listen to the guitar stuff on those first two pop records, we owe a lot to that. The production things that he was just starting to work out, that's totally how I see us. By no means do we have the kind of brain that he has, but I admire his attitude. He would just try anything, where a lot of people wouldn't have the energy.*

Eno subsequently recorded two more ambitious pop-oriented records, *Another Green World* (which featured the Velvet Underground's **John Cale** as well as future pop star Phil Collins) and *Before and After Science* (featuring the German duo Cluster, with whom Eno would collaborate often). These albums, though, were clearly informed by a new direction Eno had begun to take in music, following a 1975 car accident. While recuperating in bed, Eno found himself listening to a record with the volume turned very low. Unable to get out of bed to make the music louder, he simply let it play at a barely audible level. As he later wrote, "This presented what was for me a new way of hearing music—as part of the environment just as the colour of the light and the sound of the rain were parts of that ambience."

Beginning with his record, *Discreet Music,* Eno began to investigate music "that could be listened to and yet could be ignored"—quite similar to the goals of early 20th-century composer **Erik Satie**'s "furniture music"—which Eno termed "ambient music." The first part of *Discreet Music* involved a system of tape delay loops that processed two synthesizer melodies in various permutations, while the second part reconfigured the popular classical piece Pachelbel's *Canon* by altering the tempo of certain instruments. Both works clearly fell more in the realm of experimental composition than pop, and furthered Eno's earlier interests in self-generating and tape music.

### Jim O'Rourke, solo/Gastr del Sol

*I loved Eno. His record Discreet Music was absolutely huge, massive, gargantuan, one of the biggest eye-openers for me. He explained what he was doing in the liner notes, and that was the key because it was the first time one these records explained exactly what they were doing. That really got me into minimalism.*

Continuing along the ambient path of *Discreet Music*—which proved so calming it was used in hospitals for childbirth—Eno released a series of records to be used as aural decorations for the environment, including *Ambient #1/Music for Airports* (which was broadcast at LaGuardia Airport) and later, the evocative *Ambient #4/On Land*. Though these records are peaceful to the point of boring, Eno's ambient works definitely reward repeated listenings. While they can be blamed for giving birth to shelves of awful New Age music, they also inspired musicians over a decade later to explore the connections between tranquility and dance with "ambient house."

### Alex Patterson, the Orb

*I only met him once, like in 1984, at EG [Eno's label, where Patterson worked]. We shook hands and said hello, that was it, really. But the influence is there because I got the EG back catalogue [Eno's ambient work]. And that was the connection I put together, really. Dance music and ambient together in what became ambient house.*

While Eno's ambient works gained him few pop fans of his own, during the same years he was closely involved with a number of high-profile rock records. He produced the debut albums by Devo and Ultravox, and also compiled *No New York*, the essential document of the radical late '70s no wave scene (featuring **DNA** and **Lydia Lunch**). In addition, between 1977 and '79, Eno collaborated with David Bowie on a trilogy of albums—*Low, Heroes,* and *Lodger*—which many consider to be Bowie's artistic peak.

Eno helped shape the Talking Heads' sound by producing three of their early records. Following 1980's *Remain in Light*, on which Eno co-wrote many of the songs with Talking Heads leader David Byrne, he and Byrne collaborated on a hugely influential record, *My Life in the Bush of Ghosts*, that merged nonwestern (or "world") music with western dance beats—something he'd begun earlier with his *Possible Musics* release. Both records anticipated the next decade's ethno-techno/trance music of Banco de Gaia and Loop Guru.

## David Byrne

*We [Talking Heads] met him early on and he felt like a kindred spirit. Here's somebody who looks at music from a "what if" point of view. It's from a composer's point of view, but not from a musician with chops point of view. It was a way of breaking out of tried and true formulas. We also learned a few gimmicks, like the many uses of the Roland space echo.*

Beginning in the early '80s, Eno collaborated with Canadian producer Daniel Lanois. Early joint efforts included work on a record by Eno's brother, Roger, and with composer Harold Budd on *The Pearl.* Their best known co-credits, however, began in 1984 when they remade U2's sound on hugely popular albums, *The Unforgettable Fire* and *The Joshua Tree.* For 1991's *Achtung Baby,* Eno and Lanois earned themselves a Grammy for reshaping U2 once again. Though Lanois left to pursue other high-profile production work (including Bob Dylan and Peter Gabriel), Eno stayed on for the band's *Zooropa* album, and participated in yet another makeover on 1997's *Pop.* In 1995, Eno, along with the members of U2 (with guests including Luciano Pavarotti), recorded under the name Passengers. Their *Original Soundtracks* compiles music they'd written for imagined movies, something Eno had done decades earlier with his *Music for Films.*

The '90s have seen a bit more of everything Eno has offered in the past: more production work (for James, **John Cale**), more collaborations (with Cale, as well as **Public Image Limited**'s Jah Wobble), more ambient music (*Neroli*), and even a return to pop-oriented composition (*The Nerve Net*). Recently, composer **Philip Glass,** an important early influence, has arranged symphonic treatments of the three albums Eno made with David Bowie in the '70s. Beyond music, Eno has pursued visual art (through video works and installations), created CD-ROMs, appeared as a visiting professor, donated time to the War Child charity, published an extensive diary (*A Year with Swollen Appendices*), and even at one point conspired with Peter Gabriel and performance artist Laurie Anderson on developing a sort of multicultural avant-garde theme park in Europe. While he remains one step removed from the limelight, Eno continues to tirelessly push the limits of his own creativity—and by extension the creativity of everyone he's touched over the years.

## DISCOGRAPHY

*Here Come the Warm Jets* (Island, 1973; EG, 1982); continuing in the direction of Eno's work with Roxy Music, this first solo album is a triumph of eccentric pop.

(w/Robert Fripp) *(No Pussyfooting)* (Antilles, 1973; EG, 1981); an experimental guitar album featuring "Frippertronics."

*Taking Tiger Mountain (By Strategy)* (Island, 1974; EG, 1982).

(w/Kevin Ayers, **John Cale,** Nico) *June 1, 1974* (Island, 1974); a live album featuring former members of the Velvet Underground and Soft Machine.

*Another Green World* (Island, 1975; EG, 1982); Eno's classic, a middle ground between his pop-oriented early albums and the ambient directions he would head.

*Discreet Music* (Antilles, 1975; EG 1982); an album of highly listenable program and self-generative music.

(w/Robert Fripp) *Evening Star* (Antilles, 1975; EG, 1982).

*Before and After Science* (Island, 1977; EG, 1982); Eno's last vocal album for many years.

(w/Cluster) *Cluster and Eno* (Sky [Ger.], 1977); Eno's first collaboration with the German duo.

*Music for Films* (Antilles, 1978; EG, 1982); a collection of instrumental works created for use in films.

*Ambient 1/Music for Airports* (EG, 1978; 1982); the first full-fledged ambient work.

(w/Moebius and Roedelius) *After the Heat* (Sky [Ger.], 1978); another collaboration with the duo otherwise known as

Cluster.

(w/Harold Budd) *Ambient 2/The Plateux of Mirror* (EG, 1980).

(w/John Hassell) *Fourth World Volume 1: Possible Musics* (EG, 1980); an attempted meshing of western and non-Western music, with composer/trumpeter Hassell.

(w/David Byrne) *My Life in the Bush of Ghosts* (Sire, 1981); an acclaimed synthesis of non-Western music with techno beats.

*Ambient 4/On Land* (EG, 1982).

(w/Roger Eno, Daniel Lanois) *Apollo Atmospheres and Soundtracks* (EG, 1983); ambient music for a film about space travel to the moon.

*Working Backwards 1983–1973* (EG, 1984); an 11-disc box set containing all Eno albums in his first 10 years, plus one disc of rarities.

(w/Harold Budd) *The Pearl* (EG, 1984).

*Thursday Afternoon* (EG, 1985); the soundtrack for Eno's video piece of the same name.

(w/Cluster) *Old Land* (Relativity, 1985); a compilation of Eno's work with Cluster.

(w/John Hassell) *Power Spot* (ECM [Ger.], 1986).

*More Blank Than Frank* (EG, 1986); a collection of essential tracks from Eno's early albums.

*Desert Island Selection* (EG, 1989); a single-CD collection of Eno's own favorites from his early vocal albums.

(w/**John Cale**) *Wrong Way Up* (Opal/Warner Bros., 1990); a strong return to vocal music after over a decade away.

*The Shutov Assembly* (Opal/Warner Bros., 1992); an ambient album.

*Nerve Net* (Opal/Warner Bros., 1992); like many of his successors, Eno takes ambient into the world of dance music here.

*Neroli* (All Saints/Gyroscope, 1993); another ambient release.

*Brian Eno II/Vocal* (EG/Virgin, 1994); a box set collection of Eno's more pop-oriented vocal works.

*Brian Eno I/Instrumental* (EG/Virgin, 1994); a box set collection of Eno's ambient and experimental works.

(w/Robert Fripp) *The Essential Fripp & Eno* (EG/Virgin/Caroline, 1994); a collection from the two Fripp/Eno collaborations, including unreleased music.

(Passengers) *Original Soundtracks 1* (Island, 1995); best known as a U2 side project, this features the band and many guests, with Eno taking a larger role than his normal production duties.

(w/Jah Wobble) *Spinner* (All Saints/Gyroscope, 1995); a collaboration with the former **Public Image Limited** bassist.

*The Drop* (Thirsty Ear, 1997).

(Harmonia 76) *Tracks & Traces* (Rykodisc, 1997); a recently uncovered batch of recordings featuring **Neu!'s Michael Rother** and Cluster with Eno.

# A D R I A N   S H E R W O O D

*Producing the most whacked-out and unpredictable recordings in reggae, Sherwood has always driven the point home that musical boundaries are fluid. Sherwood's dissecting of songs is so over-the-top it baffles the mind and stomach to figure out how the ideas were ever generated. The haphazard sounds emanating from his records are a gold mine of inspiration for anyone seeking to deconstruct their music.*

**Johnny Temple, Girls Against Boys**

A white kid who grew up in England during the punk rock explosion of the '70s, Adrian Sherwood hardly fit the profile of someone destined to be a master producer of dub reggae. But in becoming just that, he brought the worlds of dub and rock closer together. With his On-U Sound label serving as the meeting ground, Sherwood applied dub's studio techniques to post-punk styles and used post-punk's wide-ranging sound palette to modernize and expand the possibilities of dub.

While he doesn't play a traditional instrument, Sherwood has done as much as anyone to define the studio itself as an instrument for creating and shaping sound. As such, Sherwood is an important reference point—particularly in the U.K.—for makers of electronic music in all genres, from techno to trip-hop to drum 'n' bass. In addition to countless projects at On-U, Sherwood has remixed some of the biggest acts of the '80s and '90s, including Depeche Mode, the Cure, Nine Inch Nails, Ministry, and Garbage, to name only a few.

### DJ Spooky (Paul Miller)

*Adrian Sherwood's On-U Sound stuff had a big impact compositionally. There's a more stark edge to the music, it sounds harder and iller [than other dub]. I grew up around the punk scene, so I have distorted guitars and bass as some of my earlier memories of social music. There's certain seminal people, and Adrian Sherwood really hit this core resonance of what music is about.*

Adrian Sherwood first became obsessed by reggae as a teen in the early '70s. In particular, he loved the eccentric studio effects of dub producers like **King Tubby** and **Lee Perry.** By 17, Sherwood was already importing and distributing Jamaican music to the U.K. through his company, Carib Gems. Though he'd soon go bankrupt, the experience provided Sherwood with contacts in reggae that he soon developed as an artist as well as a businessman.

In 1977, as punk rock ruled London's music scene, Sherwood started his own live dub reggae collective called Creation Rebel, whose debut album *Dub from Creation* he released on his new label Hit Run. Along with a second outfit called Prince Far I & the Arabs—which featured many of the same personnel—Sherwood formulated a core group of musicians and associates that would be behind most of the music throughout Sherwood's career. This included drummer Lincoln "Style" Scott, saxophonist Deadley Headley, bassists "Lizard" Logan and "Crucial" Tony Phillips, percussionist Bonjo Iyabinghi, keyboardist Dr. Pablo, and singers Bim Sherman and Prince Far I.

Early on, punk rock bands had voiced solidarity with the politically conscious reggae subculture in the U.K. (as in Jamaica) and were drawing inspiration from the music. Though Creation Rebel practiced a fairly traditional brand of dub reggae, Sherwood's posse was never very far from the punk scene, and the Clash invited the group to open for them on tour. By the early '80s, connections had been made with members of post-punk bands such as the **Slits,** the **Raincoats,** and **Public Image Limited,** and Sherwood's circle of collaborators had widened considerably.

### King Coffey, Butthole Surfers

*He pioneered the modern form of dub. There's no doubt the On-U label has been incredibly influential. At the time, every On-U record I could get my hands on seemed like a revelation. I just thought Adrian Sherwood was a god. He was challenging the very idea of what music is, using the actual studio and mixing board as an instrument. I recall when we were doing mixes of our first album, I said, "Damn, we should really do a dub remix of this stuff."*

In the late '70s new combinations of musicians formed a crop of groups around Sherwood, most notably New Age Steppers and Singer & Players, that combined post-punk's noise and roughness with dub's rhythms and studio processes. To anticipate the change in directions, in 1980 Sherwood—along with his wife Kishi Yamamoto and several partners—evolved Hit Run and other labels he'd been operating into a new umbrella label and organization he named On-U Sound. Between 1981 and '82, the label introduced no fewer than five of its major acts: In addition to New Age Steppers and Singers & Players, there were debuts by African Head Charge, London Underground, Dub Syndicate, and Playgroup, plus solo releases by Deadley Headley, Bim Sherman, and former **Brian Eno** collaborator Judy Nylon.

New Age Steppers' self-titled debut merged the On-U regulars with people like **Slits** vocalist Ari Up and **Raincoats** violinist Vicki Aspinall, as well as the Pop Group's Mark Stewart and members of Crass. Singers & Players' *War of Words* (released in the U.S. on minimalist funk label 99 Records) paired the seminal post-punk guitarist Keith Levene (of **Public Image Limited**) with On-U singers Sherman and Far I. Both releases proved dub could to be remarkably inclusive and flexible. By incorporating rock sounds and arrangements into dub, these records set an example that informs dub-influenced post-rock groups of today such as Tortoise.

---

*John McEntire, Tortoise:*
*There's a certain vocabulary that those guys use [in dub]. Adrian Sherwood has taken that vocabulary and developed it into something entirely new and exciting. It's inspiring, in terms of how far he's been able to push things.*

---

With African Head Charge, Sherwood and a group led by vocalist/percussionist Iyabinghi pursued their interest in fusing non-Western folk rhythms and African chanting (particularly African) with dance music. Inspired by the similar Brian Eno/David Byrne collaboration *My Life in the Bush of Ghosts* that had appeared earlier in the year, Sherwood titled AHC's debut *My Life in a Hole in the Ground*. Both records proved to be seminal works in the development of the ethno-techno/trance music of groups such as Banco de Gaia and Loop Guru in the '90s. While the "Style" Scott-led Dub Syndicate pursued more reggae-oriented dub, collaborations with Sherwood's eccentric hero Lee "Scratch" Perry ensured a requisite degree of madness in the music.

In the mid-'80s, Sherwood embarked on a new round of genre-hopping when he recruited the former house band at New York's premier early rap label, Sugar Hill Records. Guitarist Skip McDonald, bassist Doug Wimbish, and drummer Keith LeBlanc (whose earlier hit, "No Sell Out," introduced Malcolm X's rhetoric to hip-hop) had played on hits by Grandmaster Flash and the Sugarhill Gang and were ready for new musical adventures. The group's first On-U project, Mark Stewart and the Maffia, had them backing ex-Pop Group singer Stewart. Together with Sherwood and British M.C. ("chanter") Gary Clail, they constituted the On-U Sound System, or Tackhead Sound System; later, with the addition of vocalist Bernard Fowler, they were simply Tackhead. At its best, Tackhead combined the scorching elements of a hard funk musicianship with hip-hop beats and industrial effects. While dub was still an operative process in the music, the traditional reggae sounds were all but gone.

## Chris Connelly, the Bells/Ministry/Revolting Cocks

*Al [Jourgensen of Ministry] and I really bonded on things like Mark Stewart and the Maffia. As the Veneer of Democracy Starts to Fade, that's a noisy ass record. However, it was a rhythmic record, and that really appealed to me. Sherwood came from a more reggae background, but the records I really liked were the noisier ones. And I know Al learned a lot from him when [Sherwood] produced [Ministry's] Twitch.*

In the early '90s some of Sherwood's groups broke away from On-U completely, but Sherwood has continued to work both as a remixer for well-known artists and with newer On-U acts such as Revolutionary Dub Warriors and the techno-oriented Tribal Drift. His live dub collective, the On-U Sound System, continues to perform, carrying out its mission to bring the spirit of Jamaica's original sound systems into the next millenium.

## DISCOGRAPHY (SELECTED)

### CREATION REBEL

*Dub From Creation* (Hit Run, 1977); Sherwood's earliest, pre-On-U, release.

*Rebel Vibrations* (Hit Run, 1978).

*Close Encounters of the Third World* (Hit Run, 1979).

*Starship Africa* (On-U Sound, 1981).

(w/New Age Steppers) *Threat to Creation* (1981; Cherry Red, 1991); a joint release with another Sherwood project.

*Lows & Highs* (1982; Cherry Red, 1991).

*Historic Moments Vol. 1* (On-U Sound/Restless, 1994); a compilation of this earliest Sherwood project.

### NEW AGE STEPPERS

*New Age Steppers* (Statik, 1981); a striking debut mixing dub and post-punk sounds, with an all-star cast.

*Action Battlefield* (Statik, 1981); a follow-up featuring the Slits' Ari Up on vocals

*Foundation Steppers* (On-U Sound, 1992).

*Massive Hits Volume I* (On-U Sound/Restless, 1994); a compilation from the group's three studio albums.

### SINGERS AND PLAYERS

*War of Words* (99 Records, 1981).

*Revenge of the Underdog* (On-U Sound/Situation, 1982).

*Staggering Heights* (On-U Sound, 1983).

*Leaps & Bounds* (On-U Sound, 1984; 1991).

*Golden Greats Volume I* (On-U Sound, 1989); a compilation of the project's best material.

### AFRICAN HEAD CHARGE

*My Life in a Hole in the Ground* (On-U Sound, 1981); an Eno-inspired debut of world music in dub.

*Environmental Studies* (On-U Sound, 1982).

*Drastic Season* (On-U Sound, 1983).

*Off the Beaten Track* (On-U Sound, 1986).

*Great Vintage Vols. 1 & 2* (On-U Sound, 1989); a compilation of this group's earlier material.

*Songs of Praise* (On-U Sound, 1990, On-U Sound/Restless, 1994); features samples of religious music from around the world, with African percussion and dub effects.

*In Pursuit of Shashamane Land* (On-U Sound/Restless, 1994).

### DUB SYNDICATE

*Pounding System* (On-U Sound, 1982).

*One Way System* (ROIR, 1983); a cassette compilation of the group's early material.

(w/Dr. Pablo) *North of the River Thames* (On-U Sound, 1984).

*Tunes from the Missing Channel* (On-U Sound, 1985).

(w/Lee Perry) *Time Boom X De Devil Dead* (On-U Sound, 1987); the first of two collaborations with Perry.

*Strike the Balance* (On-U Sound, 1989).

*Classic Selection Vols 1–3* (On-U Sound, 1989; 1991; 1994); a series of compilations bringing together this group's choice cuts.

(w/Lee Perry) *From the Secret Laboratory* (Mango, 1990).

*Stoned Immaculate* (1991; On-U Sound/Restless, 1994).

*Echomania* (On-U Sound, 1993; On-U Sound/Restless, 1994).

*Ital Breakfast* (On-U Sound, 1996).

*Research & Development* (On-U Sound, 1996).

**MARK STEWART & THE MAFFIA**

*Learning to Cope with Cowardice* (On-U Sound/Plexus, 1983); industrial-style dub from the former member of the Pop Group.

*As the Veneer of Democracy Starts to Fade* (Mute, 1985).

*Mark Stewart & Maffia* (Upside, 1986); a U.S. compilation of the two earlier releases.

*Mark Stewart* (Mute, 1987).

*Metatron* (Mute, 1990).

**GARY CLAIL**

(w/Tackhead Sound System) *Tackhead Tape Time* (Nettwerk, 1988); the debut by Tackhead with British MC Gary Clail on vocals.

(w/On-U Sound System) *End of the Century Party* (On-U Sound, 1990).

**TACKHEAD**

*Friendly as a Hand Grenade* (TVT, 1989); Tackhead with singer Bernard Fowler in place of Clail.

**VARIOUS**

*Pay It All Back* (On-U Sound/Restless, 1994); a compilation featuring 13 different On-U acts and configurations.

*Reggae Archive* (On-U Sound/Restless, 1994); an On-U compilation heavy on Bim Sherman, but also featuring a variety of other Sherwood projects.

# 9

# ORIGINAL RAPPERS

Since rap music emerged as a musical genre nearly two decades ago, the question of where it came from has been much debated. But while the discussion is fascinating and informative, it's unlikely to produce a definitive answer. Suffice it to say that rapping is just the latest manifestation of a rich African and African-American tradition that includes all these and more: West African griots, the field hollers of slaves, the talking blues, church sermons of black preachers, schoolyard rhymes and backstreet toasts, the poetry performances of the Harlem Renaissance, the cadences of bebop that inspired the jazz poetry of Archie Shepp and the Beat poetry of Amiri Baraka, and, of course, the colorful boasts of Muhammad Ali.

The musical (and literary) figures included in this chapter are just a few of the most often cited precursors to the styles and attitudes we've come to know as hip-hop culture in general and rap music in particular. There is a traceable line from **U-Roy**'s talkover music to the DJs and MCs a decade later in the South Bronx, who added chanted vocals to already recorded music. The violent portrayals of criminality found in gangsta rap have their roots in **Iceberg Slim's** work. And in the music of the **Last Poets** (in the East), the Watts Prophets (in the West), and **Gil Scott-Heron** are recognizable precedents to the black consciousness and protest lyrics that have traditionally informed hip-hop music and culture.

---

### Michael Franti, Spearhead
*There was a kind of watermark stamped on hip-hop that said no matter where the music goes there has to be some kind of consciousness of black people—of liberation—in the music. Even though right now we've gone from a period where it was once "A Nation of Millions" to "How can I get millions?" I still believe that the moral foundation that those godfathers set out for all of us is something we all, at some point, have to answer to.*

---

Of course, hip-hop/rap culture, unlike rock, is still something that can be viewed as both artistically and socially revolutionary (until quite recently it seemed to be developing new manifestations and colorings at a dizzying pace), and its artists have had little interest in uncovering and championing little-known artists from the past. Until quite recently, nearly all of the best and most influential hip-hop has been commercially successful, making it technically ineligible for inclusion as "the most influential...you've never heard." However, while it would be wrong to claim that most of today's rappers have been directly influenced by the figures in this chapter, for setting precedents—and for inspiring those rhymers who influenced the rappers who taught the MCs of today—these musical precursors are worth taking a look at.

# U-ROY

*All ah we come from where Daddy Roy live, you know. Josey Wales is living in Kingston 11, you know. So is Super Cat, so is Bounty Killa, so is Beenie Man, so is Admiral Baily, so is Early B, so is many many more who come from that era there, you understand. Daddy Roy was the founder in the corporate metropolitan Kingston area in that time. So all the little youths who ah go to school, who love music and respond to musical vibes, was inspired by [him].*

**Super Cat [from Reggaematic website]**

While rap music can be tied to a long and varied line of African-American oral tradition, the specific style of rapping that developed in hip-hop music—with spoken rhymes over pre-recorded dance music—can be most directly traced to Jamaican talkover music, where a disc jockey rhymes along to the records he spins. The first DJ to popularize talkover was U-Roy, whose audience-rousing rants and amusing shout-outs to the popular songs he played at parties—and eventually released commercially—defined the art of deejaying that young Jamaicans like Kool Herc brought with them to the Bronx in the mid-'70s. And in applying U-Roy's talkover style to American funk music, these immigrant turntable showmen essentially became the first rappers.

---

**DJ Spooky (Paul Miller)**
*U-Roy was the first hip-hop MC, really. He was a huge influence. Especially I loved his vocal inflection and the way he rhymed, the rhythm patterns and the way he mixes his voice into that.*

---

Though most current rappers are too far removed from U-Roy to be aware of their debt to him, makers of rap's Jamaican equivalent (actually a precursor)—a style called dancehall—openly acknowledges U-Roy as "The Originator" of their toasting style. Popular dancehall stars such as Shabba Ranks, Buju Banton, and Super Cat, as well as reggae-flavored American rap groups such as Spearhead and the Fugees, have been directly influenced by U-Roy's vocal style. And U-Roy's earliest recordings—which are essentially previous hits with U-Roy's vocal track added—provide a

clear historical context for notorious hip-hop recyclers like Puff Daddy.

U-Roy was born Ewart Beckford in 1942 and grew up in a Kingston, Jamaica, shantytown. By his late teens, he had become involved in the world of sound systems, the popular mobile DJ setups that traveled the Jamaican countryside playing the latest R&B and ska records. These sound systems would announce locations where they were setting up outdoor dances (not unlike the more recent raves), and it was the DJ's job to offer the best mix of music while he entertained and inspired audiences to dance with funny, often rhythmic, banter known as toasting. Jamaican DJ toasting, introduced in the '50s by Count Machouki, was an outgrowth of the flamboyant announcing styles of radio DJs in the southern U.S.

### Wyclef Jean, the Fugees

*For me, U-Roy was definitely one of the founders of that toasting style. I grew up with all that stuff, because my uncle had a sound system. I'm not Jamaican, but I grew up with Jamaican music.*

As a DJ during the '60s, U-Roy developed his toasting style with sound systems such as Dickie's Dynamic, Sir George Atomic, and the popular Coxone's Downbeat Sound System. With **King Tubby**'s prestigious Home Town Hi-Fi sound system in 1968, U-Roy developed a reputation for a toasting style that was more clever and inventive, as well as faster, than any other DJ around. By 1969, when U-Roy entered Duke Reid's Treasure Isle studio to record his toasts, popular DJs such as King Stitt had already released their own talkover recordings. It was U-Roy's string of hits in 1970, though, that made talkover a commercially viable style that would spawn numerous U-Roy imitators and evolve into both dancehall and rap. His "Rule the Nation," "Wake the Town," and "Wear You to the Ball"—all recorded over **King Tubby** dubs that removed vocals from popular songs—simultaneously occupied the top three positions on the Jamaican music charts.

### Michael Franti, Spearhead

*U-Roy was probably one of the first people to every really rap on a record. To take a dub plate and put his own lyrics on it, and put it out as another record. Which is what people are doing today with sampling. "Wake the Town" is a wicked track.*

U-Roy's huge popularity can be attributed, in part, to his use of familiar backing tracks. But more, U-Roy built on the nonsensical scatting of previous DJs with eccentric catchphrases like "This station rules the nation with version" (familiar to American pop audiences through its adaptation on Musical Youth's "Pass the Dutchie") and humorous running commentary to bits of the original lyric (such as "did you hear what the man says, baby? Dig my soul brothers and soul sisters!"). As younger toasters such as I-Roy and Big Youth emerged to further advance the style he'd introduced, U-Roy became known as Daddy Roy, or simply "the King."

In 1975, U-Roy signed with British label Virgin, who introduced his music to larger audiences than ever before. By then, U-Roy had embraced Rastafarianism and his lyrics had taken on the more spiritual slant heard on *Dread in Babylon* and later releases. Back in Jamaica, he also began his own Daddy Roy Sound System, which introduced other top DJs such Charlie Chaplin and Josey Wales. Now in his late fifties and living in Southern California, U-Roy continues to record and perform around the world.

## DISCOGRAPHY

*Dread in Babylon* (Virgin 1976; Caroline, 1991); U-Roy's first album available outside of Jamaica.

*Natty Rebel* (Virgin 1976; Caroline, 1991).

*Rasta Ambassador* (Virgin, 1977; Caroline, 1991).

*Version Galore* (Front Line, 1978); this collection features many of U-Roy's early hits, and offers a good taste of the original "talkover" style.

*Jah Son of Africa* (Front Line, 1979).

*Crucial Cuts* (Virgin, 1983); a collection of the best tracks from his Virgin records.

*Music Addict* (RAS, 1987).

*True Born African* (Ariwa, 1991).

*Rock with I* (RAS, 1992).

*Smile a While* (Ariwa, 1993).

*3 Pack* (Caroline, 1994); a three-CD box set retrospective.

*Original DJ* (Caroline, 1995).

*Your Ace from Space* (Trojan [UK], 1995).

*Babylon Kingdom Must Fall* (Ariwa, 1997).

# L A S T   P O E T S

*When I look back on the things I heard, I see the Last Poets as inspirational on us as rappers and composers. They were the first ones to keep it real, to deal with the attitudes and emotions of what was going on in society. They were the first ones to inspire you to speak out and not hold it back. Express your opinion. By them doing what they did, it helped us do it on record. We're using the same heart, the same expression.*

*Darryl McDaniels, Run-D.M.C.*

Though it was not necessarily the most direct antecedent of today's rap music, the Last Poets' technique of laying rhythmic poetry on a beat provided early hip-hoppers with an important example of how vocals could be used to confront social issues and raise black consciousness. By the late '80s, groups like Public Enemy, A Tribe Called Quest, and Michael Franti's Disposable Heroes of Hiphoprisy were drawing direct connections between their music and what the Last Poets had done two decades earlier. Yet perhaps the Last Poets' example as a band of writers and vocalists working under one unified name was even more important than their message in laying the groundwork for the modern rap group.

### Michael Franti, Spearhead

*The Last Poets may not have invented rap, but they were definitely there when rap was being invented. The idea of storytelling and talking over a beat is something they advanced. It's important to look at those pioneers and see that when rap was coming out as an artform it wasn't just all about trying to get ahead and make money. Voices were reaching out and saying things, because they weren't being said somewhere else. They brought a voice to people who weren't being represented. I definitely dug what they were doing. It wasn't just singing or rhyming, you could get out there and say what you want on top of a beat, and say it in a poetic fashion.*

---

The three original Last Poets first performed together in May of 1968, at a Malcolm X birthday celebration in Harlem. They were three distinct individuals, all products of their time: David Nelson ran an antipoverty program and was closely involved with the black students' movement at Columbia University. Gylain Kain was a downtown bohemian poet in the mold of one of the group's direct predecessors, Amiri Baraka (LeRoi Jones). And Charles Franklin Davis—who would soon adopt the Yoruba religion and change his name to Abiodun Oyewole—was the middle-class product of upward mobility whose belief in integration had been severely shaken by the assassination of Martin Luther King only a month earlier.

The trio extrapolated their name from South African writer K. William Kgositsile, who wrote that the time for poetry would soon end as the revolution begins. "The goal was to revolutionize the world using poetry as our weapon," Oyewole says. "To make people wake up before the shit hit the fan." Such noble intentions required more than the strength of a single writer. "Poets are generally individuals, set aside from everyone else. But to put three strong individuals together was saying the problem is such where we have to bring ourselves to some collective to address it."

### Afrika Baby Bam (Nathaniel Hall), Jungle Brothers
*The Last Poets influenced me from a cultural standpoint. Communicating to me what was going on around the times I was born. They educated me about the way society was and to a certain degree still is. Just the spirit of the music is what influenced me to write the way I write.*

---

### Sammy B, Jungle Brothers
*My parents listened to it, and that really influenced me because they were really into the black movement and I was really exposed to it at a young age.*

---

As the Last Poets' popularity grew through performances and workshops, the possibility of recording arose. But as Kain vehemently opposed the capitalist notion of becoming a "recording artist" and Nelson returned to community organizing, only Oyewole was left to carry on the Last Poets name. By 1969, he'd brought in two new poets who had been hanging around the group: Omar Ben Hassen and Alafia Puddim. It was this new trio that Alan Douglas (Jimi Hendrix's producer) first saw on community television, and it was Douglas who first brought the group in to record their poems and chants on record.

With Douglas, the trio recorded two albums—*The Last Poets* in 1970 and *This Is Madness* in 1971—that would forever secure their reputation. Featuring the African-styled conga of percussionist Nilaja and the group's incessant chanting, the poets took turns reciting revolutionary verse to a beat. Tracks like "Niggers Are Scared of Revolution," "White Man's Got a God Complex," "Time" (later sampled by A Tribe Called Quest), and "Run, Nigger" (sampled by N.W.A.) seethed with a passionate commitment to the struggle for black empowerment. Despite radical, often inflammatory language, the Last Poets' reputation spread by word of mouth in the black community. Even without a mainstream breakthrough, the debut reached #29 on the Billboard album charts in 1970.

### Wyclef Jean, the Fugees

*That was a major influence. Conscious rap. It made me be aware of what I'm saying. Listening to the Last Poets was like street poetry. It taught you a lot of things you didn't know.*

By *This Is Madness,* though, Oyewole had dropped out(as he says, "Words weren't enough, I needed to be directly involved") and original Last Poets David Nelson and Gylain Kain believed that Puddim and Ben Hassen were unqualified to carry on the group name. With Puerto Rican poet Felipe Luciano, Nelson and Kain formed a second Last Poets, who documented their work in the film *Right On!* before dispersing shortly after. By 1972, Ben Hassen had left his version of the Last Poets as well.

That left only Puddim, renamed Jalaluddin Mansur Nuriddin after converting to Islam, to carry the Last Poets through the '70s. Along with fellow poet Suliaman El-Hadi, the group released albums such as *Chastisement* and *At Last,* which introduced increasing amounts of instrumental accompaniment and singing to the spoken word—a style they called "jazzoetry." During this time, Nuriddin also recorded work under the name Lightnin' Rod that, while less revolutionary, was at least as influential. Following an earlier recording of the traditional toast "Doriella Du Fontaine" that featured Hendrix on guitar, Lightnin' Rod released an album in 1973 called *Hustler's Convention.* The album-long epic tale of a street-player gathering featured the funk accompaniment of Kool & the Gang, as well as other known musicians. With its more danceable accompaniment and colorful story, the record became a favorite of New York deejays in the mid- and late '70s, when it was undoubtedly owned and heard by the founding fathers of hip-hop.

### Chuck D, Public Enemy

*Around '78 or '79 I got into Hustler's Convention and backtracked from there. Hustler's Convention was pretty much the thing that launched the whole rhyme scene in the Bronx. A lot of people took a lot of the verbiage off that record. Like Melle Mel—"rock your world, from the top of the world to the depths of hell"—that type of stuff.*

After a decade away from recording, Nuriddin and El-Hadi's Last Poets returned for one Bill Laswell–produced album in the '80s. This version of the group emerged once more, for a 1994 album released only in France, before El-Hadi passed away. By then, Omar Ben Hassen (now Umar Bin Hassan, since adopting Islam) had resurfaced, with a new album (also produced by Laswell), *Be Bop or Be Dead.* The record contained new poems as well as updates of Last Poets classics, and reunited Bin Hassan with original Last Poet Abiodun Oyewole.

Since 1993, Bin Hassan and Oyewole's revitalized Last Poets have released two new albums—featuring guests such as Grandmaster Melle Mel, Chuck D, and members of P-Funk—and performed in concert (in Lollapalooza '94) and the movies (in John Singleton's *Poetic Justice*). Their 1997 album, *Time Has Come,* even features Umar's rapping sons. The two remain keenly aware of the role they play as hip-hop elder statesmen, and are concerned about the direction rap has taken. Oyewole hosts an open house each Sunday in Harlem, where poets can discuss their work and current issues. Over the years, many rappers have attended as well. "It's a wonderful thing," Oyewole says. "I appreciate the relationship I have with members of the Wu-Tang, KRS-One, Rakim, MC Lyte, Brand Nubian, A Tribe Called Quest, Chuck D, on and on. There's quite a number who have given us props and who we have a lot of respect for."

## DISCOGRAPHY

*Last Poets* (Douglas, 1970; Restless Retro, 1992); the classic debut as a trio, with powerful spoken poems such as "Niggers Are Scared of Revolution."

*This Is Madness* (Douglas, 1971; Restless Retro, 1992); recorded as a duo, but featuring equally rich and ferocious proto-raps.

*Chastisement* (Blue Thumb, 1972; Celluloid, 1992); the first record with the '70s line-up of poets Nuriddin and El-Hadi, as well as added musical accompaniment.

*At Last* (Blue Thumb, 1973).

(Lightnin' Rod) *Hustlers Convention* (Casablanca, 1973; Celluloid, 1990); a classic blaxploitation record, with an extended toast by Nuriddin and funk backing by Kool & the Gang.

*Delights of the Garden* (Casablanca, 1975; Celluloid, 1985).

*Oh My People* (Celluloid, 1985); a Nuriddin/El-Hadi reunion, with slick production and cheesy dance beats.

*Freedom Express* (Celluloid, 1991).

*Retro Fit* (Celluloid, 1992).

(Umar Bin Hassan) *Be Bop or Be Dead* (Axiom/Island, 1993); Bin Hassan's return to music, which includes remakes of two early Last Poets classics.

*Scatterap/Home* (Bond Age [France], 1994); a final Nuriddin/El-Hadi record, released only in France.

*Holy Terror* (Black Arc/Rykodisc, 1995); the first of the new Last Poets releases, with Bin Hassan and Oyewole.

(Abiodun Oyewole) *25 Years* (Black Arc/Rykodisc, 1996).

*Time Has Come* (Mouth Almighty/Mercury, 1997); a partial return to the percussion and chanting style of the first records, this strong effort features a guest appearance by Chuck D.

## WATTS PROPHETS

*I knew about them because I collected records. They didn't make a lot of history books, at least not the ones I read. The Watts Prophets were the unsung heroes of spoken word. They had a different perspective, being from California. Over the years, they never diluted the message. It's surprising, because after so long not getting much mainstream attention, most people have a tendency to accommodate a larger audience somehow. That's really admirable. And they continue to be an inspiration because of their perseverance.*

**Lyrics Born**

At a time when the record industry was more regionalized, it was possible for similar movements to take hold at opposite ends of the country without one having any knowledge of the other. Given the mounting frustrations in black America and the artistic blossoming in the late '60s, it seems almost inevitable that a group would arise to voice the same percussive poetry in Watts, Los Angeles, as the **Last Poets** offered in Harlem, New York. Though lesser known than the Last Poets, the Watts Prophets laid the groundwork for an L.A. hip-hop scene that would produce both the gangsta rap of N.W.A. and the message-oriented pop of Coolio (both of whom have sampled the Watts Prophets), as well as the more clearly Prophets-influenced underground lyricism of Freestyle Fellowship.

*Aceyalone, solo/Freestyle Fellowship:*
*We did a couple shows with the Watts Prophets. It was an honor. The inspiration I get comes from being from the same area as them. And their subject matter, how they keep it positive. And they're still around in the community.*

In essence, the Watts Prophets were born out of the 1965 Watts riots. Among the people who stepped forward to help rebuild the community after the devastation was Budd Schulberg, a Hollywood screenwriter best known for writing *On the Waterfront*. He set up the Watts Writers Workshop to provide a place for young aspiring writers in the neighborhood to learn and share their work. One participant was Anthony Hamilton, an eighth-grade dropout who had recently spent time in jail and was having difficulty finding his way out of the criminal life. At a poverty program he met writer Odie Hawkins, who invited Hamilton to the Writers Workshop. Though he initially came for the free food, Hamilton ended up reciting some poetry he'd scribbled on scraps of paper. When the response from others was positive, he was hooked. "I could say a poem saved my life," he told Brian Cross in *It's Not About a Salary*. "Because from that poem I realized I could do something. I had something inside of me."

Because of its success, the workshop received extensive media attention. When schools and organizations around the country began to invite members of the workshop to come speak, the poets began to group into units for the purpose. Hamilton hooked up with Otis O'Solomon, an Alabama native who moved to L.A. in his teens, and Richard Dedeaux, who'd arrived from Louisiana around the same time. By 1968 the trio (who would soon adopt the name Watts Prophets) began performing at local gatherings as well as in well-known L.A. night clubs. Their act combined socially critical verse with theatrical performance in a way that both thrilled and outraged the audience. At one of these shows—at USC in 1969—the Watts Prophets shared a stage with the **Last Poets**. Though they had been doing similarly styled black-awareness spoken-word poetry, it was the first time either group had heard of the other.

Around this time, Laff Records—a comedy label best known for releasing Richard Pryor's first album—approached Hamilton and other Watts poets about recording an album. Because the subject matter was anything but comical, Laff set up the ALA label to release an album called *The Black Voices: On the Street in Watts*. Along with work by Odie Hawkins (who would become a well-known novelist), Ed Bereal, and Emmery Lee Joseph Evans Jr., Hamilton contributed nine provocative poems—including "I'll Stop Calling You Niggers" and "Pimping, Leaning, and Feaning"—set to Last Poets—style percussion and other instrumental background.

The following year, Hamilton brought his fellow Watts Prophets to the attention of ALA. Though the album they did for the label, *Rappin' Black in a White World,* marks the first time "rap" was used on record to describe black spoken-word performance, it was more conceptually and stylistically broad than the usual rap album, with extended suites that included character monologues like "The Master" and manifestos such as "Amerikkka" (a spelling later adopted on Ice Cube's first album). Tying it all together were the bluesy piano compositions of Dee Dee McNeil, a former Motown songwriter who had been collaborating with the trio since 1969. Her contributions, along with the use of strings and soulful singing, make *Black in a White World* as rich and varied musically as it is lyrically.

### DJ Quik

*I heard 'em when I was a kid, it was scary cause it was too radical for me. I was like five, though, when I got into it. I think the real reason I remembered it and the reason I wanted to use it was because of how blatantly scary and formidable it was, it was thought-provoking and fearful. They were the first rappers in the truest sense, they been doing it since the sixties. If what you consider rap is philosophizing over rhythmic African type beats, they paved the way for this shit. [from It's Not About a Salary (Verso, 1993)]*

Though McNeil returned to performing solo in jazz clubs shortly after, the Watts Prophets continued performing throughout the '70s. They contributed to albums by Quincy Jones (*Mellow Madness*, featuring O'Solomon's "Beautiful Black Girl"), Stevie Wonder (*Songs in the Key of Life*), and Don Cherry (*Multi-Kulti*) and did concerts at colleges and prisons across the country. When the Watts Prophets stopped performing around 1980, each focused on outside work: Dedeaux and O'Solomon did work in film and television, as actors, writers, and producers, and continued to help with community poetry projects. Hamilton became Father Amde, a leader in the Ethiopian Orthodox Church, through which he befriended Bob Marley and his family (Ziggy Marley recorded O'Solomon's "Hey World (Part I)").

In an eerie case of history repeating itself, the South Central L.A. rioting of the early '90s spurred the Watts Prophets into activity once again. Now elder statesmen in a hip-hop scene that has widely sampled their work (including DJ Quik and DJ Shadow), the trio have reemerged as outspoken community leaders. After an EP produced by the Dust Brothers, the Watts Prophets produced *When the 90's Came*, their first new album in 25 years. Featuring appearances by DJ Quik, US3, and Blackalicious on tracks that mix new material and old, the record brings the group full circle in the story of west coast rap. And with tracks like the updated "I Remember Watts" (originally written in 1967), the Watts Prophets are as relevant as ever.

## DISCOGRAPHY

*The Black Voices: On the Street in Watts* (ALA, 1970; ffrr, 1996); featuring Hamilton and other area poets, this **Last Poets**-styled poetry album is not officially a Watts Prophets creation, though it has since been credited to the group.

*Rappin' Black in a White World* (ALA, 1971; ffrr, 1996); the group's finest statement, incorporating songs and monologues into a unified conceptual suite that captures the characters and feelings of life in Watts.

*When the 90's Came* (Payday/ffrr, 1996); a newly produced reunion album featuring new poems as well as reworkings of old material, this record incorporates modern hip-hop elements and production from DJ Quik.

# GIL SCOTT-HERON

*His voice resonates with sincerity. He's not the greatest singer technically, but he has developed his own great style. He invests his voice with meaning, and people take it to heart. Gil is someone I've always respected. I've spent time talking with him about content in music. What is the moral basis of an artist? Do we just put stuff out into a vacuum—the music business and entertainment world—or does the music go out into people's cars and living rooms and find a way into their heart? He's somebody who feels very strongly that artists bring out emotions people don't always have a chance to express. And doing that comes with a responsibility.*

**Michael Franti, Spearhead**

Like the **Last Poets,** who directly inspired him, Gil Scott-Heron provided an early template for hip-hop consciousness and '90s spoken-word poetry. He's been sampled by rappers ranging from Queen Latifah to Masta Ace, and cited by street poets such as Reg E. Gaines and Mike Ladd. Much of his career, though, has been dedicated to incorporating his earlier politically aware lyrics with deeply soulful music. In doing so, he has created a series of multidimensional recordings that go beyond black power rhetoric to capture the richness of African-American life with wit and wordplay, and with powerful humanism and lots of common sense. In doing so, he's been a major inspiration to more song-oriented hip-hop groups like Spearhead and the Fugees, as well as musicians in all genres, and anybody else who's ever invoked his most famous words, "the revolution will not be televised."

### Mase, De La Soul

*The issues he would touch in his poetry was like the same thing rappers are talking about today. He had a certain type of cadence and style that he flowed to make you interested in what he was talking about. Gil Scott is definitely one of the inspiring lyricists to De La, for sure.*

Though he was born in Chicago, Gil moved to Jackson, Tennessee, when his Jamaican pro soccer playing father and librarian mother divorced, and was raised by his grandmother. By the time he rejoined his mother in New York City as a teen, Scott-Heron was already a talented writer, and his work earned him acceptance into a prestigious private high school. While still in college (Lincoln University, the alma mater of Gil's literary hero Langston Hughes) he published two novels—*The Vulture* and *The Nigger Factory*—and a book of verse, *Small Talk at 125th and Lenox.*

As Scott-Heron became more politicized in the late '60s, he decided to leave college and return to New York to focus on his increasingly political writing. When it became clear to him that he could reach more people through radio than books, Gil decided to set his volume of poetry to music and record it. Inspired by what he'd seen of the **Last Poets,** Gil's first album in 1970 (also called *Small Talk*) consisted mostly of spoken pieces set to percussion, such as "The Revolution Will Not Be Televised" and "Whitey on the Moon." In addition, songs like "Who'll Pay Reparations on My Soul?" offered Richie Havens—style singing and piano-driven gospel soul.

### Mike G., Jungle Brothers

*I was around it. Even back then, every little element of what he was doing had so much strength. Growing up in Harlem, you could see the effect it had on your elders. A pride about being black, a positive mindstate. It was about black upliftment.*

Though his deep voice, mixed with fierce intelligence and lyrical humor, was more than enough to get Scott-Heron's poetry across, it wasn't long before he drifted away from the bare-bones spoken-word style of the **Last Poets** toward the more musical approach he'd hinted at on *Small Talk*. Beginning a collaboration with keyboardist Brian Jackson, a friend and former bandmate from Lincoln University, Scott-Heron produced a series of jazz and soul ballad records in the early '70s that stand among his best work. Though 1971's *Pieces of a Man* focused on introspective material, such as "I Think I'll Call It Morning" and the title track, it included a reworked funk version of "The Revolution Will Not Be Televised" that became Scott-Heron's most enduring work—sampled, quoted, or adapted by countless rappers, writers, and even advertising executives. On 1972's *Free Will*, Scott-Heron reconciled his opposing impulses—spoken and sung, political and personal—by offering one side of full-band songs and one side of spoken word with percussion and flute accompaniment. By 1974's *Winter in America*, the music of Scott-Heron and Jackson had progressed to a level of sophistication where the socially conscious ("The Bottle") and the personal ("Your Daddy Loves You") were seamlessly integrated.

### Jenny Toomey, Tsunami/Licorice

*I love Gil Scott-Heron. I did a paper on him in high school, based on the song "The Bottle." I was writing about how clever it was to put this [anti-alcohol] message into music that was going to be played at rock clubs. He's so clever in the way he twists things. For a long time I've wanted to cover "Pieces of a Man," but how could I? I'd feel like a bad white girl singing "God Bless the Child" on Star Search.*

In 1975, Scott-Heron's music was introduced to a wider audience when he became the first act signed to Arista Records, the label started by famed record executive Clive Davis. With his newly formed Midnight Band, he and Jackson injected mid-'70s albums such as *The First Minute of a New Day* with a richer, more orchestrated sound. *From South Africa to South Carolina* produced a hit with "Johannesburg," one of the earliest pop songs to confront the issue of apartheid (it would be another 10 years before he would inspire and participate in the star-studded antiapartheid album, *Sun City*). In other songs, Scott-Heron's sharply critical lyrics focused on nuclear proliferation ("We Almost Lost Detroit") and his continued concern for the plight of urban America.

---

### Chuck D, Public Enemy
*I knew about Gil Scott-Heron when he was out in '74 and '75, but later on, finding out what he did was a big help. It just rang a lot of bells. When I decided to do Public Enemy in that particular way, it came from trying to infuse what we knew as children in the '60s into rap. I found a lot of the topics I was delving into in rap were already thoroughly covered in a different level of poetry.*

---

Though Scott-Heron split with Jackson in the late '70s and formed a new band, Amnesia Express, he continued to make music that combined soulful vocals with humanistic and socially aware lyrics. In the early '80s, current president Reagan and his conservative regime became a popular target in songs such as "B Movie" and "Re-Ron." In that more apathetic age, though, Scott-Heron's music seemed out of place. Though he continued to perform to capacity audiences, after 1982's *Moving Target* he stopped recording for over a decade.

---

### Darryl McDaniels, Run-D.M.C.
*We used to rap over his music back in the day. Before rap records were even made, if you were a DJ and didn't have his records in your crate, something was wrong. I look at Gil Scott-Heron as one of the ambassadors of his time. What made us so popular was we were speaking for the youth. Gil Scott-Heron, along with the **Last Poets,** were the artists and philosophers and men of wisdom of their time. Speaking what a lot of people were either afraid to say, or were held back from saying. They used their records and poetry to express things people weren't saying.*

---

In 1994 Gil entered a recording studio to produce *Spirits,* a strong return that bridged generations with "Don't Give Up," a song produced by Ali Shaheed Muhammed of A Tribe Called Quest. Subsequently he was seen on MTV and appeared at Woodstock '94. By then, politically aware hip-hop and spoken-word artists had acknowledged his important legacy, which Gil himself addressed in *Spirits'* "Message to the Messengers." As he reiterated for *Vibe's* James Ledbetter, "If I have any influence [with rappers], then let me use it to ask them to say something positive with theirs, to get off some of this dumb shit and to start using the influence that they have. If they admire what we did, then use it in the same fashion that we tried to. To say things that are positive for people and about people." In this, Scott-Heron continues to challenge, and lead by example.

## DISCOGRAPHY

*Small Talk at 125th and Lenox* (Flying Dutchman, 1970; RCA, 1993); a mostly spoken-word album, stylistically indebted to the **Last Poets**.

*Pieces of a Man* (Flying Dutchman, 1971; RCA, 1993); a collection of jazz and soul compositions with full-band accompaniment, including "The Revolution Will Not Be Televised."

*Free Will* (Flying Dutchman, 1972; RCA, 1993); an album split between sung piano songs and spoken word/percussion pieces.

*The Revolution Will Not be Televised* (Flying Dutchman, 1974); a compilation of the early Flying Dutchman material.

*Winter in America* (Strata/East, 1974; TVT, 1998); a varied collection of songs that remains unified in its vision.

*The First Minute of a New Day* (Arista, 1975; TVT, 1998); the first to feature the Midnight Band.

*From South Africa to South Carolina* (Arista, 1975; TVT, 1998); taking an internationalist view of social problems, this is Gil's most overtly political work since his debut.

*It's Your World* (Arista, 1975; TVT, 1998); a live double album.

*Bridges* (Arista, 1977; TVT, 1998); a solo album featuring Gil's new band, Amnesia Express.

*Secrets* (Arista, 1978; TVT, 1998).

*The Mind of Gil Scott-Heron* (Arista, 1979; TVT, 1998); a compilation of the late '70s Arista material. *1980* (Arista, 1980).

*Real Eyes* (Arista, 1980).

*Reflections* (Arista, 1981).

*Moving Target* (Arista, 1982); Gil's last studio recording before re-emerging in the '90s.

*The Best of Gil Scott-Heron* (Arista, 1984; 1991); an anthology of Gil's best known work.

*Spirits* (TVT, 1994); his first new album in 12 years, this is a surprisingly rich and up-to-date record that proves his music is still viable today.

# ICEBERG SLIM

*Although I never met the man, Iceberg Slim was to have a profound effect on my career and life. Even before I knew who he was, I knew the man's words. Ghetto hustlers in my neighborhood would talk this nasty dialect rich with imagery of sex and humor. My buddies and I wanted to know where they picked it up, and they'd told us, "You better get into some of that Iceberg stuff!"*

**Ice-T [from his introduction to *Pimp* (Payback Press UK, 1996)]**

Robert Beck—the man better known as Iceberg Slim, the "godfather of gangsta rap"—has inspired generations of rappers, from Ice-T and Ice Cube (whose names pay tribute to Slim) to Snoop Doggy Dogg (who has vied with Ice-T to play Slim in the film version of his autobiography). Slim's novels, masterpieces of pulp fiction, have introduced glossaries full of ghetto slang to rappers, readers, and fans who've never come near the 'hood. Though he was a novelist and not a lyricist or musician, he did record one album of his gritty stories set to jazz backing. But even if he'd never entered a recording studio, Iceberg Slim's huge influence on the language and themes of gangsta rap would remain.

### Lyrics Born

*His slang is the shit. When you're dealing with lyrics, you're dealing with flipping words in different ways, and hearing new slang is always intriguing. But the biggest thing that I got from him is how everyone's just trying to make a quick buck because they know it's going to be gone.*

*Everything was "cop and blow," everything is transitive. It really helps when I look at things in life, they're just so impermanent you really take advantage of the moment. One of the things you learn from reading Iceberg Slim is that everything passes, you can only be a player for so long. You can only be anything for so long. It's kind of inspirational, the theme—obviously I don't want to be a pimp—but the observations are interesting.*

---

Beck was born in Chicago in 1918. Though he grew up in Milwaukee and even attended Tuskeegee Institute for a short time in the 1930s (where he was a classmate of another African-American literary giant, Ralph Ellison), he soon dropped out and returned to the streets of Chicago. It was there, before he'd reached the age of 20, that Beck embarked on a life of crime. As a pimp he was called Iceberg Slim, a fitting name for the role he assumed as the archetypal black hustler. Tall and thin—dressed in the flashiest threads and a pricey leather overcoat—Slim used his considerable intellectect to develop a persona well-suited for his cut-throat world. Like an evil street genius, Slim studied and calculated his every move, using cruelty and intimidation to maintain control over his prostitutes. He didn't just live the life, he became the game's top student and Chicago's most enduring pimp.

Beck continued this way for decades, occasionally landing in jail for his deeds, but always returning to the life when he got out. In the early '60s, after escaping from prison and being recaptured, Beck was given 10 months in solitary. During his confinement, Beck had plenty of time to reconsider his life, and when he got out, Beck decided not to return to pimping, but to write about his experiences. The result, published in 1969 under the name Iceberg Slim, was *Pimp: The Story of My Life*. The novel let readers into a world that was rarely covered by detective novels or Hollywood gangster films: the black criminal underworld. His chilling depiction of the hustling life alternately glorified the thrills and laid down the spills without moralizing. Beck understood the tragedy of black urban life that sometimes necessitated crime. But while he had thrived and ultimately survived the game, he knew most don't.

With its street jive and rich characterization, *Pimp* became a huge success, both inside the black community—where, for better or worse, he became something of a folk hero—and outside. Universal Studios even bought the film rights to the book, though they soon determined it was too hot to handle. A movie was made of *Trick Baby*, Beck's second book, the fictional tale of a light-skinned hustler whose ability to pass as white provided advantages in crime. By then, the genre of blaxploitation—which *Pimp* had helped define—was well established, and Iceberg Slim was among the best-selling black novelists in America.

---

**DJ Spooky:**
*All these rappers read that stuff. People think hip-hop artists don't read. They do read, but they read books outside the normal zone. They'd much rather read Iceberg Slim than Ernest Hemingway. Everyone's going to read something that speaks to their own experiences more.*

---

As Beck's novels moved further away from his personal experiences—such as with *Death Wish*, an attempt to write about the Italian mafia—they were less successful. Though he'd long been criticized by groups such as the Black Panthers for glorifying his victimization of black women, by the mid-'70s his own personal guilt and his mother's disappointment weighed heavily upon him (which he reveals in his collection of essays *The Naked Soul of Iceberg Slim*). His sole recording, 1976's *Reflections,* contrasts his brutal pimp stories with "Mama Debt," a son's final plea for forgiveness. Beck began doing lecture tours at colleges—some of which had begun teaching his works as part of the "rogue novel" tradition—and speaking more directly about the emptiness and destructiveness of criminality. He also became something of an activist in the black community. From that period until his death in 1992, at age 74, Iceberg Slim lived a quiet life. Bob, as he was known to friends, married and had four kids. He continued to speak at schools and occasionally write from his home in Los Angeles. By the time he died, his works had sold over 6 million copies, and his legacy of ghetto horror stories was fast becoming the dominant flavor in hip-hop music.

### Ice-T

*Later in my life, I turned back to his works and realized that although he was a pimp, he had become a writer. It was a revelation, because nobody tells you when you're young that being a criminal or a pimp or a gangster can lead to anything positive. But because of him, I decided that although I was on the street doing wrong, I could take this experience and turn it into something else, possibly something constructive.... Like him, I wanted to be somebody who didn't just die there out on the streets. I wanted to be able to document some of my experiences, and that's what I've been trying to do in my music for the past decade. I took my rap name in tribute to him, and I've never regretted it. [from his introduction to Pimp (Payback Press UK, 1996)]*

## DISCOGRAPHY

*Reflections* (Infinite Zero, 1994); a collection of four spoken word poems, covering Slim's usual subjects, set to jazz backing.

## BIBLIOGRAPHY

*Pimp: The Story of My Life* (Holloway Publishing, 1967); Slim's autobiography that introduced him as a bard of street life. (Note: Ice-T's introduction is available only in the British edition published by Canongate/Payback Press.)

*Trick Baby: The Story of a White Negro* (Holloway Publishing, 1967); about a light-skinned black hustler, later made into a movie (note: Ice-T's introduction is available only in the British edition published by Canongate/Payback Press).

*Long White Con: The Biggest Score of His Life!* (Holloway Publishing); a sequel to *Trick Baby.*

*The Naked Soul of Iceberg Slim: Robert Beck's Real Story* (Holloway Publishing); a collection of essays in which Beck reveals guilt and remorse for the life he's led.

*Mama Black Widow: A Story of the South's Black Underworld* (Holloway Publishing); about a black homosexual in the South.

*Airtight Willie & Me: The Story of Six Incredible Players* (Holloway Publishing); a collection of short stories.

*Death Wish: A Story of the Mafia* (Holloway Publishing); Beck's attempt to stretch out, this is a largely unsuccessful portrayal of life in the Italian mafia.

*The Game For Squares*; Beck's final work, still unpublished.

*Doom Fox*; another previously unpublished work that is being made available for the first time in 1998.

# 10

# NEW YORK ROCKERS

**A**ny city that can claim to be a world capital in the areas of art, literature, theater, fashion, and media inevitably attracts creative people, even if (especially if!) they are outside of the mainstream. In the U.S., in this century, New York is such a city. And, as home to the country's most-read magazines and newspapers, New York always has plenty of music critics around to take notice of and champion the local scene when necessary.

The gritty, romantic feel of New York has been a magnet for rock artists for a long time. Musicians in the city didn't have to invent punk, it was always just part of the attitude. Though it wasn't the first band to exude New Yorkness, the Velvet Underground is a good starting point in the story of the city's underground rock. Closely tied to the downtown art scene surrounding Andy Warhol, the Velvets were dark and dirty and amphetamine-paced back when most bands were singing about sunshine and flowers and psychedelic hallucinations. What's more, they started a tradition for New York bands that produced a string of important developments in rock over the next three decades.

In the early '70s, the remnants of the Warhol/Velvets crowd emerged as a new glam scene, with brash, cross-dressing, hard-rocking bands like the New York Dolls and Wayne County. While remaining outsiders, **Suicide** mingled with these acts at the Mercer Arts Center and later emerged as the most musically significant of the lot. By the mid-'70s, a larger scene based around clubs like CBGB and Max's Kansas City had set punk culture in motion. Though acts like Talking Heads, Blondie, and the Ramones went on to more mainstream success, **Television** was most central to the scene's beginnings, while its spin-off band, **Richard Hell & the Voidoids,** left the clearest legacy for the punk rock we know today.

By the late '70s, the CBGB scene was so crowded and overhyped that the **Feelies,** a Velvets-inspired post-punk band, took refuge across the river and spawned an important rock scene in Hoboken, New Jersey. Back in downtown New York, a collection of art-punk groups deconstructed rock dynamics to create an entirely new musical movement dubbed no wave. Bands such as **DNA,** perhaps the most significant of the no wave groups, were way ahead of their time, so far that only recently has no wave started to emerge in the mainstream consciousness as an important precursor to the skronkier post-rock creations of the '90s.

While all of the original no wave groups had disappeared by the early '80s, a few underground New York bands carried on the tradition. Though Sonic Youth would bring post–no wave styles closest to mainstream popularity, the **Swans** also developed an influential sound as a no wave successor. And as those bands pushed the boundaries of punk-based music, a second movement ran concurrently in some of the same New York clubs. Impacted not only by punk, but also by the funk and disco sounds that were giving birth to hip-hop, early '80s minimalist funk bands such as **Liquid Liquid** and **ESG** were bridging the separated music worlds of uptown and downtown, with arty and adventurous sounds you could also dance to (for that story, see the next chapter).

It's important not to overstate the role New York bands played in the development of modern rock music. Key contributions also arose out of Los Angeles, Detroit, Cleveland, D.C., San Francisco, Boston, Washington State, even rural Louisiana. In fact, independent music's greatest accomplishment in past decades is the development of a network through which good music can be discovered no matter where it originates. Still, for any number of reasons, New York remains ground zero for influential underground American music.

# SUICIDE

*Not only did we not have guitars, but no drums either. That was the reason we had the kind of reaction we did. Those were the two sacred cows of rock music. No one used drum machines in bands at the time. And then we had two people. And our name. It was threatening the status quo.*

**Martin Rev, Suicide**

Suicide were making rock music that sounded like punk and new wave before those genres had a name. Their highly aggressive and noisy beginnings prefigured industrial and post-punk's unorthodox sound and instrumentation. By their first record, Suicide was an edgy synth-pop duo that anticipated (and outdid) keyboard twosomes from Soft Cell to Tears for Fears, and bands including Depeche Mode (who've been known to play Suicide records before concerts) and the Cars (who wrote the song "Shoo-Be-Do" as a tribute to Suicide).

Suicide was quintessentially New York: gritty and neon-lit, smart and aggressive, alternately cold-eyed and intensely emotional, a mix of punk, doo-wop, electronic avant-garde, and rockabilly. They arose in the no-man's-land between the '60s downtown New York scene of the Velvet Underground and the mid-'70s punk scene surrounding clubs like CBGB. In 1970 Alan Vega, a Puerto Rican Jewish artist from Brooklyn, was creating neon junk sculptures and experimenting with guerrilla theater at the Project of Living Artists, an art center in the Village that he had co-founded. There he met Martin Rev, a trained pianist from the Bronx whose free-jazz band, Reverend B, played at the Project. Vega, who'd been hugely inspired seeing Iggy Pop's stage antics and hearing the **Silver Apples'** electronic pop music, convinced Rev to quit free jazz and form a new band with him.

Along with a guitarist they called Cool P, Vega and Rev—renamed Alan Suicide and Marty Suicide—formed Suicide. Though Rev initially played drums, he soon settled on Wurlitzer organ as his primary instrument. Alan added bits of trumpet, but mostly served as the mad ranting vocalist and frontman. After Cool P and a short-lived drummer named Mari left, Suicide became a duo. "We were both trying to make something happen in a very uncompromising way," Rev says of the partnership. "I think we kind of played off each other. Alan, having very little music background, gave me the room to focus things musically. And he had a little more life experience, and brought the Iggy-inspired side that I wasn't into."

Early gigs were more a combination of manic performance art and experimental sound than rock show. Vega, dressed in leather and swinging a bike chain, would menace the audience while yelling street poetry over Rev's formless keyboard noise. Many simply considered them a spectacle and took little notice of the music, but by 1971 Suicide was already calling what they did "punk." "I had gone through the free jazz thing, and it seemed the rock world was the only place left with undiscovered territory," Rev says. "It was interesting to do free music, but with feedback and electronics and using the voice as a free instrument—all of which was not really acceptable in jazz."

---

### Nick Cave

*Suicide probably influenced me more than any contemporary rock band in the end. My vocal style—even my lyric writing to a certain extent in the early days—was influenced by Alan Vega's. And the way the music was put together, too. Like [Cave's song] "The Mercy Seat" begins with this percussive bass rhythm sound, like Suicide's "Harlem." So I know in many ways Suicide were directly influencing our music.*

---

By 1972, a new music scene—with acts like the New York Dolls and Wayne County—had begun to coalesce around the Mercer Arts Center and Max's Kansas City. While Suicide occasionally performed at these venues, their dark, confrontational style was clearly in opposition to these escapist glam groups. They remained outsiders and soon their reputation as an unruly live act made it difficult for them to get gigs. During the next few years, while the Mercer collapsed and Max's closed, Suicide laid low and continued developing material. When the duo reemerged with a more cohesive set of songs in 1975, Max's had reopened and CBGB began to emerge as a focal point for the music scene.

---

### Thurston Moore, Sonic Youth

*Suicide was the first band I saw in New York. We used to come into the city as teenagers to go to Max's. I thought Suicide was going to be another rock and roll, Kiss-type band, and that was not the case. They were in their most "accost-the-audience" period. Alan Vega had an old lady's wig and fake scars on his face, and he was crying on stage, singing "Cheree." He'd walk on the tables and tie his mic cord around people's necks and pour drinks over people's faces, and lick people on the mouth, and break glass and poke it into his chest. We were like, "My God, let's get the hell out of here!" They were such an enigma, because they were so unique and had developed their thing prior to the whole scene, somewhat in a void.*

Vega now sang actual songs, while Rev backed him on keyboard and an early $30 drum machine. Though Suicide were still outsiders, the new punk scene of bands like **Television** and Patti Smith clearly had more in common with the group. "We weren't really embraced as part of the punk scene," Rev says. "But because we were already there and our attitude was so punk, we started to get a certain amount of acceptance. At least not total confusion."

Finally, in 1977 former New York Dolls manager Marty Thau heard Suicide on the jukebox at Max's and offered to put out a Suicide album on his new Red Star label. Made in one weekend, the band's self-titled debut built songs on repetitive low-fi keyboard drones and mechanical beats. Vega sneered gritty lyrics of love ("Cheree"), nuclear terror ("Rocket USA"), and working-class frustration (the 10-minute "Frankie Teardrop") with a mix of punk intensity and showman croon. *Suicide* was to become a founding document of the next decade's synth-based new wave music.

### Henry Rollins

*I was introduced to the work of Suicide when I bought their first album in 1979. I didn't know anything about the band, just that any band who called themselves Suicide had to be intense. The picture on the back of the two members...looked menacing. I remember my friend Ian [MacKaye, of **Minor Threat**/Fugazi] and I playing the album in his attic and not knowing how to take it. It was intense, really strange. I had never heard anything like it in my life. Time went by, and I kept up with the band's records. The Rollins Band covered a Suicide song "Ghost Rider," and it became a staple of our set for years. [from 2.13.61 CD's Suicide reissue]*

Though *Suicide* failed to get much notice in the U.S., British critical acclaim led to a European tour supporting the Clash and Elvis Costello. By the late '70s, though, punk had become synonymous with guitar-based power-chord rock and audiences universally hated Suicide—riots ensued in several cities. But used to the abuse, Suicide relished it.

When the Cars, another band that integrated keyboards into punk-inspired music, hit big in the late '70s, they invited Suicide to open for them on tour and even insisted the duo be included on a popular television show they hosted. By 1980, the attention led the group to a major label for their second album, produced by the Cars' Ric Ocasek, *Alan Vega and Martin Rev: Suicide*. The record's smoothed edges and higher fidelity reflected a larger budget and better studio equipment, but while it drew comparisons to early synth-pop contemporaries **Kraftwerk,** the street attitude of songs like "Mr. Ray" and the epic "Harlem" was recognizably the work of full-blooded New Yorkers.

### King Coffey, Butthole Surfers

*"Dream Baby Dream" was the first 12-inch I bought. I played that to death. I saw them on the*

*Midnight Special, when the Cars said they'd be on the show only if they could pick the other bands. They had Suicide on. Alan Vega's presence was psychotic, it was scary. I'd never seen anything like it, just a singer and keyboard player, very over the top and confrontational.*

---

Again, Suicide was warmly greeted abroad but failed to connect at home. Though the duo never officially broke up, they slowed down in the early '80s and pursued solo projects. Vega achieved enough success in France to get him on major label Elektra in the mid '80s, though his later albums were released only in Europe (recently, they've been made available on Henry Rollins' Infinite Zero label). In 1986, amid the massive popularity in Britain of the Suicide-inspired group Sigue Sigue Sputnik, Vega and Rev reunited for a tour of the U.K. This led to two more Ocasek-produced Suicide records, in 1987 and '92. Though not without their merits, neither record ignited much interest in the band. While the possibility of further Suicide material remains, the duo have since returned to separate pursuits.

## DISCOGRAPHY

*Suicide* (Red Label, 1977; Restless, 1990); a classic record of New York punk attitude and avant-garde pop vision.

*Alan Vega and Martin Rev: Suicide* (80; Restless 90); a slicker, more upscale version of the group's unique sound.

*Half Alive* (ROIR, 1981); a collection of early unreleased recordings and live tracks.

*Ghost Riders* (ROIR, 1986); a live recording from 1981, of the band's 10th-anniversary show at Minneapolis' Walker Arts Center.

*A Way of Life* (Wax Trax!, 1989); a respectable but hardly earth-shaking return.

*Why Be Blue* (Brake Out/Enemy, 1992); a second reunion album.

TRIBUTE: *An Invitation to Suicide* (Munster [Spain], 1994); featuring Luna, Flaming Lips, Mudhoney, Spectrum's Sonic Boom, and Sonic Youth's Thurston Moore.

# TELEVISION / RICHARD HELL & THE VOIDOIDS

*Television's Marquee Moon really blew me away. It was really huge for me at the time. I had been really into [British] stuff, and hearing Television I started fixating on American stuff. It seemed more like the way I was trying to make demos and write songs. I was looking for who I was, and this was a band that sort of guided me there. And obviously later on, hooking up with Richard Lloyd, that's the big Television influence on my records.*

**Matthew Sweet**

Though less known than New York pre-punk peers such as Patti Smith, the Ramones, Blondie, and the Talking Heads, Television opened the door for all of these groups through their early gigs at CBGB, the club around which these bands coalesced to form one of the most influential music scenes in rock history. Decades later, Television remains one of the best loved "unknown" bands in rock and has earned a mythic status that belies its album sales. The group's meticulous arrangements are standard texts for post-punk guitarists and art-minded garage rockers everywhere. And Richard Hell—an original Television member who went on to front the also notable Voidoids—invented a

gritty street rebel image that would become the standard punk look for generations to come.

Television formed in 1973 in New York, but its roots go back to Delaware in the late '60s, where Tom Miller and Richard Meyers met in boarding school. Sharing an interest in music and poetry, the two became friends and conspired ways to escape their restrictive surroundings. Meyers was first to arrive in New York, where he remade himself as Richard Hell, a modern-day version of French symbolist poet Arthur Rimbaud. After a short stint at college, Miller joined his buddy in Manhattan; taking on the surname of another symbolist, he became Tom Verlaine.

### Chris Connelly, the Bells/Ministry/Revolting Cocks

*Lyrically, I'd have to say Tom Verlaine is one of my favorites. Very poetic, but very cool as well. At school, I really shone in English literature, and it was great to read the poets. But if my English teacher had come in with the album* Marquee Moon, *I would be a fucking professor by now. It spoke more to me than Shakespeare's sonnets.*

While the two pursued literary life, publishing a book of poems under the shared alias Theresa Stern, Verlaine also immersed himself in free-jazz saxophone and then guitar. Inspired by bands like the Velvet Underground, the **Stooges,** and the New York Dolls, Verlaine and Hell formed their first group in 1972. With drummer Billy Ficca (a friend of Verlaine's from Delaware) and Hell on bass by default, the Neon Boys played for one year, while they searched in vain for a second guitarist to fill out their ragged sound. After recording a six-song demo, the group called it quits.

While performing as a soloist, Tom Verlaine met the guitar compatriot he'd been searching for. With Richard Lloyd, a blues-oriented guitarist who'd recently arrived from L.A., Verlaine re-formed the Neon Boys, renaming it Television. Over the next five years, Verlaine and Lloyd rewrote the book on two-guitar arrangements in rock, with poetic styles that both worked together and played off each other in a beautiful marriage of harmony and tension.

### Carrie Brownstein, Sleater-Kinney

*Corin [Tucker, Sleater-Kinney's other guitarist] and I have been influenced by how the guitars work in Television. I love Marquee Moon, the guitars cut through in a really different way. They were able to combine two guitars without one being a soloing lead guitar. They intertwined and communicated with each other in a really interesting and dynamic way. Corin and I are conscious of not having one guitar take precedence over the other. We're interested in having them overlap, and we've become more conscious of the relationship of the guitars to each other.*

In search of a new club where Television could gig regularly, Verlaine and Lloyd chanced upon a little-known bar on the Bowery, frequented mostly by Hell's Angels. Assuring the owner that Television could play "country, bluegrass, and blues"—or CBGB—the band debuted in the spring of 1974. Soon, as Patti Smith, Blondie, the Ramones, and Talking Heads became CBGB regulars, the club emerged as a focal point for the brewing New York City punk scene of the mid-'70s, beginning a tradition that was to make CBGB the best known punk-rock establishment in the world.

### Chris Cornell, Soundgarden

*Kim [Thayill, Soundgarden's guitarist] was influenced by Television a lot. And bands like Television are the reason I started playing guitar in Soundgarden. I started writing songs that had more than one guitar part, where it wasn't just playing the same thing. There would be one color part that would come in and out, or some rhythmic thing that would happen when the other guitar was doing its thing. That was directly influenced by bands like Television.*

While Verlaine and Lloyd worked toward making the music more sophisticated, Hell was not particularly interested in becoming a master on the bass. Instead, he focused his attention on developing an image and penning early Television favorites like "Love Comes in Spurts" and "(I Belong to the) Blank Generation." But as Verlaine gradually cut Hell's material from Television's set and even began rehearsing with Blondie's bassist Fred Smith, Hell decided the time had come to quit.

In the interest of applying his street poetry to harder-driving rock, in 1975 Hell joined former New York Dolls Johnny Thunders and Jerry Nolan to form the Heartbreakers. Though Thunders' brand of muscular guitar crunch filled the bill, Hell soon found his bandmates' artless approach and drug-wasted lifestyle difficult to handle. Having contributed the band's best-known song, "(I'm Living On) Chinese Rocks," Hell left the Heartbreakers after less than a year to Thunders' leadership.

In 1976, Hell arrived at a happy medium between Television's instrumental complexity and the

Heartbreakers' energetic rock when he formed the Voidoids. As uncontested frontman—but backed by excellent backing musicians such as guitarist Robert Quine—Hell freely flaunted the personal style that would prove instrumental in defining punk attitude and fashion. Dressed in torn clothing and leather, with messy hair and a sneer on his face, Hell reclaimed his Television songs and turned them into the Voidoids' punk anthems. By 1977, the year the Voidoids released their classic debut *Blank Generation*, British kids like Johnny Rotten and Sid Vicious of the Sex Pistols had modeled themselves after Richard Hell and unleashed punk rock on the world.

### Thurston Moore, Sonic Youth

*His whole stance was really influential. The way he wore ripped t-shirts and shades, and chopped his hair and wrote on himself. And then playing this spastic punk rock music with really amazing lyrics. To me, he was the most important, more than Patti [Smith] or Tom [Verlaine]. Hell was the man, even though he wasn't the most popular. People were more into Blondie and Talking Heads, but for me personally the Voidoids were more influential.*

Meanwhile, Fred Smith's understated bass playing rounded out Television's sound just as Verlaine wanted, and in 1976 the group finally began recording. After disputes over their seven-minute single, "Little Johnny Jewel," almost split up the band (**Pere Ubu**'s Peter Laughner joined as Lloyd briefly quit), Television came together to produce its debut album, the classic *Marquee Moon*.

### Scott Kannberg, Pavement

*Marquee Moon was a great record, a big influence. How baby boomers would cite the Beatles as classic rock, I'd cite Television. On [Brighten the Corners] we definitely have a Television sound, in the dueling guitars. Like in "Transport is Arranged" or "We are Underused."*

While it never became the megahit Television's record company hoped it would be, *Marquee Moon* was quickly recognized as one of the best rock records of the decade. Along with a mix of older Television material such as "Venus" and newer workouts like "Torn Curtain," the standout title track—nine minutes of pure punk poetry—encapsulated everything that made Television great. As the guitarists perfected their tightly woven interplay through extended musical passages, Verlaine's arty street verse (voiced somewhat thinly by the lyricist) added cool commentary to the song's built-in drama.

### Eric Bachmann, Archers of Loaf

*A band like Television, the guitars never do the same thing, yet it sounds good because each player had good sounds. They were very busy, but they never walked on top of each other. Matt and Mark, our drummer and bass player, save us from sounding too much like Television. Like*

*"Form and File" [on* All the Nation's Airports] *is a blatant rip-off of "Marquee Moon," where I do this rhythmic thing and the guitar swells up over top of it. I was listening to "Marquee Moon" one day and thought, "That's a good arrangement. If I do this, maybe Eric [Johnson, Archers' other guitarist] can fill up the rest."*

A second album, *Adventure,* followed fast on the heels of *Marquee Moon* but failed to generate as much enthusiasm. Due mainly to "sophomore slump"—where a band puts its most tested material on a debut and must start from scratch on the follow-up—*Adventure* lacked the confidence and depth of the first album. A third album might have proved the band's endurance and consistency, but it never happened. By the middle of 1978, a power struggle had once again caused tensions between band members. And in July, Television performed its final show.

Both Verlaine and Lloyd launched immediately into solo careers with 1979 debuts. Verlaine was more successful, and Lloyd soon abandoned his own recordings and achieved acclaim as a guitar for hire (playing with Matthew Sweet, Lloyd Cole, and others). Fred Smith played bass with both Verlaine and Lloyd, as well as many other bands, while Billy Ficca went on to join the Waitresses, who had a hit in the '80s with "I Know What Boys Like." In 1992, Television briefly reunited and released a surprisingly vital new record. Though it was well received critically, no plans were made to continue. Richard Hell, meanwhile, has continued to make music sporadically (such as with the Dim Stars, a band featuring Sonic Youth's Thurston Moore and Steve Shelley), and has appeared in films (such as *Desperately Seeking Susan* with Madonna). In 1996, he published his first novel, *Go Now.*

## DISCOGRAPHY

### TELEVISION

*Marquee Moon* (Elektra, 1977); the group's masterpiece.

*Adventure* (Elektra, 1978); a respectable follow-up with slicker production, that failed to match the debut's power.

*The Blow Up* (ROIR, 1982); a posthumously released live album recorded in 1978.

*Television* (Capitol, 1992); a one-off reunion album that stands up remarkably well, considering the time that had passed.

### RICHARD HELL & THE VOIDOIDS

*Blank Generation* (Sire, 1977; Sire/Warner Bros., 1990); a classic punk document featuring some of Hell's best material.

*Destiny Street* (Red Star, 1982); features Quine and an otherwise different Voidoids line-up.

*R.I.P.* (ROIR, 1984); live recordings of the Voidoids from Max's in 1978 and CBGB in 1979 (and one mid-'80s track).

*Funhunt* (ROIR, 1990); Hell's career retrospective, spanning his early demos with the Heartbreakers up through the final incarnations of the Voidoids in 1984.

*Go Now* (Tim/Kerr, 1995); a spoken-word release featuring Hell reading from his novel, with Quine's guitar accompaniment.

TRIBUTE: *Who the Hell: A Tribute to Richard Hell* (Cred Factory); a limited-edition collection of local North Carolina bands, including Vanilla Trainwreck and Whiskeytown, doing Hell favorites.

# THE FEELIES

*The Feelies made me want to pick up guitar and play. I went and saw them an awful lot, and Crazy Rhythms is probably my favorite record ever. The two guitar players weren't flashy, they just worked together. Crazy Rhythms is just so textured, so beautifully produced, but it's also incredibly simple and easy to play along with. That's a band that never really got the notice they deserved.*

**Dean Wareham, Luna**

A central band in the New York and New Jersey music scenes from the late '70s through the '80s, the Feelies' low-key approach and lackadaisical career path kept them away from large-scale exposure. But during the band's long and uneven lifespan, they emerged as an important influence on post-Velvets bands of the '80s, from R.E.M. to Luna to Yo La Tengo. Though not particularly driven to perform live, the Feelies were a popular club band whose mesmerizing interpretations of other groups' songs (including everyone from **Wire** to the Monkees) inspired leagues of "fan" bands who were not ashamed to wear their influences on their sleeves.

Glenn Mercer and Bill Million (born Bill Clayton), friends in the northern New Jersey town of Haledon, formed the Feelies in 1976. Having grown up just outside New York City they'd been inspired by the direct, hard-rocking pre-punk bands like the New York Dolls and **Modern Lovers**. The Feelies (their name taken from an invention in Aldous Huxley's *Brave New World*) wished to pursue "the basic punk rock aspects of rock and roll, going back to early Rolling Stones or Chuck Berry being punk rock in a sense," Mercer says.

After a few predictably disastrous gigs in front of perplexed New Jersey high school kids, the Feelies set their sights on New York and debuted at CBGB in 1977. By then, the rock scene surrounding the club was well established, and bands like **Television** and the Talking Heads had already released albums. This proved a blessing and a curse. While the success of those bands was inspiring, the club was flooded with new bands wishing to follow in their footsteps and it became more difficult to get noticed. Still, the Feelies managed to stand out, and in 1978 they were named "New York's best underground band" by the *Village Voice*. After a number of early personnel changes, the band settled on a four-man lineup: Mercer and Million shared guitar, vocals, and songwriting, Keith Clayton handled bass, and Anton Fier, who'd been involved with a number of early Cleveland bands (such as **Pere Ubu**), played drums.

Despite the band's early acclaim, it would be years before they released a debut album. Though the CBGB scene had developed a great reputation, these bands' failure to sell records nationally (at least early on) made record companies wary. While the Feelies had some offers, Mercer and Million's insistence on producing their own records made labels especially cautious. What's more, the band—ordinary looking, plain dressing, and with songs that excelled within the rock form rather than breaking new ground—lacked a recognizable image. Then one day, Mercer remembers, "Keith got this bowl haircut and a new pair of glasses. It was such a striking image, we thought if he kept that look people might pick up on it. It kind of snowballed; people responded to it and we'd play it up a bit." By emphasizing their ordinariness the band became associated with a "nerdy" style that would later define college rock bands such as Pavement and Weezer.

---

### Stephin Merritt, Magnetic Fields/Future Bible Heroes
*The best feature of the Feelies was, you couldn't hear the words. That's where Yo La Tengo and Pavement got it from. The Feelies took the Velvets' loops and drones and made them sound rigorous and difficult just by strumming the guitar the same way on every beat, no mean feat. They didn't look anything like musicians, which was shocking and liberating.*

---

When they finally released a record, 1980's *Crazy Rhythms*, it was well worth the wait. Defined by its pleasant drone and trebly guitar strum, as well as murmured vocals and percolating drums, the record was a perfect introduction to the jangly psychedelia-laced, late-Velvets sound that would reappear throughout the decade in bands like R.E.M. and the Dream Syndicate. Originals like "The Boy with the Perpetual Nervousness" and "Fa Cé-La" placed the Feelies in a pop-oriented post-punk context, while a Beatles cover (a Stones song was added to the reissue as well) connected them to the bar-band tradition in which they thrived. The Feelies' unapologetically covers-friendly approach became one of the band's defining characteristics.

---

### Steve Wynn, solo/Dream Syndicate
*That first album, and seeing them live, was amazing. The very fast strumming guitar really appealed to me, very clean but jittery rhythms. I had a 103 degree fever when I saw them live. Maybe it was because I was sick, but it seemed like everything got faster and faster, a very drug-induced experience. I got excited by the possibility of playing a show and making people feel like they were having a psychedelic experience even without being high. In our first year together, that was something we were always trying to do.*

---

In preparation for a tour to support *Crazy Rhythms*, the band arranged to do a quiet warm-up gig in a little-known club in Hoboken, New Jersey, called Maxwell's. Just across the Hudson River from New York City, Hoboken was a low-key backwater town that attracted people who wanted to get away from Manhattan's high rents and huge crowds. Following the Feelies' lead, other bands like the Bongos, the dBs, and Yo La Tengo made Maxwell's a home base in the '80s, birthing the celebrated Hoboken music scene.

When *Crazy Rhythms* failed to take hold commercially, the Feelies were dropped from their label and Anton Fier quit the band. (Fier also quit his other band, the Lounge Lizards, and briefly joined **Pere Ubu,** before starting his own project, the Golden Palominos.) Rather than pursue a new record contract, the band became largely inactive, although they did do occasional live shows, which often coincided with a national holiday. As Mercer explains, "We just make music to make music, so if it means waiting around for inspiration to come up with a new thing or make yourself happy, we don't feel like, 'Oh, we've been out of the public eye for a while, we really need to get back in.' It's always been driven by the music."

While the Feelies largely disappeared in name during the early '80s, its members remained active. Mercer and Million wrote the soundtrack for the film *Smithereens,* which developed into the instrumental and tape-oriented group the Willies. Most of the Feelies also appeared in Yung-Wu, a group led by off-and-on Feelies percussionist Dave Weckerman, and in the Trypes, a larger band led by New Jersey keyboardist (and member of Yung-Wu) John Baumgartner. By the mid-'80s, Mercer and Million were concentrating on the Willies, who appeared in the film *Something Wild.* Having added drummer Stan Demeski and bassist Brenda Sauter, as well as Weckerman on percussion, the group moved away from instrumentals as Mercer introduced new rock-oriented songs. As it became clear that this was, by default, a re-formed version of the Feelies, the group decided to record again.

---

### Ira Kaplan, Yo La Tengo

*I certainly learned a lot from those Maxwell's bands, I was there so much. I loved the Feelies, I think some of the things we've done with percussion could be traced back to the Feelies. The first time I saw the Trypes, Glenn [Mercer] was playing drums. It was a real eye opener to see a guitarist playing drums—and playing drums like a guitarist. He did really cool things, but he wasn't a drummer. When Georgia [Hubley, Yo La Tengo's drummer] plays guitar in our group, because she doesn't technically know how to play, she does things I would never think of doing. It provides a different slant on things, a different texture. Like the song "Autumn Sweater," we started practicing it with Georgia playing the organ. That comes from being such big Feelies fans.*

---

In 1986, the Feelies released *The Good Earth,* an album co-produced by longtime fan Peter Buck, whose band R.E.M. had started out as a Feelies-inspired group and since made it big. Though still clearly influenced by the Velvet Underground, *The Good Earth*'s more acoustic and ethereal (and a bit less edgy) sound made it clear that much had changed since the group's debut. Subsequent albums in 1988 and 1991 reinforced this new approach with consistent success, both artistically and commercially, but it became more and more difficult to sustain the group financially. Following 1991's *Time for a Witness,* Bill Million quit and moved to Florida. The rest of the band remained active, but not as the Feelies. While Mercer and Weckerman formed the band WakeOoloo, each member has appeared in a variety of groups. Most notably, Stan Demeski temporarily became a member of Feelies-influenced group Luna.

## DISCOGRAPHY

*Crazy Rhythms* (Stiff, 1980; A&M, 1990); a terrific debut of jittery New York post-punk.

*The Good Earth* (Coyote/Twin-Tone, 1986); released six years after the debut, this was a more mature, acoustic effort, though still worthy of the group's reputation.

*Only Life* (Coyote/A&M, 1988); despite a major label jump, this record largely follows its predecessor and achieves similar results.

*Time for a Witness* (Coyote/A&M, 1991); a fine but unspectacular finale.

# DNA

*More than as a guitarist, I was influenced by the whole concept of what DNA were doing. The fact that Arto never played the same chords and was so free, he'd just skronk on this twelve-string he never tuned, and Ikue Mori's drumming was coming out of underground free improvisation. And Tim Wright's bass playing was extremely centric. I was completely blown away by them. There was no one that sounded like them. It wasn't like the initial English punk rock, where everybody sounded like the Pistols or the Clash. With no wave every band was completely unique, and that to me was super-influential.*

**Thurston Moore, Sonic Youth**

With its entire studio output barely long enough to fill a whole album, DNA is undoubtedly the most influential rock band in the world per minute of recorded music. As leaders of the downtown New York post-punk movement called no wave, DNA pushed the rock form to its limit by getting rid of all apparent structure and tonality. Taking its cues from the guitar deconstructions of experimental composers Rhys Chatham and **Glenn Branca,** DNA made art rock to end all art rock. And in doing so, the band—particularly the group's bespectacled guitarist and lead squawker Arto Lindsay—paved the way for generations of noise- and free-music makers, from Sonic Youth to God Is My Co-Pilot to Blonde Redhead (named after a DNA song). And Lindsay's nerd-savant approach to music has reverberated in the worlds of pop (working with David Byrne), world music, and electronica.

### DJ Spooky (Paul Miller)

*Arto Lindsay and Ikoue Mori, they're definitely big influences. Mainly with their complete discarding of normal song structure. Arto had a really artsy, poetic side to his thing, it seemed much more idealistic and open to different stuff. Also with his Brazilian stuff, he's working with people from radically different cultures, which a lot of the New York scene at the time would not do.*

Arto Lindsay was born in Pennsylvania, but spent most of his childhood with his missionary parents in a Brazilian village. Though Lindsay had no musical experience or training, his interest in experimental art led him to New York in the mid-'70s, where he met a group of like-minded noise-makers who were beginning to apply punk's irreverence to the atonality of free jazz. Out of these early gatherings came a group of bands—James Chance's Contortions, **Lydia Lunch**'s Teenage Jesus & the Jerks, Mars, and DNA—and a scene that came to be known as no wave.

Lindsay initially wrote lyrics for the earliest no wave group, Mars, though he soon began to try his hand at guitar. Rather than bothering with the mundanity of learning chords or proper tuning, Arto approached his instrument as if it had never been played before and proceeded to invent an entirely new vocabulary based around rhythms and assorted manipulations. Through his associations in the downtown New York art scene, Lindsay met two other would-be musicians with a similar lack of experience and desire to experiment: Ikue Mori, a Japanese woman who attacked her drums with anarchic expressiveness, and Robin Crutchfield, a (male) sculptor and performance artist who managed to work out enough keyboard expertise (or lack of) to fit right in when the trio—who called themselves DNA—debuted in 1977, one month after forming.

In keeping with the band's intention to push themselves at an accelerated pace, within its first year DNA released a debut single—"Little Ants" b/w "You and You"—produced by **Voidoids'** guitarist Robert Quine (who had also "reconditioned" Lindsay's guitar to better suit his approach). By this time, **Brian Eno** had become intrigued by the no wave scene and put together a compilation of the leading bands in the movement. *No New York,* as it was called, featured songs from all four of the major no wave groups, including four stand-out tracks by DNA. With Crutchfield's simple and cohesive keyboard lines, songs like the bluesy "Egomaniac's Kiss" were engaging and accessible; by the end of the year, though, creative differences led Crutchfield to form his own group, Dark Day.

---

**Matthew Sweet**

*I had the DNA 45, and I was into their whole anti-music thing. There's an element in what I do that you'd never know. I probably have done more of that experimental stuff on demos. On records, the songs usually win out, but occasionally I like to do a one note song that's really anti-melodic. And things like DNA got me into thinking that way.*

---

To replace Crutchfield, DNA acquired bass player Tim Wright, who'd been a founding member of Cleveland's **Pere Ubu.** By choosing not to add another lead instrument, Lindsay and Mori removed any melodic potential from the band. In return, they got a rhythmic bassist who could hold the more formless rumblings together without overshadowing them. It was with this lineup that the band released its only extended recording, though with just six songs in under 10 minutes, *A Taste of DNA* was hardly an epic. The record's brevity, however, was right for the music: Inspired by modern composers, far eastern folk styles, and even the Brazilian tropicalia pop Linsday had grown up on, DNA chocked so much rhythmic, tonal, and structural information into their music, it would have been exhausting to go longer than a minute and a half on any one piece.

---

**Mark De Gli Antoni, Soul Coughing**

*It was an incredible influence. I don't think I ever did anything musically similar, but DNA's freedom was a big deal to me. It's more spiritual or philosophical, where just the honesty of approach is an influence. When I watch Ikue or Arto play, it's not like you're watching a vir-*

tuoso, but through their trust in their ability comes a super-confidence. And all the gestures have meaning. For me, DNA was a big thing as far as, "How do I carry that kind of pride when I play, and what is it that gives them the confidence?"

*A Taste of* sounded like rock put through a trash compactor, full of contorted musical ideas, clustered notes, and anemic grunts of nonsensical haikus. Yet, for all its clashing tones and rhythms, the music was joyous and playful. With DNA noise wasn't an expression of nihilism, but of childlike freedom.

As it turned out, DNA's lifespan—and that of the entire no wave movement—would be just as short-lived as its music. By 1982, DNA and the rest of the *No New York* bands had split up. Mori contributed her string playing to Mars's final record, and has made albums of her own, while Wright played bass on the **Brian Eno**/David Byrne album, *My Life in the Bush of Ghosts*. Of the three, though, Arto Lindsay has maintained the highest profile. While DNA still existed, Lindsay had been a part of the Lounge Lizards, a "fake jazz" group led by saxophonist John Lurie. After appearing on that group's self-titled debut, Lindsay collaborated with another Lounge Lizard (and one-time **Feelies** drummer) Anton Fier on the first Golden Palominos record. In addition, he has appeared on albums by James Chance, Mars, John Zorn, Don King (a band comprising former members of Mars and DNA, as well as Arto's brother Duncan), Ryuichi Sakamoto, Allen Ginsberg, Laurie Anderson, and They Might Be Giants. Lindsay has also distinguished himself as a producer, of David Byrne's early solo albums as well as top Brazilian artists such as Caetano Veloso, Tom Ze, and Marisa Monte.

### Jim O'Rourke, solo/Gastr del Sol

*I'd never heard anyone play guitar like Arto Lindsay. The first time I heard him was on the first Golden Palominos record. At that time the DNA record was completely impossible to find. I think he's a great guitar player and singer. The DNA record and the stuff on No New York is awesome. They were miles ahead of all those other bands from that period.*

In the '80s, Lindsay and collaborator Peter Scherer made three albums of their own Brazilian-flavored music, ranging from experimental to dancey, as the Ambitious Lovers. In recent years, Lindsay has once again returnd to his Brazilian roots with solo albums that feature guest appearances by **Brian Eno,** clarinetist Don Byron, DJ Spooky, and members of Blonde Redhead, Cibo Matto, and Deee-Lite.

## DISCOGRAPHY

(Various Artists) *No New York* (Antilles, 1978); DNA contributed four songs to this **Brian Eno**-produced seminal document of the no wave movement.

*A Taste of DNA* (American Clave, 1980); the group's only studio release, this six-song EP, lasting less than 10 minutes, is crammed with enough musical ideas for an entire career.

*DNA* (Avant [Japan], 1993); a live recording made at the group's farewell show at CBGB in 1982, and released on John Zorn's Japanese label.

## SWANS

*Scratch Acid [Yow's previous band] was lumped into what they called "pigfuck" music, with Swans,* **Big Black,** *Sonic Youth, and Butthole Surfers. I liked the name, and I was flattered that us little kids would be lumped in with that stuff.... [I] met Michael Gira one night and asked him if he thought his lyrics were very funny. "No," he very adamantly answered, offended that I would ask. And I said, "You mean to tell me, 'Keep your head on the ground, push your ass up—here is your money,' isn't funny? How the fuck is that not funny?" The stuff I know by the Swans I think is a laugh riot. The Michael Gira/Don Rickles Christmas Special, that would be a good one, huh?*

**David Yow, Jesus Lizard**

At the peak of their strength, the Swans—both sonically and lyrically—explored the extremes of brutality, torture, and power to the point where the music seemed incapable of even the slightest glimpses of light. In his commitment to plumbing the depths of ugliness, Swans leader Michael Gira showed nothing if not a focused vision. But by the time he'd retired the band, 15 years after it began, the music had moved to a place where it revealed moments of grace and beauty. One of two primary successors to the no wave movement (Sonic Youth being the other), the Swans went on to leave their mark on everything from post-rock and electronic outfits such as Low and the Young Gods (who took their name from a Swans recording) to goth-industrial groups like Nine Inch Nails.

Though Michael Gira's first exposure to punk came while attending art school in Los Angeles in the late '70s, he was always a bit at odds with what he viewed as the fashion-oriented nature of the scene. To counter the deficiencies he saw in L.A.'s punk rag, *Slash*, Gira started his own magazine entitled *No*, which he filled with art and writing on favorite topics such as punk bands, pornography, and cadavers. Soon, though, he found himself drawn to New York and the city's no wave scene. "I responded to it immediately, because the main tool it used was raw sound instead of melodic rock structures," Gira says of the music being made by people like **Glenn Branca** and **DNA**.

By the time he arrived in New York, however, no wave was all but dead, and he found he had little in common with the early '80s dance-oriented scene. As he dissolved his first New York band Circus Mort and began to formulate the Swans, the closest things Gira found to kindred spirits were his former art school classmate Kim Gordon and her band, another no wave-inspired outfit called Sonic Youth. "There was no support system at all for the really brutal things we were doing or Sonic Youth was doing," Gira says. "No one even wanted to know about us, so Sonic Youth and us sort of banded together and supported each other."

---

### Thurston Moore, Sonic Youth

*Michael Gira...was a funny guy, he hated everything. He was always having a good time, yet he was completely nihilistic. And neither of us had a cent, so we became really tight, and I played with him a bit when he was developing the Swans. We toured with them, playing in front of ten people at most. We just stuck together and developed side by side. The cool thing was we had different esthetics—we were positive, they were negative—we were the Beatles, they were the Stones. Also, Sonic Youth always kept aware of the flux of the underground music scene and became part of it, where the Swans sort of stuck their ground and refused to be part of anything.*

---

With the Swans, Gira began to construct rhythms around tape loops, using two bassists (of which he was one) and sheets of guitar noise. The intention was to create the most physical and punishing music possible. Through the extreme darkness, Gira hoped to find a sort of freedom. "I wanted to experience making the sound, to crawl inside of it," Gira explains. "It wasn't like I was feeling angst and needed to express it, I wanted to create something, in reality, that gave me joy. The music was overwhelmingly transformative."

The Swans—which maintained a constantly changing lineup due to Gira's admitted tyrannicalness—investigated this kind of supremely heavy, minimalist metal through their 1982 debut EP and first album, *Filth*. 1984's *Cop* and their "Raping a Slave" single were even more brutal. With lyrics dealing in domination, humiliation, and mutilation—and harsh, pummeling rhythms to match—Gira's cathartic nightmare came as close as music gets to making a listener feel physically violated. The Swans' frighteningly loud and torturous live shows, taking cues from equally punishing industrial acts like **Throbbing Gristle** and **Einstürzende Neubauten,** featured band members banging on metal and manipulating tapes.

*Mark Robinson, Unrest/Air Miami*
*They had these huge sheets of metal with one guy in the front wacking them, and I think they had three bass players and a drummer. The thing that really struck me about the Swans live was how everyone in the club left. Unrest did a Swans rip-off song "Kill Whitey" that's pretty much taken from the early Swans—the really slow, metal sounding stuff.*

In 1985, a former sex worker and dedicated Swans fan named Jarboe made her way to New York from Atlanta with the intention of joining the band. Though it had been very much a boys club until then, she soon proved herself suitably tough and earned a job playing sampler. Though Jarboe's role was minor at first, on the *Greed* and *Holy Money* albums she added a melodic and ethereal element the music had never had before. "People make the clichéd assumptions that a woman gets in the group and they become soft," Gira says. "But that wasn't the case at all. She was a very hard person, and she liked the brutal music. But being that she had this tremendous musical experience, I started taking advantage of it to expand. So I started incorporating her elaborate background vocals or some orchestrations she'd help with."

By 1987, the Swans had moved a long way from their beginnings. Having become romantically involved, Jarboe and Gira embarked on a more acoustic-oriented side project called Skin, elements of which were then incorporated back into the Swans' *Children of God* record. The music had become textured and majestic—uplifting even!—with a more varied and accessible sound that fell in the territory of goth.

*Ryan Adams, Whiskeytown*
*Children of God really changed my view of music a lot. Because that was something that took rock and made it triumphant, like an opera. That record is undeniably one of the greatest records of all time. I like the way he orchestrates acoustic guitar, making it really droney. When I was 14 and 15, we would fancy these bands out in the shed after the Swans.*

In 1989, the Swans veered as close to mainstream as they would get when they signed to MCA Records and released their most slickly produced and song-oriented album, *The Burning World*. The band's major label flirtations would be short-lived, however. An overall disaster, the record brought the Swans few new fans, alienated many old ones, and left the group deeply in debt. When MCA dropped the Swans after one release, Gira felt deeply shaken by the experience. Determined to maintain complete control over his music, he started his own Young God label and steered his music away from *The Burning World's* sound.

### Lou Barlow, Sebadoh

*They started out incredibly ugly—with lyrics about being raped in a jail cell and beaten by cops, or autopsies—and slowly developed into the band that did Children of God, where they brought in male/female god themes. And that was kind of the time I met my wife, so they kind of mirrored my life for a while. From that kind of self-hatred, moving to this idea of redemption and beauty. At the time I was just young enough to allow it to speak to me. I really liked the way the band was determined to evolve and flesh out this concept. That was something that influenced me in a philosophical way: Find what you do well, even if it's the dumbest thing and people don't understand it at all.*

The Swans' '90s music has been largely defined by their synthesis of the earlier rhythm-oriented post–no wave sound with the more melodic and acoustic elements of later albums. Following 1995's return to form with *The Great Annihilator*, Gira announced that he would be disbanding the Swans following a final album and tour. He felt the group had become burdened with too many preconceptions and failed to inspire the interest it once did. With the double CD *Soundtracks for the Blind*, the Swans ended on a high note. Since the Swans' end, Gira has divided his attention between two projects, an instrumental sound-collage work called Body Lovers and more song-oriented acoustic recordings under the name Angels of Light. Now based in Atlanta with Jarboe, who has continued her solo career, Gira also plans to release new bands on Young God Records, and reissue much of the Swans' catalogue.

## DISCOGRAPHY

*Filth* (Neutral, 1983, Young God/Atavistic, 1998); reissued on 2-CD set with the 1982 debut EP and live *Body to Body* album.

*Cop* (K.422/Homestead, 1984; Young God/Atavistic, 1998); the beginning of the band's most brutal period; reissued on a double CD containing all 1984–86 material, including 1984's *Young God* EP.

*Greed* (K.422/PVC, 1985; Young God/Atavistic, 1998); a more varied sound, with the addition of Jarboe; reissued on a double CD containing all 1984–86 material.

*Holy Money* (PVC, 1986; Young God/Atavistic, 1998); a companion piece with *Greed*; reissued on a double CD containing all 1984–86 material.

*Children of God* (Caroline, 1987; Young God/Atavistic, 1997); a more textured and acoustic release; reissued in a double CD package with the collected works of the Skin side project, entitled *World of Skin*.

*The Burning World* (Uni/MCA, 1989; Young God/Atavistic, 1998); largely an anomaly, this is by far the group's most accessible album; reissued on a two-CD set with the '91–'92 studio material.

*White Light from the Mouth of Infinity* (Young God/Sky,

1991; Young God/Atavistic, 1998); a deliberate retreat from *The Burning World,* with which it is reissued.

*Body to Body, Job to Job* (Young God/Sky, 1991; Young God Atavistic, 1998); a compilation of outtakes and live tracks from the band's early years; reissued on 2-CD set with the group's first two releases.

*Love of Life* (Young God/Sky, 1992; Young God/Atavistic, 1998); reissued on a 2-CD set with all other '91–'92 studio material.

*Omniscience* (Young God/Sky, 1992); a live album of material from their 1992 tour.

*The Great Annihilator* (Invisible/Young God, 1995); a return to full strength.

*Kill the Child* (Atavistic, 1996); a live album featuring performances from 1985 to 1987.

*Soundtracks for the Blind* (Young God/Atavistic, 1996); the band's two-CD final studio album.

*Swans Are Dead* (Young God/Atavistic, 1997); a two-CD live album, one of material from the group's 1995 tour and the other of their final tour in 1997.

# 11

# MINIMALIST FUNK

In the early '90s, the bands in this chapter all worked on the periphery of a larger musical movement—hip-hop—and attempted to distill the essence of '70s funk using limited tools and/or a more focused approach. Thus they share a cetain affinity as "minimalist funk." But while **Liquid Liquid** and **ESG** stripped down the instrumentation (and recorded for 99 Records), **Trouble Funk** streamlined the song structures (with the D.C.-based go-go sound).

Go-go arose in the late '70s out of Washington, D.C.'s African-American neighborhoods. Just as DJs in the Bronx started to isolate and repeat the best section of funk records in order to create more inspiring dance music, go-go bands like Chuck Brown & the Soul Searchers did away with all but the hyper-rhythmic funk "breakdowns" in their live sets. By getting rid of the song and retaining the nonstop, full-on dance beat, go-go became the preferred music at parties in the capital area throughout the '80s, with groups like the Junkyard Band, Rare Essence, and E.U. (who gave go-go its biggest mainstream hit with 1988's "Da Butt"). With its heavy audience interaction in the form of shout-outs and call-and-response chants, go-go was by design a live, community-oriented music. For that reason, the music never translated fully on record and therefore never reached a national audience. The complex polyrhythms of bands like **Trouble Funk,** though, have lived on through their inspiration on others.

Around the same time, 250 miles north in New York City, a small record store in the Village was becoming an outpost for the post-punk sounds coming out of England. Run by Ed Bahlman, 99 Records specialized in imports that fused punk with dub reggae, spacey funk, and other experimental sounds. Bahlman decided to turn 99 into a record label in order to release the music of no-wave composer **Glenn Branca,** but soon he steered toward bands that were offering a hip, New York version of post-punk's funk and dub fusion. Though **Liquid Liquid** came out of the downtown Manhattan art scene (punks who found the groove) and **ESG** were teenage sisters from the Bronx (disco kids who fell in with the new wave), together their releases molded a unified "minimalist funk" sound for 99 Records.

---

*Thurston Moore, Sonic Youth*

*99 Records became this hangout for us. All these imports would come in and they'd play them. It became our own little slice of England. Then they put out bands like **Liquid Liquid** and **ESG** and 99 turned into this completely heavy, hip thing for us. I think there was this whole group of people like the Beastie Boys and the Luscious Jackson girls who were kind of a half-generation younger than us, teenagers who grew up [with that stuff] in New York.*

---

Go-go and 99 Records formed two distinct strands of a funk avant-garde in the early '80s. Though they were little recognized at the time—and continue to be largely overlooked today—the contributions of these scenes can be heard in everything from dance pop to hip-hop to techno to post-rock.

# T R O U B L E   F U N K

*Trouble Funk taught many of us D.C. kids the true meaning of the word "groove." Trouble's nonstop rhythms, best captured live, were mesmerizing and drew even the stiffest among us onto the dance floor. In American hardcore, D.C. was one of the first [punk] scenes to see the introduction of swing into the otherwise straight and rigid music. First in Soul Side (which included three GVSB members) and now in GVSB, we have always plumbed the depths of our low ends, searching for hidden grooves. Trouble Funk showed many of us that music could be just as sexual as it was aggressive....It was Trouble Funk that told us not to fear the groove; instead, ride it and sink way down low into it.*

*Johnny Temple, Girls Against Boys*

While Trouble Funk was not the first go-go band, or even the most commercially successful, it was certainly among the best. In accentuating the most appealing aspects of go-go pioneers, Trouble Funk stripped down the music to its groove essentials and virtually defined the genre for generations to come. What's more, in its willingness to intermingle and connect with other music worlds—including D.C.'s hardcore punk scene and New York's hip-hop scene—Trouble Funk served as the premier ambassadors of go-go. So while the go-go scene never got far beyond the capital area, Trouble Funk enabled the music's rich polyrhythms to cross into both rock and electronic dance music, and leave a significant imprint on modern music.

*DJ Spooky (Paul Miller)*

*Trouble Funk was absolutely brilliant with their multi-percussion shit. It's going to take the drum 'n' bass kids years to match that kind of complexity. All the layering and the call-and-response thing, the way they interact with the crowd, is brilliant. My drum 'n' bass is more like go-go in a way, with multiple layers, and a fusion of West African stuff with sci-fi imagery.*

Trouble Funk was together as early as 1978, but it wasn't until the following year, when the group started sharing bills with original D.C. go-go band Chuck Brown & the Soul Searchers, that it found its sound. Trouble Funk's leaders, keyboardist Robert Reed and bassist Tony Fisher, were so impressed by the Soul Searchers' ability to distill the essence of funk—the James Brown-style instrumental breakdowns that all but discarded the song in favor of the dance grooves—they decided to adopt a similar approach. Soon the group had formulated what would become the standard go-go band lineup, which included the slap bass and bright horns of most funk bands, but diminished the role of guitar, added electro-funk synthesizers (often more than one), and most of all, focused all its attention on the beat.

Trouble Funk's three percussionists built multilayered rhythms using congas, timbales, toms, and a variety of other drums and noisemakers, not the least of which was a steadily clanking cowbell. Instead of having a singer leading the group, Trouble Funk, like other go-go bands arising around D.C. in the late '70s, opted for something closer to a lead "talker." Like early hip-hop DJs, the vocalists directed the group and audience members through party chants, call-and-response games, and shout-outs to nearby towns and neighborhoods (well-known examples include: "We gonna drop the bomb on the Southeast crew!" and "Fee fi fo fum, tell me where did you come from?"). By the time the group released its debut record, 1979's *In Times of Trouble*, go-go was beginning to catch on as a distinct style and Trouble Funk were among the scene's leaders.

**Jenny Toomey, Tsunami/Licorice**

*One of the things I loved about Trouble Funk is they never leave the audience alone. They're always baiting the audience, making fun of them, getting them to dance, breaking them in half, pitting audience members against each other, and really involving the audience in the show. That's something we do with less success. I spend a lot of time baiting the audience when Tsunami plays, definitely, because I really feel like it should be an exchange.*

Three years later, go-go had grown into a major attraction at parties and dances in the mid-Atlantic. Though bands remained almost entirely centered in D.C., word of the music extended up into New York, where the local rap scene was exploding on a national level. Sensing that go-go might be the "next big thing," prominent early hip-hop label Sugar Hill (who'd introduced artists such as Sugarhill Gang and Grandmaster Flash) signed Trouble Funk and released its breakthrough album, *Drop the Bomb*. With its loose, live-in-the-studio atmosphere, the record was among the first go-go releases to successfully translate onto vinyl the party vibe so crucial to the music. But more than that, *Drop the Bomb* connected Trouble Funk and go-go with the world of rap music and a far wider audience.

**Wyclef, solo/the Fugees**

*Trouble Funk was hot, the mixture vibe of go-go: the funk, the rock, the combination. Our stuff incorporates all of that. Like if you listen to the end of "Anything Can Happen" [from The Carnival], we're using go-go beats.*

More connections between hip-hop and go-go began to raise the music's profile even further. Rick Rubin, an early go-go fan who ran the New York-based Def Jam label, sampled Trouble Funk in songs by the Beastie Boys and, most notably, LL Cool J's "Rock the Bells" (in the '90s, Rubin and Henry Rollins's Infinite Zero label would reissue two Trouble Funk collections). The group also recorded with early rapper Kurtis Blow, and later with the controversial rap group 2 Live Crew. And hoping to do for go-go what the film *Wild Style* had done for hip-hop, a film called *Good to Go* attempted to inspire wider interest in groups like Trouble Funk.

Meanwhile back in Washington, Trouble Funk was building other musical bridges. Though D.C. in the early '80s could boast of active music scenes in both go-go and hardcore punk, the two worlds rarely coincided in the largely segregated city. That changed, however, on September 23, 1983, when "The D.C. Funk-Punk Spectacular" brought together Trouble Funk with local hardcore heroes **Minor Threat** and visiting Texas punks the Big Boys. The show offered the mostly white punk kids a taste of Trouble Funk's nonstop rhythmic assault, and had an an enormous impact on the previously funk-deficient hardcore scene.

---

### King Coffey, Butthole Surfers

*The punk rockers would gather at my house and we would literally spraypaint the walls and get drunk on pink champale while listening to Trouble Funk. I'd say Trouble Funk were really influential, in the whole sense of rhythms and funk. With the Big Boys, who were huge locally in Austin, and **Minor Threat,** there was a whole crossover. Trouble Funk exposed a lot of suburban white kids to go-go music and funk in general. The whole sense of rhythm and heavy percussion, it was one of the reasons the Buttholes were excited to have two drummers in the band, just to have those extra polyrhythms.*

---

But while Trouble Funk and other go-go bands have occasionally flirted with mainstream crossover, a large scale go-go explosion never came. Mostly, this had to do with the music's appeal in primarily a live format, and its inability to translate into hit records. With 1987's *Trouble Over Here/Trouble Over There*, Trouble Funk attempted to move in a more radio-oriented direction, toward R&B and song-based funk. When it was a dismal failure, the group stopped recording altogether. As a live band, though, Trouble Funk has continued to tour the U.S. and Europe, where the group's rousing shows have converted and inspired new fans. Particularly well loved in England, Trouble Funk are cited as an influence on the rhythmically complex electronic dance music known as jungle, or drum 'n' bass. While go-go remains a popular sound in and around D.C., younger styles like jungle are applying Trouble Funk's beats to new technology and introducing it to new worlds.

## DISCOGRAPHY

*In Times of Trouble* (D.E.T.T., 1979; 1983); the rare debut album was reissued as a half live double album.

*Drop the Bomb* (Sugar Hill, 1982); the group's breakthrough, significant for its success in capturing a live sound in the studio, as well as for its release by a rap label.

*Saturday Night Live from Washington, D.C.* (Island, 1985); a terrific live album that effortlessly captures the spirit and energy of go-go.

*Trouble Over Here/Trouble Over There* (Island 1987); a largely unsuccessful attempt to expand the group's sound into more song-oriented R&B.

*Live* (Infinite Zero, 1996); an obscure, independently released live album from 1981, reissued and nationally available for the first time 15 years later.

*Early Singles* (Infinite Zero, 1997); a compilation from the group's beginnings.

## ESG

*ESG's first EP, I swear, has been sampled more than any other record. These sisters from the Bronx that looked like kids created this catchy funk, so intuitively and to the capacity of their skills. I* remember going to their shows, sweating and dancing, singing and clapping. They were like some friend of the family's band playing at a prom. When Jill [Cuniff, of Luscious Jackson] was putting together the band, she asked me, "Would you be interested in playing in an ESG cover band?" And I said, "Yeah, that sounds really cool." For us it was the same thing: a heavy bassline, a simple, funky drumbeat, and simple guitar lines. When we first started writing music for Luscious Jackson, ESG was a really big influence as far as approaching the music.

**Kate Schellenbach, Luscious Jackson**

ESG took a do-it-yourself approach to dance music, which by the late '70s had become incredibly slick and prefabricated. In doing so, they captured the attention of artsy downtown New Yorkers who wanted music that was as real and exciting as punk, but that could also move them on the dance floor. With a pure and natural musical vision, and an ability to stretch stylistic boundaries, ESG offered a New York analogue to the adventurous female post-punk being made in England by groups like the **Slits** and **Raincoats**. Because their simple and repetitive dance grooves made perfect raw material for hip-hop DJs and rappers, ESG has long been a favorite source of samples for everyone from Big Daddy Kane to Wu-Tang Clan. And at the same time, their honest, unadorned funk tunes inspired a young and eclectic early '80s New York music scene that would produce acts like the Beastie Boys, Moby, and Luscious Jackson.

*Moby*

*ESG have been sampled in millions of hip-hop and house records, and they have a couple songs that are such classics that pretty much any disco in New York could play them and everyone would scream and blow whistles.*

The Scroggins sisters grew up in a South Bronx apartment that was filled with the jazz and blues music of their white father, a struggling musician, and black mother, a former singer. By their early teens, their mother had become increasingly concerned about keeping the girls off the neighborhood streets, which had become a dangerous place for teens. To keep them occupied, she bought her daughters instruments and encouraged them to play. Sixteen-year-old Renee Scroggins took to the guitar, while younger sisters Deborah and Valerie began playing bass and drums, respectively. They learned quickly, and around 1976, the sisters formed a family group named after their birthstones (emerald, sapphire) and favorite color (gold), which they abbreviated as ESG.

Though the Scroggins sisters were fans of everything from classical music to Queen, ESG was most closely impacted by the funk and early disco music they heard in the neighborhood; it was these sounds the girls tried to recreate in their own songs. But given their limited skills and small group format, what came out was something very different. The music had the essential elements of dance music—the funky beats and basslines, with disco-styled vocals—but it moved with the simplicity and amateurism of a garage rock band. When ESG developed far enough to play live, they began appearing in various talent shows around the Bronx. Their combination of naive charm and memorable hooks was immediately appealing.

### David Pajo, Tortoise/Slint

*ESG were a huge influence, because their songs are so simple. They were one of those bands that when you see them you get really inspired to make your own music. What they do looks like anybody can do. I love when I get that feeling.*

Among those who happened to catch an early ESG talent show performance was Ed Bahlman, proprietor of 99 Records in Greenwich Village. Impressed by the teenagers, Bahlman began getting the group gigs in downtown Manhattan clubs like Hurrah's and the Mudd Club. From the start, they felt little connection with the club-hopping, coke-sniffing Soho art scene of the early '80s. The Scroggins sisters kept their distance—even to the extent of bringing their own food and drink to clubs. Richard McGuire, who as a member of **Liquid Liquid** often shared bills with ESG, says, "I always felt that they didn't understand what the hell they were doing in this scene. Everyone would love them, but they were very kind of closed to themselves. We did shows with them, and I remember their mother would come down with them and make sandwiches. It was a real family outing."

Still, ESG's stripped-down approach to groove-based music fit right in with the post-punk dance sounds at the time, and the three teenage sisters, plus a friend on percussion, became a downtown hit. In 1981, ESG met and performed for Tony Wilson, the head of well-known British indie label Factory Records. Impressed, Wilson introduced the band to producer Martin Hannett, who had planned to record Joy Division before the group's singer Ian Curtis committed suicide. With Joy Division falling apart, Hannett brought ESG into the studio instead. The result became ESG's debut U.K. single, "Moody"/"UFO," which was bolstered to six songs for their first American EP on 99 records.

### Tim Gane, Stereolab

*I bought this 12" because I liked the sleeve, and it was one of those records where you're just laughing because it's so good. I think it was the most focused record ever. You break down the parts and it was so simple, everything is unbelievably sparse. Yet it was completely realized. There's no waste on it at all.*

In no time, both the single and a follow-up 12-inch remix of "Moody" became club favorites in New York and London. The tracks were not so much songs as linear funk grooves, with echo-heavy dub percussion, a steady throbbing bass, and Renee's simple, repetitive vocal line (on "Moody"). After a second EP on 99 Records, ESG released their first album, 1983's *Come Away with ESG*. In addition to Renee, Valerie, and Deborah, the record featured a fourth sister, Marie, who joined the group on percussion. The band soon expanded even further to include the sisters' neighborhood friends, bassist Leroy Glover and guitarist David Miles, and all of the sisters shifted to percussion and began sharing vocals.

At the peak of ESG's popularity they were on the front lines of dance and punk music's intermingling, and found themselves opening for acts like Joe Jackson and the Clash. By 1984, though, as 99 Records became embroiled in legal battles unrelated to the band, ESG fell into their own disputes with Bahlman. For ESG's second album, Renee formed her own label, Emerald Saphire & Gold Records. Though they earned a club hit with the song "Standing in Line," internal problems soon split the sisters and ESG became largely inactive.

### Mark Robinson, Unrest/Air Miami

*ESG was just bass and drums, with very sparse guitar. In most bands today bass is kind of a background thing, but I've definitely thought of the bass as an instrument that could carry the song.*

Although the Scroggins women withdrew to raise families and work other jobs, their music was steadily heard—in the form of samples. Tupac, TLC, Big Daddy Kane, Public Enemy, LL Cool J, P. M. Dawn, and even nonrap artists like Unrest and Miles Davis are just some of the artists who've acknowledged sampling ESG (mostly "Moody" or "UFO"), and many more have done so without permission. In the early '90s, Renee and Val reemerged, releasing the appropriately titled EP, *Sample Credits Don't Pay Our Bills*. Recently the two sisters have enlisted their daughters—both in their teens—as the newest members of ESG, and a second-generation ESG seems to be on the rise.

## DISCOGRAPHY

*ESG* EP (99, 1981); the debut 12-inch single, featuring their best known songs "Moody" and "UFO."

*ESG Says "Dance" to "The Beat" of "Moody"* EP (99, 1982); a 3-song 12-inch single, with a remix of "Moody."

*Come Away with ESG* (99, 1983); the group's first full-length studio album.

*ESG II* (ESG Records, 1985); a second, self-released album.

*ESG* (Pow Wow, 1991); an album-length compilation of older material.

*Sample Credits Don't Pay Our Bills* EP (Nega Fulo, 1992); a five-song EP of new material.

*ESG Live!* (Nega Fulo, 1995); newly recorded and featuring a mix of older stuff with new songs.

# LIQUID LIQUID

*You could say Liquid Liquid showed me where the door was. They were taking funk rhythms and exporting them out of the party/disco context, magnifying and celebrating elements without destroying the party-ness of those elements. It was art funk that didn't sacrifice either. In Liquid songs, tiny syncopations could make enormous differences. Their way of balancing thick and thin lines, of using space—rather than more sound—to make something bigger, made an impression on me.*

### Sasha Frere-Jones, Ui

Though Liquid Liquid never produced a full-length album and lasted for only a few years, the dynamic minimalist funk it created has impacted everything from early hip-hop to modern art rock. The group's accessible dance grooves have been frequently sampled (by the likes of Deee-Lite and the Jungle Brothers), its instrumental textures and primitivist rhythms have inspired indie and post-rock bands such as Tortoise, Ui, and King Kong, and acts like De La Soul and LL Cool

J have invoked its surreal mantras. While Liquid Liquid like to call their songs "big beat" or "body music," a better label is simply "visionary."

Before Liquid Liquid, there was Liquid Idiot. Formed in 1978 by New Jersey college students Richard McGuire and Scott Hartley—one studying art, the other philosophy—Liquid Idiot was a punk-inspired ensemble featuring untrained members and an ever-changing lineup. For each performance, the band invited audience members to bring their own instruments and play along with McGuire's guitar or keyboard and Hartley's drums. When the two graduated and moved to New York City the following year, Liquid Idiot focused itself into a more guitar-driven power trio. On bass and vocals they added Sal Principato, a fellow Jerseyite who was doing experimental poetry in the city.

### Thurston Moore, Sonic Youth

*Sonic Youth probably played their first gig ever at this performance space called A. We used to hang out there, and another group that played a lot was Liquid Idiot, before they changed their name to Liquid Liquid. They were extremely rhythm-based, more sort of ethnic-influenced rhythm music, which New York bands were always influenced by, even us.*

After some gigs at CBGB and an independent single, the Idiots began to move away from their punk sound into more rhythmic, percussion-oriented territory. On the side, they'd begun playing with a 13-piece Liquid Orchestra, a percussion improv group that harked back to the original Idiot concept. When Orchestra marimba player Dennis Young joined Liquid Idiot, McGuire switched to bass, while Principato took up percussion and fiddled with voice echo devices. A name adjustment seemed appropriate, so in early '81 the quartet became Liquid Liquid. "The punk thing was over and I wanted to do something different than heavy guitar," says McGuire. "We were listening to all this heavily percussive music—Fela Kuti, reggae, Can—so it just seemed like the logical direction. Liquid Idiot had a sort of punk aesthetic to the name, and the band was getting more sophisticated and groovy. But we already had a name as Liquid Idiot, so I didn't want it to change too much."

As Liquid Liquid began gigging around New York, the group met Ed Bahlman, a hip downtown record store owner who had begun putting out his own releases. Bahlman was working with another bass-and-percussion-heavy outfit, ESG, and was interested in making a record with Liquid as well. With only the studio budget to record two songs, the band added three live tracks and released its self-titled debut EP on Bahlman's 99 Records. The unusual mix of post-punk weirdness with funk rhythms and dub effects on tracks like "Rubbermiro" (which features the trumpet of actor and original Sonic Youth drummer Richard Edson) prefigured post-rock a decade and a half before that term was invented.

### David Pajo, Tortoise/Slint

*John McEntire [of Tortoise] turned me on to them. I think that was a big influence on Tortoise before I was in the band. Tortoise does stuff that's similar to what they were doing. A lot of bass and percussion, and some electronic songs.*

By the group's second EP, *Successive Reflexes,* the band had landed in the center of a diverse early '80s art and music world. Between McGuire's pursuits in visual art and the band's eclectic sound, Liquid Liquid were at a crossroads between the burgeoning hip-hop music/graffiti-art scene uptown, rising downtown art stars like Keith Herring, no wave–inspired rock of Sonic Youth, and the post-disco dance scene of clubs like the Danceteria (Madonna's early hangout). "It seemed like there were all these overlapping worlds," McGuire recalls. "By 1980 there was this big New York New Wave Show that debuted the work of Keith and Jean-Michel Basquiat [whose graffiti partner, Al Diaz, played a homemade "metalphone" on Liquid's records] and a host of other graffitti artists. Merging all of that with the punk and new wave stuff, me included. Photographers like Robert Mapplethorpe, all those no wave people like Arto Lindsay [of **DNA**] and **Lydia Lunch**. Music and art colliding."

Liquid Liquid's most fully realized recording and their biggest success came in 1983, with the release of a third EP, *Optimo.* Tracks like "Cavern" and "Optimo" combined disco beats and aggressive basslines with obscured chants and lyric fragments to construct music that unified body and mind—dance music as art rock. "Cavern" in particular became a hit on the dance charts and a favorite at area clubs. Hip-hop DJs such as Afrika Bambaataa were spinning it regularly uptown, while downtown DJ (and future Madonna producer) Jellybean Benitez used it to close his sets at the Danceteria. Liquid was in demand at clubs all over the city, and they found themselves sharing the stage with acts like Chaka Khan and the Treacherous Three. And when a young Irish band known as U2 canceled on an opening spot for the Talking Heads' European tour, Liquid was invited to fill in.

*Darryl McDaniels, Run-D.M.C.*
*Liquid Liquid has the jam. I was definitely listening to them. Every time we did a park jam or something, we would freestyle over Liquid Liquid. As a DJ, you had to have Liquid Liquid in your crate.*

"Cavern" was so popular that it was no surprise when the song reached the ears of leading hip-hop DJ Grandmaster Flash. Yet Liquid Liquid's reaction to Flash and Melle Mel's late 1983 single "White Lines"—which was almost entirely constructed around "Cavern"'s melody and bassline and even adapted some of the lyrics—was mixed.) "We were really big fans of his [so] I was just amazed," McGuire says of "White Lines." But it was a mixture of feelings. You're excited that this guy you admire is doing this—and I remember an article at the time where [their label said they] had every intention of giving Liquid Liquid what they deserve—but then everything got kind of muddled."

"White Lines" went on to become one of the best known early rap songs (its catchphrase "something like a phenomenon" was invoked by countless rappers, and even became an album title, LL Cool J's 1997 *Phenomenon*), but Liquid Liquid did not receive a cent in royalties for over a decade. An agreement with Flash's label, Sugar Hill, was not reached until 1995, when Duran Duran's cover of "White Lines" forced a settlement. By then the cost and hassle of legal battles had long since exhausted both Liquid Liquid and 99 Records. As early as 1985, both were defunct.

McGuire, who left the group before it finally ended (and turned down an offer to join the Beastie Boys' backing band), focused on his artwork and has since distinguished himself as an illustrator in the *New York Times,* creator of children's books, toy designer, and picture book author. The other members of Liquid Liquid, who released one more 12-inch single before disbanding, have continued to be involved in music to various degrees. To a large extent, however, Liquid Liquid's contribution to modern music has been overlooked in the years since the band's demise.

In 1997, Sasha Frere-Jones, bassist in post-rock group Ui, and the Beastie Boys' record label, Grand Royal, joined forces to make Liquid Liquid's three EPs available on CD. It is the first step in what may be a radical reassessment of the band's place in the history of cutting-edge dance music. McGuire, meanwhile, is delightedly bemused: "We were a garage band, and I think it's hilarious that some of what we created ended up making its way into hip-hop culture and ultimately in a tiny way into mainstream culture. We are still being played in clubs. I would never have guessed in a million years that this quirky little band would have an afterlife!"

## DISCOGRAPHY

*Liquid Liquid* EP (99, 1981); the fantastic debut, most of which was recorded live at the group's first gig.

*Successive Reflexes* EP (99, 1981).

*Optimo* EP (99, 1983); the final EP, which contains the legendary "Cavern."

*Liquid Liquid* (Grand Royal, 1997); contains all of the quartet's recordings, on CD for the first time, and adds four live tracks from 1982.

# 12

# THE POST-INDUSTRIAL WASTELAND

hough this chapter is loosely designed to identify groups important in the early development of industrial music, not all of these bands are, strictly speaking, industrial bands. More generally, they are bands whose music in various ways uses as its backdrop the gray and decaying wasteland of post-industrial society. **Throbbing Gristle** and **Einstürzende Neubauten** did this explicitly, by incorporating industrial sounds and images into their music. The others, in more impressionistic ways, aimed to create a soundtrack for what they saw as the horror story of modern-day life.

As with other genre classifications, the question of just what constitutes industrial music is problematic. Though Throbbing Gristle is recognized as the first group to describe its music as "industrial," the ideas pursued in the music by no means started there. Important precursors include early 20th-century composers Luigi Russolo, whose 1915 essay "The Art of Noises" outlined the need for new music that reflected the sounds of the industrial age, as well as **Erik Satie** and Edgard Varese, who incorporated modern sounds into their work. Later, **John Cage** extolled the musical virtues of all sound, even those unwanted sounds generally known as noise. Postmodern literary techniques, such as those used by William Burroughs in his cutup works, were also important to the development of industrial music.

In the late '70s, with **Throbbing Gristle** and its Industrial Records label, a new crop of bands that closely identified themselves as industrial arose. These included Cabaret Voltaire, Clock DVA, and SPK, as well as other bands pursuing musical ideas along similar lines: Nurse with Wound, Laibach, This Heat. The idea was to pursue music in the context of the late industrial (or post-industrial) society, a dehumanized world increasingly alienated from nature. In addition, industrial musicians wished to focus on issues of the modern age, where propaganda and the access and control of information were becoming the primary tools of power.

### Genesis P-Orridge, Throbbing Gristle

*"Industrial" has a very clinical ring to it. It's not like that kind of romance of "paying your dues, man"; of being "on the road"—rock 'n'roll as a career being worthwhile in itself, and all that shit. So it was cynical and ironic, and also accurate. And we liked the imagery of factories—I mean, we just thought there was a whole untapped area of imagery and noise which was suggested when we thought of "industrial." [from Industrial Culture Handbook]*

A second strain of industrial music, even more indebted to Cage and 20th-century art music, arose shortly after **Throbbing Gristle** coined the term. Led by German band **Einstürzende Neubauten**—and including groups like England's Test Department and American percussionist Z'ev—these groups took the industrial idea literally and employed industrial material to make music. Using power tools and assorted metal objects, they created new instruments out of the rubble of industrial society. This was clearly industrial music in its purest form.

By the time industrial music entered mainstream consciousness in the late '80s and '90s through bands such as Ministry and Nine Inch Nails, industrial music had changed quite a bit. To a large extent, these bands were inspired by groups like **Chrome**, the **Birthday Party**, and **Big Black**, who manipulated traditional rock instruments to create metallic, industrial sounds. While popular industrial bands were inspired by the music of these early groups, new technology meant bands no longer had to use power tools to achieve the sounds of sledgehammers or electric drills. Instead, they could simply sample from earlier industrial bands who'd done the work for them.

In addition to the tools used to create industrial music, the genre itself has shifted in the '90s. No longer tied to the avant-garde, popular industrial bands have applied industrial sounds to what are essentially pop songs. Though some of the sonic characteristics remain, current industrial music has to a large extent been removed from its original context. With young bands like Gravity Kills and Marilyn Manson, industrial music has emerged as one of the defining sounds of commercial "alternative" music in the '90s.

## THROBBING GRISTLE

*[Music] is a platform for propaganda. And it's also a way to apply our ideas to show that without any musical training or background, through applying our philosophy to music, we made the music work as well....The philosophy must have something in it or the records wouldn't have worked and we wouldn't have had an influence worldwide.*

**Genesis P-Orridge, Throbbing Gristle [from *Re/Search #4/5*]**

The history of industrial music as we know it begins with Throbbing Gristle. With their label, Industrial Records, and their pseudo-corporate slogan, "Industrial Music for Industrial People," they provided the genre with a name. Not so much a band as a group of art terrorists who chose sound—noise, tape effects, documentary material, and songs as well—as the best medium for their attack. TG's reputation, then, is based less on compelling music than the power of its ideas.

---

### King Coffey, Butthole Surfers

*Throbbing Gristle threw out all the rules altogether. We had the greatest amount of respect for them, we still do. They took the promise of punk rock to the highest level, where they no longer became a rock band. They threw away any kind of structure from their songs, from the chorus-verse to the instrumentation. The whole aesthetic of making the industrial sounds of a modern society part of their music was revolutionary.*

---

As a general approach, the group claimed to fight an "information war" aimed at breaking the mass media's control over what the public sees and hears. Using do-it-yourself methods and a mischievous tendency to disseminate misinformation, TG went out of its way to cover topics clearly not found in newspapers or prime time television. They investigated a post-industrial nightmare that included fascism and its related atrocities, the dehumanization of factory labor, and social deviance in all forms. In TG's worldview, nothing was sacred and shock was an avenue to pure freedom. Much of the group's material is designed to offend, and succeeds quite well. They shrugged off accusations that they were exploitative, or irresponsible in their use of Nazi symbolism, or degenerate in their choice of subject matter. In provoking a strong reaction Throbbing Gristle felt it had done its job.

Adopting the cutup techniques of avant-garde writer William Burroughs and artist Brion Gysin, Throbbing Gristle pioneered the use of cut up and spliced tape material in the rock world. They were also early champions of cassettes—which were cheap and easy but not yet accepted as a commercial medium—and helped create a cassette underground that enabled independent and extreme music to flourish. Their musical successors include Nine Inch Nails—whose Trent Reznor has worked with members of TG—and just about anyone else who's ever set foot in the world of industrial music.

The roots of Throbbing Gristle go back to 1969's radical performance group Coum Transmissions, which was directed by future Gristlers Genesis P-Orridge (Neil Megson) and Cosey Fanni Tutti (Christine Newby). They spent a number of years shocking and provoking even the most open-minded members of the avant-garde art world with shows featuring body fluids, dead animal parts, and nude photos of Cosey (a part-time stripper), that pushed the limits of obscenity and taboo. By the mid-'70s, the group—which by then featured Peter "Sleazy" Christopherson and Chris Carter as well—determined that the best avenue for continuing their cultural assault was music. Using an array of instruments (most of which they couldn't play), as well as tape machines and various electronic effects, the quartet renamed themselves after the northern England slang for an erection, Throbbing Gristle.

---

### Lou Barlow, Sebadoh/Folk Implosion

*Stuff like Throbbing Gristle made me want to make my own music more than it made me want to listen to theirs. I just thought it was really exciting that they were exploring these really intense themes, like autopsies and all these horrible things that seemed really exciting to me at 13 or 14.*

---

Throbbing Gristle's first show, in 1976, was clearly an outgrowth of Coum's antics. The performance, a "live demonstration" that included the display of used tampons among other items, created such an uproar that it led a member of parliament to publicly brand Throbbing Gristle "the Wreckers of Civilization" (this, incidentally, came only weeks before the Sex Pistols unleashed punk's anarchy on the world). P-Orridge described TG's goal as "confounding the norm more or less for its own sake, a tried and tested subversive cultural technique."

With the formation of their Industrial Records label (which would later put out records by other important TG-inspired acts such as Cabaret Voltaire, SPK, and Clock DVA), Throbbing Gristle began releasing its series of willfully perverse, exceedingly low-fi cassette recordings. After a barely heard debut EP called *The Best of Throbbing Gristle Vol. 2,* the group made their first album, called *Second Annual Report.* A parody of the corporate music business, the cassette—of which only 785 copies were initially made—featured a black-and-white typeset cover designed to resemble a business report (a market research questionnaire was included as well). A tape collage of noise, effects, talking, electronic pulsations, and Charles Manson references, *Second* is often difficult to identify as music. "When we finished that first record, we went outside," P-Orridge told *Re/Search,* "and we suddenly heard trains going past, and little workshops under the railway arches, and the lathes going, and electric saws, and we suddenly thought, 'We haven't actually created anything at all, we've just taken it in subconsciously and *re*-created it.'"

---

### Tony Lee, Railroad Jerk

*I first got a four track after I had listened to [Throbbing Gristle] for about a year. I worked in a factory on the midnight shift, so I got the idea to bring my tape recorder and make this sound collage. I learned a lot about recording from that music. From the beginning with Railroad Jerk, we didn't talk about music. We just talked about sounds. We had a list of sounds—like a bottle rolling down the street or sand paper scratching together—that we drew from. That was our aesthetic.*

---

"United," the flipside to the single "Zyclon B Zombie" (named in "deliberate bad taste" after Nazi nerve gas) offered a rare taste of musicality, albeit a typically twisted one; though its lyrics were derived from the writings of occultist Aleister (the Great Beast) Crowley, the track sounded like a sweet electro-pop ditty. A second album, called *D.o.A.: The Third and Final Report of Throbbing Gristle,* refined the group's approach by adding shades of color. A more direct brand of humor came through with "Death Threats," which featured angry messages pulled from the group's answering machine, as well as an Abba tribute and a new 17-second version of "United" that consisted of the song being fast-forwarded. The inclusion of a solo track by each member of Throbbing Gristle lent further diversity to the record.

---

### John McEntire, Tortoise/Sea and Cake:

*It was a total shock, when I first heard it. I was like 15 years old, and I didn't know you could do things like that. It was a real departure from the straight ahead fast 4/4 punk rock stuff. It was so much more extreme than any of that shit. Their use of electronics was so far ahead of its time.*

---

*20 Jazz Funk Greats* followed shortly after *D.o.A.* and brought TG's love affair with misinformation to a climax. Along with the dreadfully misleading title, the cover art—a photo of the well-groomed, conservatively dressed group standing amid green grass and flowers—offered few clues for the uninitiated as to what was contained inside. But to confound even those who expected the worst from the group, *Jazz Funk* was their most accessible effort, often melodic and playful.

1980's *Heathen Earth*, recorded live in studio with a small crowd present, would be their last studio album. Following some soundtrack work for British cult film director Derek Jarman, Throbbing Gristle splintered into two groups: Chris and Cosey formed CTI (Creative Technology Institute) and also recorded synth pop under their own names. Genesis and Sleazy's Psychic TV more or less continued Throbbing Gristle's dark journey, though with increasingly musical results. Sleazy soon left to form Coil, and they are all active musicians today.

---

### Mark Hosler, Negativland
*Every project we've done since 1983 has been a conceptual project. Everything has some bigger concept to it, and all the packaging and the graphics, and even the press releases or ads, is all thought of as part of the art. I think that was something I got out of hearing Throbbing Gristle.*

---

## DISCOGRAPHY

*2nd Annual Report* (Industrial, 1977; Mute, 1991); the earliest release still available, a low-fi sound collage.

*D.o.A.: The Third and Final Report* (Industrial, 1978; Mute, 1991); a varied collection of solo works, tape pieces, noise, and songs.

*20 Jazz Funk Greats* (Industrial, 1978; Mute, 1991); the group's most accessible release, that injects bits of melody and definable songs between the noise.

*Heathen Earth* (Industrial, 1980; Mute, 1991); the final studio release, recorded live in front of a small audience.

*Throbbing Gristle's Greatest Hits* (Rough Trade, 1980); a compilation taken from the four albums.

*Funeral in Berlin* (Zensor [Germany] 1980; Mute, 1981); a live recording, featuring previously unreleased material.

*24 Hours* (Industrial [cassette], 1981); a "box set" of 24 one-hour live cassettes, later bolstered to 33 tapes and sold separately.

*Mission of Dead Souls* (Fetish, 1981; Mute, 1991); a live recording of the band's final show.

*Journey Through a Body* (1981; Mute, 1993) features the group's final studio recordings from 1981.

*Very Friendly, The First Annual Report* (Spurt, 1987; Genetic Terrorists, 1993); includes the group's earliest recordings, from 1975–76.

*TG CD1* (Mute, 1988); a collection of instrumental studio experiments from 1979.

## EINSTÜRZENDE NEUBAUTEN

*Growing up in Seattle was a heavy metal experience all the way. At like 16, I decided I just hated it—so much bravado and showing off—there was just nothing about it I could relate to. But there was a strong influence musically, in terms of the aggression and the starkness. And Einstürzende got me to realize there were things about heavy metal I loved, that had to be part of any band I was in. I realized you could include elements you like without having all the bullshit—the guitar solos and the four-octave range. I saw them do a free show in this park in Seattle. There were a lot of yuppies walking their dogs. All of a sudden they kicked into a song and I've never seen so many people's mouths drop at the same time. It was the most amazing show I've ever seen. They were hitting metal sheets with microphoned sticks and it sounded like the best industrial record with samples you could ever hear.*

### Chris Cornell, Soundgarden

here **Throbbing Gristle** invented industrial music as a concept and image, it was German ensemble Einstürzende Neubauten—which means "collapsing new buildings," an apt description of their sound—who made industrial a very real element in musical terms. They accomplished this by using industrial tools as percussive instruments, introducing a whole set of new sounds—made by pneumatic drills, metal sheets, hammers, chains, industrial springs, air-conditioning ducts, glass, garbage cans, metal cutters, cement mixers—and forging a revolutionary postapocalyptic tribal music. Today, these sounds are the standard aural elements in the music of Depeche Mode (who sampled the group), Nine Inch Nails (whose Trent Reznor recently signed the band to his Nothing record label), Marilyn Manson, and countless other bands, though most of these groups have taken the rather un-industrial approach of reproducing the sounds through digital sampling.

With Russolo's "The Art of Noises" and **John Cage**'s idea that "any sound is musical" as starting points, Einstürzende Neubauten set about creating new music out of the sounds that permeate our 20th-century urban environment. The visual impact of seeing Neubauten on stage with power tools and banging on metal made them as much of a performance group as they were a band, and much of their most compelling work—such as the site-specific concerts in which they "played" bridges and sides of buildings—cannot be fully appreciated on record. Einsturzende Neubauten were the ultimate do-it-yourself band, making music without even the need for musical instruments.

---

### Marcellus Hall, Railroad Jerk

*It opened up my world in helping me to realize you didn't need money to buy instruments, you didn't need to have instruments. They were exhibiting that you could just pick up anything and make music. I didn't have any obvious musical talent or training, but I always wanted to do it, so examples like that were inspiring. The way Railroad Jerk use various types of percussion—banging on metal things and stuff—would be subtly influenced by Einstürzende Neubauten.*

---

Einstürzende Neubauten were formed by guitarist Blixa Bargeld (Christian Emmerich) and American-born bassist N. U. Unruh (Andrew Chudy) in 1979, out of Berlin's thriving Dadaist art and music movement. Gudun Gut and Beate Bartel joined the group for a short while, but they were soon replaced by industrial percussionist F. M Einheit (Frank Martin Strauss) from the group Abwarts. A strange coincidence brought the group to national attention (and controversy) early on: Just weeks after the release of their first single, the brand new German Congress Center building collapsed. It seemed a fitting introduction to a band whose slogan became: "Destruction is not negative, you must destroy to build."

Neubauten's debut album, 1981's *Kollaps,* mixed post-punk guitar sounds and Bargeld's dark and guttural German vocals with layers of thrashing and grinding industrial noise to produce something that was unlike anything before it. They followed it with "Thirsty Animal," a single featuring **Lydia Lunch** and the **Birthday Party**'s Rowland Howard, that made the music's extreme physicality and aggression even more corporeal by using the percussive sounds of Bargeld's microphoned rib cage being beaten by other band members.

---

*Mark Robinson, Unrest*
*They displayed all their instruments on the back cover [of Kollaps]. Drills and hammers and a big cage they would bang on. I thought that was pretty amazing, incorporating metal and different things. At the first public Unrest concert we were banging on a Yield sign, and there's a song on our first album where we bang on metal the whole time. It was our ode to Einstürzende Neubauten.*

---

With their 1983 album, *Drawings of Patient O.T.*, Neubauten expanded to include bassist Mark Chung (from Einheit's Abwarts) and guitarist Alexander Hacke (a.k.a Alex von Borsig), who had been the group's sound technician early on. With the expanded personnel, the group ventured into more conventional territory; material such as "Armenia" (based on an Armenian folk tune) sounded liked real songs. With 1985's *Halber Mensch*, they moved even further toward accessibility with a stronger concentration on vocals (even including a capella), dance beats (with an **Adrian Sherwood** remix), and a Lee Hazlewood cover. At the same time Neubauten's live act was as trangressive as ever. Their most celebrated show came at a 1984 performance of their "Concerto for Voices and Machinery" at London's Institute for Contemporary Arts. Members of the group (along with **Throbbing Gristle**'s Genesis P-Orridge and others) began digging up the stage with their chainsaws and pneumatic drills until theater management cut the power off.

By the late '80s, Einstürzende Neubauten had defied all odds and become an accepted part of the German art—and even pop—scene. They were commissioned to compose theater work as well as Jordache jeans commercials, and were chosen to represent their country at the 1986 Expo in Montreal. Having established themselves at home, the group offered *Fuenf auf der Nach Oben Offenen Richterskala* (*Five on the Open-Ended Richter Scale*), their first record to offer original material in English, as well as string orchestration and a quieter overall sound.

---

*Alec Empire, Atari Teenage Riot*
*Einstürzende Neubauten were so important in Germany, or in Berlin especially. Every band had to sound like them in the '80s, and I didn't like that. Then I discovered the stuff later on in the '90s.*

---

Though they've cut down on activity in the '90s, Neubauten remains an active and viable band. The majority of their recent work, with the exception of 1993's *Tabular Rasa*, has been tied to the theater. They've even set up a label, Ego, to release film- and stage-related work, as well as solo projects. Their recent *Faustmusik* was written for an opera, based on the Faust tale, that featured Bargeld in the role of Mephistopheles. Increasingly, outside projects have consumed the time of individual members. Since 1983, Bargeld has been a member of Nick Cave's band, the Bad Seeds. Hacke was a member of another **Birthday Party** offshoot, Crime and the City Solution, while Einheit has explored the further devolution of environmental music with his side band Stein (stone), which uses rocks to create percussive music.

## DISCOGRAPHY

*Kollaps* (ZickZack [Ger.], 1981; 1988); their dark and transgressive debut.

*Drawings of Patient O.T.* (Some Bizarre/Ze, 1983; Thirsty Ear, 1995); a more melodic album, with an expanded lineup.

*80-83 Strategies Against Architecture* (Mute, 1983; 1994); a compilation of early material, including many of the tracks from *Kollaps*.

*2 x 4* (ROIR, 1984); a live recording made in 1982.

*Halber Mensch* (Some Bizarre/Rough Trade, 1985; Thirsty Ear, 1995); their best amalgamation of industrial percussion with song structure.

*Fuenf auf der Nach Oben Offenen Richterskala* (Some Bizarre, 1987; Thirsty Ear, 1995); a record with some original music in English.

*Haus de Luege* (Some Bizarre/Relativity, 1989; Thirsty Ear, 1995).

*Strategies Against Architecture II* (Mute, 1991); a second compilation, with a mix of album tracks and previously unreleased material from 1984-1990.

*Die Hamletmaschine* (Ego /Rough Trade, 1991); their first effort in theater music, and the first release on their Ego label.

*Tabula Rasa* (Mute, 1993); a conceptual work dealing with German unification.

*Faustmusik* (Mute, 1996); music composed for a theater production of Faust that starred Bargeld.

*Ende Neu* (Mute, 1996); featuring a streamlined group with Bargeld, Unruh, and Hacke, this was issued in *Remix* form the following year, with contributions from Jon Spencer, Alec Empire, Barry Adamson, and others.

# CHROME

*We wanted to make scary-funny music, if you can imagine that. We were definitely trying to twist it to the ends of human imagination at the time.*

**Helios Creed, Chrome**

By marrying the two seemingly incompatible sounds of '60s acid rock and '70s punk and adding bits of the latest technology, Chrome pioneered its own dark and twisted brand of freak rock, a kind of psychedelic cyberpunk. Though their music was of limited commercial appeal, the band managed to connect with a rather varied crew of new-wave rejects. Their bad-trip sci-fi rock has inspired post-hardcore maniacs like Jesus Lizard (who recorded a Chrome medley) and the Butthole Surfers (on whose records Chrome members have played), as well as goth and industrial acts from Ministry to Nine Inch Nails to Marilyn Manson. Now, younger groups like Pigeonhead and Six Finger Satellite are incorporating elements of Chrome's sound to bring the group's acid punk into the next century.

### Chris Cornell, Soundgarden

*I was a big Chrome fan. It was just like walking through a shopping mall on acid. Sounds came at you from every direction, kind of like industrial before anyone knew what that was. I've played Chrome for people who never heard them and they can't believe it came out in 1979. It sounds so much like what people are doing today. A certain amount of rhythmic, atonal guitar is probably how it translated to our band, where you didn't have to have riffs that sound like Black Sabbath. You could use the guitar as a rhythmic instrument without any melody at all.*

After studying music and art in Los Angeles with an associate of experimental composer **John Cage**, Thomas Edward Wisse headed north to San Francisco, where he assumed the name Damon Edge and formed Chrome in the mid-'70s. With bassist/violinist Gary Spain, guitarist John Lambdin and others, Edge played drums and produced Chrome's 1978 debut, *The Visitation,* on his own Siren label. It wasn't until guitarist Helios Creed (B. Johnson) joined later that year, though, that Chrome began to assert a distinctive sound and personality. Edge and Creed entered into a songwriting and producing partnership that incorporated Creed's love for Jimi Hendrix and folk music, Edge's avant-garde past, and the group's recent discovery of bands like the Sex Pistols and **Throbbing Gristle,** as well as nonmusical influences like science fiction books and horror movies, from Philip K. Dick to *Invasion of the Body Snatchers* to *A Clockwork Orange.* "I took all that stuff, put it in a bowl and mixed it up, and what came out was quite different than any of it," Creed says of Chrome's early sound.

---

### David Yow, Jesus Lizard

*Chrome was very important. I remember many, many nights of getting really drunk and taking a good bit of acid and just listening to the Chrome Box over and over. It would take us places we didn't know existed. I liked the funkiness—not in James Brown way, but in a dirty, screwy way. Some of the songs were really high-tech and clean, and some sound like a ghetto-blaster in the bathroom with a drum set.*

---

With *Alien Soundtracks,* the first fruits of the Edge/Creed collaboration, Chrome managed to cram all their disparate elements onto a simple, groundbreaking four-track recording which Creed called "industrial strength music." The album was punk in its disdain for high production values and its menacing attitude, but it was too psychedelic—with screaming guitar and electric violin solos—for most punks. And with its electronic effects and tape collages, the sound had more in common with the industrial noise of **Throbbing Gristle** than the burgeoning San Francisco punk scene. A truly inspired blend of new and old rock freakiness, the record defined Chrome's place as leaders of the pseudo-genre known as acid punk.

---

### Scott Kannberg, Pavement

*Their late '70s records are pretty crazy, warped stuff. There's a lot going on, electronic noises and minimal drums with rock guitar. They're very foreign sounding records. We were really influenced by those on our first single. We were like, "Oh, this sounds like Chrome. This is great."*

---

For their 1979 follow-up, *Half Machine Lip Moves,* Edge and Creed delved even further into futuristic ~~re~~ soundscapes. Having dismissed their bandmates for the record, the duo played all instru~~~des what they credited to a helpful computer they named John L. Cyborg. The sound is more ~~~~lectronic, and even more extreme than *Alien Soundtracks.* Songs like "Abstract Nympho" ~~Chrome Police (A Cold Clawey Bombin)" push the noise and instrumental effects to ~~nile sacrificing neither the strong rock beat nor the sense of humor.

Edge and Creed continued to go it alone for 1980's *Red Exposure*, a more polished studio record that moved closer toward the recognizably industrial sound that would be adopted by later sampler-oriented industrial bands like Nine Inch Nails. By the end of the year, though, Chrome became a full band once again when it added John and Hilary Hanes—known as the Stench Brothers—on bass and drums. Their addition made subsequent records like *Blood on the Moon* and *3rd from the Sun* tighter and more driving, plus it opened Chrome to new possibilities. "It had a better sound in a lot of ways, more energetic. Also, they enabled us to play live," Creed says.

In 1982, San Francisco indie Subterranean released the 6-LP collection, *Chrome Box*, which reissued all previous Chrome records plus two discs of new material, *Chronicles I and II*. In 1983, Edge moved with his girlfriend to France and the partnership between Edge and Creed abruptly ended. Against Creed's wishes, Edge continued recording what were essentially solo albums under the Chrome name. Released on European labels, these later Chrome releases failed to capture the metallic dementia of the group's earlier work. Left without a group, Helios Creed embarked on a solo career that came closer to carrying on the mission of the original Chrome.

In 1995, after returning to the U.S. and struggling with heroin addiction, Damon Edge died of a heart attack at age 45. The following year, Helios Creed—now a middle-aged parent of a teenage Marilyn Manson fan—re-formed Chrome with the Stench Brothers and released a new record called *Retro Transmission*. Like all past Chrome releases the album's cover features Damon Edge's collage artwork, making it the closest thing to a fully reunited Chrome record we're ever likely to see.

## DISCOGRAPHY

*The Visitation* (Siren, 1978); Edge's pre-Helios Creed release.

*Alien Soundtracks* (Siren, 1978; Touch & Go, 1990); the first of two classic Chrome albums, featuring a four-person band led by Edge and Creed.

*Half Machine Lip Moves* (Siren, 1979; Touch & Go, 1990); the second of the group's most successful records, recorded with only Edge and Creed.

*Read Only Memory* EP (Siren, 1979); a soundtrack recording.

*Red Exposure* (Siren, 1980); the second full-length record to feature Chrome as a duo of Edge and Creed.

*Blood on the Moon* (Siren, 1981); a more full-band sound, with the addition of the Stench brothers.

*3rd from the Sun* (Siren, 1982).

*No Humans Allowed* (Siren, 1982); a compilation of rare tracks and singles.

*Chrome Box* (Subterranean, 1982; Cleopatra, 1996), the three-CD box set reissue (originally 6 LPs) contains the majority of Chrome recordings made with Edge and Creed together.

## THE BIRTHDAY PARTY

*I think the Birthday Party and Led Zepellin are my two biggest influences. The structures, combining punk rock with swing, sounded kind of dangerous and a little harder to get hold of. I remember after one of the first Scratch Acid [Yow's first band] shows, listening to a tape of the show and getting really bummed out because it sounded to me like I was just mimicking Nick Cave. I remember I said, "That's gotta stop, I gotta stop doing that." I don't think I was doing it on purpose, it was just that it was the first time I'd been singing in a band and the Birthday Party was my favorite group. So I just took from them, almost subconsciously.*

*David Yow, Jesus Lizr*

The Birthday Party was eternally morbid and perverse, and played music like rabid junkyard dogs. As such, they were quickly (though reluctantly) recognized as a leading influence on the goth bands that arose in the early '80s, even as the band's dark wit and confrontational live show made them heroes to groups like the Jesus Lizard and Butthole Surfers. In the '90s, as the early legacy of the Birthday Party has been carried into adulthood through their leader Nick Cave's solo career, the group's unbridled anarchy continues to inspire bands around the world.

The Birthday Party's roots lie in Australia's Boys Next Door, a band started by singer Nick Cave, guitarist Mick Harvey, and drummer Phil Calvert while at boarding school in the early '70s. With high school graduation and the addition of bassist Tracy Pew and guitarist Rowland S. Howard, the band became part of a Melbourne punk scene split between arty college bands and junkie rockers. Though Cave enrolled briefly in art school to pursue painting, the group had more in common with the seamier, drug-addled bands inspired by aggressive American proto-punks like the **Stooges, Suicide,** and the Velvet Underground.

The Boys Next Door soon developed a reputation in Melbourne for their sometimes violent stage show, which made it difficult to get gigs and caused problems with the police. As Australia was becoming a dead end for the band, they released a debut album, 1979's *Door Door*. While they've has since disavowed the record, it proved instrumental in determining the group's future path. Unhappy with the record and everything the Boys Next Door had become, the group decided to move to England. With the release of a second album, the group changed its name to the Birthday Party.

---

### King Coffey, Butthole Surfers

*They seemed like psychotics who might kill you or each other. How could these guys not be role models? I never want to think we ripped off anyone, but this was definitely one band doing things right. There was no band like them at the time, and though there have been imitators, there's been no band like them since. They seemed like an explosion, each record seems more intense than the last. We could relate to them because they came from a punk background, but they threw off the shackles of punk and created some of the best recordings of the '80s.*

---

London did not live up to their expectations. "From Australia, London was like this dream world, where on any particular night you could see all sorts of incredible music," Cave remembers. "We came fully expecting to be confronted with this paradise and we actually found London suffering from one of the most deadly boring periods in its rock 'n' roll history. I remember two nights after arriving in London, going to see a package concert with Echo & the Bunnymen, Psychedelic Furs, Teardrop Explodes, and another band, all of whom we thought were making really cool records. And we just couldn't believe our ears, it was just so bad and so boring. And I guess the Birthday ~ty was born from that. From a contempt for what we found in England."

~r antipathy for the current music scene and bitterness over the squalid living conditions in London made the band even more extreme and nihilistic, and their chaotic live shows ~ a following. In an all-out assault on the audience, Cave would howl like a vam- ~ and accost audience members, while Harvey and Howard sprayed shrill guitar ~diculously clad in a leather S&M cowboy outfit—pummeled out his bassline.

Despite the Birthday Party's underlying humor, the band's dark and sometimes ghoulish persona caused it to be grouped with goth bands such as Sisters of Mercy, whom they passionately hated.

### Chris Cornell, Soundgarden

*That sonic approach—where it's kind of screaming and white noise but there's an energy and emotion you can't get from melody—changed my perspective quite a bit about being a singer. Until that point, the most influential band I listened to was the Beatles, where there's nothing but melody and harmonies. The Birthday Party was a band where the singing was expressive in a way that didn't really have a lot to do with melody, but was almost more effective sometimes.*

1981's *Prayers on Fire* and the following year's *Junkyard* represent the band at the peak of its powers, with increasingly assured and adventurous material. Songs like "Nick the Stripper," "Big-Jesus-Trash-Can," and "Dead Joe" further explored the band's love of black humor, the grotesque, and a twisted ramshackle take on the blues. Critically acclaimed, and with a growing cult following, the Birthday Party was ignored by the mainstream and continued to struggle to survive. In 1981, Pew was arrested and imprisoned on drug charges, causing further turmoil in the group. Magazine bassist Barry Adamson filled in for parts of *Junkyard*.

By the end of 1982, the Birthday Party were again ready for major changes. Firing Calvert (who later joined Psychedelic Furs), Harvey took over as drummer and the band became leaner and meaner. Also, the group gave up on London and moved to Berlin. "London was horrendous for us. We had no money, we couldn't get any work, we were living in appalling circumstances. When we went to Berlin, we were immediately welcomed into a strong artistic circle that was very generous and interesting. For the first time, the Birthday Party was seen by a significant number of people as a band of some importance."

### Chris Connelly, the Bells/Ministry/Revolting Cocks

*I was never into the gothic thing at all, but the Birthday Party was hilarious as well. They had really absurd songs, and also very creepy, violent songs. I know they really influenced Al [Jourgensen] and Paul [Barker] in Ministry, and it was certainly a common denominator we had. I loved the idea that the Birthday Party never really gave a fuck, they were uncontrollable. They just did what they did and to hell with everybody else. At the beginning of my involvement with the Revolting Cocks and Ministry, that was an attitude we had.*

While life in Berlin proved more artistically satisfying and economically feasible, by 1983 internal conflicts—drug problems and personal animosities—had become unbearable. In addition, Cave began to exert a dominant role in the band's songwriting that Howard, the group's other songwriter, found objectionable. "We were no longer mischievous, fun-loving boys," Cave says. "Things had gotten quite evil within the group."

Though the band recorded two more EPs, *The Bad Seed* and *Mutiny!*, their music was incre ingly evolving into what would become Nick Cave's solo career. By the time of *Mutiny!*'s release, the Birthday Party had broken up. Almost immediately, Cave formed the Bad Seeds with Harvey, Adamson, and guitarist Blixa Bargeld of Berlin's **Einstürzende Neubauten.** He also published a novel, and a book of lyrics, plays, and prose. Howard collaborated with **Lydia Lunch,** and also formed Crime and the City Solution with his brother Harry, singer Simon Bonney, and Harvey (when he was in the Bad Seeds), as well as **Swell Maps** drummer Epic Soundtracks. More recently, Harvey has recorded two solo albums of **Serge Gainsbourg** songs. Pew died of complications from epilepsy in 1986.

## DISCOGRAPHY

(Boys Next Door) *Door Door* (Mushroom [Aus.], 1979); a relatively straight rock record that the group has since disavowed.

*The Birthday Party* (Missing Link [Aus.], 1980; 4AD, 1989); the first record as the Birthday Party, made of previously released material, and reissued with *Hee Haw*, an EP released in 1979 as *The Boys Next Door.*

*Prayers on Fire* (Thermidor, 1981; 4AD, 1988); among the Birthday Party's most consistent and ferocious work.

*Junkyard* (4AD, 1982); features some of the band's best material.

*Drunk on the Pope's Blood* EP (4AD, 1982); a live release, featuring **Lydia Lunch** on one side, that captures the band's furious live shows.

*The Bad Seed* EP (4AD, 1983); first of two final EP releases, now collected with *Mutiny!* on one CD.

*Mutiny!* EP (4AD, 1983); the final studio recordings that pointed toward the direction Cave would take with the Bad Seeds.

*Peel Session Album* (Strange Fruit/Dutch East India, 1991); collects two previous Peel Session EPs.

*Hits* (4AD/Warner Bros., 1992); a 20-song collection that spans the band's entire recording career.

## BIG BLACK

*I would shoot myself in the face if I didn't have some way to blow off steam. And because I don't like sports, and because I don't like disco dancing, and because I don't take drugs, and because I don't drink, and I don't beat my head into the floor, and I don't have a wife to beat, I have Big Black.*

**Steve Albini, Big Black [from a radio interview]**

Though the idea would likely sicken him, Steve Albini can rightfully claim his place as the man behind much of the so-called alternative rock in the '90s. As a producer—or "recorder," the less grandiose term he prefers to use—Albini has played a huge behind-the-scenes role in defining the studio sound of literally dozens of notable bands, including Nirvana, PJ Harvey, Breeders, Helmet, Veruca Salt, Jesus Lizard, and Bush. Just as important, though, to Albini's legacy is his role as leader of mid-'80s band Big Black, whose dense wall of machine-gun guitars and relentless drum machine grind pioneered the current "industrial" sound made popular by bands like Nine Inch Nails and Marilyn Manson.

**Pulsford, Bush**

*...l done so many great albums and so much great work that has inspired us as a ...rk with Big Black was seminal and very important to me as a guitarist. [from ...,  February 1997]*

Steve Albini grew up in Missoula, Montana, far from any firsthand contact with the punk-rock underground of the late '70s and early '80s. Though he formed what was likely Missoula's first punk band during high school, he was anxious to find more developed music scenes. Having been accepted to study journalism at Northwestern University, Albini moved to Chicago in 1981. After a few ill-fated attempts to join other bands, he began his own musical project, Big Black. From the start, his band's basic principles (which he delineated in liner notes to *Pigpile*) included: to "avoid people who appeal to our vanity or amibition,...operate as much as possible apart from the 'music scene,'...and take no shit from anyone in the process."

Inspired as much by British post-punk bands like **Public Image Limited** and fringe noise groups like **Chrome** as by American hardcore, Albini did not feel tied to any traditional notion of what constituted punk. Big Black's first recording, 1982's *Lungs* EP, is almost entirely performed by Albini, on guitars and vocals, with an early Roland drum machine providing the beat. Though the record—packaged with "inserts" such as razor blades, firecrackers, and dollar bills—was as ugly and ferocious as any punk music around, it was rather tame compared to what was to come.

---

### Will Oldham, Palace

*The last record that we put out [Arise Therefore], that Steve recorded, had a drum machine. And it was sort of tribute to the Big Black records. The drum machine on the Big Black credits was always treated like another band member—as Roland, the Roland drum machine. We credited our drummer similarly, by giving her the name she was born with, which was Maya Tone.*

---

With 1983's *Bulldozer* and '84's *Racer-X* EPs, Big Black became an actual band when it added bassist Jeff Pezzati (of Naked Raygun) and guitarist Santiago Durango to the core of Albini and Roland (Pat Byrne of Urge Overkill provided some live drumming as well). The added guitars and studio-quality production (as opposed to *Lungs'* four-track recording), made the group's sound much fuller and infinitely more brutal. Blistering anthems like "The Ugly American" and "Texas" were packed with a sonic and lyrical aggression that spit rage at everything and anyone in shouting distance.

Big Black's potential was most fully realized between 1986 and '87, with the albums *Atomizer* and *Songs About Fucking*. With Dave Riley taking over on bass, the albums further refined the band's assault tactics. As always, Albini's lyrics dissected the dark side of middle America. Songs like "Jordan, Minnesota" and "Fish Fry" depicted the everyday cruelties and crass amorality lurking behind rural and suburban windows. Albini's take on the deep sickness portrayed was undoubtedly a combination of reality, fantasy, prophesy, and just messing around, though his ambiguous stance—he often seems to relish the depravity as much as criticize it—can be even more disturbing than the subject matter.

---

### Page Hamilton, Helmet

*I think they influenced a lot more bands than people know. A lot of industrial stuff out there right now is partially a result of what Big Black was doing—a simple old programmed drum machine, guitars, bass, and one guy adding verbal jabs of excitement to the music. The way the whole thing worked together was really powerful. The sound was really metallic and per-cussive—simple, nonvirtuoso—all about rhythm and dynamics.*

Just as *Atomizer*'s James Brown cover drew attention to the funk roots which weren't always apparent in Big Black, *Songs About Fucking*'s inclusion of **Kraftwerk**'s "The Model" highlighted the group's debt to early techno acts. By then, though, the group's marriage of punk and electronic beats was blossoming into an entirely new genre led by groups such as Ministry and Nine Inch Nails. In the summer of 1987, with Durango on the verge of entering law school, Big Black embarked on a farewell tour. They then promptly broke up, as Albini wrote, "to prevent us from overstaying our welcome." Ending as defiantly independent as they'd begun, Albini proudly noted in his *Pigpile* notes, "Nobody ever told us what to do, and nobody took any of our money."

### David Pajo, Tortoise/Slint

*Everything about them was like the coolest of the cool, we thought. The drum programming was super-cool, and the guitar tones were so brittle and machine-like. I just never heard anything like that before. And the lyrics were really cool and super-dark.*

After Big Black, Albini formed two more bands: Rapeman in the late '80s and Shellac in the '90s. He also made occasional forays into zine writing, where his punk puritanism often took the form of pointed, self-righteous attacks on those not meeting his standards. He reached his highest pro-file, though, recording other groups. Now, over a decade since Big Black last unleashed its terror-izing growl, Albini's trademark sound graces the grooves of multiplatinum records.

## DISCOGRAPHY

*Lungs* EP (Ruthless, 1982; Touch & Go, 1992); a nearly all-Albini production, with the help of Roland, the drum machine.

*Bulldozer* EP (Ruthless-Fever, 1983; Touch & Go, 1992); a fuller sound, with the addition of a second guitar and bass.

*Racer-X* EP (Homestead, 1984; Touch & Go, 1992); an even more refined sonic assault.

*The Hammer Party* (Homestead, 1986; Touch & Go, 1992); reissues the first three EPs on one CD.

*Atomizer* (Homestead, 1986; Touch & Go, 1992); the band's first full-length release finds the group at the peak of its powers.

*Headache* EP (Touch & Go, 1987; 1992); a release notable mainly for its particularly gruesome cover art, since deleted.

*The Rich Man's 8-Track Tape* (Homestead, 1987; Touch & Go, 1992); reissues on one CD of *Atomizer* and *Headache*.

*Songs About Fucking* (Touch & Go, 1987; 1992); the final studio album, which ends the group's career on a high note.

*Pigpile* (Touch & Go, 1992); a live album recorded on the band's final tour in 1987.

# 13

# BRITISH POST-PUNK

usic historians retelling the glorious tale of the Sex Pistols and the British punk explosion of 1976 can make it seem that punk was spontaneously generated by the Pistols, that nothing like it had existed before and nothing was ever the same after. But though punk rock may have represented a revival of youthful energy and subversion in rock—a rejection of the overly professional, overly pretentious megalith that rock had become—punk's sounds and ideals were almost immediately integrated into a recent past which included the very things punk orthodoxy claimed to hate: prog rock, glam rock, art rock, classic rock. As Colin Newman of the influential post-punk band **Wire** remembers of the punk era, "People weren't throwing away their Roxy Music and David Bowie records." As quickly as British punk's identity had been defined—not only by the Sex Pistols, but by the Clash, the Damned, and others—it was taken apart. Punk became fair game for anyone's use, and it was picked up not only by bands with a taste for the raw and unrefined but also by those with art rock leanings—groups that never felt a need to define themselves as one or the other, punk or prog. Therefore, nearly coinciding with punk was a genre that simultaneously took a step away from punk while it moved a step forward: for lack of a more original title, this newer music was known as post-punk.

---

### Tim Gane, Stereolab

*At the time, punk did follow the rules a bit. And that was the interesting thing about punk to me: The music it influenced was much better than the initial thing itself. Though I love a lot of the initial ideas, the Clash and so on, it really was the way it came out later—everything from Joy Division to* **Public Image** *to post-electronic music—that allowed everything to come out.*

---

Though it seemed to betray punk's anti-art stances, post-punk was in many ways a more true expression of punk's anarchistic ideals. For all its antiestablishment pronouncements, the Sex Pistols/Clash version of punk rock was, after all, the product of major labels that employed basic hard rock sounds and structures. Bands like **Public Image Limited, Wire,** and **Swell Maps** took punk's no-rules, do-it-yourself, destruction-of-rock promises literally and proceeded to create some of the most challenging, foreign, distinctive, and truly rebellious music of recent decades. This music was often so far ahead of its time that only in later decades would post-punk's musical ideas reach the mainstream, through the music of post-punk's successors: R.E.M., U2, Red Hot Chili Peppers, Sonic Youth, Butthole Surfers, and many more.

# PUBLIC IMAGE LIMITED

*Metal Box is probably my favorite album ever. I was completely blown away when I heard that. It was pure creativity.... And as years go by, it sounds more potent than it did. It sounds like everything is headed in that direction. It's very futuristic music, really. The bass and the drums, it's a lot of what people do in dance music. The repetition and groove of it all. They're a more important band than the Sex Pistols, musically. Much more important.*

**Tim Gane, Stereolab**

Though it's impossible to say definitively—and certainly the seeds were sown long before—you might pinpoint the start of the post-punk era at January 1978's final Sex Pistols gig, when singer Johnny Rotten uttered his band's famous last words: "Ever feel like you've been cheated?" and disappeared forever into history. Emerging to tear down everything his band had built up— and in doing so, actually accomplishing what punk only threatened—was the person behind the ridiculous stage name, the 22-year-old son of working class Irish immigrants, John Lydon.

Within months—before the dust had even settled on the tremendous cultural force that had been the Sex Pistols—Lydon unveiled his new band, or as he claimed, his multimedia "corporation," Public Image Limited. The goal this time was to destroy rock and start over. To retain complete control within a band, both financially and musically. To create an artistic entity that would replace the very institution of the rock band with something free to explore all avenues of creativity, musical and beyond. To mold new music rooted in sounds entirely foreign to traditional rock, part avant-garde and part world music, part nihilist and part spiritual. Though Lydon's uniquely post-punk concept of Public Image Limited would arguably prove more revolutionary than his punk assault as a Sex Pistol, PiL has been largely overlooked in music history while volumes have been written about the Sex Pistols.

### Mark Robinson, Unrest/Air Miami

*I liked how they had members in the band who didn't play instruments, and they were like a company. We tried to do that with Unrest. Our friend was in the band but wasn't really in the band—supposed to be a slide projector person. It gave me the idea you could do interesting stuff with this rock and roll thing, you don't have to just play in front of the audience, you can do all this other weird shit.*

With their first single, 1978's "Public Image," as a calling card and manifesto, Lydon let everyone know, "I will not be treated as property...the public image belongs to me." By the end of the year—with the release of the album *Public Image: First Issue*—it was clear Lydon was not about to rely on the sounds or notoriety of his former band. In the place of catchy punk rock, PiL offered a stark noise dub with little regard for song structure or melody, while Lydon's vocals traded in forceful singing for slow moans and tortured howls.

**David Yow, Jesus Lizard**

*I'd never heard anything like it before. The way the guitar and bass didn't go together—none of it went together—in a traditional way. Public Image were really influential to everyone in [Yow's first band] Scratch Acid.*

While *First Issue* contained its share of provocative lyrics, including an unrestrained attack on organized religion, unlike the Sex Pistols' formula of shock lyrics over hard rock songs, PiL focused almost entirely on musical innovation. Keith Levene, a classically trained musician who played briefly in the Clash, provided the angular and agitating guitar figures, more reminiscent of **Captain Beefheart** than Joe Strummer. Lydon's childhood friend Jah Wobble (John Wardle) weighed in on bass with an equally hypnotic and erratic groove, derived as much from German groups like **Can** as from Jamaican reggae. The remainder of the group testified to PiL's cynical experimentalism: Jim Walker on drums (soon gone), Jeanette Lee producing video, and Dave Crowe taking care of finances. And their liner notes—"Public Image Ltd. would like to thank absolutely nobody, thank you"—made their attitude perfectly clear.

**Carla Bozulich, Geraldine Fibbers**

*I thought it was great because they were doing a big "fuck you" to the punk rock thing.... Jah Wobble is the ultimate bass player. It sounds like he didn't know how to play, and it didn't matter because he was so good. The music was so simple, so stripped down, really repetitive, with all this empty space. It didn't necessarily need to rock.*

Following the terrifying "party dirge" single "Death Disco" (which included remixes, a practice virtually unheard of for rock bands of the time), Public Image dug even deeper in their aggressively uncommercial antirock aesthetic to produce their second album, *Metal Box*. This was a limited-edition set of three 12-inch 45 rpm singles packaged in a metal film canister (and later reissued as a double album called *Second Edition*). Now thoroughly rid of any traces of their punk pasts, Lydon, Levene, and Wobble (with drummer Martin Atkins, later of industrial supergroup Pigface, becoming an off-and-on member as well) created their masterpiece. A relentless deconstruction of rock that at the same time makes remarkably effective use of rock tools, *Metal Box/Second Edition* stands as the defining document of post-punk. The influence of Levene's tightly wound guitar screech would be felt immediately in bands like Killing Joke, **Gang of Four,** and the **Birthday Party,** and would soon emerge in the guitar playing of U2's Edge and Sonic Youth's Thurston Moore and Lee Ranaldo.

### Thurston Moore, Sonic Youth

*People didn't know what to think of the first record, it was such a damaged sounding thing. Uneasy listening. For us, and just about everyone I knew in bands, it was such a godhead. We had just started the band, and we were very influenced by PiL...I remember meeting Kate [Schellenbach of Luscious Jackson] when she was like 14. Her mom was a friend of [Sonic Youth's] Kim [Gordon], and she gave me this fanzine she was doing that had pictures of the Public Image gig [in New York] where they destroyed the screen and there was a riot. I was at that gig, it was great. Kate, and the Beastie Boys, were part of this whole scene of kids into hardcore and PiL*

Despite his lack of technical chops, Wobble was also recognized as a major post-punk innovator, with loping and watery basslines that introduced the more linear elements of dub and Eastern music into punk. Inner-band strife, though, led to Wobble's dismissal from the group, and 1981's *Flowers of Romance* was less successful without him. Still, Lydon, Levene, and Atkins managed to create another major breakthrough by building free-form songs around short, repetitive (at times Middle Eastern–sounding) percussion patterns. The band continued to grow in the studio and further explore their unique sound. Multimedia projects, which they'd promised from the start but hadn't followed through, began panning out as well.

By 1983, during the recording of their fourth studio album *This Is What You Want*, tensions peaked between PiL's remaining creative forces, Lydon and Levene. When the two determined they could no longer work together, Levene quit and Lydon erased Levene's guitar parts before completing the record on his own. Levene, in turn, released his own version of the album, called *Commercial Zone*, before embarking on a solo career. While "This Is Not a Love Song" became a minor hit for the band, under the sole direction of Lydon, PiL was never the same. They continued for another decade, but never produced material as defiantly transgressive as the initial trilogy of records.

### Kate Schellenbach, Luscious Jackson

*They were overshadowed by John Lydon's personality, but with their combination of the heavy dub sound of Jah Wobble's basslines and the scratchy minimalist guitar of Keith Levene, it seems like they were mixing up styles. And that applies to what we do as well. They seemed to be ahead of their time, and spawned that whole experimental world, like Sonic Youth, in the direction of post-punk. I also think they really influenced bands like Jane's Addiction, and I don't know if they get credit for that.*

Following Levene's departure, PiL became Lydon's sole property, with a revolving lineup (featuring at various points members of the Damned and Siouxsie and the Banshees) and a turn toward more cohesive, structured music. Lydon joined hip-hop pioneer Afrika Baambaataa on the memorable single "World Destruction" and also worked with world dub producer Bill Laswell on PiL's 1986 release, called *Album, Cassette,* or *Compact Disc* (depending on the format you bought). The group generally went downhill from there, and seemed to fade away after '92's *That What Is Not.* Following the release of Lydon's autobiography, *Rotten* (curiously sparse on PiL history), the Sex Pistols re-formed in 1996 for a reunion tour. Lydon released his first solo album to mixed reviews in 1997.

Wobble has made many solo records, as well as collaborations with **Brian Eno,** Holger Czukay, and Jaki Leibezeit of **Can,** and U2's Edge. In the late '80s he formed the New Age/world trance group, Invaders of the Heart, whose albums have featured Sinead O'Connor, Transglobal Underground's Natacha Atlas, and the Cranberries' Dolores O'Riordan. Keith Levene produced an album under the name Keith Levene's Violent Opposition, which included members of the Red Hot Chili Peppers, Fishbone, and Thelonious Monster as his backing band. There is no talk of a PiL reunion.

## DISCOGRAPHY

*Public Image— First Issue* (Virgin, 1978); a promising debut, though only a half-step removed from Sex Pistols-style punk.

*Metal Box* (Virgin, 1979); the earlier, limited version of *Second Edition,* packaged as three 12-inch 45s in a metal canister.

*Second Edition* (Island, 1980); a huge leap into antirock/post-punk neverland, the band's finest moment.

*Paris Au Printemps* (Virgin, 1980); a live album recorded in Paris.

*The Flowers of Romance* (Warner Bros., 1981); a percussion-heavy record that continues their experimental path.

*Live in Tokyo* (Elektra, 1983); features Lydon and backing musicians in concert.

*This Is What You Want...This Is What You Get* (Elektra, 1984); stripped of Levene's guitar, the record still has some worthwhile elements.

*Commercial Zone* (PiL, 1984); Levene's version of *This Is What You Want,* released independently.

*Album/Cassette/Compact Disc* (Elektra, 1986); the name of this first entirely post-Levene studio release depends on the format you buy, with Lydon in full control and Bill Laswell producing.

*Happy?* (Virgin, 1987); another studio album.

*9* (Virgin, 1989); and another.

*The Greatest Hits, So Far* (Virgin, 1990); a good overview of career highlights, including the weaker later stuff, with one new track and some remixes.

*That What Is Not* (Virgin, 1992); a forgettable record, probably the band's final release.

# WIRE

*This band Wire, we got their record Pink Flag, and these cats didn't know how to play, they were like art students or something. And it was just this fucking lightbulb over our heads. We said, "Man, if we do this, people will never know that we used to like Blue Oyster Cult."*

**Mike Watt, Minutemen/Firehose**

While the initial British punk explosion had, on the surface at least, some very working-class and anti-art overtones, it was immediately adopted by art school kids who saw no necessary contradiction between the art rock of the early '70s and the newer punk that had positioned itself as a reaction to art rock (anti-art, after all, was itself an artistic statement). This was particularly true for the older and more sophisticated art-schoolers of Wire, whose ideas about music were shaped by avant-garde and prog rock in the '60s and early '70s. While they were energized by punk's creative spark, and punk formed the basis of their music, the South London quartet was never motivated to follow a punk agenda. Unlike other bands that formed during the punk era, Wire had no problem being called a progressive rock band; in fact, Wire was from the start (and is still today in their solo projects) obsessed with moving forward. A driving desire never to repeat themselves has motivated just about everything the band members have done—from their records to their breakups.

Though Wire never achieved any great mainstream success in either the United States or Britain, time has revealed their tremendous influence on subsequent rock music. In the '80s, their jerky minimalism shaped the early sound of British new-wave bands such as the Cure and guitar rockers like U2 and Simple Minds, while their post-punk angularity impacted American bands from the Minutemen and R.E.M. to Fugazi and Sonic Youth. With punk-inspired alternative music and the resurgence of new wave in the '90s, Wire has popped up again as a key element in the music of bands like Elastica, Menswear, and Blur.

---

### Scott Kannberg, Pavement
*Wire was a big band for us. They're one of those bands that R.E.M. used to talk about, "Go check out Wire." I didn't understand them at first, but then I kept listening and I got it. No one sounds like them at all. "You're Killing Me," from our first single, is a Wire rip-off, in the fast guitar playing.*

---

Wire was formed in 1976 when Bruce Gilbert, then a 30-year-old studio technician working at Watford Art School, met 22-year-old student Colin Newman. Though neither had any real musical experience, Gilbert had some knowledge of avant-garde recording techniques and Newman counted himself a fan of **Brian Eno** (who occasionally guest-lectured at Watford). They came together with bassist Graham Lewis and drummer Robert Gotobed in a band called Overload, and when they kicked out the original singer for being too much of a rocker, they became Wire.

Out of necessity (because they could barely play their instruments) rather than any minimalist philosophy, Wire's sound was initially spare and simple. Like many later post-punk bands, the members of Wire came from an art tradition; they were inspired by punk but not tied to it. By 1977, they felt no need to repeat what straight punk had already accomplished, and were focused on doing new things in the punk context. "The simple idea was we didn't want to be like any other group," Newman says. "We were the next step, absolutely. The Clash were a rock band, the Sex Pistols and the Damned were comedy groups, and they were all already dinosaurs as far as we were concerned."

---

### Carrie Brownstein, Sleater-Kinney
*Wire utilize space really well in their music, and we try to leave space in songs to create a dynamic where songs can breath a little bit. A full bar chord will take up a whole range of sounds, but sometimes we're into just playing a couple notes or making it terse and simpler.*

---

Wire's debut record, *Pink Flag*, appeared in November of '77. Released on Pink Floyd's Harvest record label in a clear break from punk's anti–prog rock stance, the 21-song first album was a classic on arrival; Wire had stripped classic pop and rock songs down to their essence and rebuilt them with everything they'd learned from punk. Songs like "Strange" (later covered by R.E.M. on their *Document* album) and "Three Girl Rhumba" (whose riff is appropriated on Elastica's single "Connection") were odd and low-fi, yet unreservedly catchy, in a style Guided By Voices would later use. Every element of *Pink Flag*, from its music to its artwork (a stark image more reminiscent of Eno records that the messy collages of punk records), marked it as something different.

### Robert Pollard, Guided by Voices

*Wire is my favorite band. They just had the whole package; the album covers were great, the song titles were great, they gave you 18 to 20 songs on an album. When we put out an album we put like 19 or 20 songs on it, and I think Wire influenced me to do that. Bands get publishing deals for 12 songs on an album, so I respect any band that puts over 12 songs on a record; they don't get paid for it.*

The following year, Wire made a major leap with *Pink Flag*'s follow-up, *Chairs Missing*. Producer Mike Thorne (who also worked on the debut) introduced the band to studio techniques, which made an immediate impact. The record moved further away from punk and even closer to art rock by adding synths, manipulated sounds, and sequencers. They had also developed significantly as players, and felt comfortable being more experimental. It was in many respects their creative high point, brimming over with possibilities and exuberant in its explorations. "Everybody felt fantastic, it was a really joyous record to make," Newman remembers. "We were very aware that we were making a big step. We knew we had to jettison any sign of being a punk group at that point."

Though it may not have seemed possible, with 1979's *154* (named for the number of gigs they had played), Wire pushed their original sound even farther away and introduced an entire new world of moods and textures into the band's sonic palette. The original release even included a bonus EP of experimental noise drones (later added to *154*'s CD version), showing the influence of newer bands (that they had themselves influenced) such as Cabaret Voltaire. Like the first two records, *154* was critically adored—it was even said John Lennon was a big fan—though commercially the band remained firmly underground.

### Robin Rimbaud, Scanner

*Listening back to some demo tapes of mine from 1984/5 recently, I suddenly became aware of how influential 154 was upon my work and how it made me re-evaluate the structures of "guitar music," if such a genre ever existed. [from the liner notes to Whore: Various Artists Play Wire]*

Meanwhile, the intensity with which the band worked and the great speed at which it developed was taking its toll. Individual members were advancing creatively, but not in the same direction.

While Newman (and Gotobed) remained committed to experimentation within a pop format, Gilbert and Lewis became more immersed in noise. Wire seemed to be evolving into a collection of individual artists pursuing various avenues at the same time.

A European tour in early 1980 supporting Roxy Music (which had evolved from its **Brian Eno** days into a schmaltzy new romantic group) gave them an eerie look at what had happened to one art band that had accepted the slow pull toward commercial compromise. Wire wanted none of that; in fact, inspired by the rise of the indie music scene in the late '70s, the band wanted to move even further away from the mainstream music business, to explore the possibilities of music and video, to develop new bands, and to release solo records under one umbrella company. With their label, EMI, unreceptive to these pursuits, the members of Wire felt restrained creatively. The only other option was to fall back on already proven ideas, and instead, the members of Wire decided to call it quits. As Wire entered their first period of inactivity, they had left an already remarkable legacy. Their first three albums would pave the way for many of the most important bands of the next two decades.

### King Coffey, Butthole Surfers

*The question was, what do you do beyond punk rock? And Wire was a case example. They put out their great punk rock album, Pink Flag, but by the time you get to Chairs Missing, they're playing with all kinds of ideas, it's a real mixed bag. Then by 154 you have something very far removed from the concept of 4/4 two-minute punk songs. We admired them because they didn't keep making the same record over again. And it was such an explosion of creativity, after 154 what else could they do but break up? They were probably the ultimate post-punk band.*

A final Wire single in 1980, "Our Swimmer," pointed toward the industrial dance directions Wire would pursue when they re-formed in 1986. Prior to this, Wire members pursued solo and collaborative projects: Newman (accompanied by Gotobed) released four albums of Eno-esque pop, while Gilbert and Lewis recorded industrial and dance music under many names, including Dome, Duet Emmo, Cupol, 3R4, P'O, He Said, and simply as Gilbert and Lewis. The two also joined in multimedia collaborations with visual artist Russell Mills and choreographer Michael Clark.

When Wire re-formed in 1986, it was as a progressive synth pop band. Unwilling to fall back on earlier material, they toured the U.S. with a Wire tribute band that opened with the group's older songs. Though hints of the original Wire resurfaced, it was essentially an entirely new group, more commercially successful but also less distinctive. Over six albums, Wire pursued rhythmic pop in a "monophonic monorhythmic repetition" style, close to New Order's sound, which they gave the onomatopoeic name "dugga dugga."

### Page Hamilton, Helmet

*Their philosophy, their vibe influenced me immeasurably, the music was so creative and artful, yet so direct. They would talk about things in very abstract ways; having a conversation with Bruce Gilbert is like going on a magic carpet ride. They see music not as a technical pursuit in any way, they implement color and texture like paint brushes or something.*

By 1991's *The First Letter,* drummer Gotobed felt the band's electronic dance sound made a live drummer unnecessary and quit. In deference to the departure of one quarter of Wire, the band released their last album as Wir. Though a second reunion is not out of the question, Wire members have remained busy with solo work. Newman and his wife Malka Spigel formed the electronic label Swim, Lewis has pursued his H.A.L.O. and He Said projects, and Gilbert has created a new musical life as techno DJ Beekeeper. In May of 1996, Wire re-formed for one night in celebration of Bruce Gilbert's 50th birthday.

## DISCOGRAPHY

*Pink Flag* (Harvest, 1977, Restless Retro, 1989); the classic post-punk debut, unifying punk energy with progressive experimentation.

*Chairs Missing* (Harvest, 1978, Restless Retro, 1989); the landmark second record, capturing the band at the peak of their creativity.

*154* (Warner Bros., 1979, Restless Retro, 1989); the final record of Wire's first incarnation, bringing the band's explorations to its furthest point.

*Document and Eyewitness* (Rough Trade, 1981, Mute, 1991); a live album from their notable "Dadaist cabaret" show, it also includes the final single.

*And Here It Is...Again...Wire* (Sneaky Pete, 1984); a compilation of early material.

*Wire Play Pop* (Pink, 1986); another compilation of early material.

*Snakedrill* EP (Mute, 1986); the first studio work since *154,* a four-song return with a new sound.

*The Ideal Copy* (Mute, 1987); the first full-length since returning, the record features one of the group's minor hits, "Ahead."

*A Bell Is a Cup Until it is Struck* (Mute, 1988); a successful later-era studio album.

*It's Beginning to and Back Again* (Mute, 1989); an interesting idea—taking live recordings and reworking them digitally—with mixed results.

*The Peel Sessions Album* (Strange Fruit/Dutch East India, 1987; 1991); an expanded version of the Peel Sessions EP released in 1987.

*On Returning (1977–1979)* (Restless Retro, 1989); compilation of early material.

*Manscape* (Mute, 1990); a studio album, essential only for collectors.

*The Drill* EP (Mute, 1991); consisting of nine remixed versions of the song "Drill" from *Snakedrill.*

(Wir) *The First Letter* (Mute/Elektra, 1991); the reunified group's final recording, without drummer Robert Gotobed.

*1985–1990: The A List* (Mute/Elektra, 1993); a best of compilation, voted on by fans.

*Behind the Curtain: Early Versions 1977 & 78* (EMI, 1995); a compilation of early songs.

*Turns and Strokes* (WMO, 1996); a collection of unreleased live tracks and demos from the early years.

*Coatings* (WMO, 1997); a collection of unreleased tracks and alternate mixes from the later years.

TRIBUTE: *Whore* (WMO, 1996); various artists do their favorite Wire songs, featuring members of Sonic Youth, Ministry, Lush, the Minutemen, and the all-Wire cover band, Ex-Lion Tamers.

# BUZZCOCKS

*The Buzzcocks were better than overrated acts like the Beatles, and Singles Going Steady is one of the best pop albums ever. It was catchy, and best of all, it was punk! The Buttholes, at heart, are an experimental punk band that write pop songs (if covered in layers of absurdity). Bands like the Buzzcocks proved that you could write catchy songs and still be punk about it. Bands like Green Day were probably inspired by the Buzzcocks, but the Buzzcocks were there 20 years earlier and did it right the first time.*

### King Coffey, the Butthole Surfers

While the first wave of English punk rockers purported to completely wipe away the accepted musical conventions of the past, some musical traditions proved too enduring to stay away long. By incorporating classic pop song structure and melody into punk, bands like the Buzzcocks made clear just how much their music was part of a British pop continuum that stretched back at least as far as the Beatles and Kinks, and almost certainly even further.

Though they formed a short time after the classic English punk bands—the Sex Pistols, Clash, Damned—the Buzzcocks' embrace of pop and distance from punk polemics make them distinctly post-punk. And 15 years later, when bands like Green Day introduced punk to the American pop charts, their hard-driving but melodic sound and relatively low anger-and-angst quotient, could be traced directly back to the Buzzcocks.

### Page Hamilton, Helmet

*The Buzzcocks are just pure unadulterated punk rock, writing pop songs that completely cut the bullshit. Hearing that was so fresh for me, having grown up in the '70's overblown, pompous horseshit era of music.*

Manchester University schoolmates Howard Trafford and Peter McNeish were so thrilled after seeing the Sex Pistols perform in London they not only organized a concert to bring the Sex Pistols up to their home town, 150 miles north, but also decided to start a band of their own. Renaming themselves Howard Devoto and Pete Shelley, and assuming the roles of vocalist and guitarist, the two recruited drummer John Maher and bassist Steve Diggle to round out their new band, the Buzzcocks.

*Bob Mould, Sugar/Hüsker Dü*
*In that first wave of punk bands there was the Sex Pistols, the Clash, the more spitting, safe-ty-pin type bands. The Buzzcocks were very different. They had a much better knack for clas-sic pop songwriting, but all the energy of a punk band. That left a pretty good impression on me. I liked punk rock but a lot of it seemed a little too simplistic, whereas the Buzzcocks' song-writing is more sophisticated.*

Removed from London, the center of British punk sounds and styles, the Buzzcocks were less influenced by fashion trends and free to develop their own personality. Instead of expressing polit-ical and socioeconomic frustrations, the Buzzcocks turned to more traditional subjects for their songs: love, sex, teen alienation. Stil, Maher's high-energy precision drumming and the slashing gui-tars of Shelley and Diggle asserted the Buzzcocks' punk heritage.

Within months of forming, the Buzzcocks had developed a reputation in both Manchester and London as one of the best bands to emerge from the punk scene. By December of 1976 the group had formed its own label—appropriately called New Hormones for the sexual tension in many of the band's songs—and released an EP, *Spiral Scratch*. Recognized as the first notable indie punk record in the U.K., the record was to be the original lineup's only enduring document. One month after its release, singer Devoto quit the group to return to school (though he would soon form the adventurous post-punk group Magazine).

In his absence, the creative control that Devoto and Shelley had shared fell almost entirely on Shelley. Shelley became the group's main singer and songwriter. Steve Diggle switched from bass to guitar, and bassist Steve Garvey joined (after a brief stint by Garth Smith), securing a lineup that remained intact until the end.

In true British pop tradition, the Buzzcocks made a name for themselves on the basis of great sin-gles. The band signed a contract with United Artists in late 1977 and released their first and perhaps most memorable single, a hilarious Shelley/Devoto holdover dedicated to compulsive masturbation called "Orgasm Addict." Despite being too dirty for radio airplay, the song caused a huge stir through more underground channels and began a chain of memorable '45s that included "What Do I Get?," "Everbody's Happy Nowadays," and "Ever Fallen In Love?" (later covered by the Fine Young Cannibals).

*Dave Dederer, Presidents of the United States of America*
*I remember in 10th-grade, going into this music store and putting on the turntable the U.S. sin-gle version of "Why Can't I Touch It?" and "Everybody's Happy Nowadays." It just completely blew my mind, the energy and intensity of it. It opened up a whole new world of music for me.*

A debut album called *Another Music in a Different Kitchen*—which in true punk fashion origi-nally came in a bag labeled "Product"—came at the start of 1978, and a second LP called *Love Bites* was released by the end of that year. While the first record reinforced the perfectly crafted pop-punk style of the early singles, the second showed the group maturing quickly. Written by both

Shelley and Diggle, the songs were longer and incorporated influences beyond straight pop and punk, including psychedelia. Outside the band, Shelley was already experimenting with electronic sounds, using tape loops and drum machines in his early solo work.

By 1979 it became clear the burst of energy that marked the Buzzcocks' early singles had faded. *A Different Kind of Tension,* a third album released late in the year, was not very well received. An American tour in 1980 failed to revive interest in the Buzzcocks, either from fans or the band itself, and before the end of the year the group had called it quits. In less than four years, they had inspired new generations of punk, particularly in the American hardcore tradition that stretches from Hüsker Dü to Superchunk and Nirvana. The band also created a legacy of great punk songwriting that impacts rock music today, perhaps more than ever.

### Mac McCaughan, Superchunk

*I listened to the Buzzcocks so much. They were the perfect combination of what I wanted to hear, being catchy and poppy but really loud and fast. The first album and Singles Going Steady have all the catchiest songs and no fat, but Love Bites is probably my favorite; it had all that but was also a bit weirder. We got from them the combination of being loud and fast but really catchy at the same time.*

With the Buzzcocks' demise, Shelley launched straightaway into a solo career that explored more synth-oriented pop, such as his hit "Homosapien." Devoto, too, pursued a solo career once Magazine had run its course, while Diggle and Maher collaborated in a new band, Flag of Convenience. A 1989 Buzzcocks' box set called *Product* revived interest in the band and led to a reunion tour that featured the band's classic lineup of Shelley, Diggle, Garvey, and Maher.

Though Garvey and Maher soon departed, Shelley and Diggle continued and recorded new material. Following a four-song EP in 1991, the Buzzcocks released *Trade Test Transmissions* in '93. Tame by current standards and lacking the spark that made the band special a decade earlier, the record nevertheless proved they were able to compete with the younger groups that had taken a cue from their marriage of mannered pop and punk riffing. A second postreunion album, 1996's *All Set*, was less successful and the future of the Buzzcocks remains uncertain.

## DISCOGRAPHY

*Spiral Scratch* EP (New Hormones, 1977; Document, 1991); a rare first release, the only recording that features original vocalist Howard Devoto.

*Another Music in a Different Kitchen* (United Artists, 1978); the band's classic debut, full of energy and unforgettable pop-punk songs.

*Love Bites* (United Artists, 1978); a second record that branches out stylistically but remains catchy.

*A Different Kind of Tension* (United Artists, 1979; IRS, 1989); the band's final studio release, which shows the band's fatigue but still offers a set of terrific songs.

*Singles Going Steady* (IRS, 1979); the essential release, a definitive collection of their great singles and B sides (many not available on the three studio albums).

*Lest We Forget* (ROIR cassette, 1988); live recordings taken from 1979 and '80.

*Live at the Roxy Club April '77* (Absolutely Free, 1989; Receiver, 1990); more live recordings, not available domestically in the U.S.

*Product* (Restless Retro, 1989); a box set featuring the original albums and singles (though not *Spiral Scratch*), which sparked new interest in the band and led to the reunion.

*The Peel Sessions Album* (Strange Fruit, 1989; Strange Fruit/Dutch East India Trading, 1991); an extended version of the original EP from 1988.

*Operators Manual: Buzzcocks Best* (IRS, 1991).

*Alive Tonight* EP (Planet Pacific, 1991); a reunion release that revealed the potential for starting up again.

*Entertaining Friends: Live at the Hammersmith Odeon March 1979* (IRS, 1992); a previously unreleased live recording.

*Trade Test Transmissions* (Castle Communications/ Caroline, 1993); a promising return; the first new Buzzcocks album in 13 years.

*French* (IRS, 1996); a live album taken from a post-reunion tour.

*All Set* (IRS, 1996); a second post-reunion studio album.

TRIBUTE: *Something's Gone Wrong Again: The Buzzcocks' Covers Compilation* (C/Z, 1992); featuring covers by Alice Donut, Porn Orchard, Naked Raygun, Lunachicks, and others.

# THE FALL

*The thing that blew me away about the Fall was there didn't seem to be any rules or formulas. Random mishaps that could occur during the songs were okay, sort of expected as part of the music. Mark E. Smith cracks me up because he's such a raw nerve, a spoiled pudding. A bratty, upset person; it's wonderful. I interviewed him once for Ben Is Dead [zine], and the interview went so poorly we didn't print it. My friend who was with me asked if he was aware of Pavement, and if he felt they were knocking him off. And he got really angry about it; he said something like, 'Yeah, these scags go around just blatantly ripping me off year after year!' Total bitter tirade. He's right, but I think they mean it as a complete tribute.*

**Carla Bozulich, Geraldine Fibbers**

The **Buzzcocks** were the first major band of the punk era to emerge from the northern industrial city of Manchester, but the Fall were the true forerunners of Mancunian rock music of the '80s and '90s. Proudly regional in a way that indie rockers would later become, the Fall created a twangy post-punk sound it called "Mancabilly." It's even rumored that one of the best known Manchester groups, the Smiths, took their name in tribute to a local hero, the Fall's irascible leader Mark E. Smith.

The Fall's influence stretches far beyond its hometown. By drawing as much on German bands like **Can** and **Faust** as on punk rock, the Fall provided a blueprint for the most significant indie rock bands of the '80s and '90s, including Sonic Youth and Pavement. Their love of obscure references, peculiarly detailed lyrics, odd song titles, ramshackle collage album art, deadpan singing, and jagged guitar work all show up in countless groups who came later. With Fall leader Mark E. Smith's patented smarter-than-thou indie attitude, the Fall may be the first distinctly post-punk college rock band.

---

**Steve Wynn, Dream Syndicate**

*We were ripping off the Fall as much or more than the Velvets. People were less familiar with the Fall and didn't catch that as much. A lot of things on [the Dream Syndicate's] Days of Wine And Roses I was trying to make sound like Hex Induction Hour, Slates and stuff like that. We were really into the way they would just find a groove and stay on it forever. We liked doing that too.*

---

Over the band's 20-year (and ongoing) career, members have joined, quit, been fired, returned, and left again. The one constant has been Smith, the group's founder and vocalist. In 1977, 20-year-old Smith quit his office job to explore his musical fascination with krautrock, rockabilly, and, of course, punk. Taking an unapologetically intellectual perspective, he named his band after a favorite existential novel by Albert Camus. The Fall's original lineup included guitarist Martin Bramah and drummer Karl Burns, though within two years, more than 10 instrumentalists had come and gone, leaving Smith the only original member. Smith, a curmudgeon with a sullen (if darkly humorous) take on life, was not easy to get along with.

Despite the revolving-door membership, the Fall developed quickly and earned the attention of Mark Perry, leader of the cult punk group Alternative Television, who signed them to his Step Forward label. Both the three-song debut EP *Bingo Master's Breakout* and the first album *Live at the Witch Trials* revealed a band with much more to offer than three-chord punk rock. The music was bleak and minimal, and drew on everything from British skiffle bands to the Velvets to Teutonic art rock of the '70s. The ambitious *Witch Trials,* which the band recorded in one day in 1978, was an early indication of how much further punk could be stretched when freed of the limited style that had defined it.

### Marcellus Hall, Railroad Jerk
*It was totally amazing to me when I heard the Fall. I was really impressed that you could speak over music in an authoritative way, it had a real power to it, and I realized we could use that too, talking through a song in an urgent way. We do it all the time: "Ballad of Railroad Jerk," "Talking Railroad Jerk Blues," are directly from the Fall's declarative singing (and Woody Guthrie type talking blues of course).*

From the start, Smith emerged as a distinctive vocalist, with his cool monotone, pissed-off talksing, northern drawl, and curious habit of drawing out the final syllables of lines. Among the most successful earlier Fall releases is 1980's *Grotesque*, where Smith focuses on Manchester as a subject, with both fondness and scorn, in songs like "Mancabilly" and "The North Will Rise Again." With 1982's *Hex Enduction Hour,* another fan favorite, the Fall added a second drummer for a more intricately rhythmic sound.

Personal and personnel changes put the Fall at a crossroads in 1983. Smith's partner Kay Caroll, who served as the band's manager, ended her involvement with Smith and the Fall, and guitarist

Marc Riley, a key Smith collaborator since he joined in 1978, left as well. At the same time, Smith met American guitarist Laura Salinger, who under the name Brix would join the Fall and eventually marry Smith. More than any other past or current Fall member except Smith himself, Brix would exert a huge influence on the band. With *Perverted by Language*, the first Fall record featuring Brix, the band took a distinct turn toward a more accessible, pop-oriented sound. Despite a tribute to krautrock band **Can**'s lead singer ("I Am Damo Suzuki"), 1985's *This Nation's Saving Grace* showed Smith more willing to sing—however flatly—than ever. Still it wouldn't be until their cover of the Kinks' "Victoria" on 1988's *Frenz Experiment* that the Fall would score their first U.K. hit.

### Mac McCaughan, Superchunk

*The Fall was my favorite band, I probably have more Fall records than any other band. I really like the Brix period. They were still weird, with a great rhythm section, heavy basslines and drums, but also getting really poppy, with catchy songs. And they still make good records, that's why I like them so much, they've managed to stick around for 20 years and still do interesting stuff.*

While the band was experiencing its first taste of mainstream success, it was also pushing its music further. In 1986 Smith wrote music about papal politics, and in 1988 the group composed the score to a ballet called *I Am Kurious Oranj*. By 1990, though, Smith had alienated his closest collaborator, and Brix left both their marriage and band. Smith soldiered on with *Extricate*, which featured production work by British dub guru **Adrian Sherwood** and techno wizards Coldcut. The record was a clear indication that, after a decade and a half, Smith still had plenty more areas to explore.

As young bands who were clearly informed by the Fall's music emerged in the '90s, it looked as if Smith and company would cash in on its reputation and influence. 1991's *Shift-work* provided the Fall—now streamlined down to a four piece—with its biggest U.K. hit yet, and two years later the band released the first of two records for influential American indie label Matador Records (the label of Fall devotees such as Pavement and Railroad Jerk).

### Scott Kannberg, Pavement

*A lot of the vocal delivery that Steve [Malkmus, Pavement singer] does, and I do in some songs, comes from Mark Smith. A song like "Forklift," the talk-singing and using language not found in most songs. We tried to get Gary [Young, original Pavement drummer] to do that weird, syncopated drums, too. "Condo for Sale" is a total Fall rip-off, and "Two States."*

Smith's guest appearance on Inspiral Carpets' 1994 album indicated that a new generation of Manchester acts was acknowledging their debt to the Fall. But despite an ever-growing willingness of American acts to admit the Fall's influence, the band remains as underground as ever in the U.S. Recent albums, which explore electronics and mark the return of Brix to the band (though not the marriage), have not even been released domestically. Recent internal fighting and legal trouble have put the band's future in question.

## DISCOGRAPHY

*Bingo Master's Breakout* EP (Step Forward, 1978).

*Live at the Witch Trials* (Step Forward/IRS, 1979).

*Dragnet* (Step Forward, 1979).

*Totale's Turns (It's Now or Never)* (Rough Trade, 1980; Dojo, 1992).

*Grotesque (After the Gramme)* (Rough Trade, 1980; Castle Classics, 1993).

*Early Years 77–79* (Faulty Products, 1981).

*Slates* EP (Rough Trade, 1981); along with the *Hex* record, often viewed as the finest Fall material.

*Hex Enduction Hour* (Kamera, 1982); the high point of the Fall's early period.

*Room to Live* (Kamera, 1982).

*A Part of America Therein, 1981* (Cottage, 1982; Dojo 1992); live album, reissued with *Slates* EP.

*Perverted by Language* (Rough Trade, 1983); the first record to feature Brix, and thus the start of the Fall's more accessible middle period.

*Kicker Conspiracy* EP (Rough Trade, 1983).

*Fall in a Hole* (Flying Nun, 1983).

*The Wonderful and Frightening World of...* (Beggars Banquet/PVC, 1984).

*Hip Priest and Kamerads* (Situation Two, 1985; Beggars Banquet, 1995).

*This Nation's Saving Grace* (Beggars Banquet/PVC, 1985).

*The Fall* EP (PVC, 1986).

*Bend Sinister* (Beggars Banquet, 1986).

*Domesday Pay-Off* (Big Time, 1987).

*The Peel Sessions* EP (Strange Fruit, 1987); tracks collected from the band's appearance on the British show, John Peel's Radio 1.

*The Fall In: Palace of Swords Reversed* (Rough Trade/Cog Sinister, 1987); a fine compilation of early '80s stuff.

*The Frenz Experiment* (Big Time, 1988).

*I Am Kurious Oranj* (Beggars Banquet/RCA, 1988); featuring music written for a ballet to commemorate William of Orange's accession to the British throne.

*Seminal Live* (Beggars Banquet, 1989).

*Extricate* (Cog Sinister/Fontana/Polygram, 1990).

*458489 A Sides* (Beggars Banquet/RCA, 1990); compilation of '45s from the '84–'89 period.

*458489 B Sides* (Beggars Banquet/RCA, 1990; 1995); double CD of the B sides from *A Sides'* singles.

*Shift-work* (Cog Sinister/Fontana/Phonogram, 1991).

*Code: Selfish* (Cog Sinister/Fontana/Phonogram, 1992).

*The Collection* (Castle Communications, 1993); a U.K. compilation of early '80s material.

*Kimble* EP (Strange Fruit/Dutch East India, 1993); more Peel sessions, including cover of **Lee Perry**'s "Kimble."

*The Infotainment Scan* (Matador/Atlantic, 1993); the first of two records made for U.S. indie Matador, home to a number of Fall-influenced groups.

*Middle Class Revolt/The Vapourisation of Reality* (Matador, 1994); the second and last Matador release.

*Cerebral Caustic* (Permanent, 1995); unavailable domestically in the U.S., the record marks the return of Brix.

*The Twenty-Seven Points* (Permanent, 1995), a double live CD with some demos thrown in.

*The Legendary Chaos Tape* (Scout/Rough Trade, 1995); CD version of Live in London cassette from 1980.

*Light Users Syndrome* (Jet, 1996); a recent studio album exploring new directions, such as drum 'n' bass, as well as old rockabilly styles.

*Levitate* (1998).

# GANG OF FOUR

*Gang of Four is the first rock band I could truly relate to, the first to make me want to go crazy and dance and fuck and feel like I was part of something cool.... It completely changed the way I looked at rock music and sent me on my trip as a bass player.... I hear their influence on really great bands, too, like Fugazi and Jane's Addiction.... "Not Great Men" is the first thing I put on my*

*turntable to show somebody what shaped the sound of the rookie Red Hot Chili Peppers.*
**Flea, Red Hot Chili Peppers [from the liner notes to the Songs of the Free CD]**

The English group Gang of Four turned funk inside out and melded it with punk polemics, taking George Clinton's great funk dictum "free your ass and your mind follow" to a whole other level. With music that simultaneously made listeners dance and think, the band created a "politics of dancing,"where crowded discos become social movements and regimented dance steps subtle forms of solidarity. And with the gray economic climate of early-'80s Britain, dancing—even as an escape from everyday frustrations—was political in a very real way.

While some of the issues Gang of Four addressed may have faded, the group's influence is more apparent than ever. Their agit-prop lyrical style has been adopted by bands such as Fugazi and (somewhat clumsily) Rage Against the Machine. Musically, the stark punk-funk of jerking guitars and walloping bass can be heard in many of the major "alternative" bands of the past decade: the Cure, U2, Red Hot Chili Peppers, Nine Inch Nails.

### Tom Morello, Rage Against the Machine
*When I first heard [Andy Gill] play I thought it was the most atonal crap I had ever heard. Only later did I realize the genius of those jagged rhythms, unpredictable honks, and unapologetic stutter-funk grooves. His deconstructed playing perfectly offset the band's neo-Marxist politics. [from Alternative Press, November 1996]*

Gang of Four took its name from the radical post-Maoist Chinese political faction that was still recent news when the band formed at Leeds University in 1977. Though punk was in full bloom throughout Britain by then, from the start the group's reference points included funk and R&B as well. "We were happy to be part of any movement we felt would bring about change in England, but I wouldn't have felt comfortable being called a punk," bassist Dave Allen says. "We didn't follow the punk fashion or lifestyle, but we thrived on the energy of it all because it was knocking down lots of doors."

The group became politicized, partially, in reaction to the growth of ultra-nationalist skinhead groups in England, particularly in depressed northern cities like Leeds. Through their camaraderie with outspoken black groups such as Steel Pulse (both bands later toured as part of Rock Against Racism), the influence of reggae and dub music seeped into the Gang of Four's sound. Gang of Four gigged their way through '77, '78, and much of '79 before putting out a full-length record. This allowed the band to blend its many influences into a cohesive sound that hit with maximum intensity when they finally put out their first album, at the end of 1979.

### Bono, U2
*Hard, angular, bold...Andy Gill's chin is the very black hole of '90's music we should have all disappeared into...a dimple atop the body pimple, a pimple on the arse of pop. A Gang of Four*

metal gurus, a corporation of common sense, a smart bomb of text that had me "at home feeling like a typist." [from the liner notes to Songs of the Free]

---

*Entertainment!* captured the band's spare, uptight live sound perfectly. The alienation expressed in the lyrics to songs like "At Home He's a Tourist" and "Damaged Goods," the tightly-wound rhythms of Hugo Burnham's drums and Allen's bass, with Andy Gill's irregular chainsaw-jerking guitar, conveyed a profound discontent. It shredded funk into a joyless grind, amassing as much tension as it released. This was dance music that had been clawed through by punk, a symptom of British decline, and unlike the punk music of other angry English kids, vocalist Jon King's lyrics were smart enough to explain it all.

---

**Michael Stipe, R.E.M.**
*Entertainment!* shredded everything that came before it. The Gang of Four know how to swing. I stole a lot from them. [from the liner notes to Songs of the Free]

---

While Gang of Four were not the first band to confront problematic social issues with intelligence rather than anger, they did it better than any punks before them. And they backed up their uncompromising words with actions: the group's commercial potential was permanently damaged when, after refusing to excise the word "rubbers" from a song, their debut performance on the British television show *Top of the Pops* was canceled.

Following another two full years of touring, both with Rock Against Racism and on their own, Gang of Four returned in 1981 with a long-awaited follow-up entitled *Solid Gold.* They employed an R&B producer to smooth out the sound, and *Solid Gold* is more polished and mature than *Entertainment!*, certainly a worthy successor. Where Andy Gill's guitars seem to have eased slightly from their trebly assault, Dave Allen's bass takes on a heavy dub sound and becomes more disorienting than ever on songs like "Paralysed."

---

**Carrie Brownstein, Sleater-Kinney**
I just love them rhythmically, how they put their songs together with interesting time changes. I love the way Andy Gill's guitar sounds. I'd say for [Sleater-Kinney's album] *Dig Me Out, I was listening to Entertainment!* more than any other record. It just has an energy that's inspiring.

---

A difficult record to make, *Solid Gold* proved to be the one that ripped the group apart. Feeling a "sense of completion" and wanting to explore dub further, Allen quit, and by the end of 1981, Sara Lee had taken over on bass. While Lee proved every bit as capable of handling the substantial low-end throbs that drove Gang of Four, the group never again captured the intensity of the original lineup.

### King Coffey, Butthole Surfers

*The first two albums were really influential to me personally as a drummer, because they had a real tribal sense, it wasn't "kick-snare-kick-snare," they were laying into the toms. It was a very different style of drumming.*

With 1982's *Songs of the Free*, the group proved they had some life—if little muscle—left in them. Shifting into a looser funk that incorporated slick background vocals and electro dance elements, the band nearly produced a hit song with the catchy and hilarious "I Love a Man In Uniform." With the cold existentialism of "We Live As We Dream, Alone," though, it was clear the angst and social alienation were not gone entirely.

By the time the group released 1983's *Hard*, however, they truly seemed to have gone soft. Reduced to a trio (drummer Burnham was fired to make way for a drum machine) and backed with lightweight string arrangements, the record sounds like a lame stab at the pop charts. Even with glossy production, the Marxist funk rockers were way out of step with current trends, and following a farewell show that included an encore with original members Burnham and Allen, Gang of Four disbanded in 1984.

After leaving Gang of Four, Dave Allen formed the band Shriekback and later the groups King Swamp and Low Pop Suicide (he also composed music with Jon King for the film *The Karate Kid*). Allen also founded World Domination Records, which he continues to run today. Both Lee and Burnham did for-hire work, with the B-52s and Bryan Ferry respectively, while Gill produced the Red Hot Chili Peppers' debut album (and more recently, Jesus Lizard). Burnham eventually retired as a musician, though he continues in the business today as a successful record executive.

Following the 1990 release of the Gang of Four's career overview, *A Brief History of the Twentieth Century*, new interest in the group led Andy Gill and Jon King to re-form the group with session musicians. Two releases—1991's *Mall* and '95's *Shrinkwrapped*—are mildly interesting, though largely irrelevant to the career and subsequent impact of the original group.

## DISCOGRAPHY

*Damaged Goods* EP (Fast Product, 1978); a debut single never released domestically.

*Entertainment!* (Warner Bros., 1979; Infinite Zero, 1995); the classic debut that finds the group at its tightest and most agitating; the reissue includes the 1980 EP *Gang of Four* [a.k.a. *Yellow*].

*Solid Gold* (Warner Bros., 1981; Infinite Zero, 1995); a very good recording of the band in transition between the debut's raw power and the later electro-funk; the reissue includes the 1981 EP *Another Day, Another Dollar*.

*Songs of the Free* (Warner Bros. 1982; Infinite Zero, 1996); a generally successful move toward pop styles, including the classic "I Love a Man In Uniform."

*Hard* (Warner Bros., 1983); a slickly produced drum machine record that ended the band on a low note.

*At the Palace* (Phonogram, 1984); a live album recorded in Hollywood during the band's final tour.

*The Peel Sessions* (Strange Fruit/Dutch East India Trading, 1990); a record collecting the group's appearances on the John Peel's U.K. radio show.

*A Brief History of the Twentieth Century* (Warner Bros., 1990); an excellent collection that spans the pre-reunited band's career and is appropriately heavy on early material.

*Mall* (Polydor, 1991); though not without its merits, this reunion record is generally flat.

*Shrinkwrapped* (Castle, 1995); largely irrelevant.

# SWELL MAPS

*Swell Maps was a big influence on our early records, one of those bands that we heard and were like, "Oh, we can do this." They had these songs they fucked up somehow to make sound really dirty and low frequency, but they had these great songs underneath all this mess. And that's what we tried to do on the first couple singles. I actually met Nikki Sudden recently in London. He heard we were big fans and came to our show.*

**Scott Kannberg, Pavement**

For most of its existence, Swell Maps was little more than two suburban teenage brothers and their neighborhood friends, copping mysterious pseudonyms and low profiles to hide their mundane reality, and messing around at home with tape recorders and instruments they couldn't play. What they created might have amounted to nothing special, except for how extraordinarily "nothing special" it all was. Their dingy racket helped inspire many subsequent suburban teens—most notably Pavement (whose early sound and career mirrors that of Swell Maps)—to make use of whatever skills and tools they had on hand to express themselves musically. Using punk as a method more than as a style, Swell Maps were among the primary architects of an aesthetic that would later be dubbed "low-fi."

Adrian Nicholas Godley and his little brother Paul began making music from their home in the town of Solihull (near Birmingham) around 1972, when they were 15 and 12 years old, respectively. At the time, the two—who would rename themselves Nikki Sudden and Epic Soundtracks—were inspired by popular glam rockers like T. Rex, American garage rock like the **Stooges,** and somewhat later by German groovers **Can.** When they expanded the group during the punk explosion of 1976, Nikki became singer and guitarist and Epic drummer; Nikki's schoolmate Steve Bird (who became Jowe Head) joined on bass, neighbor Richard Earl (Biggles Books) came aboard on guitar, and buddies David Barrington (Phones Sportsmen) and John "Golden" Cockrill helped out with "occasional vocals and cacophony."

Inspired by pioneer do-it-yourself punk band Desperate Bicycles (whose slogan was "it's easy, it's cheap, go and do it"), Swell Maps decided to make and independently release (on Rather Records) a single in late 1977. At 1 minute 27 seconds, "Read About Seymour" was a shriveled pop gem; an obscure, tossed-off classic. A year and a half later these unambitious part-time punks got around to recording again and released their debut album, *A Trip to Marineville*. The record combined straight punk sounds with krautrock, acid rock, and industrial elements to make one great sloppy, off-key and off-kilter, collection of sculpted noise and song. Tracks were haphazardly recorded, often created on the spot, and featured whoever happened to be around that day.

### Lou Barlow, Sebadoh/Folk Implosion

*I heard Swell Maps when I was pretty young. It was cool to hear those records back then because it sort of strengthened my convictions, like "Wow, you can do this." Even if only one person in the world goes and buys your record that you recorded on your own tape machine, at least someone did. I mean, how did I find the Swell Maps? That was really inspirational to know that someone will listen to it.*

"Listening to our early records I can hear us fumbling around for a style," Epic Soundtracks said. "We weren't a punk band; we just thought we were us, really. Because the people in the band were all into different music, it came out as a lot of things thrown together and mixed up. It confused a lot of people." The sleeve prefectly completed the record's disorientingly random quality, reading: "Try it at 16 rpm, 33 rpm, 45 rpm and 78 rpm! It is probably funniest at 33!! And most musical at 16!"

### Tim Gane, Stereolab

*"Read About Seymour" is a minute and a half long and it's just pure independence personified. Done in a low-fi studio, it sounds amazing. Everything I like in rock dynamics. Real excitement. When I first bought A Trip to Marineville I must have played it a hundred times or more, just to listen to every single second of it.*

While *Marineville* received good reviews and did well on the indie charts, the band was difficult to maintain. By 1980, Epic had begun attending college in Portsmouth and Nikki had moved to London, Jowe was living in Manchester and Richard was in Bath. Still, Swell Maps continued when they could, releasing their best-known single, "Let's Build a Car," as well as a second album, *Swell Maps in "Jane from Occupied Europe."* Both noisier and at times more tuneful, *Jane* showed real growth in studio editing techniques and greater instrumental range with added keyboard and saxophone.

### Thurston Moore, Sonic Youth

*The first Swell Maps 45 I bought (for no reason 'cept what th' fuck) was "Let's Build a Car" which still to this day gives me a soul scorched buzz 'n' rush. As soon as that Nikki Sudden gtr comes slicing slabbing and all out fuzzifying off that crackling vinyl groove you know yr gonna rock. It's the best of both whirls: fist-in-the-heart guitar burnin' rock and ahead-of-it's-time songsmith awareness. So fuck, it was amazing. The Swell Maps had a lot to do with my upbringing. [from liner notes to* Collision Time Revisited]

The band did a short tour of Europe, but the members soon realized they didn't get along well enough to stay together. As Epic aptly summed up in the notes to the *Collision Time Revisited* compilation: "Formed March '72—Made first record Sept. '77—Self-destructed March '80. We grew up together but we grew apart. Anyway it was fun."

Jowe made a few solo albums before joining celebrated English indie band Television Personalities. Richard Earl put together a solo record on his own label before quitting music. Nikki and Epic formed the Jacobites (later Nikki Sudden and the Jacobites), which had some success during the '80s. Sudden, who evolved into a New Romantic strummer of dark love ballads, made records solo and with Dave Kusworth. Epic became the drummer for Crime and the City Solution (which featured Simon Bonney), These Immortal Souls (with Roland Howard of the **Birthday Party**), and, briefly, **Red Crayola.** With the encouragement of Sonic Youth guitarist Lee Ranaldo (with whom he'd worked), Epic became a solo artist in the '90s and released a series of surprisingly gentle and beautiful piano ballad records. Guests on his albums included members of Sonic Youth and Dinosaur Jr. Late in 1997 (a month after being interviewed for this book), Epic died of heart failure at home in London.

## DISCOGRAPHY

*A Trip to Marineville* (Rather/Rough Trade, 1979; Mute, 1991); the debut record that made an art out of sloppily compiled, all-over-the-place, punk-inspired pop.

*In "Jane from Occupied Europe"* (Rather/Rough Trade, 1980; Mute, 1991); the second and last studio album, which showed the band still developing as it was breaking up.

*Whatever Happens Next...* (Rather/Rough Trade, 1981; Mute, 1991); a collection of outtakes and demos from their short career.

*Train Out of It* (Antar, 1987; Mute, 1991); compilation featuring 26 singles and outtakes.

*Collision Time Revisited* (Mute, 1989); a 27-song remastered version of the 1981 *Collision Time* compilation of singles, favorites, and rarities.

# 14

# RIOT MOMS AND OTHER ANGRY WOMEN

When you consider that slightly more than half the people in the world are female, the idea of classifying "women in rock" as a sort of specialty genre seems absurd. Still, popular music reflects the culture in which it arises, and there has been a definite male dominance in rock. So while in an ideal world "women in rock" would have long ago been accepted as a given, the growing equality of the sexes in music continues to be newsworthy. And certainly it is one of the defining stories in rock music of the '90s.

But the fact that women in the past decade have made a larger contribution to rock and related genres than ever before is simply a matter of statistics. What's more interesting is the proliferation of music that, on one level, speaks directly to women's experience and on another, more esoteric level seeks to express, in a purely sonic language, a feminine nature and sense of creativity. While there are certainly more distant examples of female-oriented music, punk rock offered a philosophy that proved particularly inspiring and fertile for women. By placing itself defiantly outside the mainstream culture and purporting to throw out all the rules, punk presented itself as a natural arena for women to empower and define themselves. Patti Smith, who came out of the pre-punk downtown New York/CBGB scene of the mid-'70s, was a crucial first step and has provided a powerful role model for women in the post-punk world of rock. Though she never claimed a kinship with Smith, **Lydia Lunch** emerged out of the same scene with a similar poetry-and-rock approach. But where Smith tends to be universalist in her writing—speaking equally to men and women—Lunch has been confrontationally female-oriented with words that target sexual abuse, gender inequality, and her own (female-specific, she'd claim) inner torment.

Taking shape around the same time, but across the ocean in England, the punk-rock explosion spearheaded by the Sex Pistols gave birth to an even more accomplished succession of female bands. **X-Ray Spex,** one of the earliest female-led punk bands in London, mocked the expectations society has for little girls and the consumer culture that manipulates them. The **Slits** started out in a similar vein, but soon developed to a point where they transcended punk's musical limitations and began to define a post-punk sound that was characteristically female in sound and structure. The **Raincoats,** meanwhile, progressed along a nearly identical course as their friends the **Slits,** but lasted longer. At their best, the Raincoats rose above their punk roots to make a music that was a completely intimate expression of their own female creativity: detailed and rhythmic, nonlinear and open-ended, flowing and richly textured.

---

*Jean Smith, Mecca Normal*
*I started listening to a lot of punk bands from London, specifically the ones with aggressive women in them. The **Raincoats, Slits, X-Ray Spex,** Poison Girls, Crass, Frightwig. All*

*those bands were monumentally inspiring for one thing, and would certainly be the reason I started feeling confident enough to express the ideas I was shuffling through: political and feminist concerns, anarchist concepts, general social ideas from a dissatisfied prospective.*

Of course, these groups were not inspirational only to women. Regardless of gender, the music they made belongs in the company of the best post-punk had to offer: **Wire, Public Image Limited, Gang of Four,** and so on. Indeed, everything written about those bands in the chapter on British post-punk also applies to groups like the **Slits** and **Raincoats**. But for their role in setting a precedent and providing a model for "riot grrrl" groups like Bikini Kill and Sleater-Kinney, grunge-oriented bands like Hole and Babes in Toyland, and even for distinctly female musical voices such as Tori Amos and PJ Harvey, these groups deserve a chapter of their own.

## L Y D I A   L U N C H

*She has a really commanding presence. She's a really articulate storyteller. She gets into the side of being a woman that I find really excellent, where a woman lets somebody think they're in control because they get off on that, but the woman really knows it's not that way at all, that she's really in control. We have a song called "Song About Walls" about being in a situation where the girl is playing that game with her boyfriend. It's an interesting dynamic Lydia Lunch brings to light really well. And it's something I obsess over, so that's one reason I love Lydia Lunch.*

**Carla Bozulich, Geraldine Fibbers**

Since she began as a teenager over two decades ago, Lydia Lunch has been a nearly constant source of the angriest, most pained and cathartic outpourings in the worlds of music and poetry. Lunch's earliest music earned her a position as one of the first and strongest female voices in post-punk and experimental rock, and her subsequent career as outspoken radical feminist poet and all-around angry woman has made her the ass-kicking aunt to riot grrrls everywhere. More directly, her fearless examination of taboo subjects and personal traumas has made her an important role model to women rockers of the '90s such as Courtney Love and Kat Bjelland of Babes in Toyland.

At age 14, Lydia Koch began running away from her parents' home in Rochester to visit New York City. Escaping the sexual abuse she has since documented in her work, she found a scene where poets and punk bands intermingled and liberated themselves through expression. By 16, Koch had left home for good, taken a waitressing job at CBGB, and remade herself as Lydia Lunch. Soon, she'd hooked up with saxophonist James Chance and drummer Bradly Field, with whom she formed her first band, Teenage Jesus & the Jerks. Along with the bands Mars and **DNA**, which both practiced in the space where Lunch lived, the Jerks formed a new scene of like-minded friends interested in pursuing a more radical deconstruction of rock than what punk was offering. Before she'd turned 18, the "teenage Jesus" had landed in the center of an influential downtown movement she herself had named "no wave."

## Thurston Moore, Sonic Youth

*Punk rock was becoming something to be cynical about. You started hearing about how Macy's was having a punk rock window, or how major labels thought the best way to promote this music was to call it new wave and make it less dangerous. And so you started having people like Lydia Lunch, who to me was super-influential, saying things in the local newspapers like, "Oh, I don't really have time for Patti Smith, she's a hippie. I don't have time for* **Television** *because they play long wanky lead guitar songs." Here was somebody my age coming to town, saying, "fuck that stuff, we're into total destruction." That attitude in general was influential.*

While Chance soon departed to form his own no wave group, the Contortions, Lunch, Field, and a rotating cast of bass players continued bashing out what Lunch described as "aural terror." Featuring Field's one-drum percussion with Lunch's noise/slide guitar and tortured vocals, Teenage Jesus & the Jerks songs like "The Closet" and "Red Alert" lasted little more than a minute or two, but offered a lifetime of emotional release. Dedicated to a "less is more" principle, Lunch's band became known for its 10-minute live shows. Similarly, Teenage Jesus offered only minimal recorded work. In its four-year existence, the band put out two singles and an EP (produced by Robert Quine of **Richard Hell & the Voidoids**) and contributed four songs to the crucial no wave compilation, *No New York.*

Concurrent with her time in the Jerks, Lunch also played in a short-lived band called Beirut Slump. By 1980, though, Lunch was ready for a change in direction; disbanding both groups, she embarked on a solo career. In place of the Jerks' numbing blows, her debut album *Queen of Siam* offered a mellow and murky cross between the **Residents** and lounge jazz, with Lunch as a relatively sedate torch (or was it *torture?*) singer. Though much of the music—including full orchestral pieces—was effective, Lunch's vocals were not, and within the year Lunch had formed a new, harder-rocking group, called 8 Eyed Spy.

A quintet featuring bassist George Scott (who played with **John Cale** as well as the Contortions) and Beirut Slump/Jerks member Jim Sclavunos (now in Nick Cave's Bad Seeds), 8 Eyed Spy presented Lunch as hard rock frontwoman on avant blues originals like "Swamp Song" and punked-out covers like "I Want Candy" (before Bow Wow Wow got to it) and "Diddy Wah Diddy." With Scott's heroin overdose in 1980, the band ended before it had released a record, though two posthumous recordings have appeared. Following an even shorter-lived turn in the unrecorded Devil Dogs, Lunch headed west to Los Angeles where she formed yet another group, 13.13.

After collaborating on a book of poetry with X's Exene Cervenka (they'd collaborate again on a 1995 spoken-word album), the ever-restless Lunch left Los Angeles for Europe, where she recorded with **Einstürzende Neubauten** and collaborated with the **Birthday Party** on a number of projects. In addition to recording songs with the group (which later appeared on *Honeymoon in Red*), Lunch worked with the group's guitarist Rowland Howard and wrote "fifty one-act plays" with vocalist Nick Cave.

---

### Nick Cave

*She had quite an impact on our lives. Her scope, of doing readings and all of this sort of stuff, and moving out of just strict rock and roll music, had some influence as well.*

---

In 1984, when Lunch was barely 23 years old and had already passed through a half-dozen music projects in nearly as many cities, she returned to New York to start her own company, Widowspeak, so that she could release the spoken-word material that was becoming a major part of her art. Here she entered into an even more intense phase of activity, writing and acting in the gritty East Village films of Richard Kern (*The Right Side of my Brain* with Henry Rollins, and *Fingered*) and making music with just about anyone who could catch up with her, including her lover Jim Thirwell (a.k.a. Clint Ruin, a.k.a. Foetus), members of X and Red Hot Chili Peppers, members of Sonic Youth (separately and collectively), Mars (on a soundtrack to one of Kern's films), Rowland Howard (again), and Nick Cave (again) with Thirwell and Marc Almond (as part of a touring group called the Immaculate Consumptives).

In the '90s, though Lunch has continued to write (books, comics, and plays), teach classes, and, relatively recently, make music again, it is in her spoken-word performance that her creative fires have burned brightest. Through her live monologues and spoken-word recordings such as *The Uncensored Lydia Lunch*, *Oral Fixation*, and *Conspiracy of Women*, Lunch rips out her own blood and guts and puts them on display for anyone to see. In her stories, confessions, damnations, and tirades she can be alternately shocking, hilarious, and admittedly often a nag. But it's here, at her most naked, where Lunch's true voice emerges, and where the implications of her message are clearest. As she says in an interview for the book, *Angry Women*, "I'm only using my own example for the benefit of all who suffer the same multiple frustrations: fear, horror, anger, hatred. And the stories aren't just personal—often they're very political."

---

### Will Oldham, Palace

*On the Uncensored cassette, the kinds of stories she told and the way she modulated her voice in telling the story, she inspired discomfort in the listener and built it very well even before the really brutal aspects of the piece came around. I listened to that tape a lot, and I learned some things from her about understatement in expressing morbid or confrontational ideas. As a writer and a speaker.*

---

## DISCOGRAPHY

### TEENAGE JESUS & THE JERKS

(Various Artists) *No New York* (Antilles, 1978); the band contributed four tracks to the **Brian Eno**-produced no wave compilation.

*Teenage Jesus & the Jerks (Pink)* EP (Migraine/ Lust/Unlust, 1979); this pink vinyl release collects the group's singles.

*Pre-EP* (Ze, 1979); Lunch's earliest recording, featuring TJ&J's original lineup with James Chance on sax.

*Everything* (Atavistic, 1995); a reissue containing all of the band's recorded material.

### 8 EYED SPY

*Live* (ROIR, 1981); a document of the band's 1980 live performances.

*8 Eyed Spy* (Fetish, 1981; Atavistic, 1997); a part live, part studio album released after the band had broken up.

### SOLO AND COLLABORATIONS

*Queen of Siam* (Ze, 1980; Widowspeak, 1985); a subdued solo debut, heavy on the noir-jazz numbers.

*13.13* (Ruby, 1982; Widowspeak, 1988); recorded with an L.A.-based band of the same name.

(w/**Birthday Party**) *The Agony is the Ecstasy* EP (4AD, 1982); a live Lunch gig in London appears on one side of this EP, while the other features the Birthday Party's *Drunk on the Pope's Blood.*

(w/Michael Gira) *Hard Rock* (Ecstatic Peace, 1984); a spoken-word cassette that also features the **Swans'** leader.

(w/Lucy Hamilton) *The Drowning of Lucy Hamilton* (Widowspeak, 1985); an instrumental soundtrack to *The Right Side of My Brain,* a film starring Lunch.

*In Limbo* EP (Doublevision, 1984; Widowspeak, 1986); a six-track record featuring Sonic Youth's Thurston

Moore, reissued together with *Lucy Hamilton* in 1989 as *Drowning in Limbo.*

*Hysterie* (Widowspeak/CD Presents, 1986); a double album compilation featuring the best of Lunch's past bands, as well as some collaborations.

*Honeymoon in Red* (Widowspeak, 1987; Atavistic, 1996); an album recorded in '82 and '83 as a **Birthday Party** collaboration, remixed and featuring Thurston Moore.

(w/Thurston Moore) *The Crumb* EP/(w/Clint Ruin) *Stinkfist* EP (Widowspeak, 1988; Atavistic, 1996); two EPs collected onto one CD.

(Harry Crews) *Naked in Garden Hills* (Widowspeak, 1989); a project with Sonic Youth bassist Kim Gordon.

*The Uncensored Lydia Lunch/Oral Fixation* (Widowspeak, 1989); two spoken-word albums, the first originally from 1985, collected on one CD.

(w/Henry Rollins, Hubert Selby Jr., Don Bajema) *Our Fathers Who Aren't in Heaven* (Widowspeak, 1990); a spoken-word double album, split with three other writer/ poets, including former **Black Flag** vocalist Rollins.

*Conspiracy of Women* (Widowspeak, 1991); another spoken-word album.

(w/Roland S. Howard) *Shotgun Wedding* (Triple X, 1991); a collaboration with the former **Birthday Party** guitarist.

*Crimes Against Nature* (Triple X, 1993); a three-CD box set of Lunch's spoken-word material.

*Universal Infiltrators* (Atavistic, 1995); further spoken-word adventures.

(w/Exene Cervenka) *Rude Hieroglyphics* (Rykodisc, 1995); a spoken-word collaboration with X's lead singer.

(w/Glyn Styler) *The Desperate Ones* (Truckstop/Atavistic, 1997); a three-song return to music recordings.

# X - R A Y   S P E X

*I thought [X-Ray Spex singer] Poly Styrene was such a great singer. Her songs were really full-flight, with soaring vocals. The topics just mystified me, like "Warrior in Woolworths," the weird allitera-*

*tion of this loopy kind of line, with her accent and this rich flowing vocal. That was really a stylistic attraction. That would've been my ideal, but physical limitations prevented me from it. I just connected with the power and energy and determination and tried to bring it out of myself, and what came out of me I realized was as valid as what came out of anyone. I really trusted that.*

**Jean Smith, Mecca Normal**

Though X-Ray Spex produced only one album of note, it was enough to inspire entire movements. Though her time in the group was short, Lora Logic's blaring saxophone would prove a notable precursor to future female-led, sax-driven bands of the '80s such as Romeo Void and the Waitresses. But X-Ray Spex's main contributions came from their lead singer, Poly Styrene. With her combination of youth and awareness, girlishness and nasty wit, strength and joyousness, Styrene realized punk's potential for expressing the frustrations and displaying the intelligence of girls, just as it had for disaffected boys. Her voice—bursting with enthusiasm and giddy shrieks—provided a model for female punk singers everywhere.

---

**Kathleen Hanna, Bikini Kill**

*[People said] "Oh, you sing just like Poly Styrene." And I was like, "Yeah! Great!" A lot of girls had never heard of Poly Styrene; maybe they'll hear me and then buy an X-Ray Spex record.... I don't care if I sound like Poly Styrene—I think Poly Styrene is great! [from Angry Women In Rock]*

---

While the first rumblings of England's punk-rock explosion were led by white males, they effectively empowered social misfits of all sorts to express themselves. Among the scores of kids inspired to action after seeing a Sex Pistols gig was a chubby, brown-skinned (half-Somali), 15-year-old girl with braces named Marion Elliot. What she lacked in rock star looks made her a perfect antihero, while her muscular pipes and precocious wit made her a compelling new voice in punk. After putting out a little-noticed solo single, Elliot adopted the nom-de-punk Poly Styrene—an expression of dual interests, in mass culture and artificiality—and set about forming her very own punk band.

Along with an all-male back-up band consisting of guitarist Jak Airport, bassist Paul Dean, and drummer B. P. Hurding, Styrene recruited another powerful female presence in skronky 16-year-old saxophonist Lora Logic (Susan Whitby). Named for a kitschy toy Poly received from her cousins in America, X-Ray Spex hit their stride very quickly; by their second gig, the group was playing

London's top punk club, the Roxy. When a song from this show was included on the 1977 compilation *Live at the Roxy*, X-Ray Spex began to receive press attention, which led to their recording a studio version of the song and releasing it as a debut single. "Oh Bondage Up Yours!"—a powerful statement of girl rebellion delivered fearlessly by an actual teenager—became a huge punk hit. With its defiant opening line—"Some people think little girls should be seen and not heard. I say, Oh bondage! Up yours!"—and the sarcastic submissiveness of the lyrics, Styrene virtually invented riot grrrl attitude.

### Alec Empire, Atari Teenage Riot

*X-Ray Spex influenced us a lot, especially [ATR singer] Hanin Elias. She was influenced a lot by the way Poly Styrene sings and the energy. When Hanin and I had our first punk bands in the '80s we wanted to do things like X-Ray Spex.*

With follow-up singles such as "The Day the World Turned Dayglo" and "Identity," Styrene began to confront topics only hinted at with "Bondage": the devasting effects of consumer culture on girls' self-images and the artificiality of the everyday world. In early 1978, Lora Logic quit to return to school (she later formed her own band, Essential Logic) and was replaced by Rudi Thompson. By fall, X-Ray Spex had released their debut, *Germ-Free Adolescents*. The record, whose cover showed band members dressed in dayglo, trapped inside large test tubes, was an early manifestation of the bright colors and futuristic imagery that would carry over into new wave. And though the music was catchy and fun enough to compete with the best pop, its heart was undeniably punk. Full of bratty intelligence and wit, songs like "Art-I-Ficial," "Warrior in Woolworths," "I Am a Poseur," and "I Am a Cliché" tempered Styrene's articulate search for identity with the screaming glee of youth and freedom.

### Kate Schellenbach, Luscious Jackson

*The fact that they had a 15-year-old girl singer with braces was really appealing and exciting as a teenager, to think I could do this too, and make these incredible statements. To hear her singing with this incredible confidence and voice was so inspirational. Listen to Bikini Kill and it's like a carbon copy of X-Ray Spex.*

As quickly as they had risen, though, X-Ray Spex came undone. As Styrene matured (though still barely 18!), she felt uncomfortable continuing with the brashness and squealing intensity that had defined her. Not only did she want to move the band toward slower, more acoustic songs, she was searching for a more stable—and in her eyes, more meaningful—existence. The release of their "Highly Inflammable" single marked the end of the band.

While Styrene thought she'd found some peace through joining the Hare Krishnas and leaving the music business, she returned to singing in the '80s with sporadic solo records and guest appearances on albums by Boy George and the Dream Academy. The other former X-Ray Spex members continued to make music, and Paul Dean (believe it or not) formed Canadian '80s cheese rockers Loverboy. Following a 1991 reunion show in London, the original band—featuring Styrene, Dean, and Lora Logic—re-formed and in 1995 released a new album. Though few noticed their return, *Germ Free Adolescents* (finally made available in the U.S. in 1992) had by then become essential listening for girls (and boys) in revolt.

## DISCOGRAPHY

*Germ Free Adolescents* (Blue Plate/EMI, 1978; Caroline, 1992); the one and only X-Ray Spex album in its original incarnation, a Brit punk classic.

*Live at the Roxy* (Receiver [UK], 1991); recorded at a live show that predates their debut album, this import features Lora Logic on sax.

*Conscious Consumer* (Receiver [UK], 1995); a new record by a reunited X-Ray Spex, featuring Poly, Lora, and Paul Dean.

# THE SLITS

*When I first saw them I was in the Beastie Boys, and Adam Yauch [of the Beasties] had a Slits poster on his wall. We were all really into them, but it was extra-special for girls. Cut is still in my all-time top ten, I would never want to be without it. If they came around now, people would understand them so much better. They brought out the dub bass and scratchy guitar, which was originally Luscious Jackson's approach. For me, Jill [Cuniff], and Gabby [Glazer, in Luscious Jackson], they were seriously heroes. When some girls would be playing Barbie, we would play dress-up like the Slits.*

### Kate Schellenbach, Luscious Jackson

With a name that evoked both punk's violence and—in the crudest terms—womanhood, the Slits offered a female version of first-generation British punk bands that appeared in the late '70s. But as they came into their own musically, the group transcended punk and shaped an adventurous post-punk sound that celebrated femininity in more abstract and complex ways. In a short career that produced only two studio albums, the Slits presented a unique musical vision. And, along the way, they inspired musicians across the entire spectrum: from riot grrrl, with their feminist polemics, to PJ Harvey and Mecca Normal, with their more metaphysical approach, to anyone—regardless of sex—interested in pushing the boundaries of punk.

Before forming, members of the Slits had been part of the inner clique of British punk kids surrounding bands like the Sex Pistols and the Clash. Fourteen-year-old Arianna Forster had recently left boarding school to move to London with her mother, a German heiress named Nora, who through her daughter's punk connections would meet and eventually marry the Pistols' Johnny Rotten. Forster befriended Paloma Romero (renamed Palmolive by Clash bassist Paul Simonon), a 22-year-old Spanish woman who'd been living with the Clash's Joe Strummer. Before they'd even tried to play their instruments, would-be guitarist Arianna—renamed Ari Up—and drummer Palmolive recruited guitarist Kate Korus and bassist Suzi Gutsy to form the Slits.

In the time between forming and actually playing a gig, Korus and Gutsy were replaced by Viv Albertine and Tessa Pollit, two young punks who'd spent some time in Sid Vicious's pre-Pistols band, Flowers of Romance. Like many of the punk bands forming in 1976 and '77, the early Slits were more of a social unit that called themselves a band than an actual music group. Appropriately, they appeared at the time in Derek Jarman's punk fantasy film *Jubilee* as a street-roaming girl gang. And their lack of ability was made even more clear when they debuted as the Clash's opening act in March of 1977. A sort of punk version of the **Shaggs**, the early Slits teetered at the brink of falling apart with songs like "A Boring Life" and "Once Upon a Time in a Living Room." Live, the band banged along in cacophonous abandon while members stopped occasionally to yell at each other.

---

### Amy Rigby

*They were just a mess, and I really like that about them. The way they dressed, and covered themselves with mud and were naked on the cover of their record. They were very powerful females and they weren't afraid of flaunting their attractiveness, but it was in a way they wanted to do it and to their own purposes. It wasn't some art director who took them and said it would be a cool idea.*

---

Within the year, though, the Slits had perfected punk's standard fast riffing style and worked up enough material to record for radio DJ/producer John Peel. By the time they signed a record con-tract in late 1978 the group had moved beyond punk and developed a more rhythmic, reggae-inflected style, with surprisingly complex vocal parts and song structures. When Sex Pistols impresario Malcolm McLaren attempted to assume management of the group, Palmolive's opposition to McLaren—as well as other artistic differences—led to her departure. Months later, she reappeared as the **Raincoats'** drummer. In the midst of recording an album, the Slits called in their friend Budgie (Peter Clark) to sit in on drums.

Though it was their first record, 1979's *Cut* documents the band at a rather late stage in its evolution. By then, the group had fully come into its own as a strong—and distinctly female— post-punk voice. The provocative album featured the young women posed against the backdrop of a pleasant English garden, but topless and covered in mud. The photo confounded notions of sexuality and civility, and positioned the group as

modern primitive feminist rebels—girls not afraid to be natural, sexual, and formidable.

Even more powerful than the photo was the music, which reinvented punk rock as a forum for young women. In opposition to the driving aggression of male-oriented punk, *Cut* was more rhythmic and textural, while the lyrics to songs like "Spend, Spend, Spend," "Shoplifting," and the single "Typical Girls," alternatively celebrated the liberation of girl delinquency and confronted consumer culture's manipulation of female self-esteem. A post-punk classic, *Cut* set the standard for all female-oriented punk to come.

### Jean Smith, Mecca Normal

*I went out and bought* Cut *and tried to figure out what the hell they were trying to do. It was my first close look at really wondering about a band, because the whole focus was on the women in an inviting way. It seemed much more open. And I felt I had the go-ahead to see what came out of me in much the same way that these people seemed very genuine in their own noisemaking.*

As Budgie left to join Siouxsie and the Banshees and the Pop Group's Bruce Smith took over as fill-in drummer, the Slits continued to incorporate reggae music and consciousness into their music. Between *Cut* and the 1981 follow-up, *The Return of the Giant Slits*, the group released a series of singles such as "In the Beginning There Was Rhythm" that explored their growing interest in rhythm as a sort of life force. Songs like "Earthbeat" on *The Return* took their richly drawn primitivism and mother earth vibe even further with more subtle and organic music. The record was a worthy successor to *Cut*, but its foray into esoteric structure alienated fans of *Cut*'s more pop-oriented music, and the album failed to earn much attention. By the end of 1981, the Slits had called it quits.

Ari Up has continued her involvement in reggae music with **Adrian Sherwood**'s New Age Steppers and Prince Far-I & the Arabs. She now lives in Jamaica with her family (and remains John Lydon's stepdaughter). Viv Albertine also appeared in the New Age Steppers, and was more recently involved in the Courtney Love-directed soundtrack to the film *Tank Girl*.

## DISCOGRAPHY

*Cut* (Island, 1979); a debut album that came fairly late in the band's development, it is nevertheless the ultimate document of female punk.

*Untitled (Retrospective)* (Y/Rough Trade, 1980); this "official bootleg" collects the group's earliest music, which never appeared on a studio album.

*The Return of the Giant Slits* (CBS UK, 1981); unreleased in the U.S., this studio follow-up to *Cut* shows the band developing a more dub, rhythm-oriented sound.

*The Peel Sessions* (Strange Fruit, 1989); a collection from two Peel studio sessions in 1977 and 1978, featuring earlier versions of some songs later on *Cut*.

# THE RAINCOATS

*The Raincoats were not very well known in the States—I don't know about the U.K. or Europe. In fact, I really don't know anything about the Raincoats except that they recorded some music that has affected me so much that whenever I hear it I'm reminded of a particular time in my life when*

*I was (shall we say) extremely unhappy, lonely, and bored. If it weren't for the luxury of putting on that scratchy copy of the Raincoats first record, I would have had very few moments of peace.*
**Kurt Cobain, Nirvana [from the liner notes to The Raincoats CD reissue]**

In their amazing ability to apply punk's freedom to create an equally strong and feminine sound, the Raincoats took what the **Slits** started to an even more sublime level. Unlike any "girl groups" of the past, the power of the Raincoats' music came from its emotional fearlessness. They could be striking without flaunting sexuality, and experimental without alienating listeners. As a key early '80s post-punk group, the Raincoats inspired bands like Throwing Muses and Sonic Youth. By the time they reappeared in the '90s, they'd become important mother figures for bands like Sleater-Kinney, Hole (who covered the Raincoats' "The Void"), even Nirvana. In fact, Kurt Cobain felt such an emotional debt to the Raincoats, he convinced his record company to reissue the Raincoats' catalogue.

### Kristin Hersh, Throwing Muses

*I did listen to the Raincoats, and it was wild to hear a band more fragile and feminine than we were. I don't mean girlie, I mean shooting off in all directions and paying more attention to details. And they were purely unconscious. They made such beautiful sounds that we thought what we were doing was okay. We were pretty much in a boy's club at the time.*

Inspired by female punk bands like the **Slits** and **X-Ray Spex** that had cropped up in the wake of the British punk explosion, two recent arrivals to London—Gina Birch from northern England and Ana Da Silva from Portugal—formed the Raincoats in 1977. Though they debuted in November of that year with a male guitarist and drummer, the group went through a number of lineup changes before they started gigging regularly. When they recruited former **Slits** drummer Palmolive (Paloma Romero) and found violinist Vicky Aspinall (they placed an ad for someone who played an unusual instrument), the Raincoats—with Birch on bass, Ana on guitar, and all of them sharing vocals—became a focused and steady musical unit.

With the exception of Aspinall, none of the women were trained on their instruments. Growing together as musicians enabled the group to develop a shared musical language, one that was not necessarily connected to any prior rules or conventions. "It was a great period for learning and achieving the surprises that were our songs and our sound," Da Silva writes in the notes to *The Raincoats* CD reissue. "The punk idea that you just needed to know three chords to start something was a very encouraging concept, and I think it still stands."

### Amy Rigby

*The Raincoats were really important to me. I love the way they just created their own kind of music. It was personal in a way that the other punk groups I loved didn't speak to me. "Fairytale in a Supermarket" was a big revelation to me when I first heard it. I loved what they did with their voices. They took their musical limitations and made them work for them. I found that inspiring. And they couldn't have made that music if they hadn't been women.*

After attracting the interest of influential London label Rough Trade, in 1979 the Raincoats released their first single, "Fairytale in the Supermarket." Despite subtle lyrics that were unrhymed and unstructured, the song soars on its screeching violin and rocks along to the rumble and thrash of the drums and guitar. Six months later, the group followed with a self-titled debut album. Produced by **Mayo Thompson** of the **Red Krayola** and featuring former **X-Ray Spex** saxophonist Lora Logic, *The Raincoats* established the band as one of the most distinct voices in post-punk. Even when the songs sounded familiar—such as with their cover of the Kinks' ode to sexual ambiguity "Lola," or with their reworking of Palmolive-penned **Slits** song "Adventures Close to Home"—the Raincoats seemed completely original—incapable of either copying anyone else or of being copied.

As the group began writing its second album, Palmolive quit in search of a more spiritual existence (she traveled to India, and has since become a born-again Christian), and the band was left temporarily without a drummer. The songs on *Odyshape* (the title is an amalgamation of "oddly-shaped" and "body shape") are less rhythmic, accented by percussion more than driven by it (though almost an afterthought, drums were contributed by Richard Dudanski, who'd been one of the group's earlier members, as well as Robert Wyatt and Palmolive's short-lived replacement, Ingrid Weiss).

---

### Carrie Brownstein, Sleater-Kinney

*I can listen to a Raincoats album and I don't know how they were able to do it. It's such an incredible mix of musicianship and melody. The voices are amazing too. The first time I heard the Raincoats I was definitely amazed. It seemed like classical music, except it was punk. It had the complexity and hugeness of a symphony, except it was being performed by three women.*

---

Like the **Slits,** the Raincoats moved away from punk—away from even post-punk—with their second record, toward a sound more reminiscent of dub reggae (particularly Birch's bass) and British folk music (particularly Aspinal's violin). While *Odyshape* contained fewer memorable songs than the debut, it showed the group developing as a tightly woven musical unit. Though not as overtly female-centered as the **Slits,** *Odyshape* expressed feminine creativity even more eloquently—so much so, in fact, that it made little sense in the context of the current rock scene.

**Kim Gordon, Sonic Youth**
*I loved the **Slits** but it was the Raincoats I related to most. They seemed like ordinary people playing extraordinary music. Music that was natural that made room for a cohesion of personalities. They had enough confidence to be vulnerable and to be themselves without having to take on the mantle of male rock/punk rock aggression. [from the liner notes to the Odyshape CD reissue]*

While the group maintained a core of Birch, Da Silva, and Aspinall, the early '80s saw the addition of a number of drummers, percussionists, and multi-instrumentalists, including This Heat's Charles Hayward. Despite the polish of their third record, 1984's *Moving*, it shows the Raincoats in search of a clear direction, lacking focus; they split up following the album's release. As Aspinall wrote later in the liner notes, "The title of this album describes the process it encapsulated for us as individuals, and by the time it was recorded we had all moved on to some other place...."

The Raincoats' members remained artistically active, though out of the public eye, for nearly a decade until longtime fan Kurt Cobain initiated the reissue of the Raincoats' three studio albums. This renewed interest spurred the women back into action in 1993, and with a lineup of Birch, Da Silva, and new violinist Anne Wood, the band began touring again. Though plans to open for Nirvana did not materialize (Cobain committed suicide), the Raincoats continued to develop strong new material and went on to record an EP (with Sonic Youth drummer Steve Shelley) and an album (with Tiger Trap's Heather Dunn).

With Birch now fronting a new band called the Hangovers, the Raincoats' future is uncertain. The band, though, seems well aware of their place in the history of women's rock. As Da Silva wrote, "The efforts to open doors for women have been fruitful (though painfully slow) and we hope that...our three albums can still inspire those who want to voice their feelings, ideas, opinions, etc. through music and otherwise."

## DISCOGRAPHY

*The Raincoats* (Rough Trade, 1979; DGC, 1993); the low-fi and amateurish punk classic debut.

*Odyshape* (Rough Trade, 1981; DGC, 1993); a quieter, but equally eccentric, follow-up.

*The Kitchen Tapes* (ROIR, 1983); a live recording from the group's 1982 U.S. tour, including stronger versions of many songs from *Moving*.

*Moving* (Rough Trade, 1984; DGC, 1994); the group's most eclectic work, recorded as they were on the verge of breaking up.

*Extended Play* EP (Smells Like, 1994); a four-track live in-studio release taken from the John Peel radio show, with the group's first new songs in a decade.

*Fairytales* (Tim/Kerr, 1995); a limited edition release featuring tracks from three Rough Trade albums and pressed on blue vinyl.

*Looking in the Shadows* (DGC, 1996); a new full-length that showed the women still capable of creating captivating music.

# 15

## AMERICAN HARDCORE

**P**unk rock may have had its roots in American bands like the **Stooges** and the Ramones, but by 1978 punk's most recognizable face was undeniably British. The Sex Pistols had exploded, and London became the place where tourists from around the world came to take souvenir photos of purple-haired teens with safety-pinned cheeks and spray-painted leather jackets.

At first, most U.S. punk kids—particularly in California—gladly adopted England's made-to-shock styles. But inevitably, a more distinctly American expression of punk rock began to re-appear. Rather than the punk of London kids with grim economic prospects, this punk was made by predominantly suburban Americans who had grown up in relative comfort and faced the boredom of continued prosperity. In places like the beach communities surrounding L.A., kids raised on arena rock and consumer culture wanted music that would excite them, music that was louder, faster, harder than anything before.

And so by the early '80s, Americans had reclaimed punk's cutting edge. The music of bands like **Black Flag** in Southern California, **Hüsker Dü** in Minnesota, and **Minor Threat** in Washington, D.C. became known as hardcore punk, or simply hardcore. While hardcore's first concern was making high-energy rock, the band stook an additional step by turning punk's rejectionist stance into something constructive. Where British punk's best-known bands worked within the same business structure in place for years, American hardcore (like British post-punk) placed a high value on the do-it-yourself (D-I-Y) ethic. These bands wanted to set up an entirely new system where groups served as their own record label, manager, and booking agent; they wanted the punk scene to form entirely new distribution networks and tour circuits.

---

### King Coffey, Butthole Surfers

*Hardcore brought the message home that Brits don't have sole property over punk rock. In fact, nobody did it as fiercely and with as much intensity and meaning as early '80s American hardcore. It was through the bands I saw back then, and the records coming out on local and regional labels, that we had a sense of community—that we were truly the counterculture. I have never been so excited about any music, ever, as I was back then. It was really mind blowing—mind expanding—maybe parallel to what it would've been like when hippies first realized they had their own subculture going. I will forever view the world through punk rock eyes.*

---

Of course, for every kid attracted by hardcore's constructive elements there were probably ten impressionable followers drawn to its nihilistic and violent tendencies. In the end, the bands with the most commitment and self-respect left the most important legacy. While the bands determined to maintain autonomy from the record industry had little hope of achieving commercial success, their styles and ideals greatly influenced a younger generation of punk fans. The hard/fast innovations of American hardcore set the stage for '90s groups like Nirvana and Green Day, while the early punk labels made today's highly developed indie music scene—with labels like Kill Rock Stars and D-I-Y artists such as Ani Difranco—a feasible alternative to the corporate record industry.

---

### Thurston Moore, Sonic Youth

*It's funny, when those rock documentaries on PBS last year did punk rock, they couldn't deal with the '80s. They were like, "Oh, the Pretenders and reggae became a big influence on the new wave. And not much happened until later, there were some bands in Seattle." And Steve [Shelley, Sonic Youth's drummer] turned to me and said, "The '80s are still a secret." Nobody knows what happened. We know, we were there. And all those people like Kurt [Cobain] and Krist [Novoselic, Nirvana's bassist], they were the kids in the fucking audience.*

---

## T H E   G E R M S

*I can't believe anyone's even interested anymore. I haven't been bothered by it for years myself, but sometimes these famous guitarists will come up and tell me I'm the reason they started playing guitar.... I never even owned a guitar the whole time I was in the band, I bought my first guitar for the reunion gig.*

### Pat Smear, the Germs/Nirvana/Foo Fighters [from liner notes to *A Small Circle of Friends*]

While the Germs weren't the first L.A. punk band, they were certainly one of the most celebrated—and the first to leave a undeniable legacy on subsequent punk music. Too short-lived and erratic to ever reach their potential, the Germs nevertheless played a crucial role in translating British-style punk back into American terms. By making the look, attitude, and energy of punk American, the Germs opened the doors for the hardcore bands that would soon develop nearby. From there, a definitively American style of punk would spread—east to Washington, north to Seattle, and everywhere in between.

---

### Thurston Moore, Sonic Youth

*At first, we thought the L.A. scene was completely copying British bands, like dress-up punk, and New Yorkers thought that was silly. But at some point L.A. developed its own identity. They weren't singing about the death of their social system like in England, it was mostly, "I don't wanna grow up and be a rich banker like my daddy, because that's boring." It was a whole American thing New Yorkers didn't even think about, and it related much more to middle America. That's why hardcore was more influenced by the Germs than by [New York band] 8 Eyed Spy.*

---

Jan Paul Beahm and George Ruthenberg formed their first band while attending an experimental high school for troubled kids. Called Sophistifuck and the Revlon Spam Queens, it was more a concept than actual group since neither played nor owned an instrument. In early 1977, Jan (who'd take the punk name Darby Crash) and Geroge (who became Pat Smear) met two young ladies while waiting in a hotel for the chance to the meet the members of Queen. The four—Darby, Pat, and the equally inexperienced bass player Lorna Doom and drummer Dottie Danger—decided to form a band, which they named the Germs. Despite their lack of musical ability, they soon debuted at the Orpheum Theater, opening for the Weirdos and the Zeros. (By then, Dottie had been replaced by her friend Donna Rhia; the following year Dottie reclaimed her given name, Belinda Carlisle, and formed the Go-Gos.)

In a matter of months, the Germs had emerged as the most notorious band on the burgeoning L.A. punk scene. With stage moves, audience-baiting, and peanut butter–flinging antics borrowed from the **Stooges'** Iggy Pop, Darby was ringleader of his band's unrefined chaos. He slurred his words, showing little concern for lyrics or melody or whether he was singing into the microphone, while the rest of the Germs—Smear's noisy untuned guitar, Lorna's erratic and lumbering bass, and Donna's precariously uneven drum tempos—sounded about as loose as a band could be without actually falling apart.

Nevertheless, the Germs became L.A.'s equivalent to the Sex Pistols; just as the Pistols had their loyalists, the Bromley Contingent, Germs fans were dubbed the Germs (or Darby Crash) Contingent. As the group's notoriety (fueled by riots and food fights) escalated, though, gigs were increasingly difficult to secure. Few clubs would agree to book the Germs a second time. To trick venues into booking them, the group began billing themselves under a code name: G.I.(for Germs Incognito).

---

### Mike Watt, Minutemen/Firehose
*It was funny, some of the early Hollywood [punk] bands were like, "We're going to be stars, this is the new rock and roll." But the Germs were like, "We're going to make our own music." They were coming up with their own sound, and were copied by all the Orange County bands. A lot of the Hollywood bands had elitism, but Darby was into expanding it out. In a way he was kind of an ambassador.*

---

By the summer of '78, Rhia had been replaced by a succession of drummers—including Nicky Beat of the Weirdos and future X drummer DJ Bonebrake—and the Germs had earned the right to be called "most improved band." They'd tightened up and increased the tempo of their songs in keeping with the high-speed hardcore trend that was emerging from the L.A. suburbs. The band didn't settle on a (relatively) permanent beat-keeper, though, until Don Bolles arrived from Phoenix. In 1979, with their strongest and most stable lineup in place, the group entered the studio with producer Joan Jett (who they idolized from her days in the Runaways) to record their first and only album, *(GI)* [actually self-titled and credited to Germs (GI)]. Featuring a black cover with the band's blue circle logo, the record was an instant punk classic, hailed by fans and critics alike as the first great post-Sex Pistols American punk album. The band managed to turn out dynamic and confident performances on songs like "What We Do Is Secret," with Crash's throaty growl setting the standard for punk vocalists of the future.

---

### Ian MacKaye, Minor Threat/Fugazi

*The Germs, and the whole L.A. punk scene, were a big inspiration for us. It was so totally insane, but their music—and particularly Darby's lyrics—can't be replicated. The Germs were the center of an intense crew of really fucked-up kids in L.A., and this was their art. I think that Germs album is close to perfect.*

---

As it turned out, though, the American version of the Sex Pistols would implode just as quickly as their British counterparts. Darby, while borrowing vocal affectations from Johnny Rotten, more closely resembled Sid Vicious with his heroin habit, dumb nihilism, and fascist flirtations. As Darby fostered his own cult of personality by encouraging followers to wear the Germs logo on armbands and scar their arms with cigarettes (Germs burns), he seemed to lose touch with reality. Toward the end of 1979, Darby fired Don Bolles and took off to London. Having seen Adam and the Ants there, he returned to L.A. a few months later sporting a mohawk and Indian face paint. By then, Lorna had quit the Germs and the band had folded.

Darby and Smear soon formed the Darby Crash Band, but the group fell apart after a handful of gigs. In December of 1980, Darby convinced Pat, Don, and Lorna to re-form the Germs for one final gig. Having earned enough money from the show to buy a lethal dose of heroin, Crash overdosed and died—one day before John Lennon's assassination—at age 22. While Lorna Doom did not continue as a musician, Don Bolles has played in a number of bands, including Celebrity Skin.

Pat Smear played with Nina Hagen and the Adolescents—as well as original Germ turned pop star Belinda Carlisle—then made records in the late '80s as a solo artist and half of the duo Death Folk. After recording with Courtney Love for a Germs tribute album, Smear met Love's husband and fellow Germs fan Kurt Cobain. Invited to join Nirvana as a second guitarist on their 1993 tour, he remained part of the band until Cobain's death. Afterward, he and Nirvana drummer Dave Grohl formed the Foo Fighters, which he quit in 1997 to focus on life as an MTV personality and other pursuits.

## DISCOGRAPHY

*(GI)* (Slash, 1979); the only studio release, this can be found in its entirety on *(MIA)*.

*What We Do Is Secret* EP (Slash, 1981); collects first two singles and two other songs; found in its entirety on *(MIA)*.

*Germicide: Live at the Whiskey* (Bomp/ROIR, 1981); a live recording of an early show from June 1977.

*Let the Circle Be Unbroken* (Gasatanka, 1985); a live recording.

*Lion's Share* (Ghost o'Darb, 1985); half live, half recordings from the soundtrack to *Cruising* [which appear also on *(MIA)*].

*Rock N' Rule* (XES, 1986); a live recording..

*(MIA) The Complete Anthology* (Slash, 1993); the definitive collection which includes all of the studio recordings.

TRIBUTE: Various Artists, *A Small Circle of Friends* (Grass, 1996); a collection of Germs songs done by Matthew Sweet, L7, the Meat Puppets, members of Sonic Youth, Hole, and Dinosaur Jr., as well as others.

## B L A C K   F L A G

*Black Flag's early records virtually defined hardcore, and their records were required listening, part of the essential syllabus for every U.S. punk, then and now. Few records had as much rage, few shows were as powerful. "Rise Above" is perhaps the ultimate hardcore anthem, a gauntlet Black Flag threw down that inspired U.S. punks to create something indigenous: HARDCORE ('77 Brit punk seemed tame in comparison). The Butthole Surfers came from the hardcore underground and therefore are indebted to bands like Black Flag for inventing it in the first place.*

**King Coffey, Butthole Surfers**

Black Flag played hardcore punk before there was a name for it. And by the time the genre had been defined, the band could take credit for having influenced just about every group that had formed in its wake. With superfast riffing and all-out fury, Black Flag's take on punk would, for the first time since the Brit punk explosion, define the style as uniquely American. More than musically, though, the group put forth a hardcore ethic that backed punk's rebellious rhetoric with an actual rejection of the "system." By releasing records and booking tours on its own, Black Flag created a model for do-it-yourself bands and started a network for underground music. And by the time they were through, Black Flag—through their record label's releases, their side projects, and their punk-metal hybrids—had laid the foundation for much of the so-called grunge and alternative rock of the '90s.

---

### Scott Kannberg, Pavement

*They were my favorite band when I was 14, 15 years old. The first singles were a huge influence on me. I was scared to play them in front of my parents, it was just a whole different sound I'd never heard before.... Their whole aesthetic of working really hard, touring a lot, was inspiring. I think Steve [Malkmus, of Pavement] got a lot of guitar inspiration from Greg Ginn.*

Before he'd even picked up a guitar, Greg Ginn had cultivated many of the gifts that would make him a key force in the creation of an entirely new punk paradigm, American hardcore music. As a child Ginn hated the commercialism of pop music, and instead of listening to music he kept busy making things: He built electronics, then wrote and published his own magazine in high school. After studying economics at UCLA, Ginn set up his own company making ham radio antennas, which he named Solid State Transformers, or SST.

In college, Ginn started playing guitar and immersing himself in various music styles, from jazz to avant-garde classical to pre-punk bands like the **Stooges**. When he finally decided to form a band, it was 1977 and Ginn was already 24 years old. He recruited Charles "Chuck" Dukowski on bass, Brian Migdol on drums, and Keith Morris to be lead vocalist in the Hermosa Beach-based band he formed, called Black Flag. While inspired by the punk scene brewing in Hollywood, Black Flag began to project a separate musical identity for outlying communities such as theirs.

Unlike the more glitzy city punk, where dyed hair and black leather were the standard, Black Flag was strictly short hair, T-shirt, and jeans. And oblivious to genre classifications, Black Flag owed as much to Black Sabbath's metal as they did to the Sex Pistols' Brit punk. While early Black Flag songs like "Nervous Breakdown" and "Wasted" were harder and faster than any punk before, they were for the most part meat and potatoes American-style hard rock. Though it hadn't yet been named, this was the beginning of hardcore.

To release Black Flag's first EP, *Nervous Breakdown,* Ginn mutated SST Electronics into SST Records. Despite personnel changes that included replacing Morris (who left to form the Circle Jerks) with singer Ron Reyes, the band's EP and powerful live shows solidified Black Flag's reputation. Unlike the intentionally provocative punk bands, Black Flag wanted to play as much as possible and had little interest in controversies that would make it difficult to get gigs. Miles away from the **Germs** nihilism, Black Flag developed a nonstop work ethic.

---

### Thurston Moore, Sonic Youth
*Black Flag were the first band that got in a van and just played in people's rec-rooms all across the country, and they created this whole network of people doing it for themselves. Sonic Youth was just coming of age as far as touring, and we were totally into that: "We'll book our own tour and put our own records out, and we'll play with these bands." A lot of them were great, Black Flag were fantastic.*

---

By the end of the '70s, Black Flag had switched to a third vocalist, Dez Cadena, and was reaching its widest audience yet. Songs like "Six Pack," and "TV Party" appealed both to fans who appreciated the irony of lines like "We've got nothing better to do/Than watch TV and have a couple of brews" and those who actually identified with it.

---

### Eric Wilson, Sublime
*I was always into the "Six Pack" thing and "TV Party." Definitely the lyrical content influenced me, just them talking about being young, growing up, and having a good time.*

---

As the band developed a national reputation through constant touring, Black Flag could draw hundreds of young hardcore fans in cities like San Francisco and New York. After one fan, named Henry Garfield, sang with them at a show in New York, they asked him to quit his job as manager of a Washington, D.C. ice cream store and become their new singer. With Garfield—now calling himself Henry Rollins—doing vocals and Cadena switched to rhythm guitar, Black Flag released their first full album, *Damaged,* on SST in 1981. Containing much of the band's most memorable material—the "party" tunes as well as intensely emotional songs like "Depression" and the anthemic "Rise Above"—the album became a definitive document of American hardcore.

*Lou Barlow, Sebadoh/Folk Implosion*
*When I was 14 or 15, I went to see them play live. Wow, that pretty much killed me. Black Flag was so stripped down. They had all these emotional issues, and that was pretty inspiring.*

As the band's popularity grew, Black Flag aligned itself with the MCA-affiliated Unicorn Records, a larger company that could better distribute their album. However, MCA executives deemed *Damaged* an "anti-parent" record and refused to release it. A two-year legal battle ensued, during which the band was barred from releasing records under the Black Flag name (1982's outtake collection *Everything Went Black* listed band members' names on the cover). Through 1982 and most of 1983, Black Flag spent what could have been their most fruitful years without any new releases. By the time Unicorn went bankrupt and freed Black Flag, the band was down to three members: Ginn (who also played bass under the pseudonym Dale Nixon), Rollins, and former Descendents drummer Bill Stevenson (Dukowski remained active in SST but not the band).

By the time they released *My War*, their long-awaited second studio album, Black Flag had evolved away from the full-on assault of their earlier hardcore punk. Tempos were slower and Ginn had developed a lead style that brought in more metal and prog rock influences. Meanwhile, Rollins had discovered a new avocation in spoken-word poetry, which appeared on the band's half-instrumental *Family Man* album in 1984.

That same year, with the addition of bassist Kira (Roessler)—a rare female in the male-dominated world of hardcore—Black Flag released two more albums: the hard rocking *Slip It In* and *Live '84*. Three more releases came in 1985: *Loose Nut, The Process of Weeding Out*, and *In My Head*. While the *Process* EP offered punk-jazz fusion instrumentals, the others defined a punk/metal hybrid that would reach mainstream ears a half-decade later as grunge.

*Mark Robinson, Unrest*
*I saw them when they put out My War. It really struck me how they were playing more of a King Crimson-ish prog rock kind of punk—doing different things within the punk construct—it wasn't straight-ahead stuff. With Unrest, we were really into King Crimson and also into punk, so the fact that Black Flag could cross over the two genres was appealing to us.*

By late 1985, internal tensions in the band led to the departure of both Stevenson and Kira (who married **Minutemen** bassist Mike Watt and formed the duo Dos with him). Rollins, meanwhile, became more interested in spoken-word and writing projects (and started hanging out with fellow rising stars like Michael Stipe and Nick Cave). Ginn, who had formed the instrumental side band Gone to better explore new directions, decided to end Black Flag in the summer of '86.

While Ginn has continued with Gone and solo albums, he has devoted much of his time to running SST with Dukowski. With releases by hardcore forefathers the **Minutemen, Bad Brains, Hüsker Dü,** and the Descendents—as well as future alternative rockers the Meat Puppets, Sonic Youth, Dinosaur Jr., and Screaming Trees—SST became the preeminent indie of the '80s. Apparently,

Ginn's industriousness also rubbed off on Rollins, who has put out seven solo albums (mostly spoken word), and another seven as leader of the Rollins Band. In addition, Rollins has run a record label (Infinite Zero) and publishing company (2.13.61), written books of poetry and prose (including the Black Flag tour diary *Get in the Van*), appeared in films (including 1997's *Lost Highway*), and done ads for Apple Computers. He participated in the first Lollapalooza and now records for the Spielberg/Katzenberg/Geffen label Dreamworks.

## DISCOGRAPHY

*Damaged* (SST, 1981); their debut album and first release featuring Henry Rollins, this hardcore classic includes "Rise Above" and "TV Party."

*Everything Went Black* (SST, 1982); a double album of alternate takes from pre-Rollins recordings and radio promos.

*The First Four Years* (SST, 1983); collects all the pre-Rollins EPs and singles, including 1978's *Nervous Breakdown* and '80's *Jealous Again*.

*My War* (SST, 1983); a long-awaited follow-up to *Damaged*, showing a move away from traditional hardcore to slower and more complex songs.

*Family Man* (SST, 1984); features both instrumentals and Henry Rollins spoken word.

*Slip It In* (SST, 1984); an uneven mix of the band's further explorations into a punk-metal hybrid.

*Live '84* (SST, 1984); a cassette-only live recording.

*Loose Nut* (SST, 1985); a slight return to punk roots, including the late-career classic "Annihilate This Week."

*Process of Weeding Out* (SST, 1985); an instrumental four-song EP, with a punk/jazz fusion bent.

*In My Head* (SST, 1985); the final studio recording, ending the band on a relative high note.

# D E A D   K E N N E D Y S

*When I first head the name Dead Kennedys, I thought it was the fucking funniest thing. I knew it was for me, it was so totally offensive. Once I heard the Dead Kennedys I denounced everything else—it became as close to a religion as anything—I wrote "DK" on everything I owned.*

**Micky "Gene Ween" Melchiondo, Ween**

With outrageous songs delivered with equal parts frenzy and intelligence, the Dead Kennedys gave American punk rock a political voice. And when confronted with a challenge to its free speech rights, the band fought the system wholeheartedly—even to the point that it consumed and destroyed them. Their commitment to backing up words with action makes them an inspiration to politically oriented groups in punk and beyond, while their twisted humor and unorthodox take on punk has paved the way for bands like the Butthole Surfers. Through their music as well as their label—which has fostered the careers of many younger bands—the Dead Kennedys' legacy continues long after the band has gone.

### King Coffey, Butthole Surfers

*They were probably most influential on us for the sheer fact that they put out our first two records. They also took us out on tour, which exposed us to the rest of the world. They were kind of our mentors to a large degree.*

Before he became Jello Biafra, he was Eric Boucher of Boulder, Colorado. Politicized at a young age by events such as the Vietnam War and later Watergate, Boucher early on developed a healthy skepticism for government and a contrarian attitude. While most kids in school enjoyed the Eagles, Boucher sought out the **Stooges** and **MC5**. After a trip to London in the summer of 1977—where he encountered **Wire** and other punk bands—Boucher moved to the Bay area for college. Inspired by early San Francisco punk bands like the Nuns and the Dils, and more artsy groups like the **Residents,** Boucher dropped out of school after one semester to form his own band.

After only a week's rehearsal in July 1978, Boucher—now Jello Biafra—and his band the Dead Kennedys debuted. Joining him was bassist Klaus Flouride, drummer Bruce Slesinger (a.k.a. Ted), guitarist East Bay Ray (Glasser), and briefly, the enigmatic 6025 (a.k.a Carlos). Centered in what has long been a hotbed of liberal activism, the Bay area punk scene was naturally more politically oriented than the L.A. scene, and the Dead Kennedys thrived in this environment. Their first single "California Uber Alles," released in 1979 on the band's own Alternative Tentacles label, targeted then-governor Jerry Brown and his mob of "zen fascists." A few months later, Biafra caused further controversy by running for mayor of San Francisco on the slogan, "There's always room for Jello." Despite the campaign's absurdity, Biafra proved himself an intelligent and impassioned public speaker, and even earned 3½ percent of the votes.

Leaving political aspirations behind, in 1980 Biafra and the Dead Kennedys released an equally provocative second single called "Holiday in Cambodia" and a debut album, *Fresh Fruit for Rotting Vegetables*. On songs like "Kill the Poor" and "Let's Lynch the Landlord," Biafra railed against militarism, consumer culture, conformity, and complacency in a quavery voice that all but codified American punk's political agenda. Overshadowed by the rhetoric, but equally impressive, were East Bay Ray's dynamic guitar and a garage pop rhythm section that kept the songs moving in unpredictable directions. Like Biafra's lyrics, the band's music challenged existing conventions—even punk ones.

*Lou Barlow, Sebadoh/Folk Implosion*
*Hearing "Holiday in Cambodia" was so exciting, they sounded really aggressive and kind of psychedelic too. It appealed to me in a way Hendrix had appealed to me when I first heard "Purple Haze"—"How do they make those sounds?" The combination of surf guitar, psychedelic, heavy metal—but played really fast—appealed to me a lot. After that I just got into faster and faster music.*

When the band's next single, "Too Drunk to Fuck," became a hit in England, the DKs decided to use Alternative Tentacles to export American punk to Europe. While British punk styles had influenced American music for years, with the 1981 compilation *Let Them Eat Jellybeans,* American bands like **Black Flag, Flipper, Half Japanese,** and **Bad Brains** were able to have a large impact on expanding European punk sounds. At home, the Dead Kennedys' EP *In God We Trust, Inc.* took aim not only at organized religion and the Reagan administration, but also at divisive elements within the punk scene ("Nazi Punks Fuck Off"). While the record's faster pace reflected an influence of newer hardcore bands like **Hüsker Dü** (released by Alternative Tentacles in Europe), 1982's *Plastic Surgery Disasters* returned to the more varied sounds of *Fresh Fruit,* with songs like "Terminal Preppie" and "Winnebago Warrior."

### Kristin Hersh, Throwing Muses

*DKs were my soundtrack for a whole year, when I was 16. I was just making copies of demos and sending them off to record companies all day and night, and doing terrible paintings for art school. I played the DKs all the time.... I sang like Jello for years. I thought it was a really cool voice, but now there are little chickies who think they sound like me when really they sound like Jello Biafra, who they've never heard of.*

As the Dead Kennedys' appearances at demonstrations—including rallies at the 1984 Democratic and Republican conventions—established the band as punk's most committed agitators, their third album, *Frankenchrist,* landed them in the midst of a political battle of their own. The album's poster insert featured a work by well-known Swiss surrealist H. R. Giger which depicted uniform rows of penises as a comment on consumerism and conformity. California law enforcement deemed the image pornographic and, in a raid on Alternative Tentacles offices, seized all copies of *Frankenchrist.* Charged with "distribution of harmful matter to minors," Biafra and four others faced a possible year in jail and a $2,000 fine.

The attention and resources devoted to Biafra's obscenity trial exacerbated tensions within the band. By the time their long-delayed fourth album, *Bedtime for Democracy,* came out—filled with inserts detailing Biafra's case and the right-wing crusade against music—the Dead Kennedys had already decided to call it quits. Though Biafra eventually won his war against censorship when his case was dismissed (the jury deadlocked), with his band dissolved and his records banned from stores across the country, he seemed to have lost most of the battles along the way. What remained, though, was his integrity and a new career as an anti-censorship spokesperson.

### Michael Franti, Spearhead

*I always admired the fact that he was doing things for himself, and kept that spirit alive. He tries to balance making music that people want to listen to and music that's saying something.*

After the DK's breakup, Biafra appeared on talk shows, gave lectures about his court battle, and recorded a number of spoken-word albums on that and other subjects. In addition, he has continued to make music with a variety of groups—including members of Ministry (as Lard), D.O.A., NoMeansNo, and Mojo Nixon—and to run Alternative Tentacles. Both Klaus Flouride and D. H. Peligro made solo records, while East Bay Ray plays in a band called Candy Ass.

## DISCOGRAPHY

*Fresh Fruit for Rotting Vegetables* (Alternative Tentacles, 1980); a classic debut, containing early singles "California Uber Alles" and "Holiday in Cambodia."

*In God We Trust, Inc.* EP (Alternative Tentacles, 1981); a faster, more hardcore eight-song collection included on the CD version of *Plastic Surgery Disasters.*

*Plastic Surgery Disasters* (Alternative Tentacles, 1982); a less successful blend of hardcore with outside styles.

*Frankenchrist* (Alternative Tentacles, 1985); originally containing the H.R. Giger artwork that spurred an obscenity trial, this is the DKs' best latter-day record.

*Bedtime for Democracy* (Alternative Tentacles, 1986); a studio finale with typically topical songs, though lacking the color of earlier records.

*Give Me Convenience or Give Me Death* (Alternative Tentacles, 1987); a posthumous collection of their best singles and less-than-essential rarities.

TRIBUTE: Various Artists, *Virus 100* (Alternative Tentacles, 1992); for AT's 100th release, artists such as L7, Kramer, Disposable Heroes of Hiphoprisy, and Mojo Nixon record Dead Kennedy's songs.

## THE   MINUTEMEN

*In the late '80s, early '90s I thought music had sunk pretty low. But hearing Superchunk, I heard our whole scene in them, and I realized that this thing will never die."*

**Mike Watt, Minutemen**

In the SST dynasty that produced the greatest documents of '80s hardcore, Black Flag ruled the roost while the Minutemen were always next in line for the throne. In many ways, though, the Minutemen were American punk's most endearing band, hardcore's great populists. Their intimate sound and nonflashy appearance made them favorites of the "regular guy" punks drawn into the music not by its sense of danger or spectacle, but rather by the camaraderie of the scene. The Minutemen came across as the kind of band you wanted to be friends with. After all, the band always functioned as an extension of its members' friendships.

### Doug Martsch, Built to Spill

*It could be said the Minutemen were the most important band ever. In so many ways they were perfect to me. They were the band I thought all punk bands were like. They seemed like completely decent people who understood priorities the way I did, and the importance of love. They were totally people I wanted to know.*

Though the Minutemen didn't actually form until 1979, their roots go back to 1970, the year 12-year-olds Dennes Dale (D.) Boon and Mike Watt met on a playground in San Pedro, the blue-collar port town on the Los Angeles harbor. In a case of mistaken identity, D. Boon pounced down from a tree onto Watt—a military brat who'd recently moved to town—and soon they were best friends. Years later, when D.'s mom bought her son a guitar to keep him off San Pedro's increasingly dangerous streets, she arranged for Mike to take up the bass. Soon the two were learning Creedence Clearwater Revival songs off records.

In high school, Mike and D. started hearing about a new music called "punk," and when they discovered punk was not much different than the amateurish guitar rock they'd been playing at home, it became clear that their music could be more than something to pass the time. After graduating in 1976, they started checking out the Hollywood punk scene that was developing around bands like the Weirdos and the **Germs,** where they found misfit kids like themselves transforming the accepted notions of rock. Inspired and empowered, Boon and Watt decided to form a band.

With their friend Martin Tamburovich as singer and San Pedro High classmate George Hurley on drums, Boon and Watt formed the Reactionaries. Though Hurley was wary of punk (as Watt explains, "In Pedro, 'punk' was what you called someone who let some guy fuck him in jail for cigarettes") he was quick to pick up on the energy. As punk began to reach outlying towns like San Pedro, the group identified with the populism of hardcore bands like **Black Flag,** which was very different from Hollywood punk's insularity. They decided to apply democratic principles to everything they did and got rid of their singer, who they felt took too much of the limelight and didn't contribute enough musically. As a trio, they renamed themselves the Minutemen to reflect the length of their songs.

---

### Scott Kannberg, Pavement

*Minutemen were a band for the masses. They should've been huge. I saw them like ten times in high school. They made you feel like yelling—yelling anything they said to yell. They had passion and great songs, too. We had a Minutemen party on the tour bus a couple weeks ago where we listened to Ballot Result. It was so fun, we hadn't heard it in so long. We were just bouncing off the walls.*

---

After opening for **Black Flag,** the Minutemen were invited in early 1980 to release a record on Black Flag's SST label; they made *Paranoid Time* in one day for $300. With seven songs in less than seven minutes, the single perfectly delineated the Minutemen's early approach: Short bursts of energy, with jerky riffs and politically charged haiku lyrics. The following year's debut album *The Punch Line* made even more clear that while the band was hardcore in spirit and association, the music eschewed overpowering guitar chords for a sound that better expressed the equality of the band's three members.

Boon's guitar combined punk's speed with the angularity of **Captain Beefheart,** while it respected the other instruments' territory by staying in treble range and never getting too rhythmic. As Watt explains, "D. Boon was very political about the music. He wanted three fiefdoms, and nobody in the way. He thought the heavy guitar bogarted the bass." Watt's bass, in turn, held its own with a springy, melodic style. With the sonic landscape divided, and Watt and Boon sharing vocals, the trio created an amazingly dynamic sound that was sometimes labeled "jazz-punk."

---

### Kristin Hersh, Throwing Muses:

*D. Boon's guitar style was influential in showing you didn't have to take up so much space. If you have a great rhythm section the song will keep going.*

---

### Eric Wilson, Sublime

*I'd never heard anybody play bass like Mike Watt before. He'd just go off. He wouldn't be doing the slap thing—I hated how everyone was into slap bass—Mike Watt would just lay into it with his fingers, playing the real shit. I pretty much picked up that style listening to him.*

With an EP on the Thermidor label and the formation of their own New Alliance Records, the Minutemen asserted an identity apart from SST. They returned, though, for *What Makes a Man Start Fires?* and the *Buzz or Howl Under the Influence of Heat* EP, both of which retained the group's character while pushing them into new stylistic territory. In 1984, as labelmates **Hüsker Dü** offered their definitive musical statement with the double album *Zen Arcade,* the Minutemen set about creating a similarly sprawling and powerful work. The result, a 75-minute 46-song opus called *Double Nickles on the Dime,* was the ultimate expression of the band's personality. Political and personal, anthemic and jokey, acoustic and psychedelic, the record touched on styles from garage and country rock to moody avant jazz and at the same time was a completely unified slice of San Pedro no wave funk.

### Lou Barlow, Sebadoh/Folk Implosion

*They were part of that hardcore proto-indie thing, when hardcore could mean anything. It had nothing to do with the mainstream, just with people discovering their own style, making the most of what they had and stretching the boundaries of their influences in a way that wasn't precious or pretentious or condescending. As far as full-bodied inspiration, the Minutemen were totally it for me.*

In 1985, the Minutemen released *Project: Mersh,* a self-parody of a band on the verge of going commercial (or "mersh"). But with arrangements of horns, synths, backing vocals, fadeouts, and slower tempos, the EP veered dangerously close to becoming everything it ridiculed. After a tour with R.E.M. offered another taste of where greater accessibility might lead them, the group's *3-Way Tie (For Last)* indicated a more pop-oriented approach was not necessarily a joke. Within days of the album's release, though, questions whether the Minutemen were destined for the mainstream became irrelevant. D. Boon's van crashed in the Arizona desert, and he died at age 27. The Minutemen were suddenly a thing of the past.

### Jeff Tweedy, Wilco

*I was really a huge fan. I feel lucky that I got to see them before D. Boon died. Those records meant a lot to me and I think early Uncle Tupelo [Tweedy's first band] took a lot from the Minutemen.*

After D.'s death, Watt and Hurley remained largely inactive (though Watt was part of Sonic Youth's Ciccone Youth project), until a devoted fan named Ed Crawford (edfromohio) convinced them to form Firehose with him. Though the group made a number of memorable albums before disbanding in 1994, they remained in the shadow of the Minutemen. Hurley has since played part-time with the **Red Krayola** and other groups, while Watt continued his side project Dos with then-wife (and former **Black Flag** bassist) Kira.

Watt's 1995 solo album, *Ball-Hog or Tugboat?*—which featured appearances by members of Nirvana, Pearl Jam, Soul Asylum, Sonic Youth, the Beastie Boys, Dinosaur Jr., Screaming Trees, and Geraldine Fibbers—underscored the Minutemen's influence on '90s rock. More recently, Watt toured as a member of Porno for Pyros and released a "punk opera," *Contemplating the Engine Room,* that brings his career full circle. A celebration of three sailors' camaraderie, it's an obvious allegory for the Minutemen. Of Boon (cast as "the boilerman"), Watt sings, "I'm a lucky man, to know that man/a hell of a man, the boilerman."

---

### David Yow, Jesus Lizard/Scratch Acid

*It seemed like jazz-punk, all the syncopation and odd times were influential. I know with [Yow's first band] Scratch Acid, [drummer] Rey Washam had a truckload of respect for George Hurley. Their song "Cut" drove me fucking nuts. I remember the Minutemen played Tacoland in San Antonio—this really small place with a low stage—and I was really drunk, right in Mike Watt's face all night going, "PLAY 'CUT!' PLAY 'CUT!' PLAY 'CUT!'" I felt like a fool when I found out what I'd done. I talked to Mike Watt years later and he remembered some stupid little idiot in his face in San Antonio.*

---

## DISCOGRAPHY

*Paranoid Time* EP (SST, 1980); the band's seven-song-in-under-seven-minutes burst of passion.

*The Punch Line* (SST, 1981); a mini-album along the lines of the debut.

*Bean Spill* EP (Thermidor, 1982), a five-song extended single.

*What Makes a Man Start Fires?* (SST, 1982); the album where the Minutemen begin to stretch out songs and hone their eclectic sound.

*Buzz or Howl Under the Influence of Heat* EP (SST, 1983); an eight-song collection that shows the band's expanded sound.

*Double Nickels on the Dime* (SST, 1984); a sprawling masterpiece of a double record that captures everything great about the Minutemen.

*The Politics of Time* (New Alliance, 1984); a compilation of outtakes and obscure early recordings.

*My First Bells 1980–1983* (SST cassette, 1985); collects everything up through *What Makes a Man Start Fires?*

*Project: Mersh* EP (SST, 1985); a six-song, tongue-in-cheek stab at writing mainstream rock songs.

*3-Way Tie (For Last)* (SST, 1985); a final studio album that further shifts the band toward accessibility.

(w/**Black Flag**) *Minuteflag* EP (SST, 1986); a mostly instrumental four-song collaboration featuring the members of **Black Flag.**

*Ballot Result* (SST, 1987); a double live album whose tracks were voted on by fans.

*Post-Mersh, Vols. 1–3* (SST, 1987); the first volume collects *The Punch Line* and *What Makes a Man Start Fires?*; the second includes *Buzz or Howl* and *Project Mersh*; while the third compiles *Paranoid Time*, the "Joy" single, *Bean Spill, The Politics of Time*, and *Tour Spiel.*

TRIBUTE: Various Artists, *Our Band Could Be Your Life* (Little Brother, 1994); features Tsunami, Meat Puppets, Dos, Jawbox, and members of the Beastie Boys, Sebadoh, and Sonic Youth doing Minutemen songs.

# HÜSKER DÜ

*They were the embodiment of it all: incredibly prolific, earnest, catchy, raw, nice, and hard work-ing. They'd take other cool bands like Soul Asylum on the tour and help them make records. The were the next step of it all...they got a major label deal.*

**Jenny Toomey, Tsunami/Licorice**

Where some American punk bands fell apart too soon and others remained part of the underground until the end, Hüsker Dü allowed their music to evolve as the members' goals and priorities changed. While reviled by some hardcore loyalists as the first band to "sell out" to a major record company, Hüsker Dü remained true to themselves, for better or worse, the whole way. And while careerist ambitions threatened to tarnish their reputation in underground rock, Hüsker Dü stands today as one of the truly pivotal groups in punk rock's transition from '80s underground to '90s mainstream. Though they paid the price for daring to cross over, bands from Soul Asylum to Nirvana to Green Day have them to thank for their paychecks.

Growing up in a small New York town near the Canadian border, Bob Mould had little contact with rock music beyond what he heard on the radio. He loved the Beatles and the Byrds until his teens, when he began to search out bands like the Ramones, **Television,** and the New York Dolls, which he read about in magazines from New York City. By 1978, when Mould went off to college in Minneapolis, British punk had exploded and Mould loved the **Buzzcocks** for blending his twin loves of punk rock and classic pop. Soon after arriving at school, Mould befriended Grant Hart and Greg Norton, a couple of local record store clerks who shared his tastes in music.

With Hart on drums, Norton on bass, and Mould on guitar, the three decided to form a band. Adopting the name Hüsker Dü from a children's board game of the '50s (it's Swedish for "do you remember?"), the trio came together in early 1979 and within a year had secured a place in a local punk scene that included future members of the Replacements and Soul Asylum (whose debut album Mould would produce in 1984).

---

**Art Alexakis, Everclear**
*Bob Mould's guitar playing was very simple, open key—distorted but melodic. It was the first time I heard the Beatles meeting punk rock. And I started fucking around with distorted open tunings and that kind of melodicism.*

---

Early on, the Huskers' reputation for short, fast songs and an intensely powerful live act made them Minneapolis's punk ambassadors. Bands like the **Dead Kennedys** stayed with them when pass-ing through town, and as they released a single on their own Reflex label, the Huskers began to arrange tours to the West Coast. After meeting **Black Flag** at a gig in Chicago in late 1981, word of the band spread to the **Minutemen,** who called to see if Hüsker Dü wanted to put out a record on their New Alliance label. Without enough money to go into a studio, the band recorded a live show in Minneapolis that was released as their debut album, *Land Speed Record*. While the record's furi-ous pace conveyed the band's energy, poor recording quality reduced much of it to a noisy racket.

### King Coffey, Butthole Surfers

*Hüsker Dü tell me I wrote them their first out-of-state fan letter. I was so impressed by Land Speed Record—it was incredibly fast, with lots of energy behind it—I wrote them a letter. And they were so flattered somebody outside Minneapolis thought they were worthwhile, they wrote back and answered my stupid little fanzine questions I asked. Then when they came through Texas I roadied for them and got paid $5 a day.*

After an uncharacteristically political single revealed a **Minutemen** influence, Hüsker Dü released its first studio (mini-)album, *Everything Falls Apart*. More cohesive and better produced than the debut—though still fast and noisy—the record showcased the songwriting abilities of Mould and Hart, while their cover of Donovan's "Sunshine Superman" unveiled the band's long-suppressed pop sensibilities. On 1983's *Metal Circus* EP—their first for SST—songs like "Diane" and "It's Not Funny Anymore" marked an increasingly melodic approach, a stretch beyond the standard hardcore sound.

Even given Hüsker Dü's popularity within the hardcore scene, few fans expected a work as ambitious as 1984's double album concept record, *Zen Arcade*. Bringing outside elements (piano, acoustic guitar, tape effects) into their music without sacrificing hardcore's ferocity, Hüsker Dü took the hardcore form to its furthest limits. Tough and spacey, melancholic and celebratory, *Zen Arcade* connected hardcore to rock traditionalism, and opened the form up to countless new possibilities. Along with the equally successful, if less sprawling, follow-up *New Day Rising*, Hüsker Dü hit full stride—marrying pop and punk in a way that didn't lessen the impact of either—and jumped to the head of the class in American punk rock.

### Kristin Hersh, Throwing Muses

*I was really unhappy at art school—RISD was full of these morose people dressed in black—and I was sleeping on a friend's floor one night, really disillusioned, when he put on Zen Arcade. And it was just the most beautiful sound I'd ever heard, like the hardcore bands I grew up with but much prettier. They were stomping around, yelling and screaming, and still sounded like wind. I thought pop songs were evil, but they taught me that pop songs were okay. I don't know if other people would call Hüsker Dü a pop band but I'm pretty sure they were.*

### Will Oldham, Palace

*New Day Rising was one of those records where I called the store every day for three weeks waiting for it to come out.*

By 1985's *Flip Your Wig*, their first record to emphasize vocal clarity over raging guitar walls, Hüsker Dü was crossing over the borders of hardcore. Rather than retrench and risk repeating themselves, they decided they had no choice but but to move beyond SST and the punk underground. Late in the year, Hüsker Dü signed with Warner Bros., and 1986's *Candy Apple Gray* became the first hardcore album recorded for a major label. Though not substantially different from *Flip Your Wig*, the record marked an end to hardcore's first generation. By then, both **Black Flag** and the **Minutemen** were through, and for Hüsker Dü, priorities had changed.

### Van Conner, Screaming Trees

*Right after New Day Rising and Flip Your Wig, whenever we'd tour, the local band of high school or college kids who opened up for us always sounded like Hüsker Dü, probably in the same way bands nowadays sound like Nirvana or Soundgarden.*

For a younger generation of hardcore kids weaned on records like *Zen Arcade*, *Candy Apple Gray* was blasphemy; it seemed the band had alienated as many core fans as they gained from larger exposure. By 1987, though, Hüsker Dü were facing larger threats to its existence, including intensified alcohol and drug use, and a long-brewing power struggle between Mould and Hart. Their double album and final studio release, *Warehouse: Songs & Stories*, sounds weary and lifeless despite some strong material. The liner copy reads like a suicide note, making no attempt to hide the band's sense of regret and despair: "Sometimes you feel real old, older than you are....The demands of life. Responsibilities, Responsibilities....You can't go if you don't know, and you can't know if you don't go..." Following the actual suicide of Hüsker Dü's office manager, the band finally fell apart in early 1988.

Greg Norton left music to become a chef, and Grant Hart returned to SST as a solo artist before forming the band Nova Mob. Bob Mould also spent a few years as a solo artist (recording with former **Pere Ubu** members Tony Maimone and Anton Fier), then reverted back to the power-trio format (and indie status) with the band Sugar. More recently, he has resumed his solo career.

## DISCOGRAPHY

*Land Speed Record* (New Alliance, 1981; SST, 1987); the super-fast live debut.

*Everything Falls Apart* (Reflex, 1982; Rhino, 1993); first released as a minialbum, the reissue *Everything Falls Apart and More* includes singles, outtakes, and demos.

*Metal Circus EP* (SST, 1983); seven songs that showcase the band's songwriting ability.

*Zen Arcade* (SST, 1984); the classic document of American hardcore punk in a two-record concept album.

*New Day Rising* (SST, 1985); everything great about *Zen Arcade*, but stripped down to one record.

*Flip Your Wig* (SST, 1985); a portrait of a band aching for something bigger. ·

*Candy Apple Gray* (Warner Bros., 1986); the major label debut, with a predictably cleaner sound.

*Warehouse: Songs and Stories* (Warner Bros., 1987); the final studio album, two records of a great band grown stale.

*The Living End* (Warner Bros., 1994); a posthumous live album taken from the band's final tour in 1987.

TRIBUTE: Various Artists, *Dü Hüskers: The Twin Cities Replay Zen Arcade* (Synapse, 1993); local Minneapolis/St. Paul groups including Walt Mink, the Blue Up, Balloon Guy, and Arcwelder remake the Huskers' classic record in its entirety.

# B A D   B R A I N S

*Like most of the truly inspirational bands who really made a difference—the ones that took the machetes out and chopped their way through the jungle—you can't contain the Bad Brains, you can't fucking put a leash on them. They're never going to appeal to the mainstream because they're groundbreakers. But the Bad Brains have had more effect on music than most people could hope to realize. A lot of the popular bands of the past ten years, while maybe they haven't been direct-ly inspired by the Bad Brains, they've certainly been inspired by bands who've been inspired by the Bad Brains.*

**Ian MacKaye, Minor Threat/Fugazi**

Four African-American kids from the Washington, D.C suburbs, Bad Brains were destined to be hard-core's great anomaly. But, as true outsiders—racially, musically, religiously—in a subculture that cultivated "outsiderness," Bad Brains were perhaps the purest manifestation of hardcore ideology. And in the end, their impact would be as great (if not greater) than any of their hardcore peers. From Living Colour's so-called "black rock" music, to the Red Hot Chili Peppers' punk-funk, to Seattle's metallic grunge, Bad Brains' long shadow has reached across regions, styles, and decades of American punk-based music.

The members of Bad Brains had all been born in D.C.'s mostly black inner city, but moved with their parents to the Maryland suburbs around 1970, when gentrification pushed middle-income families out to make room for high-rent renovations. Singer Paul Hudson (known as H.R.) and his drummer brother Earl met guitarist Gary Wayne Miller (called Dr. Know, or Doc) and bassist Darryl Jenifer in high school, where they formed the jazz fusion band Mind Power. While the untrained foursome developed their jazz chops by copying Al DiMeola and Chick Corea records, each also played in more mainstream funk bands.

When the band started hearing the punk music coming out of England in 1977, they identified with its sense of marginalization and rebellion, and thought they could apply that spirit to their own music. As Mind Power moved toward a punk sound, the band renamed itself Bad Brains to connote awareness (like the original name), blackness ("bad" as slang for good), and punk rock (as in the earlier Ramones song "Bad Brain").

*Michael Franti, Spearhead*

*They had a large impact on the scene because they weren't only playing punk but were carrying within their music reggae and the spirit of Rastafari. For me to see bands out there who weren't just R&B singers, but who still came from a very African perspective, was crucial. They showed me, as a black artist, you didn't have to do what the mainstream of black music was doing.*

Right away the band gravitated to groups like the Clash and the Specials who saw a kinship between punk and reggae, and the influence was reflected in the way Bad Brains would shift between lightning-fast punk songs and laid-back reggae grooves. From the punk-reggae connection, Bad Brains came into contact with Rastafarianism, the religion of many Jamaican musicians, and adopted it as their own faith. Not only did the group introduce local punk audiences to reggae, but by advancing Rastafarianism's asceticism they would influence the D.C. scene's later embrace of clean living, straight edge punk.

Punk's reputation for high-energy shows made D.C. clubs unwilling to book bands like Bad Brains. Instead, the group played wherever it could organize a gig, including its own basement and a brownstone co-op in D.C.'s Adams Morgan neighborhood called Madame's Organ. Attended by a motley crew of friends, hippies, and teenagers—including future **Black Flag** singer Henry Rollins and **Minor Threat** leader Ian MacKaye—these shows earned Bad Brains a reputation as the fastest, most exciting punk band in D.C. But still frustrated with local clubs' unwillingness to book them (as they detail in the song "Banned in D.C."), the group moved to New York in 1980.

*Kate Schellenbach, Luscious Jackson:*

*Bad Brains was one of the bands that I—along with other kids my age like Jill and Gabby [of Luscious Jackson] and the Beastie Boys—would see every time they played. Not only was seeing them very exciting, it was also this social event. I met a lot of my good friends there....When I was in the Beastie Boys, their songs were some of our favorites to try and figure out. They were very accomplished musicians, so they inspired us to step up on our musicianship.*

*Adam Yauch, Beastie Boys*

*The Bad Brains influenced me more than any other band in the world.*

Though Bad Brains first recorded as early as 1979, it wasn't until 1982 that they finally released a cassette-only debut album on ROIR. The tape (with liner notes written by Yo La Tengo's Ira Kaplan, then a music critic) mixed high-energy classics such as "Big Take Over" and "Sailin' On" with reggae tracks like "Jah Calling" for a sound that was as fast and ferocious as any hardcore album (if not more so), while maintaining tight structures and quick changes. As the band's reputation grew, it stepped up a touring regime that brought them to California, where they headlined a show featuring the first-ever gig by Bad-Brains fanatics, the Red Hot Chili Peppers.

### Dave Grohl, Nirvana/Foo Fighters

*My goal has always been to be as powerful live as the Bad Brains. We're not that close yet, but we're getting there. [Allstar Daily Music News, 1/26/98]*

Having garnered enough attention to warrant a full-scale LP, Bad Brains released *Rock for Light* in 1983. Though it contained some of the same songs as the ROIR cassette, the material was re-recorded by Ric Ocasek of the Cars. The album's slicker sound did little to detract from the music's power; it even added greater dynamism. Within a year, though, H.R.'s desire to pursue reggae exclusively led him to quit Bad Brains for a solo career, and the group entered a two-year period of inactivity.

After an H.R. solo album, Bad Brains re-formed in 1986 and released *I Against I* on **Black Flag**'s SST label. Both a triumphant return and stylistic departure, the record was not explicitly hardcore and not at all reggae, but rather a seminal album in the development of the black rock style typi-fied by Living Colour, the grunge sound of bands like Soundgarden, and the funk-inflected metal of later bands like Rage Against the Machine. But after a lengthy 1987 tour yielded three live albums, H.R. quit the band again (along with Earl) to record a second solo album.

### Chris Cornell, Soundgarden

*I Against I was a record that everyone in the band poured over. Everyone in the Seattle scene, we'd sit around in rooms and listen, song to song, and talk about them.*

Determined to continue Bad Brains without H.R. and Earl, Doc and Darryl briefly recruited mem-bers of Faith No More and the Cro-Mags to tour, though H.R. returned once again for 1989's metal-oriented *The Quickness*. Disbanding once again, the group remained inactive until 1993, when they were signed by Epic, a major label that had been successful with Living Colour. Joined by a young H.R. sound-alike named Israel Joseph I, Doc and Darryl made *Rise*, a record that augmented their recent metal funk leanings with cheesy synths and dancehall beats. The album was unsuccessful both commercially and creatively, and Epic soon dropped the band.

A second chance at revival came in 1994, when Madonna's Maverick label reunited H.R. and Earl with Doc and Darryl to record *God of Love*. Ric Ocasek was producing again, and the band was invited to join a Beastie Boys' tour. Bad Brains seemed poised for another comeback. However, early into the tour H.R. showed signs of instability, due possibly to anxiety, drugs, or a more serious mental condition (or what Doc laments as H.R.'s "fear of the big time"). After dropping off and then rejoining the Beasties, the group embarked on their own tour.

While performing in Lawrence, Kansas, H.R. became agitated by an audience member he believed was heckling him and he smashed the heavy steel base of his microphone stand over the kid's head. The victim sustained severe head injuries (but survived), while H.R. spent over a month in jail before being released. Not surprisingly, Bad Brains split up again, this time perhaps for good. Meanwhile, the musical style that Bad Brains invented now fills arenas.

## DISCOGRAPHY

*Bad Brains* (ROIR 1982, 1996); the classic debut cassette that captures the band's early sound, recently reissued on CD.

*Rock for Light* (PVC 1983, Caroline 1991); their first widely available album, featuring slicker production by Ric Ocasek.

*I Against I* (SST, 1986); a strong comeback album of all new material, including some of their best songs.

*Live* (SST, 1988); a concert recording from the band's 1987 tour.

*Quickness* (Caroline, 1989); the most consistently metallic of Bad Brains albums, but retaining hard funk elements.

*The Youth Are Getting Restless* (Caroline, 1990); a live recording from the 1987 tour.

*Spirit Electricity* (SST, 1991); yet another live album recorded in 1987.

*Rise* (Epic, 1993); featuring new singer Israel Joseph I and drummer Mackie, the band's uneven and ill-considered major label debut.

*God of Love* (Maverick/Warner Bros., 1995); H.R.'s return (and perhaps the band's swan song) is one step better than *Rise*, but a far cry from the '80s recordings.

*Black Dots* (Caroline, 1997); the band's first recordings, from D.C. in 1979, including early versions and some never-released songs.

# M I N O R   T H R E A T

*All I ever wanted was to belong to a community. D.C. is a very transitory town. The main industry is government, which I have no connection to, and the people who come work for the government are gone within a few years. In the black community there's a deeper sense of community, because it's larger and people don't split. But in the white community you can feel very marginalized. So growing up there was a real desire—maybe even a necessity—to create something to belong to, some way to measure life.*

**Ian MacKaye, Minor Threat**

Minor Threat was among the most passionate and exciting—as well as most musical—hardcore groups of the early '80s, but the band's chief significance came in its relationship to its community. The Washington, D.C. punk scene—an insular society made of bands, labels, zines, skateboarding teens, and high school misfits of all sorts—wasn't the first of its kind. But through the efforts of artists like Minor Threat's MacKaye—who fostered a the local scene that could sustain itself through shared interests and common ideals—D.C. punk became a template for the entire punk subculture.

## Mac McCaughan, Superchunk

*Minor Threat was probably the first hardcore record I bought. I heard other stuff on the radio and thought they were pretty cool, but those first Minor Threat 7-inches are so catchy, so raw and fast....Once I started thinking about the aesthetic of running a label—down to the ads and album covers, how to keep records cheap—Dischord [Minor Threat's label] definitely influenced Merge [McCaughan's label]. Their idea of being a label not so much centered around a band, but around a community. The idea of putting out bands you like and keeping it for people who are into this music.*

Though MacKaye has long been agnostic and disdainful of organized religion, it's easy to see how his church background informed the ethics he later applied to punk. MacKaye's father, a theologian and former religion editor for the *Washington Post,* was a leader in a liberal inner-city church involved with grassroots political action. Following the King assassination in 1968, six-year-old Ian marched with his parents and church members.

With his earliest exposure to rock coming through church functions and activism, Ian always tied music to politics and social gatherings. After seeing the *Woodstock* film 16 times, MacKaye decided he wanted to throw a free music festival of his own someday. As a teen, Ian loved Ted Nugent's music, wildman image, and outspoken sobriety, but discouraged by the professionalism of '70s arena rock, MacKaye instead took up skateboarding. With a group of D.C. kids that included his best friend, future **Black Flag** vocalist Henry Garfield (Rollins), he formed a completely independent, unsponsored skateboard team.

MacKaye started getting into punk bands like the Ramones and the Sex Pistols when he entered high school in 1977, though it wasn't until his junior year that he discovered his calling. At a college radio benefit concert featuring the **Cramps,** MacKaye and his friends got a first taste of live punk rock and it forever changed the way they viewed music. Feeling like a participant—as opposed to a faraway spectator at arena rock shows—MacKaye found the social/musical community he'd been looking for. From there he discovered a small underground of punk outcasts he could identify with (as one of the few socially active high schoolers who didn't drink or do drugs, he felt like a deviant himself). Though D.C.'s older art punks viewed MacKaye's crowd as "teeny punks," they soon established themselves as the heart of the local scene.

With the support of his parents, MacKaye decided to skip college and form a band instead. After playing bass in a short-lived group called the Slinkees, MacKaye and Slinkees drummer Jeff Nelson formed the Teen Idles. During its year-long existence the group managed to arrange a West Coast tour (with Henry Rollins as roadie) in search of early hardcore heros like **Black Flag** and the **Dead Kennedys** and put out a single on its own label, Dischord. When the Teen Idles folded, MacKaye and Nelson regrouped with guitarist Lyle Preslar and bassist Brian Baker to form Minor Threat. Along with bands like Henry Rollins' State of Alert (Dischord's second release) and Government Issue, Minor Threat pushed the D.C. hardcore scene into motion.

Minor Threat built on the sounds of **Bad Brains** and **Black Flag** with Preslar's high-tempo reverb guitar riffing, Nelson's impulsive drum pounding, and MacKaye's melodic yet sneering vocals. They perfected a hardcore style bands still copy. Balancing power and intimacy, songs like "I Don't Wanna Hear It" and "Small Man, Big Mouth" attacked blind followers, liars, and bullies, and spoke directly to and about the lives of band members and people around them.

---

### Jenny Toomey, Tsunami/Licorice

*There's a lot of heart in what Ian does, he really challenges himself. Minor Threat just had perfect songs. It's no surprise an entire genre of punk has grown up to copy them. [Simple Machines, Toomey's label] gets demo tapes to this day of fifteen-year-old boys and girls singing in that exact same style.*

---

The Minor Threat song that probably had the biggest impact was "Straight Edge." As D.C. punks connected with lyrics such as, "I've got better things to do/Than sit around and smoke dope./Always gonna keep in touch/Never want to use a crutch," they began to advocate sobriety as an act of rebellion against mainstream society's rampant substance abuse. Though it never constituted a majority in the punk scene (or even a majority of Minor Threat fans), "straight edge" became the name and rallying cry of a drug- and alcohol-free punk faction that spread across the country (and world), and still exists today.

---

### Eric Wilson, Sublime

*I loved them even though I wasn't straight edge. I wouldn't even listen to the lyrics, the music was so good. I'd be riding to school with a Walkman cranking, "I don't drink, I don't smoke," while I was smoking a roach. The music was just so pure and full of energy.*

---

MacKaye resisted the straight edge tag once the movement showed signs of becoming tyrannically fundamentalist, but because he remained outspoken in the punk community it was difficult to separate the message from the original messenger. Idealism aside, though, straight edge had an important pragmatic role. While getting into shows was a problem for MacKaye and his still-underage friends, the young punks convinced venues to let them in provided they didn't buy alcohol. To alert bartenders not to serve them, the kids marked their hands with the "x" that later became a symbol of straight edge affiliation.

As Dischord resumed activity in 1981 and '82—releasing Minor Threat's first two EPs *Bottled Violence* and *In My Eyes*—Jeff and Ian moved into Dischord House, their home and base of business operations. Following Minor Threat's community-minded practices such as insisting their shows be open to fans of all ages and cost no more than $5 per ticket, Dischord kept its record prices low as well. After a brief breakup while Preslar did a semester in college, Preslar rejoined and Baker switched to second guitar, while Steve Hansgen joined on bass. With a bolstered lineup, Minor Threat recorded an album, *Out of Step,* in early 1983.

Showing a maturation from its earlier finger-pointing rants, Minor Threat's lyrical concerns on songs like "Sob Story" and "Betray" focused on the punk scene's own shortcomings, while "Look

Back and Laugh" revealed a new sensitivity. Indeed, as the D.C. punk scene grew in the early '80s and slam dancing (moshing) attracted more violent elements, it became increasingly difficult to maintain cohesion. Meanwhile, Minor Threat's rising national prominence made it more difficult to maintain the band's community orientation. When a major label record deal became a possibility, tensions flared within the band, and Ian and Jeff—unwilling to separate their band from their label—disbanded Minor Threat for good. A final single, "Salad Days," pointed toward the future without relying on nostalgia for the past: "Look at us today/We've gotten soft and fat/Waiting for the moment/It's just not coming back.../But I stay on, I stay on."

### Mark Robinson, Unrest

*I was impressed with Dischord Records locally, and the guys in Minor Threat. That was definitely a huge label influence on me. It was cool seeing bands around here doing shows and putting out records. It was almost like the country didn't exist, people were famous just in D.C. and that was okay. I also liked their design elements. The TeenBeat [Robinson's D.C.-based label] logo is kind of fashioned after it.*

Remaining an integral part of the D.C. punk scene, MacKaye and Nelson devoted their energy to Dischord, which continued to release albums by local bands such as Scream (featuring future Nirvana/Foo Fighters member Dave Grohl) and Dag Nasty. MacKaye also continued his role as activist and participated in D.C. punk's "Good Food October" and "Revolution Summer," movements that attempted to distance the scene from negative elements and reshape punk aesthetics. In 1985 he formed Embrace, a band that defined a more mature and expressive post-punk sound, "emocore." Nelson collaborated with MacKaye on Egghunt, then played in the bands Three and High Back Chairs. In 1987, MacKaye teamed up with another well-known D.C. frontman, Rites of Spring's Guy Picciotto, to form Fugazi, a band that is in many ways the ideal successor to D.C. hardcore. Both Fugazi and Dischord continue to enjoy success, entirely on their own terms, while MacKaye remains a vital part of a local scene that wouldn't be the same without him.

## DISCOGRAPHY

*Bottled Violence* 7-inch (Dischord, 1981); an eight-song debut single.

*In My Eyes* 7-inch (Dischord, 1982); a four-song follow-up single.

*Out of Step* (Dischord, 1983); a mini-album featuring 12 songs.

*Salad Days* 7-inch (Dischord, 1983); a final three-song single.

*Minor Threat* (Dischord, 1984); collects the first two singles together on one album.

*Complete Discography* (Dischord, 1988); collects all the band's recordings on one CD.

# 16

## AVANT PUNK USA

T he bands classified here as avant punk fall somewhere between the British post-punk movement, which attempted to explore the outer reaches of punk sounds and structures, and the American hardcore scene, which tried to take punk's hard-fast-short-loud aesthetic to it's furthest point and build on punk's do-it-yourself ethic. American bands like **Flipper** and **Mission of Burma** had a definite artistic kinship with the British post-punks, and were too arty (and not enough punk) to be hardcore.

By the late '80s, with hardcore bands like **Minor Threat** and **Hüsker Dü** either gone or diminished, younger groups that had descended from their tradition were left in a position to move beyond hardcore. Bands like **Slint** incorporated other influences into their music to create a more progressive, avant-garde brand of American punk and opened up entirely new possibilities for a style that only a few years earlier seemed to be running out of ideas.

For the most part, the bands in this chapter came out of—or operated within—the punk scene, side by side with hardcore and post-punk bands. And, while it was appropriate to group them together here, it's important not to overlook the fact that neither the artists nor their fans ever had to choose sides. Despite their pop sensibility, the **Wipers** could easily share a bill with **Black Flag** and exert an influence on the same group of people.

## WIPERS

*I wasn't aware you had to look a certain way to be accepted in punk. Living in Portland, I wore flannel shirts, which I guess was the most uncool thing you could wear. A lot of people thought it was funny, they'd call me a logger. It's funny how old photos from that era translated to what was going on in the early '90s with the grunge thing. So all of a sudden I became a leader of that.*

**Greg Sage, Wipers**

A the first notable punk band from the northwest, the Wipers are the earliest link in a chain that leads directly to Nirvana and the rest of the Seattle bands of the '90s. Despite this, and despite the fact their songs have been covered by bands like Nirvana (twice) and Hole, the group has managed to stay out of sight in the United States (they are better known in Europe). Though the Wipers' relative obscurity may be partly due to their ahead-of-its-time indie approach, in large part it can be attributed to their leader (and only constant member) Greg Sage, a talented songwriter and guitarist whose career has been uncompromising to the point of being self-defeating.

Musically, it would be unfair to give the Wipers too much credit for starting the heavy metal/punk amalgamation that was dubbed "grunge" (credit for that goes more to Aberdeen, Washington's Melvins). The Wipers, though, were a great band with great songs, whose greatest influence lay in the way they cleared a path in independent music for later Northwest bands to follow. From their base in Portland, the Wipers' sent out a message of "be yourself" and "do-it-yourself" that was heard throughout Oregon and up to the punk rock centers in Olympia and Seattle, Washington.

### Van Conner, Screaming Trees

*The Wipers were—still are, actually—an influence for everybody in the Trees. The Wipers were just so far before their time. They were our favorite band for years and years. The idea of us taking everything a little more seriously came from the Wipers. Having fun doing it, but putting a little heart and blood into it. That's not something that sells records, but it's something people notice.*

From elementary school on, Greg Sage was interested in the recording process. His reason for writing songs as a teenager was more so he'd have something to record than out of a desire to express himself. Around 1977, he started playing music with his friends Dave Koupal (on bass) and Sam Henry (on drums). Though he had little knowledge or experience with punk rock at the time, when his band—which he named the Wipers—got invited to play live, he fell into Portland's small punk scene. As a distant outpost of the early West Coast punk scene, Portland bands at the time were more of the "dress up" kind, imitating the leather and chains punk styles they saw in magazines. The Wipers, with their flannel shirts and jeans, clearly didn't fit in, but when the band's music caught on it sent a powerful message that good music was independent of fashions.

### John McEntire, Tortoise/Sea and Cake

*He was kind of the first person to ever do stuff in [Portland, where McEntire grew up]. He was this amazingly enterprising guy who built his own studio in days when nobody did that, and put out his own records. It was before a lot of the hardcore bands were around. There was the same sort of independent idea happening, but before it was formulated and solidified by a larger community. I was a little too young to be fully impacted, but in time I came to understand how it developed on a local level.*

Being from Portland proved problematic when the Wipers recorded their first single, "Better Off Dead," and Sage tried to release it on his own label, Trap. "We'd call the distributors on the East Coast, and they'd ask where our label was based. I'd say Portland, Oregon, and they'd laugh and hang up," Sage remembers. It necessitated a move to New York, though the Wipers eventually returned to Portland. With the release of their debut album *Is This Real?* in 1980, Sage had developed a plan for how he wanted to make music. "My goal was to put out 15 albums in 10 years, and never play live, never do interviews, never put out photos," he says. "To get people to listen I wanted to create a mystique, because the more that people know, the less they look into what you're doing for the answers. But working with other people made it impossible. It was just a constant bombardment of 'You have to do this, you have to do that.'"

### Carrie Brownstein, Sleater-Kinney
*Greg Sage and the Wipers are totally legendary here [in the Northwest]. His lyrics really sum up this weird sort of depression of being in the Northwest a lot, without really targeting anything. I know that Corin [Tucker of Sleater-Kinney] totally loved his guitar playing in a way that influenced her.*

Though he never achieved his recording goal, Sage was able to maintain a low profile and his independence by not signing multi-album deals with record companies, retaining complete control of the writing and production of Wipers material, and doing as little promotion as possible. Of course, his unwillingness to go along with established record company practices also limited his commercial viability. Still, *Is This Real?* and the 1981 EP *Youth of America* established the Wipers as the leading punk band in the northwest. At a time when **Black Flag**'s hardcore sound was coming to dominate punk scenes on the West Coast, Wipers songs like "Return of the Rat" (covered by Nirvana) were a throwback to the more melodic, hook-laden punk of the Ramones, while "Is this Real?" was reminiscent of Elvis Costello. With *Youth of America*, Sage and a new Wipers lineup moved even further away from the current "short and fast" punk style with a 10-minute epic title track and more new wave/post-punk explorations.

### Chris Cornell, Soundgarden
*We played shows with them and they were a really big influence on our band overall. They were an example to me of a band that could have punk aggression and post-punk sensibilities in their instrumental approach, but at the same time write songs that would stick with you and be as important to you as any band you'd grown up listening to. The first time I ever met our drummer Matt [Cameron] he played me a bunch of 4-track demos he'd recorded, and they sounded really cool. And then he played the Wipers, and I asked him, "Is that you, too?" And he just kind of rolled his eyes and said, "I wish."*

As the '80s progressed, the Wipers settled into a comfortable anonymity. Without much attention from the music press or radio, Sage continued to produce increasingly polished and consistently good albums such as *Over the Edge*—which featured standouts like "Doom Town" and the title track that Hole later covered—as well as *Land of the Lost*. In 1985, Sage also released his first solo album, which he recorded (like all Wipers material) in his own studio. Then, as the '80s ended and the Northwest rock scene was teetering on the verge of national prominence, Sage moved away from Portland. Disappointed with the growing metropolitanism of the region, he took refuge in the wide-open desert near Phoenix, where he built a new recording studio, pursued solo work, and produced other groups.

## Ryan Adams, Whiskeytown

*Greg Sage is the king songwriter. His solo record, Straight Ahead, is probably the most influential thing I've ever heard. It's all songwriting, no bullshit. And Wipers songs like "Doom Town," I think that's where I got my fascination with naming songs with "town" in them, like "Inn Town" and "Mining Town." Some songs on [Whiskeytown's] Strangers Almanac, like "Turn Around," are extremely influenced by Greg Sage.*

After a second solo album in 1991, Wipers drummer Steve Plouf joined Sage in Arizona and they began recording the first new Wipers album in nearly five years. *Silver Sail*, released in 1993, coincided with the band's growing prominence as a result of endorsements by Kurt Cobain (who told *Melody Maker* in 1992, "The Wipers started grunge in Portland in 1977") and a Wipers tribute album. Though it easily could have been the Wipers commercial breakthrough, Sage deliberately sabotaged himself. He says, "When Nirvana and Hole and a bunch of other well-known bands were making it fashionable to cover Wipers songs, the record company was calling me up saying, 'This is your time.' I had some stuff I was going to record but I got cold feet because I was afraid of jumping on my own bandwagon. So I ended up rewriting *Silver Sail* to be something so off-base, a lot less distorted and mellower. I just didn't like the feeling, after all the work I'd done before, of just becoming popular because of a fluke."

Sure enough, the record went nowhere. A second Phoenix-based Wipers record, 1996's *The Herd*, was a strong return to form that gained widespread critical praise. By the end of the year, though, Sage and Plouf played their final gig as the Wipers and forever retired the band (in name, at least). Sage, meanwhile, continues to record—both his own music and that of others—and design studio equipment. After 20 years, he's still doing his thing; still independent and still largely unknown.

## DISCOGRAPHY

*Is This Real?* (Park Avenue, 1980; Sub Pop, 1993); the debut album featuring many of the group's best-known material, reissued with the earlier *Alien Boy* EP.

*Youth of America* EP (Park Avenue, 1981; Restless, 1990); a six-song collection, including the adventurous 10-minute title track.

*Over the Edge* (Brain Eater, 1983; Restless, 1987); though hard to find, this is considered by many a favorite Wipers release.

*Wipers Live* (Enigma, 1985); a concert recording that fails to capture the band's real energy or sound, but contains some otherwise unavailable songs.

*Land of the Lost* (Restless, 1986).

*Follow Blind* (Restless, 1987).

*The Circle* (Restless, 1988).

*The Best of Wipers and Greg Sage* (Restless, 1990); a good but poorly packaged collection of singles and standouts that span the years 1977–1989.

*Silver Sail* (Tim/Kerr, 1993); just as grunge-fever kicked in, Sage took a softer approach to ensure continued obscurity.

*Complete Rarities '78–'90* (True Believer, 1993).

*The Herd* (Tim/Kerr, 1996); a strong return to rocking, just in time to be the band's final release.

TRIBUTE: *Fourteen Songs for Greg Sage and the Wipers* (Tim/Kerr, 1993); a compilation of Wipers songs done by a selection of indie bands, and a few larger ones—Nirvana, Hole, Sonic Youth's Thurston Moore—as well.

# M I S S I O N   O F   B U R M A

*The minute we died I could feel us getting bigger. As I drove back from our last gig I told a friend, "In three or four years, people will refer to us as the Velvet Underground of the '80s. I'm not saying we are, but that's how they'll refer to us." And lo and behold, in a few years it was in print: "The Velvet Underground of the '80s." It's just absurd the stuff they'll say.*

*Roger Miller, Mission of Burma*

By incorporating avant-garde and progressive techniques into rough-hewn punk rock, Mission of Burma put an American face on the post-punk style spearheaded by British bands like **Wire** and the **Fall**. And in doing so, they brought an uptight and angular sound firsthand to the ears of contemporaries like **Hüsker Dü** and younger bands such as R.E.M., who would follow their lead in crafting the alternative rock sound of the '90s. Though Mission of Burma were always smart and often subtle, they could rock as fiercely as any punk group. It was this love for loudness, ultimately, that was their undoing. Yet their premature demise has only added to the band's mystique and legend.

It would seem Roger Miller was destined from childhood to lead America's premier art punk band. He grew up in Ann Arbor, Michigan, where as a kid in the late '60s he witnessed the **MC5** and **Stooges** do their part in inventing punk rock. But Ann Arbor was also a college town, and as the son of a professor, Miller had access to the world of 20th-century art music as well. In his late teens he pursued both strains, playing briefly with Ron Asheton's post-Stooges band, Destroy All Monsters, and studying atonality and serialism at music school.

By the late '70s, though, Ann Arbor was no longer the place to be. Having heard about the diverse music scene brewing in Boston, Miller moved east. "I was going to play piano with tape loops and synthesizer, maybe a saxophone, that was my ideal at the time. But when I came to Boston, the punk scene was really good. The first show I saw was the Girls, La Peste, and Human Sexual Response, the three art punk bands in Boston. My jaw dropped. I said, 'I came to the right town.' So I joined a rock band, I couldn't help it."

Miller soon joined Moving Parts, a band led by two friends who would both become important collaborators with Miller (though in separate bands). When the band broke up in 1978, Miller—a multi-instrumentalist who was then playing guitar—formed Mission of Burma with Moving Parts bassist Clint Conley. (Two years later, Miller would reunite with Moving Parts' Erik Lindgren in his keyboard-oriented instrumental side band, Birdsongs of the Mesozoic.) Conley shared Miller's love for English groups like **Wire**, Magazine, and the **Fall** that were incorporating progressive elements into punk.

---

*Lou Barlow, Sebadoh/Folk Implosion*

*I was really into the way they played. They were this American band taking that **Gang of Four**/early '80s jagged guitar sound from England, but they made it even more listenable and added more space to it, and the songs were just gorgeous. The way Roger Miller played guitar was a huge influence on the way I play now. He uses a lot of cool chords, and doesn't rely on your usual consonant folk chords. He just changed the fingerings a bit and rattled the strings.*

---

With the recruitment of drummer Pete Prescott from local band the Molls, Mission of Burma began gigging as a trio in early 1979. But soon, in the true post-punk style of bringing avant-garde elements into rock, the group incorporated a fourth band member, Martin Swope. Swope was not an instrumentalist—he wasn't even on stage with the band—but rather he operated a tape machine behind the mixing board that added strange effects and electronic loops to the rather traditional guitar/bass/drums lineup.

### Scott Kannberg, Pavement

*They were a big influence on our early records. I'm really into bands that use electronics and tape loops as an accompaniment to rock, and they were that type of band. We tried to do it like that. They're an under-acclaimed band, they should've been a lot bigger.*

From the start, Burma was largely a democracy, with Conley's anthemic rock songs on equal ground with Miller's more experimental and challenging material (later, Prescott wrote songs as well). In fact, the group was made stronger by the variety; Miller's compositions fulfilled the group's impulse to explore the boundaries of punk, while Conley's tightly wound melodies—such as the group's first single, 1980's "Academy Fight Song" (later covered in concert by R.E.M.)—became alternative rock classics.

### Eric Bachmann, Archers of Loaf

*[Burma's] "That's When I Reach for My Revolver" is the first song I ever learned on guitar. Some of my guitar parts have obvious references, just because that was the first thing I learned. To me, it's like a foundation. Listen to our "Harnessed In Slums" and to "Academy Fight Song," there are parts that are similar.*

Burma's 1981 EP *Signals, Calls, and Marches* produced a second standout, "That's When I Reach for My Revolver" (later covered by Moby). Led by a metallic bassline and droney guitar that invited comparisons with their English contemporaries, **Gang of Four,** the song combined raw passion and dry humor with an unforgettably insistent chorus.

It wasn't until 1982 that Burma finally released a full-length album, *VS.* (a title likely borrowed by Pearl Jam for their 1993 record *Vs.,* and definitely adopted by the band Versus). The album found the band at its creative peak. Many of the songs seemed to strike a perfect balance between the band's pop and experimental impulses. Unusual chord progressions and rhythms were integrated with driving guitar tunes. While no song on *VS.* was as independently memorable as "Academy" or "Revolver," it stands as the band's most unified and successful statement.

By the time they released *VS.,* though, Burma was fast on its way to breaking up. Miller had long suffered from tinnitus—a hearing disorder caused by his repeated exposure to intense volume— and by early '83 the condition had worsened to a point where it became clear he'd have to pursue quieter music. And so, just as the rave reviews for *VS.* promised to push Mission of Burma toward a larger audience, the band amicably called it quits.

*Jenny Toomey, Tsunami/Licorice*

*Mission of Burma are just amazing. Their lyrics are incredibly ambitious. They really don't pander to their audience at all, and they're not being willfully obscure. I wish there were more bands out there that really inspired you to think. It's like they were precursors for what became emo-core, the idea of emotional songs as part of the punk thing. They're a band I go back to all the time. They're so much of what became the later indie rock style. Running open chords up the neck of the guitar. A lot of times I'll come up with a really good pattern and realize it's part of a Mission of Burma song.*

Though posthumous Burma releases continued for years—including a live album with **Stooges** and **Pere Ubu** covers—the individual members quickly moved on. Miller and Swope made Birdsongs of the Mesozoic, a quieter, more experimental "rock chamber music" group, their primary focus. Miller left Birdsongs in the late '80s and continues to perform and record, under his own name and with groups such as No Man and Binary System. Swope left Birdsongs shortly after and currently lives in Hawaii.

Clint Conley produced Yo La Tengo's debut album in 1986, but has since left music to work as a television news producer, while Pete Prescott went on to front the Volcano Suns, Kustomized, and his current band, Peer Group. The former bandmates have remained friends, and in 1996 Conley and Miller reunited to record a single under the group name Wrong Pipe. While more material may follow from them, as long as Miller wishes to keep his tinnitus stabilized there's no hope of hearing Mission of Burma together again.

## DISCOGRAPHY

*Signals, Calls, and Marches* EP (Ace of Hearts, 1981; Rykodisc, 1997); a six-song debut, with "Revolver," reissued together with the "Academy Fight Song" single.

*VS.* (Ace of Hearts, 1982; Rykodisc, 1997); the one and only album, the fullest realization of the band's power.

*The Horrible Truth About Burma* (Ace of Hearts, 1985; Rykodisc, 1997); a posthumous live album, revealing their rougher live sound, taken from various shows on their 1983 tour.

*Peking Spring* (Taang!, 1987); a collection of unreleased recordings made between 1979 and 1982; some of which was originally released as a self-titled EP.

*Forget* (Taang!, 1987; 1994); a second less essential collection, featuring different unreleased recordings from the same sessions.

*Mission of Burma* [CD] (Rykodisc, 1988); an out-of-print release that collects all the formally released material, including singles, the first EP, and *VS.*

# FLIPPER

*Flipper were a huge influence on me. I got their first single and it blew me away. Just the fact that they were lumped in with these hardcore bands but they were really slow. The guitar wasn't making any effort to stick to the standard punk rock bar chord thing. It was just a total mess, and no one else really played like that. The churning noise, this wall of muddy agitated slug groove, with these really amazing anthemic lyrics. They were the first real heavy sludge band. Grunge was really influenced by that.*

**Lou Barlow, Sebadoh/Folk Implosion**

ust at the point where hardcore made punk rock a whole lot faster than ever before, Flipper was heading in the other direction with a dissonant, lumbering sound that got heavier and dirtier the slower it became. Almost two decades since their debut, Flipper don't sound nearly as snail-paced today as they no doubt seemed when compared to speedy contemporaries like **Bad Brains.** But the unrelenting din of their most plodding work still sounds like it's taking its sweet time and going nowhere in particular.

Flipper's sense of humor and disdain for convention—even punk convention—made them favorites of bands like the Butthole Surfers, who broadcast a radio show on the Internet named after the Flipper song "Brainwash." And from Flipper's sludge rock, of course, it was only a short step to grunge. The Melvins, a heavy rock band from Aberdeen, Washington, liked Flipper so much they covered one of the group's best songs, "Sacrifice." And Flipper clearly had a huge impact on the Melvins' "little brother" band, Nirvana.

### King Coffey, Butthole Surfers
*They were a hardcore band but they played so slow, and they played forever, and were really confrontational. Like every great band they had a lot of myth about them, like they'd play "Brainwash" and lock the doors to the club so everyone would be forced to hear the same song for four hours. I really respected Flipper for being a hardcore band that wasn't playing hardcore. The Butthole Surfers were like that as well.*

Flipper formed in 1979 out of the San Francisco band Negative Trend, which featured bassist Will Shatter (born Russell Wilkinson) and drummer Steve DePace. The group was part of an early Bay area punk scene that included bands like the **Dead Kennedys,** the Avengers, and the Nuns, with groups like **Chrome** and **Residents** on the more damaged side. When Negative Trend collapsed, Shatter and DePace recruited guitarist Ted Falconi and vocalist Bruce Lose (Calderwood). Lose had been known in the punk scene more as an audience member than a musician because he'd invented a dance, called the Worm, where he'd throw himself on the floor and flop around. He was just the theatrical nutcase the others were looking for, and soon Lose and Shatter entered into a creative partnership, where they switched off on bass and vocals, and wrote songs together.

After placing their muddy and slinking "Earthworm" on a compilation by local punk label Subterranean, Flipper released a debut single in 1980: the nuclear fallout noise of "Love Canal" backed with the mocking "Ha Ha Ha." The following year they released their best-known song, "Sex Bomb," an open ended dirge-jam with stupid lyrics repeated over and over for effect. It was the ultimate statement of their supremely loose, unmitigated racket.

Flipper managed to get a full-length record together in 1981. Naming it *Album: Generic Flipper*, the group beat **Public Image Limited** to the punch (and when Public Image released their generic *Album* five years later, Flipper responded with the live *Public Flipper Limited*). Most songs—catchy and compelling despite the band's obliviousness to song structure—relied on a simple heavy riff and bassline that repeated throughout the whole song. Though it sounded downright polished next to the early singles, the record was by most standards a masterpiece of artfully inarticulate slop. Tempos had increased slightly as well, though various details—handclapped beats, blaring saxophones, sound effects (like the bomb drop noise in a re-recorded "Sex Bomb")—made clear this was not your typical hardcore band.

### Krist Novoselic, Nirvana

*I listened to Generic Flipper and it was a revelation. It was art. It made me realize it was art. It was valid, it was beautiful. 'Cause I gave things validity by going, like, "Is it as good as Physical Graffiti?" And Flipper was suddenly, like, "Sure it is! If not better." [from Route 666: On the Road to Nirvana, by Gina Arnold]*

With their second album, *Gone Fishin'*, Flipper was clearly stretching itself. Still gleefully twisted and heavy, the record cut down the noise quotient—or at least directed it better—and added new instruments such as piano, clavinet, and congas. Neither as extreme nor as successful as the first record, *Gone Fishin'* was an interesting development for a band so resolutely sloppy. It pointed to real potential once the group gained full control of its talents.

### Tim Gane, Stereolab:

*Flipper were kind of punk but mixed with electronics and strange vocal effects. That to me was another key to something, mixing hardcore with electronics. They were my ideal band back then.*

The original Flipper, however, would never return to the studio to produce a follow-up album and discover where it had been heading. Instead, the group toured through the mid-'80s and attracted a following for their always-loud, always-fun live show. In 1987, Will Shatter—leaving a wife and unborn son behind—died of a heroin overdose. Though the remaining members would replace Shatter in the '90s and release their first new record in a decade, the new Flipper lacked the irreverence and looseness (despite Lose's name change to Bruce Loose) that made them memorable in the beginning. In an early '90s music world where Flipper-inspired bands were topping the charts, the re-formed Flipper couldn't compete.

## DISCOGRAPHY

*Album: Generic Flipper* (Subterranean, 1981; Def American, 1992); the essential debut album.

*Gone Fishin'* (Subterranean, 1982); the more ambitious second studio record, that traded musical variety for sublime sludge.

*Blow'n Chunks* [tape] (ROIR, 1984; 1990); recorded live in 1983 at CBGB.

*Public Flipper Limited Live 1980–1985* (Subterranean, 1986); a double album of live recordings, spanning the group's career.

*Sex Bomb Baby!* (Subterranean, 1987; Infinite Zero, 1995); a collection of singles and compilation tracks, including much of their most inspired material, with three tracks added on the reissue.

*American Grafishy* (Def American, 1993); an uninspired '90s reunion record without Will Shatter.

# SLINT

*Slint were the most name-dropped band of the '90s probably. I don't know that anyone has done that style of music—which did become a style—as well as they did. Codeine, Karate, a million bands. They proved slow and quiet could be more powerful and earnest than fast rock songs.*

**Jenny Toomey, Tsunami/Licorice**

Because Slint is the youngest band in this book, it's not yet possible to gauge the influence they've had and will continue to have on rock. By all accounts, though, they are destined to be one of the great underground reference points for generations of post-rock bands to come. During Slint's brief career—1987 to 1991—the group released only two albums (plus a posthumous single). Their amalgam of avant hardcore and prog rock, though, has already been adopted by enough indie bands—Rodan, June of '44, Codeine, and so forth—to make "Slint-esque" a meaningful label. Even bands much older than Slint are likely to name the group as one of the truly inventive rock creations of the '90s. At this late hour in rock's history, that's quite an accomplishment.

Slint represents the artistic pinnacle of the small, closely intertwined punk scene in Louisville, Kentucky that has produced (or played some part in) indie bands as diverse as Palace, King Kong, Tortoise, and Gastr del Sol. The group was formed by guitarist Brian McMahon and drummer Britt Walford, who at the ripe old age of 17 had already made two highly regarded records as part of the hardcore band Squirrel Bait. When McMahon recruited guitarist David Pajo, and Pajo's friend Ethan Buckler joined as bassist, the quartet was complete.

Though they weren't sure how they'd go about it, from the start Slint meant to be a reaction to the hardcore sound that by '87 was way past its prime. "Bands all started to sound the same. There wasn't anything new and exciting," Pajo remembers. "We talked about doing something out of frustration with what was around. It sounded pretty fun, so we just started playing." Slint was primarily interested in exploring dynamics and textures as opposed to writing traditionally structured songs. Though they'd later add some words—often spoken rather than sung—the emphasis was always on crafting perfectly economical instrumentals.

Creating rock music as intricate as what they envisioned proved demanding, and it required the band to focus much more energy on practicing than would be prudent for a more informal punk band. But barely out of high school, the four members were content to live with their parents and work odd jobs while ironing out Slint's sound. "We weren't really driven to make lots of records or tour," Pajo says. "We were serious but didn't obsess over it. But we'd practice a lot compared to how much we played out or recorded. And I think it shows in how intricate the songs are."

Anxious to document their initial material, Slint drove north to Chicago in the fall of 1987 to record with one of their biggest musical influences, **Big Black**'s Steve Albini. Though it wasn't released until 1989—and then only on the micro-indie Jennifer Hartman Records and Tapes—the band's debut, *Tweez*, was an immediately distinctive statement of purpose. With songs named after band member's parents (and pets) and album sides named after toilet manufacturers, it was clearly a record with a sense of humor. However, the music was surprisingly dramatic, with sudden leaps between its fractured song segments. Though the music was rarely melodic, it managed to stay more focused and fluid than most instrumental rock.

Buckler, who found his ideas on music didn't fit with the other Slint members, disapproved of *Tweez* and left soon after to pursue more whimsical and groove-based music with King Kong. The addition of new bassist Todd Brashear, as well as the maturing of the others, changed Slint's sound greatly in the two years before they recorded their follow-up, *Spiderland*. "Our taste in music started to change. We all started listening to a lot more Delta blues and old country music and Leonard Cohen. With *Tweez* there's tons of inside jokes and weird noises, but with *Spiderland* it's completely straight. We tried to keep it pure, which I think was part of us being into all this old music."

For *Spiderland* (which featured a cover photo taken by their friend, Will Oldham of Palace), Slint worked with producer Brian Paulson (who also worked with Wilco, Beck, and many others) to create something that took their ideas to an entirely different level. Songs were tighter and better executed, with even more subtlety to the instrumental dynamics. McMahon's vocals—such as the quietly intoned narrative of "Breadcrumb Trail"—became more prominent, though never intruded on the primacy of the arrangements. *Spiderland*'s impact on certain segments of the indie rock world was, much to the band's surprise, immediate and deep.

### Jim O'Rourke, solo/Gastr del Sol

*I can't heap enough praise on the second Slint record. They found something new. It's an original representation of Americana, in its place and time. It couldn't have been made elsewhere. It's a very pure record, distilled to its essentials. It has a real articulateness that I had never heard before in music like that. Any time somebody falls upon something like that I'm very inspired, like, "Ah ha! Excellent! Let's get back to work...."*

Slint, though, would not last long enough to capitalize on its notoriety. By the time *Spiderland* came out in 1991, McMahon had quit and the group effectively dissolved. Britt Walford had a short stint as the Breeders' drummer (credited as "Mike Hunt"), then played with Evergreen; David Pajo joined Chicago's Tortoise and also pursued M, his Louisville-based band; McMahon formed the For Carnation, and then worked for a record company in Los Angeles. Each member of Slint, at various points, has also taken part in Will Oldham's Palace. And though Slint re-formed for a short time in 1993, no new recordings resulted and the group has no plans to play together again.

## DISCOGRAPHY

*Tweez* (Jennifer Hartman, 1989; Touch and Go, 1993); the Steve Albini–recorded debut, a lighthearted post-hardcore record that hinted what was to come.

*Spiderland* (Touch and Go, 1991); the group's masterpiece, a founding document of '90s indie rock.

*Slint* [single] (Touch and Go, 1994); a posthumous two-song release featuring extended instrumentals recorded between the two albums.

# BIBLIOGRAPHY

Arnold, Gina. *Route 666: On the Road to Nirvana*. New York: St. Martin's Press, 1993.

Bergman, Billy, and Richard Horn. *Recombinant Do Re Mi: Frontiers of the Rock Era*. New York: Quill, 1985.

Buckley, Jonathan, and Mark Ellingham, eds. *Rock: The Rough Guide*. New York: Penguin Books, 1996.

Bussy, Pascal, and Andy Hall. *The Can Book*. Wembley, England: SAF Publishing Ltd., 1989.

Christgau, Robert. *Christgau's Record Guide: The '80s*. New York: Pantheon Books, 1990.

Cope, Julian. *Krautrocksampler*. Great Britain: Head Heritage, 1996.

Cross, Brian. *It's Not About a Salary...Rap, Race + Resistance in Los Angeles*. New York: Verso, 1993.

Eden, Kevin S. *Wire...Everybody Loves a History*. Wembley, England: SAF Publishing Ltd., 1991.

Erlewine, Micheal, et al., eds. *All Music Guide,* 3rd ed. San Francisco: Miller Freeman Books, 1997.

Fernando, S.H., Jr. *The New Beats*. New York: Doubleday, 1994.

Gagne, Cole. *Soundpieces 2*. Metuchen, N.J.: Scarecrow Press, Inc., 1993.

Gimarc, George. *Punk Diary: 1970–1979*. New York: St. Martin's Press, 1994.

Graff, Gary, ed. *MusicHound Rock: The Essential Album Guide*. New York: Visible Ink, 1996.

*Grand Royal*. Issue 2. Los Angeles, 1995.

Harding, James. *Erik Satie*. London: Secker & Warburg, 1975.

Hardy, Phil, and Dave Laing. *The Faber Companion to 20th-Century Popular Music*. London: Faber & Faber, 1990.

Hebdige, Dick. *Cut 'N' Mix*. New York: Methuen & Co., 1987.

Heylin, Clinton. *From the Velvets to the Voidoids*. New York: Penguin Books, 1993.

Jancik, Wayne, and Tad Lathrop. *Cult Rockers*. New York: Simon & Schuster, 1995.

Juno, Andrea, ed. *Angry Women in Rock*. New York: Juno Books, 1996.

Kostelanetz, Richard. *John Cage*. New York: Da Capo Press, Inc., 1991.

McNeil, Legs, and Gillian McCain. *Please Kill Me*. New York: Penguin, 1997.

Mertens, Wim. *American Minimal Music*. New York: Alexander Broude Inc., 1983.

Neal, Charles. *Tape Delay*. Wembley, England: SAF Publishing Ltd., 1992.

Nyman, Michael. *Experimental Music*. London: Studio Vista, 1974.

Palmer, Robert. *Rock & Roll*. New York: Harmony Books, 1995.

Pop, Iggy. *I Need More*. Los Angeles: 2.13.61.

Reynolds, Simon, and Joy Press. *The Sex Revolts*. Cambridge: Harvard University Press, 1995.

Rich, Allen. *American Pioneers: Ives to Cage and Beyond*. Singapore: Phaidon Press Limited, 1995.

Robbins, Ira, ed. *The Trouser Press Guide to '90s Rock*. New York: Simon & Schuster, 1997.

Robbins, Ira, ed. *The Trouser Press Record Guide*, rev. ed. New York: Macmillan Publishing, 1989.

Rollins, Henry. *Get in the Van: On the Road with Black Flag*. Los Angeles: 2.13.61, 1994.

Romanski, Patricia, et al. *The New Rolling Stone Encyclopedia of Rock*, rev. ed. New York: Fireside, 1995.

Schaefer, John. *New Sounds*. New York: Harper & Row, 1987.

Schafner, Nicholas. *Saucerful of Secrets: The Pink Floyd Odyssey*. New York: Delta, 1991.

Toop, David. *Ocean Sound*. New York: Serpent's Tail, 1995.

_____. *The Rap Attack*. Boston: South End Press, 1984.

Vale, V., ed. *Search & Destroy #1–6: The Complete Reprint*. San Francisco: V/Search Publications, 1996.

————, ed. *Search & Destroy* # *7–11: The Complete Reprint*. San Francisco: V/Search Publications, 1996.

————, and Andrea Juno, eds. *Re/Search #6/7: Industrial Culture Handbook*. San Francisco: RE/Search Publications, 1994.

————, and Andrea Juno, eds. *Re/Search #13: Angry Women*. San Francisco: RE/Search Publications, 1991.

————, and Andrea Juno, eds. *W.S. Burroughs/ B. Gysin/ Throbbing Gristle*. San Francisco: RE/Search Publications, 1982.

Weisbard, Eric, and Craig Marks, eds. *SPIN Alternative Record Guide*. New York: Random House, 1995.

Whitburn, Joel. *The Billboard Book of Top 40 Albums*, 3rd ed. New York: Watson-Guptill Publications, 1995.

————l. *The Billboard Book of Top 40 Hits*, 6th ed. New York: Watson-Guptill Publications, 1996.

White, Timothy. *The Nearest Faraway Place*. New York: Henry Holt & Co., 1994.

# INDEX

**Notes on the Index:** Pages on which quotations from commentators can be found are listed with the commentator's name, in *italic type*. For artists and groups whose work is discussed in a major section of the book, the page range for that section is listed in **boldface type**.

"Academy Fight Song," 261

*Academy in Peril*, 20

Aceyalone (Freestyle Fellowship), *145*

*Achtung Baby*, 132

Adams, Ryan (Whiskeytown),
94-95, *106*, 169, *259*

Adkins, Hasil, 102

*African Head Charge*, 135

Afrika Baby Bam (Nathaniel Hall)
(Jungle Brothers), *142*

Airport, Jak, 224

*Akhnaten*, 24

Albertine, Viv, 226, 228

Albini, Steve, 63, *194*, 195

*Album: Generic Flipper*, 264

Alexakis, Art (Everclear), *246*

Alexander, Dave, 54, 55

Ali, Muhammad, 138

*Alien Soundtracks*, 190

Allen, David, 213, 214, 215

Alternative Television, 210

Alternative Tentacles, 240, 241, 242

Ambient music, 11, 131

Amon Düül, 108

Amos, Tori, 220

Anderson, Laurie, 24, 132, 167

*Animal Justice*, 20

Antoni, Mark De Gli, *10, 11, 13,
15, 128-129, 166-167*

Aphex Twin (Richard James), 22,
24, *115*

Archers of Loaf, 9, 130, 160-161, 261

Ardent Records, 40, 42, 43

Art & Language, 78

Art music, 7

"The Art of Noises," 8, 182

*The Art of Walking*, 76

Asheton, Ron, 53, 54, 55, 56, 260

Asheton, Scott, 54

Aspinall, Vicky, 229, 230, 231

Atari Teenage Riot, 60, 61, 188, 225

Atkins, Juan, 116

Atkins, Martin, 199, 200

Atlas, Natacha, 201

*Atlas Eclipticalis*, 16

*Atomizer*, 195, 196

Atonal music, 7

*Autobahn*, 115-116, 117

Avant garage, 74

Avant-garde music, 7

Avant punk, 256

Aztec Camera, 66

B-52s, 56, 69, 215

Baambaataa, Afrika, 116, 200

Babes in Toyland, 220

Bachmann, Eric (Archers of
Loaf), *9, 130, 160-161, 261*

*Back in the U.S.A.*, 53

Bad Brains, 238, 241, **249-252**, 253, 263

Bad Religion, 53

Bahlman, Ed, *172, 177, 179*

Baker, Brian, 253, 254

*Ball-Hog or Tugboat?*, 245

Banco de Gaia, 24, 63, 109, 131, 135

Banton, Buju, 139

Baraka, Amiri (LeRoi Jones), 138, 142

Bardot, Brigit, 37

Bargeld, Blix (Christian Emmerich),
187, 194

Barlow, Lou (Sebadoh, Folk
Implosion), *43, 51, 55, 61, 69, 82,
89, 170, 184, 217, 238,*

240, 244, 260, 262, 266

*Barrett*, 65

Barrett, Syd, 50, 57, **63-65**

Barrington, David, 216

Bartel, Beate, 187

Barthelme, Frederick (Rick), 77

Barton, Lou Ann, 59

Basquiat, Jean-Michel, 180

Bastard Theater, 25

Bauhaus (school), 108, 117

Baumgartner, John, 164

Beach Boys, 13, 30, 31

Beastie Boys, 127, 174, 176, 181,
245, 250, 251

Beahm, Jan Paul. *See* Crash, Darby

Beat, Nicky, 234

Beat Happening, 29, 44, **45-49**

Beatles, 9, 13, 22, 25, 87, 108, 110, 113

Beck, 16, *36*, 48

Beck, Robert. *See* Iceberg Slim

Bell, Chris, 40, 41, 42, 43

Bell and Sebastian, 98, 100

Bin Hassan, Umar (Omar Ben
Hassen), 142, 143, 144

Benitez, Jelly Bean, 180

Bereal, Ed, 145

Berry, Chuck, 162

Biafra, Jello (Eric Boucher), 240,
241-242

Big Boys, The, 175

Big Black, 63, 168, 183, **194-196**, 266

Big Star, 29, **39-43**, 102

Big Youth, 140

Bikini Kill, 220, 224

Birch, Gina, 78, 229, 230, 231

Bird, Steve, 216

Birdsongs of the Mesozoic, 260
Birdstuff (Man Or Astroman?), *101*
Birken, Jane, 38
Birthday Party, 103, 183, 187, 188, **191-194,** 200, 218, 222
Bjelland, Kat, 220
Blackalicious, 146
Black, Frank, 67, 74, 76
Black Flag, 47, 54, 232, **235-239,** 241, 243, 245, 246, 248, 250, 251, 253, 256, 258
Black Sabbath, 237
Blake, William, 99
The Blasters, 105
Blonde Redhead, 165, 167
Blondie, 106, 153, 157, 159
Blow, Kurtis, 174
Blur, 202
Bolles, Don, 234, 235
Bomp Records, 105
Bonebrake DJ, 234
Bonney, Simon, 194, 218
Bono (U2), *128, 213-214*
Boon, Dennes Dale (D.), 242-243, 244
Boucher, Eric. *See* Biafra, Jello
Boulanger, Nadia, 22
Bounty Hunters, 51
Bowie, David, 22, 23, 24, 33, 56, 63, 109, 116, *119,* 120, 131, 132
Box Tops, 40
Boy George, 225
Boyd, Joe, 99
Boys Next Door, 192
Bozulich, Carla (Geraldine Fibbers), *199, 209, 220*
Bramah, Martin, 210
Branca, Glenn, 2, 9, **25-28,** 165, 168, 172
Brashear, Todd, 266
Breeders, 194, 267
Brel, Jacques, 34
British post-punk, 197
Brix (Laura Salinger), 211
Brown, Chuck and the Soul Searchers, 172, 173
Brown, George Washington, 31
Brown, James, 196
Brown, Jerry, 240
Brownstein, Carrie (Sleater-Kinney), *46, 159, 202, 214, 230, 258*

*Bryter Layter,* 100
Buck, Peter, 164
Buckler, Ethan, 265, 266
Budd, Harold, 132
Buffalo Daughter, 119
Built to Spill, 45, 48, 87, 242
*Bull of the Woods,* 58
*Bureaucratic Sonatina,* 10
Burnham, Hugo, 214, 215
*The Burning World,* 170
Burns, Karl, 210
Burroughs, William, 182, 184
Butthole Surfers, 11, 48, 50, 54, 59, 77, 82-83, 88, 89, 103, 134, 156-157, 175, 183, 189, 192, 204, 206, 215, 232, 235-236, 239, 247, 263
Buzzcocks, **206-209,** 246
Byrds, 30, 95, 96
Byrne, David, 20, *21, 22, 24, 26-27, 68, 72, 90,* 110, *126,* 131, *132,* 135, 165, 167
Byrne, Pat, 195
Byron, Don, *11-12,* 14, 167
Cabaret Voltaire, 182
Cadena, Dez, 237
Cage, John, 10, 11, 13, **14-17,** 18, 25, 77, 109, 111, 129, 182, 187, 190
Cale, John, 10, **17-21,** 55, 90, 100, 130, 132, 221
Calvert, Phil, 192, 193
Camus, Albert, 210
Can, 2, 108, **109-112,** 179, 199, 201, 209, 211, 216
*Candy Apple Gray,* 248
Cannanes, 45
The Cardigans, 100
Captain Beefheart, 3, **66-70,** 71, 76, 199, 243
Cardew, Cornelius, 9, 129
Carlisle, Belinda, 234, 235
Carlos (6025), 240
Caroll, Kay, 210
The Cars, 90, 154, 156, 251
Carter, Chris, 184, 186
*Cartridge Music,* 16
Cave, Nick, 20, 33, 36, *56, 103,* 105, *155,* 188, 192, 194, 222, *222,* 238
CBGB, 26, 102, 153, 157, 159, 162, 163, 220
Cervenka, Exene, 222
*Chairs Missing,* 203

Chamberlain, Jesse, 78-79
Chance, James, 166, 220, 221
*Charmed Life,* 85
Chatham, Rhys, 165
Cherry, Don, 18, 146
*Children of God,* 169
Chilton, Alex, 40, 41, 42-43, 102
Christopherson, Peter "Sleazy," 184, 186
Chrome, 5, 183, **189-191,** 195, 264
Chuck D (Public Enemy), *143, 144, 149*
Chung, Mark, 188
*Church of Anthrax,* 20
Cibo Matto, 167
Ciccolini, Aldo, 11
Circle Jerks, 237
Clail, Gary, 135
*Clang of the Yankee Reaper,* 32
The Clash, 53, 126, 134, 156, 178, 197, 199, 226, 250
Clapton, Eric, 67
Clark, Michael, 204
Clark, Peter (Budgie), 227, 228
Classical music, 7
Clayton, Keith, 163
Clem, Jay, 71
*Climate of Hunter,* 35
Clinton, George, 213
Cluster, 109, 120, 130
Cobain, Kurt (Nirvana), 45, *83,* 87, *228-229,* 231, 235, 259
Cockrill, John "Golden," 216
*Coconut Hotel,* 77, 78
Cocteau, Jean, 10
Codeine, 265
Coffey, King (Butthole Surfers), *48, 50, 54, 57, 82-83, 88, 103, 134, 156-157, 175, 183, 192, 204, 206, 215, 232, 235-236, 239, 247, 263*
Cohen, Leonard, 266
Coldcut, 211
Cole, Lloyd, 161
Coleman, Ornette, 18, 68
Collins, Phil, 130
*Colossal Youth,* 44
Coltrane, John, 52
*Come Away with ESG,* 177
*Composition 1960 #7,* 18
Concert music, term of, 7
Conley, Clint, 260, 261, 262

Connelly, Chris, *33, 136, 158, 193*

Conner, Van (Screaming Trees),
*47, 52, 54, 58, 248, 257*

Conrad, Tony, 4, *17,* **17-21,** 114, 115

*Contemplating the Engine Room,* 245

Cooder, Ry, 67

Cool P, 155

Coolio, 145

Cope, Julian, 33, *120*

Copeland, Aaron, 24

Corea, Chick, 249

Cornell, Chris (Soundgarden), *52, 65,
68, 88, 99, 159, 186, 189, 193, 251, 258*

Cornershop, 92, 125

*Corrected Slogans,* 78

Cosey Fanni Tutti (Christine
Newby), 184, 186

Costello, Elvis, 53, 95, 156

Coum Transmissions, 184

Count Five, 50

Country rock, 05

County, Wayne, 153, 155

Cowell, Henry, 14

The Cramps, 42, 47, 94, **101-104,** 105, 253

Cranberries, 201

Crash, Darby (Jan Paul Beahm), 234, 235

Crawford, Ed, 244

*Crazy Rhythms,* 163-164

Creation Rebel, 134

Creed, Helios (B. Johnson), *5, 189,
190, 191*

Crenshaw, Marshall, 33

Crime and the City Solution, 188,
194, 218

Cross, Brian, 145

Crutchfield, Robin, 166

Cunningham, Merce, 15

Cunningham, Steve, 77, 78

The Cure, 98, 134, 202, 213

Curtis, Ian, 177

*Cut,* 227, 228

Cutler, Chris, 76

Czukay, Holger, 109, 110, 111, 112, 201

Dadaist movement, 187

Dag Nasty, 255

*Damaged,* 238

The Damned, 53, 54, 197, 200

Danger, Dottie, 234

Da Silva, Ana, 229, 231

Davis, Clive, 148

Davis, Michael, 51, 53

Davis, Miles, 178

The dBs, 39, 164

Dead Boys, 75

Dead Kennedys, **239-242,** 246, 253, 264

"Deadlier Than the Male," 34

Dean, Paul, 224, 226

Debussy, Claude, 9, 10

Dedeaux, Richard, 145

Dederer, David (Presidents of the
United States of America), *37,
71, 92, 207*

Dee-Lite, 167, 178

De La Soul, 127, 147, 178

Demeski, Stan, 164

Denny, Martin, 12

DePace, Steve, 264

Depeche Mode, 116, 134, 154, 187

Descendents, 238

Desperate Bicycles, 44, 217

Destroy All Monsters, 53, 56, 260

Deuys, Margaret, 26

Devo, 131

Devoto, Hamilton, 206, 207, 208

Diaz, Al, 180

Dick, Philip K, 190

Dickinson, Jim, 42

Diddley, Bo, 67

Diermaier, Werner, 114

DiFranco, Ani, 233

Diggle, Steve, 206, 207, 208

DiMeola, Al, 249

Dim Stars, 161

Dinger, Klaus, 116, 117, 119, 120

Dinger, Thomas, 120

"Dinner Music for a Pack of Hungry
Cannibals," 12

Dinosaur Jr., 51, 86, 218, 238, 245

Dischord Records, 253

*Discover America,* 32

*Discreet Music,* 130-131

DIY. *See* Do-it yourself

DJ Beekeeper, 205

DJ Quik, *146*

DJ Shadow, 146

DJ Spooky (Paul Miller), *13, 15-16,
122, 134, 139, 151, 165, 167, 173*

DNA, 26, 66, 84, 131, 153, **165-167,**

168, 180, 220

Do-it-yourself, 44, 47, 71, 187, 236

Doom, Lorna, 234, 235

*Door Door,* 192

The Doors, 55, 56

Dotson, Ward, 105, 106

*Double Nickles on the Dime,* 244

Douglas, Alan, 142

Downbeat Sound System, 125, 140

Drake, Gabrielle, 99

Drake, Nick, 94, **98-101**

Dream Academy, 98-225

Dream Syndicate ('80s rock band),
17, 19, 39, 51, 114, 163, 209

The Dream Syndicate. *See*
Theater of Eternal Music (The
Dream Syndicate)

*Dried-Up Embryos,* 10

Dub, 121, 122, 123, 133, 134, 135

*Dub Housing,* 75

Dub Narcotic Sound System, 48

Dub Syndicate, 135

Dudanski, Richard, 230

Dukowski, Charles, 236, 238

Dunbar, Sly (Sly and Robbie), 38, 124

Dunn, Heather, 231

Duran Duran, 180

Durango, Santiago, 195

La Dusseldorf, 120

Dust Brothers, 146

Dylan, Bob, 87, 132

The Eagles, 95, 96

Earl, Richard, 216, 218

*Easter Everywhere,* 58

Eastern influences, 8, 24
Cage, John, 14, 16
Glass, Philip, 22
Young, La Monte, 18

Edge (U2), 112, 200, 201

Edge, Damon, 190, 191, 200

Edson, Richard, 179

*Ege Bamyasi,* 111

8 Eyed Spy, 221, 222

Einheit, F. M. (Frank Martin
Strauss), 187

*Einstein on the Beach,* 23

Einstürzende Neubauten, 169,
182, 183, **186-189,** 194, 222

Eitzel, Mark, 33

Elastica, 202

Electronic music
emergence of, 8
Scott, Raymond, 13

Electronium, 13

Elektra Records, 52, 55

Elfman, Danny, 14

El-Hadi, Suliaman, 143

Elliot, Marion, 224

Ellison, Ralph, 151

Embrace, 255

Empire, Alec (Atari Teenage Riot),
61, 188, 225

Engel, Noel Scott, 34

Eno, Brian, 2, 3, 20, 23, 24, 109, 120, 122,
128-133, 135, 166, 167, 201, 202, 204

Eno, Roger, 132

Epic Soundtracks, 217, 218

Erickson, Roky, 57-60, 77

ESG, 4, 154, 172, 175-178, 179

Esquivel, 12

Ess, Barbara, 26

Ethridge, Chris, 96

E.U., 172

Europeras, 17

Eurythmics, 112

Evans, Emmery Lee Joseph, Jr., 145

Everdear, 246

Everything But the Girl, 44, 45

Everything Falls Apart, 247

Experimental music, term of, 7

Fahey, John, 77

Fair, David, 83, 84, 85, 86

Fair, Jad, 83, 84, 85, 86

Fairport Convention, 99

Faith No More, 251

Falconi, Ted, 264

The Fall, 78, 109, 209-212, 260

Familiar Ugly, 77

Farrar, Jay, 96

Fastbacks, 47

Faust, 18, 19, 112-115, 209

Feelies, 76, 153, 161-165, 167

Feldman, Eric Drew, 76

Ferry, Bryan, 130

Ficca, Billy, 158, 161

Field, Bradly, 220, 221

Fier, Anton, 76, 163, 164, 167, 248

Fine Young Cannibals, 207

Firehose, 245

Fire of Love, 105-106

Firley, Doug (Gravity Kills), 118

First Construction, 15

Fisher, Eddie, 33

Fisher, Tony, 173

Fisk, Steve, 48

Five Leaves Left, 99, 100

Flea (Red Hot Chili Peppers), 212-213

Fleming, Don, 85

The Flicker, 19

Flipper, 256, 262-265

Flip Your Wig, 248

Flouride, Klaus, 240

Fluxus art movement, 16, 18, 25

Flying Burrito Brothers, 96

Folk Implosion, 11, 69

Fontana Mix, 17

Foo Fighters, 235, 255

Forster, Arianna, 226

4'33", 10, 13, 16

Frankenchrist, 241

Franti, Michael (Spearhead), 124-
125, 138, 140, 141-142, 147, 241, 250

Franz, Johnny, 34

Freak Show, 72

Free Will, 148

Freestyle Fellowship, 145

Frenz Experiment, 211

Frere-Jones, Sasha (Ui), 178, 181

Fresh Fruit for Rotting Vegetables, 240

Fripp, Robert, 130

Fry, John, 40

Fugazi, 104, 202, 235, 255

The Fugees, 123, 140, 143, 174

Fun House, 55, 56

Furniture Music, 11

Gabriel, Peter, 110, 132

Gaines, Reg E., 147

Gainsbourg, Charlotte, 38

Gainsbourg, Serge, 29, 36-39, 194

Gall, France, 37

Gandhi, Mohandas, 24

Gane, Tim (Stereolab), 23, 48, 61,
64, 71, 113, 117, 118, 177, 197,
198, 217, 264

Gang of Four, 69, 199, 212-216,
220, 260, 261

Garbage, 134

Garage rock, 50, 74, 83, 240

Garfield, Henry. See Rollins, Henry

Garvey, Steve, 207, 208

Gastr del Sol, 14, 19, 20, 24, 31-32, 77-
78, 79, 100, 114, 131, 167, 265, 267

Geraldine Fibbers, 105, 199, 209,
220, 245

German rock music, 108-109

Germ-Free Adolescents, 225

The Germs, 54, 233-235, 237, 243

Gershwin, George, 25

Gibbs, Joe, 126

Giger, H. R., 241

Gigolo Aunts, 63

Gilbert, Bruce, 202, 204, 205

The Gilded Palace of Sin, 96

Gill, Andy, 213, 214, 215

Gilmour, David, 64

Ginn, Greg, 236, 237, 238, 239

Ginsberg, Allen, 167

Gira, Michael, 168, 169, 170

Girls Against Boys, 122-123, 133, 173

Glass, Philip, 9, 13, 18, 21-25, 132

Glasser, East Bay Ray, 240

Glassworks, 24

Glynn, Homer, 71

Goddess, Tony (Papas Fritas), 31, 41, 91

God Is My Co-Pilot, 165

Godley, Adrian Nicholas, 216

Go-go, 172, 173, 174

Gone Fishin', 264

Good Bless the Red Krayola and All
Who Sail with It, 78

The Good Earth, 164

Gordon, Kim (Sonic Youth), 26, 168, 231

Gotobed, Robert, 202, 204, 205

Government Issue, 253

Grandmaster Flash, 135, 174, 180

Gravity Kills, 118, 183

Green Day, 206, 246

Gregory, Bryan, 102

Gregory, Pam "Balam," 102

Grohl, Dave (Nirvana, Foo
Fighters), 235, 251, 255

Grotesque, 210

Grubbs, David (Gastr del Sol), 14,
77-78, 79, 114

Grunge rock, 52

Guided By Voices, 62, 74, 203, 266

Guns N' Roses, 1, 75

Gun Club, 94, 103, **104-107**

Guru Guru, 109, 119

Gut, Gudun, 187

Guthrie, Robin, 106

Gutsy, Suzi, 226

Gysin, Brion, 184

Hacke, Alexander (Alex von Borsig), 188

Hahn, Christine, 26

Half Japanese, 2, 45, 66, 80, **83-86,** 241

*Half Machine Lip Moves,* 190

Hall, Marcellus (Railroad Jerk), 64, 75, 92, 187, 210

Hall, Tommy, 58, 59

Halo Benders, 45, 48

Hamilton, Anthony, 145

Hamilton, Page (Helmet), 26, 27, 195-196, 205, 206

Hanna, Kathleen (Bikini Kill), 224

Hannett, Martin, 177

Hansen, Al, 16, 18

Hansgen, Steve, 254

Hardcore punk rock, 232

Hardy, Françoise, 100, 101

Harmonia, 120

Harris, Emmylou, 97

Harrison, Jerry, 90

Harry, Debbie, 106

Hart, Grant, 246, 247, 248

Hartley, Scott, 179

Harvey, Mick, 36, 192, 193, 194

Harvey, PJ, 36, 66, 67, 76, 194, 220, 226

Hawkins, Odie, 145

Hayward, Charles, 231

Hazelwood,Lee, 95, 188

Head, Jowe, 216, 217, 218

Headley, Deadley, 134, 135

Heartbreakers, 159-160

Hell, Richard, **157-161**

Helmet, 26, 27, 194, 195-196, 205, 206

Hendrix, Jimi, 34, 51, 61, 62, 143, 190

Henry, Joe, 16, 69

Henry, Pierre, 8, 121

Henry, Sam, 257

*The Herd,* 259

Herman, Tom, 76

Herman's Hermits, 81

Herring, Keith, 180

Hersch, Kristin (Throwing Muses), 229, 241, 243, 247

*Hex Enduction Hour,* 210

*Hi, How Are You,* 88

"High Coin," 30

High Llamas, 19, 27-28, 30, 72, 114-115

High music, low music compared, 7, 8-9

*High Time,* 53

Hillman, Chris, 96

*Histoire de Mélodie Nelson,* 38

Hitchcock, Robyn, 63, 98

Hohman, Thomas, 116, 117

Hole, 44, 220, 229, 256

Holly, Buddy, 95

Honegger, Arthur, 11

Hosler, Mark (Negativland), 119-120, 186

Houston, Whitney, 38

Howard, Rowland S., 187, 192, 194, 218, 222

Howie B, 13

H.R. (Paul Hudson), 249, 251, 252

Hudson, Earl, 249, 251

Hughes, Langston, 147

Human League, 117

Hummel, Andy, 40, 41, 43

Hurding, B. P., 224

Hurley, George, 79, 243, 244, 245

Hüsker Dü, 74, 232, 238, 241, 244, **246-249,** 256, 260

Hütter, Ralf, 116, 117, 118, 119

Huxley, Aldous, 162

*I Against I,* 251

Iceberg Slim, 138, **150-152**

Ice Cube, 146, 150

Ice-T, 150, 152

Ice Water, 40

*Imaginary Landscape No. 1,* 16

*Imaginary Landscape No. 5,* 17

Industrial Records, 182, 183, 184

Industrial sound, musical incorporation of, 8, 182-183

*In God We Trust, Inc.,* 241

Inspiral Carpets, 211

"Instrumental with Six Guitars, 26

Interior, Lux (Erick Purkhiser), 102

International Pop Underground, 29, 45, 47

*Is This Real?,* 258

Ives, Charles, 31, 32

Iyabinghi, Bonjo, 134

Jackson, Brian, 148, 149

Jackson, Joe, 178

Jackson, Michael, 116

Jacobites, 218

Jagger, Mick, 97

James, Richard, 115

Jarboe, 169

Jarman, Derek, 186, 227

Jarry, Alfred, 74

The Jayhawks, 39, 43, 95, 98, 109

Jean, Wyclef (The Fugees), 123, 140, 143, 174

Jenifer, Darryl, 249, 251

Jessamine, 60

Jesus Lizard, 67, 102, 168, 189, 190, 191, 194, 199, 215, 245

"Je T'Aime...Moi Non Plus," 38

Jett, Joan, 234

John, Elton, 98

Johnson, Calvin, 29, 45, 46, 47, 48

Johnson, Daniel, 86

Johnson, Robert, 106

Johnston, Daniel, 57, **86**-89

Jones, Jim, 76

Jones, LeRoi (Baraka, Amiri), 142

Jones, Quincy, 146

Jon Spencer Blues Explosion, 51, 101

Joplin, Janis, 58

*The Joshua Tree,* 132

Joy Division, 4, 177

*Jump!,* 32

June of '44, 265

Jungle Brothers, 142, 148, 178

*Junkyard,* 193

K Records, 45, 46, 47, 48

Kain, Gylain, 142, 143

Kannberg, Scott (Pavement), 75, 110, 130, 160, 190, 202, 211, 216, 236, 243, 261

Kaplan, Ira (Yo La Tengo), 81, 85, 164, 251

Karoli, Michael, 110

Keranen, Curly, 91

Kern, Richard, 222

Kgositsile, K. William, 142

*Kick Out the Jams,* 52, 53

Killing Joke, 4, 199

King, Jon, 214, 215

King Kong, 45, 266

King, Martin Luther, Jr., 142

King Tubby, 121, **122-124,** 126, 134, 140

Kira (Kira Roessler), 238

Kirkwood, Curt (Meat Puppets), *58, 68*

Kleinow, "Sneeky Pete," 96

Knox, Nick, 102

Koch, Lydia. *See* Lunch, Lydia

Kool Herc, 139

Korus, Kate, 226

Kosmische music, 108

Koupal, Dave, 257

Kraftwerk, 3, 60, 109, **115-118,** 119, 156, 196

Kramer, 85, 88

Kramer, Wayne, *51, 52, 53,* 88

Krauss, Scott, 75

Krautrock, 108

Kronos Quartet, 14

Kusworth, Dave, 218

Ladd, Mike, 147

La Dusseldorf, 120

Lambdin, John, 190

Lampe, Hans, 120

Landau, John, 53

*Land Speed Record,* 246

Lanegan, Mark (Screaming Trees), *104-105,* 107

Lanois, Daniel, 132

Last Poets, 3, 138, **141-144,** 145, 147, 148, 149

*Las Vegas Story,* 106

Laswell, Bill, 143, 201

Laughner, Peter, 74, 75, 160

Leadon, Bernie, 96

Leary, Paul, 59, 89

LeBlanc, Keith, 135

Lee, Sara, 214, 215

Lee, Tony (Railroad Jerk), *185*

Leeds, Gary, 33

Leibezeit, Jaki, 110, 201

Lennon, John, 203, 235

Les Six, 11

*Let It Bleed,* 97

Levene, Keith, 199, 200, 201

Lewis, Graham, 202, 204, 205

Lewis, Heather, 46

*Lick My Decals Off, Baby,* 68

Lightnin' Rod, 143

Lindsay, Arto, 165, 166, 167, 180

Lindsay, Duncan, 167

Linklater, Richard, 88

Liquid Liquid, 4, 154, 172, 177, **178-181**

Liquor Giants, 106

Living Colour, 249, 251

LL Cool J, 178

Lloyd, Richard, 159, 160, 161

Logan, "Lizard," 134

Logic, Lora (Susan Whitby), 78, 224, 225, 230

Lohn, Jeffrey, 26

"Lollipops (Les Sucettes),'' 37

Looney Tunes cartoons, 12, 13

Los Angeles Free Music Society, 84

Lose, Bruce (Calderwood), 264, 265

Lounge Lizards, 76, 164, 167

Louris, Gary (The Jayhawks), *43, 95, 98, 109*

Louvin Brothers, 95

Love, Courtney, 220, 228, 235

"Love Her," 34

Loverboy, 226

Low music, high music compared, 7, 8-9

LSD, 13th Floor Elevators, 57-58

Luciano, Felipe, 143

Luna, 36, 37, 42, 48, 90, 161-162, 164

Lunch, Lydia, 26, 104, 131, 166, 180, 187, 194, 219, **220-223**

Lunsford, Bret, 46

Lurie, John, 167

Luscious Jackson, 36, 44, 102, 175-176, 200, 225, 226, 250

Lydon, John (Johnny Rotten), 120, 160, 198, 199, 200, 201, 226, 228, 235

Lyrics Born, *144, 150-151*

MacKaye, Ian, *104, 235, 249, 250, 252, 253, 254, 255*

MacLise, Angus, 18

*The Madcap Laughs,* 64

Mad Professor, 127

Madonna, 161, 180, 251

Magazine, 207

Magic Band, 67

Magnetic Fields, 44

Maher, John, 206, 207, 208

Mahler, Gustav, 25

Maimone, Tony, 75, 76, 248

"Make It Easy on Yourself," 34

Malcolm X, 135, 142

Malkmus, Steve (Pavement), *85*

*Man-Machine,* 117

Man or Astroman?, 101, 102

Mapplethorpe, Robert, 180

Marilyn Manson, 183, 191

Marks, Toby (Banco de Gaia), *24, 63, 109*

Marley, Bob, 38, 126, 146

Marley, Ziggy, 146

*Marquee Moon,* 160

Mars, 166, 220, 222

Martin, George, 13, 122

Martsch, Doug (Built to Spill), *45, 242*

Mase (De La Soul), *127, 147*

Masta Ace, 147

Matthews, Eric, *10, 32, 33, 41, 99*

Maus, John, 33

Max's Kansas City, 26, 62, 153

Maxwell, Tom (Squirrel Nut Zippers), *12*

Maxwell's, 163

May, Derrick, 116

MC5, 50, **51-53,** 55, 83, 240, 260

McCarty, Kathy, 88

McCaughan, Mac (Superchunk), *208, 211, 253*

McDaniels, Darryl (Run-D.M.C.), *141, 149, 180*

McDonald, Skip, 135

McEntire, John (Tortoise), *79, 135, 185, 257*

McGuire, Richard, 177, 179, 180, 181

McLaren, Malcolm, 227

McMahon, Brian, 265, 266, 267

McNeil, Dee Dee, 146

McNeish, Peter, 206

Meat Beat Manifesto, 63

Meat Puppets, 58, 68, 238

Mecca Normal, 47

Melchiondo, Micky "Gene Ween," *70, 239*

Melvins, 47, 257, 263

Mercer, Glenn, 162, 163, 164

Merritt, Stephin (Magnetic Fields), *163*

Meyer, Russ, 104

Meyers, Richard See Hell, Richard, 158

*Miami,* 106

Microtonal music, 8
  Branca, Glenn, 27

Migdol, Brian, 236

Mike G (Jungle Brothers), *148*

Milhaud, Darius, 11, 22

Miller, Gary Wayne (Doc), 249, 251, 252

Miller, Roger, *260,* 260, 261, 262

Miller, Tom (*see also* Verlaine, Tom), 158

Million, Bill, 162, 163, 164

Mills, Russell, 204

Minimalism
  Branca, Glenn, 25-26
  Glass, Philip, 22-23

Minimalist funk, 172

Ministry, 134, 136, 183, 193, 196, 242

Minor Threat, 104, 156, 175, 232, 250, **252-255,** 256

The Minutemen, 47, 56, 66, 79, 238, **242-245,** 246, 247, 248

Mission of Burma, 256, **260-262**

Moby, *100, 105, 176,* 261

*The Modern Dance,* 75

The Modern Lovers, **90-93,** 162

Moebius, Dieter, 120

Monkees, 31, 113, 162

*Monster Movie,* 110

Monte, Marisa, 167

Mooney, Malcolm, 110, 111, 112

Moonshake, 109

Moore, Thurston (Sonic Youth), *14-15, 18, 25, 26, 52, 53-54,* 56, *84, 111, 155-156,* 160, 165, 168, *172-173, 179,* 200, *217-218, 221, 233, 237*

Morello, Tom (Rage Against the Machine), *213*

Mori, Ikoue, 165, 166

Mori, Romi, 106

Morphine, 105, 106

Morris, Keith, 236

Morrison, Jim, 55, 56, 192

Morrissey, 98, 103

*Mother Juno,* 106

Mothers of Invention, 67

Mould, Bob, *74,* 76, *207,* 246, 247, 248

Moving Parts, 260

Moxham, Philip, 44, 45

Mudhoney, 56, 57

Muhammed, Ali Shaheed, 149

Moxham, Stuart, 44, 45, 48

Murvin, Junior, 126

*Music for a New Society,* 20

*Music for Babies,* 13

Musical Youth, 140

*My Life in the Bush of Ghosts,* 131, 135

"My Ship Coming In," 34

*My War,* 238

Naïve rock, 80

Name, Billy, 18

Negative Trend, 264

Negativland, 119-120, 186

Nelson, David, 142, 143

Nelson, Jeff, 253, 254, 255

Neon Boys, 158

Nettlebeck, Uwe, 113, 114

Neu!, 117, **118-120**

Neutral Records, 27

New Age Steppers, 135, 228

Newby, Christine, 184, 186

Newman, Colin, 197, 202, 203, 204

New Order, 205

New York Dolls, 153, 155, 158, 246

New York rock, term of, 153-154

Nikki Sudden, 216, 217, 218

Nilaja, 142

Nine Inch Nails, 134, 168, 177, 183, 187, 191, 196, 213

99 Records, 27, 172, 179, 178, 179, 180

Nivana, 45, 83, 87, 194, 208, 228-229, 231, 233, 235, 245, 246, 255, 256, 259, 264

Noise, musical incorporation of, 8

Nolan, Jerry, 159

*No New York,* 166, 167, 221

Normal, Mecca, 226

Norton, Greg, 246, 248

Novoselic, Krist (Nirvana), *264*

No wave, 153, 165-166, 168, 220

NRBQ, 83

Nuel, 4

Nugent, Ted, 253

Numan, Gary, 117

The Nuns, 240, 264

Nuriddin, Jalaluddin Mansur (Alafia Puddim), 142, 143

N.W.A., 143, 145

Nylon, Judy, 135

Ocasek, Ric, 156, 157, 251

O'Connor, Sinead, 201

*Odyshape,* 230

O'Hagen, Sean (High Llamas), *19, 27-28, 30, 72, 114-115,* 116

"Oh Bondage Up Yours!," 225

Oingo Boingo, 14

Oldham, Will (Palace), *35, 195, 222-223, 248, 267*

Ono, Yoko, 16, 18

On-U Sound, 133, 134, 135, 136

*Optimo,* 180

*Orange Crate Art,* 32

The Orb, 10, 116, 131

O'Riordan, Dolores, 201

O'Rourke, Jim (Gastr del Sol), *20, 24, 31-32, 78, 79, 100, 131, 167,* 267

O'Solomon, Otis, 145, 146

"The Ostrich," 19

*Out of Step,* 254-255

Overload, 202

Oyewole, Abiodun (Charles Franklin Davis), 142, 143, 144

Pablo, Augustus, 124

Pablo, Dr., 134

Pachelbel's *Canon,* 131

Pajo, David (Tortoise, Slint), *177, 179, 196,* 265, 266, 267

Palace, 35, 195, 222-223, 248, 265, 267

Palmolive (Paloma Romero), 226, 227, 229, 230

Papas Fritas, 31, 41, 91

*The Parable of Arable Land,* 77

*Parade,* 10, 11

*Paranoid Time,* 243

*Paris,* 20

Parks, Carson, 30

Parks, Van Dyke, 29, **30-32**

Parsons, Gram, **94-98**

Patterson, Alex (The Orb), *10, 116, 131*

Patterson, Carl, 123

Paulson, Brian, 267

Pavement, 36, 74, 75, 85, 110, 113, 130, 160, 190, 202, 211, 216, 236, 243, 261

Pavarotti, Luciano, 132

Pavitt, Bruce, 46

Pearl Jam, 87, 245, 261

Pee Shy, 86

Pentangle, 99
Peel, John, 227
Percussion, Cage, John, 15
Pere Ubu, 66, **74-76**, 77, 78, 160, 163, 164, 166, 248, 262
Peron, Jean-Hervé, *112*, 114
Perry, Lee "Scratch," 121, 124, **124-128**, 134, 135
Perry, Mark, 210
*Perverted by Language*, 211
*Pet Sounds*, 30
Pew, Tracy, 192, 194
Pezzati, Jeff, 195
Phillips, Tony "Crucial," 134
*Philosophy of the World*, 82
Picasso, Pablo, 10
Picciotto, Guy, 255
*Pieces of a Man*, 148
Pierce, Jeffrey Lee, 105, 106, 107
Pigeonhead, 48, 189
Pigface, 199
PiL. *See* Public Image Limited
*Pink Flag*, 203
Pink Floyd, 50, 63, 64, 65
*Pink Moon*, 100
Pixies, 74
Plank, Conrad, 119
*Plastic Surgery Disasters*, 241
Plouf, Steve, 259
The Police, 103
Pollard, Bob (Guided By Voices), *62, 74, 203, 266*
Pollit, Tessa, 226
Pontiac Brothers, 106
The Pop Group, 135, 228
Pop, Iggy, 54-57, 155, 234
Pop music, term of, 29
Porn For Pyros, 245
P-Orridge, Genesis (Neil Megson), *182, 183*, 184, 185, 186, 188
Portsmouth Sinfonia, 130
The Posies, 39, 43
Post-industrial music, 182
Post-punk rock, 44, 75, 119, 122
  British, 197
  women and, 219
"Powerhouse," 12
Powers, Congo Kid, 103, 105, 106
*Prayers on Fire*, 193

Prescott, Pete, 261, 262
Presidents of the United States of America, 37, 71, 92, 207
Preslar, Lyle, 253, 254
Presley, Elvis, 95
Primitives, 19
Primus, 70
Prince Far I, 134, 228
Prince Jammy (Lloyd James), 124
Principato, Sal, 179
Pryor, Richard, 145
Psychedelic Furs, 193
*The Psychedelic Sounds of the 13th Floor Elevators*, 58
Psychic TV, 186
Public Enemy, 11, 141, 143, 149, 178
Public Image Limited, 66, 109, 110, 112, 132, 134, 195, 197, **198-201**, 220, 264
Puff Daddy, 140
Pulsford, Nigel (Bush), *194*
Pulp, 20, 33
Punk rock, 51, 55, 56, 120, 153, 156, 160, 201-202, 232 women and, 219
"Punky Reggae Party," 126
Purkhiser, Erick (Lux Interior), 102
Queen Latifah, 147
*Queen of Siam*, 221
Quine, Robert, 160, 166, 221
Radcliffe, Leroy, 91
*Radio City*, 41
Rage Against the Machine, 51, 213, 251
Railroad Jerk, 64, 75, 92, 185, 187, 210
The Raincoats, 78, 134, 176, 219, 220, 227, **228-231**
Ralph Records, 71
Ramones, 25, 153, 157, 232, 246, 250, 253
Ranaldo, Lee, 26, 88, 200, 218
Ranks, Shabba, 139
Rap, 123, 138, 145-146
*Rappin' Black in a White World*, 145-146
Rauschenberg, Robert, 78
Ravel, Maurice, 9
Ravenstine, Allen, 75, 76, 78
*Raw Power*, 56
Reactionaries, 243
"Read About Seymour," 217
Reagan, Ronald, 149
Recording studios, technology and, 121
*Red Exposure*, 190

Red Hot Chili Peppers, 67, 201, 212-213, 215, 222, 249, 251
Red Krayola, 66, 76, **77-79**, 230, 245
Reed, Lou, 19, 20, 56
Reed, Robert, 173
Reich, Steve, 18, 22, 23
R.E.M., 14, 39, 50, 57, 63, 162, 164, 203, 214, 244, 260, 261
The Replacements, 39, 246
The Residents, 66, **70-73**, 84, 221, 240, 264
Rev, Martin, *154*, 155, 156, 157
Rexsmith, Ron, *34*
Reyes, Ron, 237
Reznor, Trent, 184
Rhia, Donna, 234
Richard Hell & the Voidoids, 153, **157-161**, 166, 221
Richards, Keith, 97
Richman, Jonathan, 45, 47, 80, **90-93**
Rigby, Amy, *80, 81, 227, 229*
Riley, Dave, 195
Riley, Marc, 211
Riley, Terry, 13, 18, 20, 22
Rimbaud, Arthur (Scanner), 158
Rimbaud, Robin, *203*
Rites of Spring, 255
*Roaratorio*, 17
Robinson, David, 90
Robinson, Mark (Unrest, Air Miami), *169, 178, 188, 198, 238, 255*
Rocket from the Tombs, 74
*Rock for Light*, 251
Rodan, 265
Roedelius, Hans Joachim, 120
Roeder, Klaus, 117
Rolling Stones, 67, 95, 97
Rollins, Henry, *156*, 157, 174, 222, 237, 238, 239, 250, 253
Romeo, Max, 126
Romeo Void, 224
Romero, Paloma. *See* Palmolive
Rorshach, Poison Ivy (Christine Wallace), 102
Rother, Michael, 117, 119, 120
Rotten, Johnny. *See* Lydon, John
Roxy Music, 25, 35, 130, 204
Rubin, Rick, 174
Run-D. M. C., 141, 149, 180

Run On, 98
Rush, Tom, 35
Russolo, Luigi, 8, 182
Ruthenberg, George. *See* Smear, Pat
*Sabotage*, 20
*Safe At Home*, 96
Sage, Greg, 46, 47, *256*, *257-259*
Sakamoto, Ryuichi, 167
Salinger, Laura (Brix), 211
Sammy B (Jungle Brothers), *142*
Sandman, Mark (Morphine), *106*
Satie, Erik, **9-11**, 14, 131, 182
*Satyagraha*, 24
Scanner, 203
Schaeffer, Pierre, 8, 121
Schellenbach, Kate (Luscious Jackson),
    *102*, *175-176*, *200*, *225*, *226*, *250*
Scherer, Peter, 167
Schmidt, Irmin, 109, 110
Schneider, Florian, 116, 118, 119
Schneider, Fred (B-52s), *56*
Schoenberg, Arnold, 14
Schulberg, Budd, 145
Schult, Emil, 117
Sclavunos, Jim, 104, 222
Scott, George, 221, 222
Scott, Lincoln "Style," 134
Scott, Raymond, **11-14**
*Scott* (also *Scott 2*, *Scott 3*, *Scott
    4*), 34-35
Scott-Heron, Gil, 138, **147-150**
Scratch Orchestra, 129
Screaming Trees, 47, 49, 51, 52, 54,
    58, 104-105, 238, 245, 248, 257
Scroggins sisters, 176-178
Sebadoh, 43, 51, 55, 61, 69, 82, 89,
    170, 184, 217, 238, 240, 244, 260,
    262, 262, 266
Seeds, 50
Serialism, 7
Sex Pistols, 55, 91, 120, 160, 190,
    197, 198, 199, 201, 206, 219, 224,
    226, 227, 232, 234, 237, 253
Sexton, Charlie, 59
The Shaggs, 80, **81-83**, 90, 227
Shakespeare, Robbie (Sly and
    Robbie), 38, 124
Shankar, Ravi, 22
Sharpe, D., 91

Shatter, Will, 264, 265
Shellac, 196
Shelley, Pete, 206, 207, 208
Shelley, Steve (Sonic Youth), *38*,
    56, 88, 231
Shepard, Sam, 20
Sherman, Bim, 134, 135
Sherwood, Adrian, 122, 127, **133-137,**
    188, 211, 228
Shonen Knife, 45
*Signals, Calls, and Marches*, 261
Sigue Sigue Sputnik, 157
"Silent Music," 12
*Silver Apples*, 2, **60-63,** 155
*Silver Sail*, 259
Simeon, *60*, *61*, *62*, *63*
Simon, Paul, 22, 24
Simonon, Paul, 226
Sinatra, Frank, 30
Sinclair, John, 52, 53
Singers and Players, 135
Singh, Tjinder (Cornershop), *92*, *125*
Singleton, John, 144
Siouxsie and the Banshees, 200, 228
6025 (Carlos), 240
Sixteen Horsepower, 105
Sleater-Kinney, 46, 159, 202, 214,
    220, 230, 258
Slesinger, Bruce, 240
Slint, 79, 256, **265-267**
The Slits, 134, 176, 219, 220, **226-
    228,** 229, 230
Smear, Pat (George Ruthenberg),
    *233*, *234*, *235*
*Smile*, 30, 31
Smith, Bruce, 228
Smith, Fred "Sonic," 51, 53, 159, 160, 161
Smith, Garth, 207
Smith, Jean, *59*, *219-220*, *223-224*, *228*
Smith, Mark E., 209, 210, 211
Smith, Patti, 25, 53, 102, 156, 157, 219
The Smiths, 79, 209
Snoop Doggy Dogg, 150
*So Far*, 114
Soft Boys, 50, 63
Soft Cell, 154
Soft Machine, 64
"Soixante Neuf Année Erotique," 38
*Solid Gold*, 214

*Sonatas and Interludes*, 15
*Song Cycle*, 31
*Song of the Bailing Man*, 76
*Songs About Fucking*, 195, 196
*Songs for Drella*, 20
*Songs for Liquid Days*, 24
*Songs of Fire*, 215
*Songs the Lord Taught Us*, 102, 103
Sonic Youth, 9, 14-15, 18, 25, 26,
    27, 36, 38, 51, 53-54, 66, 86, 87,
    88, 119, 153, 155-156, 160, 161, 165,
    168, 172-173, 179, 200, 217-218, 221,
    222, 233, 237, 238, 244, 245
Son Volt, 95, 96
*Soothing Sounds for Baby*, 13
Sosna, Rudolf, 114
Soul Asylum, 43, 245, 246
Soul Coughing, 9, 10, 11, 13, 15, 128-
    129, 166-167
*Soundgarden*, 52, 65, 68, 88, 99,
    *159*, *186*, *189*, *193*, *251*, *258*
*Soundtracks for the Blind*, 170
Southern Culture On the Skids, 102
Spain, Gary, 190
Spacemen, 3, 77
Spearhead, 124-125, 138, 140, 141-
    142, 147, 241, 250
The Specials, 250
Spectrum, 60
Spector, Phil, 33, 122
*Spiderland*, 266-267
Spinanes, 86
Spiritualized, 20
SPK, 182
*Spiral Scratch*, 207
Springfield, Dusty, 34
Springsteen, Bruce, 32, 53
Squirrel Bait, 79, 265, 266
Squirrel Nut Zippers, 12
SST Records, 236, 237, 238, 242,
    243, 247, 248, 251
Stalling, Carl, 13
Static, 26
Statton, Alison, 44, 45
Steel Pulse, 213
Stein, Chris, 106
Stephens, Jody, 40, 41, 43
Stereolab, 12, 14, 23, 36, 48, 60, 61,
    64, 71, 77, 111, 113, 117, 118, 197,

198, 217, 264

Stevens, Cat, 34

Stevenson, Bill, 238

Stewart, Mark, 135

Stipe, Michael, *214*, 238

Stockhausen, Karlheinz, 60, 108, 110, 116

The Stooges, 53, **53-57**, 55, 83, 120, 158, 192, 216, 232, 234, 236, 240, 260, 262

Strummer, Joe, 199, 226

Styrene, Poly, 224, 225, 226

Sublimer, 237, 244, 254

Sub Pop, 46

Subterranean Records, 191, 264

Sugar Hill Records, 135, 174, 180

Suicide, 54, 60, 153, **154-157**, 192

"Sun Ain't Gonna Shine Anymore," 34

*Sun City,* 149

Sun Ra, 52

*Super Ape,* 126

Super Cat, *139*

Superchunk, 208, 211, 253

"Surf's Up," 30

Suzuki, Damo, 110, 111, 211

Swans, 27, 98, 153, **168-171**

Sweet, Matthew, 39, *42*, 97, *157*, 161, *166*

*Sweetheart of the Rodeo,* 96

Swell Maps, 44, 78, 194, 197, **216-218**

Swope, Martin, 261, 262

Sylvian, David, 112

*Symphony No. 1-3,* 27-28

Tackhead, 135

*Tago Mago,* 111

Talking Heads, 21, 66, 69, 90, 131, 132, 153, 157, 162, 180

Talkover, 123

Tamburovich, Martin, 243

*A Taste of DNA,* 166-167

Taylor, Dan, 60-61, 62

Technology, recording studios and, 121

Teenage Fanclub, 39

Teenage Jesus and the Jerks, 26, 220, 221

Teen Idles, 253

Television, 4, 102, 153, 156, **157-161**, 162, 221, 246

Television Personalities, 218

Temple, Johnny (Girls Against

Boys), *122-123, 133, 173*

Test Department, 183

Tharp, Twyla, 24, 28

Thau, Marty, 156

Theater of Eternal Music (The Dream Syndicate), **17-21**

*Theatre Piece,* 16

Theoretical Girls, 26

They Might Be Giants, 14, 70, 90, 167

13th Floor Elevators, 50, **57-60**, 77

Thirwell, Jim, 222

*This Is Madness,* 142-143

Thomas, David, 74, 75, 76

Thomas, Dylan, 20

Thompson, Dennis, 51, 53, 56

Thompson, Mayo, 76, **77**-79, 230

Thompson, Richard, 98

Thompson, Rudi, 225

Thorn, Tracy, *44*

Thorne, Mike, 203

*Three Pear-Shaped Pieces,* 10

Throbbing Gristle, 113, 169, 182, **183-186**, 187, 188, 190

Throwing Muses, 229, 241, 243, 247

Thunders, Johnny, 159

"The Ticket Puncher," 36

Tiers, Wharton, 26

*Tilt,* 35

*Tokyo Rose,* 32

Toomey, Jenny (Tsunami, Licorice), *47, 148, 174, 246, 254, 262, 265*

Toots and the Maytals, 125

Tortoise, 77, 79, 135, 179, 185, 257, 267

Toscanini, Arturo, 30

"Toy Trumpet," 12

Trafford, Howard, 206

*Trans-Europe Express,* 117

Treasure Isle Studios, 123, 140

T. Rex, 63

A Tribe Called Quest, 143, 149

*Trio for Strings,* 18

*A Trip to Marineville,* 217

Tristan, Brian, 105

*Trois Gnossiennes,* 10

*Trois Gymnopédies,* 10

Trouble Funk, 172, **173-175**

*Trout Mask Replica,* 67-68

Trypes, 164

Tsunami, 45, 47, 148, 174, 246, 254,

262, 265

Tucker, Mo, 86

Turner, Ike and Tina, 33

Tweedy, Jeff (Wilco), *31, 90, 96, 244*

*Tweez,* 266

12-tone music, 7

Cage, John, 14

2 Live Crew, 174

Tyner, Rob, 51, 53

Ui, 178, 181

Ultravox, 119, 131

Underground garage movement, 50

*The Unforgettable Fire,* 132

Unrest, 169, 178, 188, 198, 238, 255

Unruh, N. U. (Andrew Chudy), 187

U-Roy, 123, 126, 138, **139-141**

US3, 146

U2, 32, 109, 128, 132, 180, 200, 202, 213-214

Van Vliet, Don. *See* Captain Beefheart

Varese, Edgard, 11, 182

Vaselines, 29, 45

Vega, Alan, 154, 155, 156, 157

Vega, Suzanne, 24

Veloso, Caetano, 167

Velvet Underground, 16, 18, 19, 55, 90, 114, 108, 153

Verlaine, Tom, 158, 159, 160, 161

Versus, 261

Veruca Salt, 45, 194

*Vexations,* 10

Vicious, Sid, 160, 226

Violet Femmes, 90

Volcano Suns, 261

*VS.,* 261

Waitresses, 161, 224

Waits, Tom, 66

Walford, Britt, 265, 266, 267

Walker, Jim, 199

Walker, Scott, 4, 29, **33-35**

Walker Brothers, 33-34

Wallace, Christine (Poison Ivy Rorshach), 102

Wallinger, Karl (World Party), *110*

Wareham, Dean (Luna), *37, 42, 44, 90, 161-162*

Warhol, Andy, 18, 20, 153

Warren, Stanley, 62

Waters, John, 56

Waters, Roger, 64

Watt, Mike, 56, 57, 79, *201, 234,*
*242,* 243, 244, 245

Watts Prophets, **144-146**

Webern, Anton, 18

Weckerman, Dave, 164

Ween, 70, 239

Weirdos, 243

Weiss, Ingrid, 230

Whiskeytown, 94-95, 106, 169, 259

The Who, 25, 50, 51, 52

Wiggin, Austin, Jr., 81, 82

Wiggin, Betty, 81, 82

Wiggin, Dorothy (Dot), 81, 82

Wiggin, Helen, 81, 82

Wiggin, Rachel, 82

Wilco, 31, 43, 87, 90, 96, 244

Williams, Hank, 95

Williams, John, 12

Williams, Lucinda, 98

The Willies, 164

Williamson, James, 55, 56

Wilson, Brian, 13, 30, 31, 32

Wilson, Eric (Sublime), *237, 244, 254*

Wilson, Robert, 23

Wimbish, Doug, 135

Wipers, 46, **256-259**

Wire, 2, 162, 197, **201-206,** 220, 240, 260

*Wish You Were Here,* 64

Wisse, Thomas, 190

Wobble, Jah (John Wardle), 112,
132, 199, 200, 201

Women, rock and, 219

Wonder, Stevie, 146

Wood, Anne, 231

Wood, John, 100

*Words for the Dying,* 20

World Party, 110

Wray, Link, 102

Wright, Richard, 65

Wu-Tang Clan, 144, 176

Wyatt, Robert, 230

Wright, Tim, 166

Wynn, Steve, *39, 51, 163, 209*

X, 105, 222, 234

X-Ray Spex, 78, 219, **223-226,** 229, 230

Yauch, Adam (Beastie Boys), *250*

Yeats, W. B., 61

*Yip/Jump Music,* 88

Yo La Tengo, 48, 60, 81, 85, 86,
87, 164, 251

Young Gods, 168

Young, La Monte, 10, 16, **17-21,** 22,
109, 114, 129

Young, Neil, 87, 93

Young Marble Giants, 29, **43-45,** 48

*Youth of America,* 258

Yow, David (Jesus Lizard), 67, *102,*
*168, 190, 191, 199,* 245

Yung-Wu, 164

Zappa, Frank, 9, 15, 67, 68, 108, 114

Zazeela, Marian, 18

Ze, Tom, 167

*Zen Arcade,* 244, 247

Z'ev, 27, 183

Zorn, John, 9, 86, 167